Lives of the Archbishops of Canterbury: Anglo-Saxon Period, Volume 1

Walter Farquhar Hook

LIVES

OF THE

ARCHBISHOPS OF CANTERBURY.

VOL. I. NEW SERIES.

Reformation Period.

LONDON
PRINTED BY SPOTTISWOODE AND CO.
NEW-STREET SQUARE

LIVES

OF THE

ARCHBISHOPS OF CANTERBURY.

BY

WALTER FARQUHAR HOOK, D.D. F.R.S.

DEAN OF CHICHESTER.

VOL. I. NEW SERIES.

REFORMATION PERIOD.

History which may be called just and perfect history is of three kinds, according to the object which it propoundeth or pretendeth to represent; for it either representeth a time, or a person, or an action. The first we call Chronicles, the second Lives, and the third Narratives or Relations. Of these, although Chronicles be the most complete and absolute kind of history, and hath most estimation and glory, yet Lives excelleth in profit and use, and Narratives or Relations in verity or sincerity.   LORD BACON.

LONDON:

RICHARD BENTLEY, NEW BURLINGTON STREET.

Publisher in Ordinary to Her Majesty.

1868.

The right of translation is reserved.

70.264

LIVES

OF THE

ARCHBISHOPS OF CANTERBURY.

VOL. VI.

LIVES

OF THE

ARCHBISHOPS OF CANTERBURY.

BY

WALTER FARQUHAR HOOK, D.D. F.R.S.

DEAN OF CHICHESTER.

VOLUME VI.

History which may be called just and perfect history is of three kinds, according to the object which it propoundeth or pretendeth to represent: for it either representeth a time, or a person, or an action. The first we call Chronicles, the second Lives, and the third Narratives or Relations. Of these, although Chronicles be the most complete and absolute kind of history, and hath most estimation and glory, yet Lives excelleth in profit and use, and Narratives or Relations in verity or sincerity. Lord Bacon.

LONDON:

RICHARD BENTLEY, NEW BURLINGTON STREET,

Publisher in Ordinary to Her Majesty.

1868.

The right of translation is reserved.

LONDON:
R. CLAY, SON, AND TAYLOR, PRINTERS,
BREAD STREET HILL.

CONTENTS

OF

THE SIXTH VOLUME.

BOOK IV.
THE REFORMATION.

CHAPTER I.

INTRODUCTORY.

CHAP. II.

WILLIAM WARHAM.

CHAP. III.

THOMAS CRANMER.

LIVES

OF THE

ARCHBISHOPS OF CANTERBURY.

BOOK IV

THE REFORMATION

CHAPTER I.

INTRODUCTORY.

The one Duty of an Incorporated Society.—The Church a Society incorporated by Christ our Lord.—Its special Duty to propagate the Gospel.—Study of Theology necessary to an Ecclesiastical Historian.—No exertion of Intellect can discover that there is a future State of Existence.—This can only be known by a Revelation from God.—Revealed Religion is a transmissive Religion.—Compulsion allowable to induce Men to accept Revealed Truth.—Men compelled by Education, and by the Institutions of their Country.—Intolerance of Man.—Intolerance of Literary and Scientific Men.—Intolerance of Politicians.—Moral Persecutions in the Religious World.—Evils of anonymous Journalism.—Persecution forbidden in Scripture.—All the Reformers intolerant.—Struggle of the Church of England from the Conquest against Popery.—Reformers.—Wiclif.—Reformers at Pisa, Constance, and Basle.—Luther.—Modern Romanism established as a Sect at the Council of Trent.—English Reformation.—All the Reformers repudiated Chillingworth's Dogma.—The Bible only the Religion of Protestants.—Confessions of Faith.—English Reformation the Re-establishment of Primitive Christianity.—Romish Reformation at Trent established Mediævalism.—Continuity and Perpetuity of the Church of England.—The old Catholic Church reformed.—No new Sect.—Malignant or party Use of the title Catholic.—Royal

CHAP.
I.

Introduc-
tory.

To the constitution and characteristic peculiarities of incorporated societies the attention of the reader has been directed in the introductory chapter of the preceding book. A body corporate is a legal fiction, invested with a living power; and possesses an immortality which does not pertain to any of its component parts. I revert to the subject now to remark, that when a society is incorporated, the design is not the personal aggrandizement of its members; but the furtherance of some definite and extrinsic object. In consequence of their association, honours may accrue to the members; but this is an accident of the institution, and not the purport of its organization. The officers of a regiment are honoured by the commission they hold, and through the regiment they may rise to distinction; nevertheless, the regiment was raised not to stimulate or reward personal merit, but, through the valour of its members, to fight the battles of the country. In a municipal corporation, the magistrates are dignified; but the royal charter embodied them, not for their own sakes; but that, by their combined energy and wisdom, justice may be administered and the public peace maintained.

The reader will bear this in mind while we call to his recollection the fact, that in Holy Scripture the Church Universal is presented to our contemplation as an incorporated society: "We being many," says St. Paul, "are one body in Christ;" "We are all baptized into one body;" "Now ye are the body of Christ, and members in particular." *

The Universal Church is a society divinely incorporated under its Divine Head; it is governed by a succession of officers divinely appointed: we are admitted into it by the Sacrament of Baptism.

Having realized this idea, we pass on to the next. The Church has been incorporated for some special purpose. Over and above the duties devolving upon individuals there is one common object, to promote which is the object of its incorporation.

The Church was not incorporated to inculcate a code of morals. This it has done, but it has done it incidentally. It is not the will of God to do by miracle, what can be accomplished by the natural powers of the human mind, duly cultivated, taught by experience, and properly exercised. The ethical writings of the heathen philosophers still exist to bear testimony to what can be accomplished by the unassisted human intellect; and to show that a miracle was not required for the development of a system of ethics. The Lord did not descend from heaven to become a moralist and lawgiver. He is such; but the inculcation of morality is an accident of Christianity, and not of its essence.

The Church was not incorporated as a school of philosophy. The members of an incorporated society cannot do their duty in or to the society, unless they adhere to its rules; they are to labour for a special object, but only through legitimate means. There must, therefore, be dogmatic teaching in the Church. The members of the Church are to impart to one another what the Head of the Church has enjoined, and to instruct them in all that the Lord has commanded. But this again is only an incidental, though an important, duty.

* Rom. xii. 5; 1 Cor. xii. 12, 13; Ephes. iv. 4.

The special duty of the Church, the object for the furtherance of which it was organized, the one end for which it was incorporated, its peculiar function as a body corporate,—is declared by its Divine Founder: "Go ye and disciple all nations;" "Go ye into all the world, and preach the Gospel to every creature."

Each individual is to seek his own salvation. In the battle-field, every soldier is instinctively impelled to adopt measures for the protection of his person and the preservation of his life. Every individual is to acquire a knowledge of the Divine law, as he has the opportunity. In a municipal corporation, each magistrate must study the laws of the land. But, in addition to these, the personal duties of each individual member, there is the one duty of the incorporated society, the object for which it was organized, chartered, commanded into existence. This duty, in the case of the Church, is to disciple nations; to preach the Gospel, as God provides the opportunity, to every creature, baptizing them in the name of the Father, and of the Son, and of the Holy Ghost. It is to continue for ever, by the accretion of new members, that Divine corporation to which this duty has been assigned.

Words, however, are so often used to which no meaning, or an inadequate meaning, or a wrong meaning, is attached; that, when we have ascertained what was the special object which our Lord had in view when Christians were incorporated, a further question arises, and we are obliged to ask, What is meant by the Gospel?

In giving an answer to this question, we enter into the province of theology, and for so doing no apology is necessary. To divorce theology from ecclesiastical history is impossible, if by history we mean anything more than annals or a dry statement of facts,—a corpse without a soul. It is only in favour of theology that the Church acts, and to a person ignorant of the Christian religion the conduct of Christians must appear frequently offensive, and always unaccountable.

To meet the question before us, we must repeat what has been advanced before : that God only reveals what man, without revelation, is unable to discover ; or what is necessary to preserve its tradition.

No exertion of intellectual power could discover the fact that there is a future state of existence—a world beyond the grave. Reason, by its intuitions, may regard the thing as probable ; the understanding, by its logic, may prove that it is not impossible ; upon the possibility and the probability the imagination may love to dwell. But the fact that there is a heaven and that there is a hell ; this, if it be a fact, must be revealed—made known to us by miracle.

Again, no ratiocinative skill, no logical process, can discover what we are to do if, when we have received a revelation upon the subject, we desire to make that future state an eternity of happiness.

It has been made known to us, that a future world exists, in which an order of things is constituted analogous to that with which we are familiar ;—that which we denote when we speak of the laws of nature. Our life is not renewed, but continued. Death can make no alteration in our character ; as the child is said to be father to the man, so man in time is father to man in eternity. There is a change in our circumstances, but, as these circumstances are subject to the same law of nature, there is a sequence of cause and effect ; hence what we are doing in this world may be the cause of what will be experienced in the next.

There are circumstances in this world which may admit of explanation by a reference to the laws of nature, but present themselves as mysteries to the

mind of the moralist. Suffering and misery are dis-
connected from vice; and virtue frequently becomes its
own reward, and nothing more. A man by accident
falls into a pit; there is no blame to be attached to
him, but the result in death is the same, whether it
be an accident or a suicide. A pious son is struggling
with poverty, not from any fault of his own, but
because an improvident father hazarded his all at a
gaming table. Another person is ruined because, in
his charity, he has become surety for a friend, whom
he trusted and by whom he has been deceived. We
have had repeated instances of great families reduced
to distress through the attainder of an ancestor, the
innocent victim of party malice or of royal injustice.

For these things we cannot account; we must take
them as they are, and act accordingly. It is in
accordance with this order of things, that the human
race, through no fault of its members now existing,
has, in its corporate capacity, become a disobedient
race. A disobedient race cannot answer the end and
object for the furtherance of which it was originally
created, and is therefore in a state of condemnation.
Each man who is born into this world is, under present
circumstances, incapable of obeying God. Until it is
revealed to him, he knows not what God requires of
him; he is even ignorant of his position as a sinful
creature. It is revealed to us, that the inevitable
consequence of any deviation from the Divine will,
whether intentional or not, is misery; misery is the
effect of which a deviation from God's will is the
cause. Although gleams of happiness are vouchsafed
to him from time to time, yet man goes on adding sin
to sin, and, in consequence, incurring a never-ceasing
increase of misery. When he has reached a certain
height, his descent is rapid; through the weakness of
old age he sinks into a second childhood, and, passing

a sinner into the next world, he is eternally miserable, because he is eternally sinning. Reason can never discover any change in the laws of nature, when the boundaries of this world shall have been passed; and certainly death is not a Saviour to atone, or a Paraclete to regenerate.

Under this state of things, God has been pleased to make known to us that a miracle of mercy has been performed; another force has been brought to bear upon the forces in existence, and a Saviour has been provided to restore the human race as such, and those among its individual members who will conform to the conditions imposed, to that high position in which man was seen, when, by the created intelligences who surround the throne of glory, the voice of God was heard declaring that whatever He had made was very good. Good news, glad tidings are these; that for fallen man, in his corporate capacity, an Almighty Saviour has been provided, and, for the regeneration of each penitent individual, the Divine Comforter. This is the Gospel which the Church is to preach, and such is the Divine Saviour under whose dominion it is to endeavour to reduce every creature. The Church cannot secure the salvation of all who are enrolled among its members; in an earthly kingdom a subject of the king may be condemned to death for robbery, murder, or treason; but the Church can bring to all men the privileges of the Gospel, and it must labour incessantly, to make all the kingdoms of the earth the kingdoms of the Lord.

It is useless to conceal the fact, so unwelcome to a large portion of the governing classes, that while the Church exists, it must exist as a Church militant. The spirit of syncretism, at this time prevalent in England, made its appearance, only to fail, in the Roman Empire. And such must ever be the case. It is not an opinion or a wish that is now stated; it is simply an historical fact. At certain times and in some localities the Church may be indifferent and corrupt, or the world may seem to triumph over it; but the mandate of its Founder is unalterable. According to His command, whether it shall bring peace upon earth or a sword, the Church will never rest until it has subdued to Christ "flesh and blood, principalities and powers, the rulers of the darkness of this world, spiritual wickedness in high places." It will, by recourse to all lawful means and measures, compel men to become, at least nominally, Christian.

To the word *compulsion*, as applied to religion, many will demur, who are nevertheless among the first to compel. We have recourse to compulsion, whenever we resort to any measure, except that of argument, to induce men to profess and call themselves Christians. The Christian father, who believes that the whole world is under sentence of condemnation, brings his unconscious infant to baptism, that he may place him in a state of salvation. He invests him with privileges; but the child, without being consulted, is involved also in responsibilities. It is a sweet compulsion, nevertheless compulsion it is, when the young mother teaches her babe to lisp the Saviour's name; and to call God his Father. When the child passes from the nursery to the school-room, he finds himself surrounded by preceptors and books, the avowed purpose of whom and of which is, to prejudice his mind in favour of Christianity; and to train him in the way that a Christian, though scorned by the world as narrow-minded, thinks that he ought to go. The Christian parent, whether he reasons on the subject or not, is aware that a prejudice by no means implies a wrong opinion: it is simply an opinion which, without examination, we have received from others. Persuaded that his own convictions on the subject of religion are right,—prepared perhaps, if need should be, to die for them,—the Christian parent is anxious to transmit the truth he has received to his posterity.

The present controversy on the subject of education is based on the right claimed by various parties to compel the young to adopt or to eschew certain opinions and principles, by prejudicing their minds in favour of them, or against them. The divisions of Christendom prove to be the strength of infidelity. The infidel, however, in seeking to eliminate Christianity from our schools, is acting on the same principle. He seeks to compel the rising generation to become infidel, by exciting a prejudice in its mind against all dogmatic teaching. He would cajole the unstable, without offending established prejudices ; he would retain the name of Christian, but speak of Christ, not as a Saviour, but as a fallible moralist ; he repudiates the epithet of godless, but the God in whose favour he would prejudice the minds of his children, whether spoken of as Jehovah, Jove, or Lord, is, in his estimation, not a Person.

We summon him, therefore, into the witness-box, to bear testimony to the fact, that man cannot arrive at those practical conclusions which are to shape his course of life through any processes of the understanding, independent of external circumstances. It is to a few subjects only that the deepest thinker can apply the whole force of his intellect, and adjust the intuitions of reason to the deductions of the understanding. Independently of education, the logical power exists pretty nearly the same in all sound minds. It is in information rather than in logical capacity, that the learned differ from the unlearned. The counsel learned in the law, when addressing a jury of illiterate persons, makes them acquainted with certain points of law and fact of which they had been previously ignorant, in full confidence that, when they have been rightly informed, there is in them sufficient logical power to enable them to arrive at a unanimous conclusion. If, indeed, we depended upon the understanding only, we should not behold those wonderful differences, not only in the character of individuals, but in the whole tone of mind and cast of thought, by which entire nations and whole races are distinguished from each other. Diversities of character absolutely antagonistic are to be found between the English and the French, the German and the Italian; and, more marked still, between ourselves and our brethren in the United States of America. We may ask why is one whole nation, with a few exceptions, Protestant; and, with similar exceptions, another race of human beings Papistical; or, forming the most populous and ancient of all branches of the Christian family, members of the Greek Church?

The truth is, we become what we are by the training which in early life our affections have received, and by the bias given to the grateful mind through the traditions of our elders; by the example of our associates; by the customs to which we have been habituated; by the manners we have formed; by the silent impression of national institutions; by the prevalent tone of society; by the laws to which we have been taught to submit: by all these and similar circumstances, which seem to endow us with new and peculiar instincts before our reasoning powers are developed, or the understanding has been taught to exert itself. When reason dawns, the mind has already accepted certain opinions transmitted to us as true, and these are so woven into our whole system of thought that they are regarded as intuitions. The business of the educated understanding may be to go in quest of new truths, but these truths when discovered have to be harmonized with truths already received; it may have to winnow out the errors attendant more or less upon all transmitted information, to correct or to corroborate; but though the inherited doctrine be amended or enlarged, it has been the basis of our reasoning and discoveries. A heart has been given us as well as a head, to enable us to steer with safety through the shoals and quicksands of this troublous world; and by self-control we are to temper excesses on either side.

We find the book of God's word in perfect harmony with the book of God's works. It has been through tradition that God has made known His will to the several generations of mankind; His religion is to be transmitted from father to son. When it pleased God to make that revelation of a future state to which we have adverted, this is the only conceivable way through which the fact revealed could be brought to bear upon the mass of mankind.

If God had thought fit to reveal this great fact to each man as he comes into the world—the fact of his immortality and the preparation required to make it a state of happiness—the whole course of nature would have been changed. A creature different from what he now is, man would have become, if the probationary circumstances under which he is placed were different. An entirely new creature would have been called into existence. Man remaining as he is, we can only conceive that plan to have been feasible, which by Divine wisdom has been adopted.

When the revelation made to Adam had become virtually obliterated from the mind and memory of man, it was renewed by Divine mercy to Abraham; and we are told why Abraham was selected. In the language of Scripture it is said, " I know him that he will command his children and his household after him, and they shall keep the way of the Lord." A miracle was in one instance wrought, but God would not interfere further with the ordinary course of nature than the circumstances of the case actually required.

When Abraham's family expanded into a nation, there was again a miracle, or a series of miracles wrought, in order that, through the political system imposed upon a stiff-necked people, the grand fact of revelation, as received in the patriarchal Church, might be engraven on the public mind : "I know that my Redeemer liveth, and that He shall stand at the latter day upon the earth."

In the Christian Church the continuance of the same system of transmissive religion was implied, when Timothy was pronounced to be blessed by St. Paul because his religion was an inheritance. Having profited by the instructions of his mother and his grandmother, who taught him to expect the Messiah, he stood on vantage-ground when St. Paul offered proof to show, that the Lord Jesus is He. The good Bereans inherited the Scriptures ; and when to the knowledge which had been transmitted to them the Apostles would make an addition, they then, without ignoring the past, but resting upon it as their foundation, searched the Scriptures to see "whether those things were so."

We are taught the duty of compelling men, in these and similar ways, "to come in," by a greater than St. Paul. To remind us of this duty, and to enforce its observance, our Lord Himself delivered more than one of His parables.

Our Divine Master, having made all things ready for the salvation and sanctification of human souls, opens His house—the Church Universal—and sends out an invitation to all men to partake of the blessings He has prepared for them. Having effected our salvation by a miracle, He leaves the Church to expand itself in accordance with the ordinary laws of nature. He sends forth His messengers, and continues to send them forth, to invite men into the visible Church. They are to employ the arts of persuasion when addressing the educated, and to have recourse to argument. We are told in the parable the various excuses that are made by the busy men of the world; and if on them we depended exclusively for the propagation of the Gospel, we should be still in the darkness of heathenism. The messengers of the Lord are then sent into the streets and lanes of the city, and they are commanded to bring in the poor and the maimed, and the halt and the blind. The express injunction of the Master is, "Compel them to come in, that My house may be full."

When we make a spiritual application of these parables, we must admit, that by the poor and maimed, and the halt and the blind, can be meant, and meant only, the ignorant, the uninstructed, the great mass of mankind; the poor in circumstances, in intellect, in information.

The peculiarity of Christianity is, indeed, that the Gospel is preached to the poor. The heathen philosopher contemned the poor, because to the poor, the uneducated, he could not render his speculations intelligible; but by an appeal to their gratitude and to their interests, by educating, and training, and prejudicing them, they may be made members of the visible Church.

That we cannot, by these means alone, secure their future salvation, our Lord warns us, by mentioning the severe punishment to which the sinner was subjected, who, though admitted to the house, had not on, when the Lord appeared, the wedding-garment. He instructs us, that in the day of judgment, although a man has entered into the Church, he will only suffer

CHAP.
I.

Introductory.

the severer punishment, if, having had advantages placed within his reach, he in wilfulness or in careless-ness neglects to avail himself of the same. But be-cause we cannot array a man in a wedding-garment, which must be his own act and deed, it does not follow that we are not to bring him to the Lord's house, where he may obtain it if he will. The com-munion of saints is one thing, the visible Church is another. The visible Church man can extend; the sanctification of souls pertains to another agency. We cannot make a man a loyal subject, but we may enlarge our Master's kingdom.

The Christian believes that the Messiah has come; and he would prepare his own soul, and the souls of all over whom his influence may extend, to share, by faith in Him, the blessings which He came to procure for all. The Christian also believes, that the Messiah, having a special work to perform in the final subjugation of the rebels against the Divine government—fallen angels, as well as fallen man—is again to appear upon earth; and the Church, in zeal for His glory, and in love to our fellow-creatures, is incorporated to prepare the way for His reception.

In bringing men to Christ, the question is not *how* were they brought; but, What is their present position? Have they accepted Christ as their Saviour? Are they willing to learn what His commandments are, and, being enlightened, will they seek to obey? One may be brought by conviction through argument; another through affection; the majority from the instruction of a Lois or Eunice. We do not despise even the inferior motives. A man may commence with the inferior motive, as did the Apostles, when they regarded our Lord as having come to establish a temporal kingdom; and, as in their case, from a worldly he may rise to that high principle which is consecrated by the blood of martyrs. There are some who come to church to enjoy the music there, but who remain to pray.

Into this theological statement we have been induced to enter, that, before reverting to the corruptions of the thirteenth and fourteenth centuries which rendered a Reformation necessary, we may see and acknowledge our obligations to the pre-Reformation Church.

It was the duty of those missionaries who, under God, were the founders of the Church of England, to preach the Gospel to the poor; to tell them of a Saviour almighty to save, and to induce them to receive the Lord Jesus as such. They continued to be the only friends of the poor, at a time when any one beneath the dignity of a knight was treated by the supercilious noble as less worthy of his regard than his war-horse, his hawk, or his hound. They compelled the poor to listen, by advocating their cause, and by an appeal to their gratitude. This, however, was not sufficient. They sought to indoctrinate the young, and to enlighten the ignorant, by surrounding them with a Christian atmosphere, and by making the Church a national institution.

The tendency of mankind is to look upwards, and we become, unconsciously, the imitators of those we admire and respect. In every kingdom, therefore, of the so-called Heptarchy, the founders of our Church addressed themselves, in the first instance, to the king and his council. If these were won, they knew that the people would follow. When the king, the council, and the people agreed, the name of the Church was inscribed on every institution of the land, and even on the banners of the battle-field. The nation became a Christian nation, because its laws were based on Christianity.

It may safely be affirmed, that at no period subsequent to the Reformation could the Church of

England have received its present organization. The whole tendency of the religious mind, since the close of the sixteenth century, has been to individualize Christianity. Religion is treated as entirely subjective, and so has become more and more selfish. The simple question has been,—How does Christianity bear upon my salvation? What is the state of my own soul? Not, What is my duty as a sworn soldier and servant of the Great Captain of our salvation? The object for which the Church was incorporated, though partially sustained by missionary exertions, is almost forgotten.

It was by the Church before the Reformation that our dioceses were formed, very nearly as they now are; and, at the same time, the parochial system was established; a minister of the Gospel is planted in each rural district, which otherwise the glad sounds of salvation would only occasionally and fitfully have reached. To the exertions of our ancestors, in ages far remote, we owe the endowments of our Church; endowments for which we are indebted to private benevolence, and not to the State; except so far as the State has extended to them the same protection, which it is required to extend to other owners of property. If St. Paul's was rebuilt, and other Cathedrals have been restored, still the foundations were laid before the Reformation, and it is to pre-Reformation piety that we are entirely indebted for what still remains of these establishments. Although in our universities some of our colleges have been founded subsequently to the reign of Henry VIII, yet the universities themselves are mediæval institutions. Our Book of Common Prayer was not the composition of the illustrious men by whom the Reformation of our Church was conducted; but it existed in the "Use of Sarum," which was itself an anticipation of the Prayer-book;

being an attempt to reduce the various rituals of the
Church of England to one book.

So far we have spoken of compulsion effected by
recourse to legitimate measures;—measures which,
injurious to no one, are the means of alluring the
young, the weak, and the ignorant into the narrow
path that leadeth to eternal life. Among true
Christians, then, if a question arises on this subject
it cannot have reference to compulsion, considered
abstractedly; it refers to the employment of legitimate
or illegitimate means, to effect the end they have in
view. There can be no doubt, that the abuse of this
principle has led to persecution; but a principle is not
to be condemned because in its abuse it may terminate
in criminal action. The truth is, that, when it does so,
it becomes a new principle with an old name. Accustomed, in the nineteenth century, to test our opinions
by a reference to Scripture, we at once condemn as
irreligious, while we denounce as horrible, the acts of
intolerance and persecution of which, not only in the
sixteenth and seventeenth centuries, but in almost
every age before and since, we read the history. The
wars of Charlemagne, the Crusades, the fires of
Smithfield, the severities of Crumwell and of Bonner,
the battles of the Puritans, the treatment of the
Covenanters, to say nothing of the Inquisition, and
the miserable war, in which that institution found
its birth or at all events its first sphere of action,
are denounced with one universal cry of reprobation;
and yet it will be observed there is no religious
party, sect, school, or faction, from which the ac-
cursed spot can be washed out. No mistake can
be greater, than that which would represent the Reformation as a struggle for freedom; this mistake,
however, has rendered the name of Protestant dear to
the politician who, regardless of religion, has inscribed

"civil and religious liberty" on the banner of his
party.

The notion of religious liberty, or even of toleration, never entered into the mind of any Reformer
of the sixteenth century. With Lutheran, Zuinglian,
Romanist, Anglican, the simple question was, What is
the truth? Each party claimed to be in possession
of the truth; each struggled for the mastery, in order
that it might compel its opponents to accept the
truth to which, it was imagined, God gave the Divine
sanction when, through the operation of Divine Providence, He gave to the one party the success which
He denied to the other. By degrees men learned,
that visible and immediate success in this world was
not a criterion of the truth; and for the toleration we
enjoy we are indebted rather to the mutual interests
than to the generosity of mankind. In the uncertainty
of human events, the party in the ascendant to-day
may be in a miserable minority to-morrow; and all
parties have come to a tacit understanding, that the
security from persecution, to be enjoyed by each, can
only be secured by extending an exemption from
physical persecution to all. This is the result of that
which, abstractly considered, is a calamity—the disunion of Christendom and the formation of those
sects, which came into existence during, or after, the
Reformation of the sixteenth century. Disunion is a
great calamity; for reunion the heart of man begins
to yearn. But the Christian always sees the hand
of Providence behind the darkness and the cloud,
unceasingly employed in educing good out of evil.
It would, humanly speaking, have been impossible for
the corruptions of the Church to have been removed,
and for a spirit of toleration to have been gradually
created, if men had not been made to feel, that their
own security depends upon the granting to others,

of that toleration of which they may themselves soon stand in need.

Hence we hear no more of the rack or the stake. But the *spirit* of persecution is as rife and as general in the nineteenth century as it was in the sixteenth. When godless mobs are inebriated by concealed fanatics to attack unpopular churches; when parliamentary senility invokes authority to treat æstheticism as a crime ; we are inclined to think, that an absence of persecution is to be attributed to want of power rather than to want of will. When we observe the rancour with which, with a few honourable exceptions, that portion of the public press which assumes to itself the character of religious, is accustomed to vilify the great and the good, whose doctrinal principles or ecclesiastical taste are impugned ; we feel, that we are indebted for our safety, not to religious charity, but to a well-ordered police. The truculent letters by which all are assailed, almost daily, who occupy a prominent position in Church or State, are sufficient to prove that, if Bonner's hand be paralysed, Bonner's heart still beats in many a breast.

It is sometimes assumed, that this bitterness of spirit is peculiar to religious controversy ; but we must not forget, that the *odium geologicum*, though more unreasonable, is quite as bitter as the *odium theologicum*. We are painfully reminded of the controversies into which men of science and literature, with less excuse, have been precipitated. Unregenerate man is by nature intolerant, and of those who imagine themselves tolerant there are many who are merely indifferent. When the intellect alone is in activity, and the passions are unconcerned, to display a spirit of toleration towards those who differ from us in opinion may be comparatively easy. Very different is it found to be, when the affections are enlisted in

the cause; still more so, when emotions of vanity and
self-love are excited. That the passions are easily
roused and with difficulty appeased, in theological
discussions, it will be our duty, in the present book,
to state and lament; but we must remind the reader,
that they have been, and still are, exhibited, with
equal intensity, in every pursuit to which thoughtful
men have given up their hearts. The hard language
that passed between Newton and Flamstead reflects
no honour on their noble science or on their personal
self-control. After Newton's death, the fluxional controversy is a blot upon the page of science. Hot
as fire were the controversies on phlogiston and
hydrogen. Recently the question whether a gorilla's
hippocampus minor did or did not diminish the
similarity of his brain to that of man, provoked a
fierce personal altercation between two eminent natu-
ralists; because each staked, to a certain extent, his
own scientific reputation on the result.

If we proceed from science to literature, especially
at the revival of learning, the reader is grieved or
amused, when he finds a man like Scaliger heaping on
the gentle and refined Erasmus, epithets of contumely,
which he certainly did not find in his favourite classic;
and which suggests the idea that he must have occasionally visited the fishmarket. Erasmus is described
as a drunkard, a hangman, a parricide, a monster, a
Porphyry, a Luther, and an infidel,—and all because,
in his "Ciceronianus," he accused the Ciceronians of
admiring Cicero too much. It is equally painful, at a
later period, to find Salmasius, a man of learning and
a courtier, cruelly describing Milton, because he was a
republican, as

"Monstrum horrendum informe ingens cui lumen ademptum;"

and we are sorry to be informed, that our sublime

poet, instead of treating the rudeness with contempt, in his just indignation at the personalities of his opponent, employed language equally pungent.

In the present age, literary men are aware, that, by their criminations and recriminations, they amuse, without exciting an unsympathising public by exposing themselves to ridicule; and our most painful instances of intolerance are to be sought for in the political world. *

It is because the intensity of feeling, brought to bear upon religion in the sixteenth century, is directed,

---

* By the system of anonymous journalism controversialists have discovered the means of giving a keener edge to the dagger they would aim at a rival's heart. By assuming the first person plural instead of the first person singular, the modern Scaliger can make it appear, that his opponent is a hangman, a parricide, and a monster, not merely in his own opinion, but in the opinion of the whole world, represented by the mysterious WE. Much may be said in favour of the anonymous in Political journalism. It may not always be expedient to produce the authority on which a statement is made. As in tournaments of old, some unknown knight would come unexpectedly to the rescue; so in the political contest, in aid of his party, a great man may come, from the council-board or the senate, down to the printing office, whose influence in his proper sphere would be diminished if he assumed the position also of a political writer. But in favour of anonymous *criticism* scarcely a word can be said. When the question relates to the merits or the demerits of a literary or scientific publication, the public ought to be informed, whether the critic, who represents the plurality of voices by whom judgment is pronounced, is a man competent to sit in judgment upon the author. We know before-hand, that from political or religious partisanship an author will be undeservedly praised in one place, and as undeservedly censured in another. The opportunity offered for the indulgence of private malignity and revenge is obvious. The system is nearly exploded in France, and we are following the example, though with our usual caution, in England. The reviews of distinguished authors are now republished as essays; but still the vituperative and anonymous system is carried so far, that some distinguished men may be named, who, while lending a large amount of literary assistance to others, have refused to come forward as authors themselves.

in the present age, to the subject of politics, that
the course of conduct which, when apparent in the
theologian, is held up to reprobation, is, inconsistently, vindicated whenever it may chance to be
applied to the assertion or maintenance of political
principles. In favour of persecuting political offenders,
or men regarded as such, modern historians have much
to advance. In a political age, their defence of persecution for the furtherance of political ends, is received
with very general applause. We might quote passages
from more than one of the most popular historians of
modern times, in which the execution of such men as the
Earl of Strafford and of King Charles I. is treated with
a levity sufficient to show, that their tolerance in what
relates to religion is the tolerance, not of principle
but of indifference. *Crudelitatis odio in crudelitatem
ruitis.* The death of a king is treated as a jest,
and that of a hostile statesman with exultation.
Upon this subject I am not at present concerned
to give an opinion; we only contend, that we must
deal justly to all men; and what is said in justification of a political persecution must be, in all fairness,
adduced in palliation of the evil deeds of religious
enthusiasts.

By the writers to whom I refer it is asserted—and
to the assertion the public in general assents—that
as you execute a robber and condemn a murderer
to death, so to death you may condemn the king or
the statesman, who robs the citizen or subject of his
property, his just rights, or his liberty. If we admit
the lawfulness of capital punishment in any case, we
cannot deny, that to a traitor's death a king, found
guilty of treason against the country over which he
is appointed to preside, may be justly doomed. But
if we accept this principle at all, we cannot censure
its application in the case of heresy. Innocent III.

adverted to the executions which abounded in his time, for offences against the laws enacted for the protection of life and property ; and then he continues :—"He that taketh away the faith of a man stealeth his life, for the just shall live by faith." If you condemn a man to death because he has robbed somebody of his life in this world ; *à fortiori*, the pontiff argues, you may inflict capital punishment on the man who robs another of his spiritual and eternal life. The same line is taken by Thomas Aquinas. That great man argues, that, if false coiners be punished with death, much more is such a doom deserved by heretics, forasmuch as a corruption of faith whereby the soul has its life is far worse than a falsification of money. In like manner, another Dominican, Humbert de Romanis, inculcates the duty of punishing heretics, and declares, that if even the pope were a heretic—a supposition which our Church historian observes was not in that age supposed to be impossible—he should be subjected to punishment.*

It was not, indeed, for *holding* erroneous opinions, as is sometimes supposed, that men were punished, but for *propagating* those opinions. Until the passions were roused in the sixteenth century, and so long as the discussions were confined to the schools of

---

* See Robertson, Hist. of Christian Church, iii. 561. Upon this subject we shall never probably be consistent until capital punishment for any offence is abolished. How far it may be considered possible, with a due regard to life and property, to abolish capital punishments, I am not concerned to say. But if you slay the man who attacks your property or life, you are undoubtedly open to the retort, that you only condemn those who would inflict a similar punishment on the propagators of heresy, because you value life and property, but do not value the human soul. Because we value the human soul, instead of condemning the criminal, under any circumstances, to death, ought we not to give him time for repentance ?

learning, considerable latitude was allowed on all that pertained to theological opinion. Just before the commencement of the Reformation, we have seen that complaint was made, that the bishops of the Church of England were lukewarm in the suppression of heresy. When the passions were once excited, and the aid of political revolutionists was invoked by religious reformers, then began the tale of horror which we shall have to recount.

Although we contend, that a spirit of intolerance is natural to man in his unrenewed nature, we must at the same time affirm, that a resort to acts of persecution, under any plea whatever, is more criminal in a Christian than it is in any other person or party. When the Christian was directed to have recourse to all legitimate means for propagating the Gospel, he was expressly warned, that his weapons were not to be carnal. This, the first warning against persecution, was given in Scripture, at the very time that zeal for the propagation of revealed truth was required. Men were warned not to rush from one extreme to another. An action which in its proper place is a virtue may, when urged to excess, become a vice. It is good to be "zealously affected in a good cause:" but zeal without love may be a mere human, and is sometimes a diabolical, passion.

The reader of these volumes is well aware, that what is called the Reformation was not, as is commonly supposed, an improvised revolution for which men had not been prepared. The history of our Church, from the time of the Conquest, is the history of a continued struggle, varying in its intensity in different ages, against the papacy. It was not a struggle confined to the laity; the laity rather came to the aid of the clergy, who were the first to suffer from the papal aggression. The struggle would have come to a crisis earlier, if it had not been, that it was too generally the interest of the king to side with the pope, and so to evade the law. The statutes of Provisors and Præmunire, though, at a subsequent period, turned against the clergy, were originally enacted for their protection against the pope. No man in the kingdom was more devoted to the papal interests than King Henry VIII. until his passions separated his interests from those of the pontiff. When he determined upon that separation, he found everything relating to the independence of the Church of England, prepared to his hand. The nation, ripe for no other reforms, was ready to assert its independence, and to renounce the jurisdiction of the foreign prince, prelate, state, and potentate who had been, all along, resisted in his usurpations by the laws of the land.

We have seen how the powerful intellect of John Wiclif, when led by his politics to examine the subject of papal pretensions, went at once to the root of the evil. He proclaimed, that the whole Church system required revision and reform; he pointed out that we could only discover what the errors were which the Western Church unconsciously held, by a reference to some authority admitted by all. That the Bible was written by inspired men all agreed in asserting; the authority of the Bible therefore could not be denied, nor could it be denied that a doctrine condemned by the Bible could not be true; therefore, that all might have insight into the corrupt state of the Church, the Bible was translated by Wiclif.

It did not, however, follow that the man, who invented the needle-gun, should himself know how to use it; Wiclif might prepare a weapon to attack corruptions of the Church without employing it properly. He was himself led into many fallacies from not perceiving, that though the Bible is the authority, yet it is an authority only when it is rightly interpreted. He pointed his weapon against his opponents, and, not being properly wielded, the weapon sometimes recoiled upon himself. When the time of his departure came, while there were many who, piously and in secret, studied the sacred volume he had placed in their hands, yet he left behind him, not a religious party, but only a violent political faction, which in his name propagated what would now be called the principles of Socialism. This so alarmed the conservatism of Europe as to delay an effectual reformation for more than a century.

Dismayed by the spread of Lollardism, the illustrious reformers, who, at Pisa, Constance, and Basle, contended for the liberty of the Church, and asserted its superiority over the pope, failed in their labours by deviating into an opposite extreme. Their denunciation of the malpractices of ecclesiastics, particularly of monks, was vehement and loud; but they were careful to deny, that any correction of doctrine was required. They even accepted as an article of faith what till then had been only a prevalent opinion in the Church, the "Thomistic figment" of transubstantiation. They thought to reform the Church, by taking steps to rectify the administration of its discipline, to bring the canons to bear on all alike, and to make both pope and people amenable to general councils to be periodically convened.

Such was the state of things, when the voice of Luther was heard; and his reformation, with differences in detail but identical in principle with that of Zuingle and Calvin, soon extended from the northern provinces of Germany to the Rhine and the Seine; from Würtemburg to the Lake of Geneva and the

Alpine Valleys : it approached England, like the Gulf Stream, influencing our moral atmosphere, touching but not penetrating our theology.

The principle of Wiclif was accepted and modified. It was agreed, that what could not be read in the Bible, or proved thereby, ought not to be enforced as an article of faith. It was contended, that every doctrine received in the Church, if disputed, was to be brought to this test. But the fanatical notion propounded by Chillingworth in the following century, that the Bible, and the Bible only,—understood by the private judgment of each individual, however *idiotic* he may be,—is the religion of Protestants, never entered into the minds of those great men, Luther and Melancthon, to whom the title of Protestant was first applied; or of that great theologian to whom the same title, in modern parlance, applies, John Calvin. The confessions of faith, which no man within their sway could reject without peril of life, survive to bear witness to the principle, that when they referred to the Bible, they meant the Bible rightly interpreted. Whether they can be justified in the position they assumed, that their own interpretation of the Bible is the only interpretation admissible, may be doubted; *more* than doubted, when we find that, on some material points, they differed from one another. There can, however, be no doubt, that while they agreed with Wiclif in making the inspired volume the test of truth, they sought to escape from the serious errors into which his followers, if not Wiclif himself, had been hurried. This they endeavoured to do by drawing up those confessions of faith which contain their view of fundamental truths.

The necessity of a Reformation having been long acknowledged and declared by the whole Western Church, the Church of Rome undertook to reform

itself and all the Churches which continued to adhere to the papal system. To reform the Church
the Council of Trent was convened. The first session
was held on the 13th of December, 1545 ; when there
were present, besides the three papal legates, four
archbishops and twenty-two bishops ; the last session
took place on the 3rd of December, 1563. It concluded in establishing modern Romanism in the secta-
rian sense of the word.

That the Council of Trent did not represent the
Catholic Church is an historical fact, which can be
denied by those and only those who make Catholicism
and Romanism convertible terms.* The great Catholic
Churches of the East, or the Greek Church, were not
represented ; and, besides the Church of England,
there were other European Churches which refused
to send delegates to the synod.

Several wise measures were adopted, by which the
foundation was laid for a reformation of ecclesiastical
discipline ; but in regard to doctrine, instead of ac-

---

* The pope had decreed, that the title to be given to the Council
should run in this form : " The Holy Œcumenical and General
Council of Trent." To this the Gallican bishops, together with
many of the Italians and Spaniards, objected ; asserting that the
following words should be added, " representing the Universal
Church." To this proposed addition the legates would not give
their consent. It had been the form used at Constance and Basle,
and they feared that the rest of the form of those councils would
follow, " which derives its power immediately from Jesus Christ,
and to which every person of whatever dignity, not excepting the
pope, is bound to yield obedience." The reader will observe, that
the council itself did not claim to be binding upon all Churches,
and he will also perceive how this corroborates the statement frequently made that the Ultramontane notion had no date anterior to
the time of Martin V. The English Church, therefore, adhering to
the principles of the great councils of the fifteenth century, was, in
its reformation, pursuing a consistent course.

cepting the Bible, rightly interpreted, as the standard by which to ascertain how far, in the lapse of ages, the Church had deviated from primitive truth; they asserted Christianity to be a continuous revelation to the Catholic, which was, in their sense, the Roman, Church. It was not their duty to contend for the faith, which, as we learn from Scripture, was once, and once for all, delivered to the saints; but their business was, through the miraculous inspiration of the Holy Ghost, to add such articles of faith to the existing dogmas of Christianity as the exigencies of the time or the demand of the faithful might require.

Among the sacred books of the Church, the Bible stood the first, and for the purposes of devotion it ought to be studied, under proper regulations and restrictions; but as the guide of the Church or the test of the truth, it was such neither to individuals nor to the Church in general. Although among the Tridentine fathers there were many good and pious men, who desired to pursue a different course, yet they were overruled and silenced. Therefore not an attempt was made on disputable points to compare the existing theology with the theology of the fathers, or with Holy Scripture; the business of the Synod was rather to confirm and methodize the doctrines of the Middle Ages; and many doctrines which had previously been merely pious opinions still open to discussion, were, at this time, made articles of faith.*

* It is observed by Mosheim, that not only was every doctrine that had been established by mediæval councils received, but many maxims of the scholastic doctors on intricate subjects, which had formerly been left undecided, and had wisely been permitted as subjects of debate, were by the council absurdly adopted as articles of faith, and imposed with violence on the consciences of men, under pain of excommunication. For example, the use of indulgences, as relating to the release of souls out of purgatory, by the pope's authority, was prevalent before the Council of Trent, and

Before the Council of Trent had entered upon its first session, the foundation had been laid for the reformation of the Church of England, which was gradually carried on until its completion in 1662.

gave rise to the Lutheran movement, yet the first of the (so-called) general councils which decreed in favour of indulgences was that of Trent. The same is to be said of the Roman Canon of Scripture. which includes the Apocrypha. The Council of Trent was the first council which enforced by anathema the acknowledgment of seven sacraments. The Council of Trent was the first to decree concerning the necessity of the priest's intention in order to the validity of sacraments. It had been put forth by Pope Eugenius in his letter to the Armenians in the Council of Florence, but was not confirmed by the authority of that council. The Tridentine doctrine is as follows :—'If any man shall say that there is not required in the ministers, when they administer the sacraments, the intention of doing what the Church does, let him be anathema.' It was now also that the doctrine of the 15th century, which placed a council above the pope, was finally cancelled. Of the infallibility of the Church the councils had no doubt, but with them the voice which uttered the infallible judgment was the council. The Tridentine doctrine is, that, after taking counsel, the pope was to speak, and that through him the infallibility of the Church was to be pronounced. We have as much right to affirm that the Church of Rome was founded at the Council of Trent, as that our Church was founded at the Reformation. It is most important to observe the difference between Post-Reformation Romanism, the Romanism of the Council of Trent, and Pre-Reformation Catholicism. The editor of Mosheim, adds the following observation on the drawing up of the Forty-two Articles by the English Church in the reign of Edward VI.— "This body of doctrine received the unanimous consent of Convocation at the end of July, 1563. The prelates authenticated it immediately by their subscriptions ; the Lower House did this after some delay. It is worthy of remark that Romanism could not appeal to a similar authentication till the year 1563. The Council of Trent then ceased its sessions, and gave authority to that mass of doctrine, uncontained, it seems to ordinary readers or students, in Scripture, which Pius IV. has embodied in the celebrated creed which bears his name. Thus, in fact, the English Church preceded the Roman in the formal enunciation of her principles. To the Tridentine divines, forming a body chiefly Italian and

Although the divines who commenced the Reformation in England were many of them influenced, at first, by a sympathy with Luther ; and afterwards, as regards some of them, with a greater sympathy with Zwingle ; yet their work differed materially from what was going on contemporaneously, or nearly so, among the Protestants on the Continent. Ours was, in the strict sense of the word, a Reformation, which theirs was not.

The Protestant reformers on the Continent were, by circumstances over which they had no control, excluded from the Church. Their proceedings, in consequence, resulted in a new creation rather than in a reformation, the latter word implying a pre-existing entity. While we admire or criticise their splendid exertions to remedy an inevitable evil, we lament that they had no Church to reform, and had therefore to deviate into sects. Instead of a succession of ministers from the Apostles, they had, in each sect, to create the ministers ; and if a succession be observed, the succession dates from the founder of the sect.

To confound the Church of England with the various sects thus created at the Reformation, is the policy of the Romanists in this country ; they presume upon the acknowledged ignorance of even educated Englishmen as regards the history of their country, and especially of their Church. In hostility to the Church, the infidel makes common cause with the Romanist ;

Spanish, sitting in the 16th century, not to any society or other unquestionable sanction, the Church of Rome is indebted for the formal authentication of her peculiar or post-Reformation creed. Englishmen must have had as great right to deliberate on theological difficulties, which had hitherto been universally open to debate ; and they certainly took the safer side, in exacting no man's belief to such doctrines as were undoubtedly destitute of any certain warranty in Scripture, and, as many scholars thought, were equally destitute of any safe authority from Catholic tradition."

and we have to regret that, under the same feeling, the same course is pursued by some of the foreign Protestants. They fail to perceive that, in upholding the real position of the Church of England as possessing peculiar advantages, they strengthen what was called, in former times, the bulwark of the Reformation.

When we speak of the continuity and perpetuity of the English Church, we only affirm an historical fact. But, as historical facts are not unfrequently mis-stated, or perverted for party purposes, it is advantageous to the cause of truth to be able to state these facts in the eloquent words of a writer who has studied history impartially, and with the mind of a liberal philosopher. Mr. Gladstone, with Sir William Page Wood, Lord Lyttelton, Sir Roundell Palmer, and a few eminent statesmen and lawyers, has divorced religion from party politics; and if, as a man, he contends for the civil rights of the people, he labours with equal zeal, as a Christian, for the promotion of God's glory.

"I can find," he says, "no trace of that opinion which is now common in the mouths of unthinking persons, that the Roman Catholic Church was abolished in England at the period of the Reformation, and that a Protestant Church was put in its place; nor does there appear to have been so much as a doubt in the mind of any one of them, whether the Church legally established in England after the Reformation was the same institution with the Church legally established in England before the Reformation. When Whitgift died, with the memorable words, *Pro Ecclesiâ Dei*, on his lips, the image that hovered before the mind of the aged and faithful primate was no device of the human fancy, no creature of civil law; but a determinate, transmitted gift of God, the Church of all times and of all places, to him represented, but not limited, by its

local organization in England. In short, the spirit of
the English Reformation, with respect to the continuity
of the Church, cannot be better exemplified than by
the words of the *congé d'élire*, in which Elizabeth
empowered the Dean and Chapter of Canterbury to
elect Parker to the Metropolitan See. '*Cum Ecclesia
prædicta per mortem naturalem reverendissimi in
Christo Patris et Domini Reginaldi Pole. . . . jam
vacat, et pastoris sit solatio destituta;*' therefore, it
proceeds, we give you our licence as Founder to proceed
to a new election, and recommend accordingly." *

He points out how different it was with respect to
the Religious Revolution,—for so it was rather than a
Reformation,—in Scotland. He names the year when
in Scotland the Catholic Church was *un*-established :
the Act was passed in 1560, in the Scottish Parliament,
which forbade the ministrations of the ancient priesthood.

In England he states, that the course of events was
widely different. " Her Reformation, through the providence of God, succeeded in maintaining the unity
and continuity of the Church in her apostolical ministry. We have, therefore, still among us the ordained
hereditary witnesses of the truth, conveying it to us
through an unbroken series from our Lord Jesus Christ
and His Apostles. This is but the ordinary voice of
authority ; of authority equally reasonable and equally
true, whether we will hear, or whether we will forbear ;
of authority which does not supersede either the exercise of private judgment, or the sense of the Church at
large, or the supremacy of Scripture ; but assists the
first, locally applies the second, and publicly witnesses
the last."†

* Gladstone, The State in its Relations with the Church, ii. 127.
† Ibid. ii. 95.

In another work Mr. Gladstone asserts the fact more clearly still. "We follow the institution, which, existing in this country for sixteen hundred years or more, was founded among us by missionaries undoubtedly apostolical : which has kept unmutilated among us the Divine Word : which has handed down the performance of its offices by uninterrupted succession, from man to man, through a line of bishops : which has given us the primitive creeds of the Church as limits of its interpretation of Scripture : which has, with whatever doctrinal abuse, never forsaken those great Scriptural positions which are brought out in her ancient symbols : and which, therefore, coming to us in the first instance with clear and sufficient marks of the Christian Church upon her, has never at any time so far degenerated as to lose those marks ; as to abandon those truths and those sacraments which are appointed for the salvation of the soul. And we still bear strong, even if unconscious testimony to her claims in her familiar appellation, the Church *of England.*" *

"But some of Protestant opinions," he observes, "say that this institution, though remaining outwardly the same, lost its identity as a Church before the Reformation, in consequence of the corruption of doctrine and prevalence of idolatry. This, however, is an opinion that will hardly be maintained in serious discussion. The *primâ facie* grounds for it are exceedingly weakened when we consider that the Scriptures remained uncorrupt, that their essential doctrines held their place undisputed in the Creeds, and that the prevalent errors, however grievous, firstly, were such as did not directly overthrow or deny, as Hooker says, the foundation ; secondly, that they had not then been generally recognised and established as of faith by any Council of the

* Gladstone, Church Principles, 290.

Church, much less by any decree in which the Church of England had taken part. We may therefore assume, on the part of all those who believe in the perpetual visibility of the Church of Christ, that it was actually existing by unbroken succession in this country at the period of the Reformation." *

To this we may add the fact, that by both Church and State measures had been adopted to annihilate the Papal authority in England, long before any notion was entertained of dealing with any points of doctrine. In the twenty-eighth year of Henry's reign, when king and parliament and Church were vehement in their opposition to Protestantism, some of the chief acts against the pope and his pretensions were passed in parliament. The Commons followed the example of the House of Lords; and in the House of Lords the lords spiritual formed a decided majority. Such were the acts prohibiting appeals to Rome; for the payment of first-fruits to the crown; for repudiating all the exactions of the court of Rome; for enforcing the act of convocation in the assertion of the royal supremacy; the renunciation of papal bulls, faculties, and dispensations, together with the act for utterly extinguishing the usurped authority of the See of Rome. The Church of England was antipapal before it was reformed.†

At the commencement of the dispute between the Church of England and the court of Rome, in the

* Gladstone, Church Principles, 307. There are three works of Mr. Gladstone to which reference is made, and which, as expository of the doctrine and history of the Church of England, will always be regarded as standard works: 1, Church Principles. 2, The State in its Relations to the Church. 3, Remarks on the Royal Supremacy. The last was published in 1850.

† 24 Henry VIII. c 12; 25 Henry VIII. c. 19; 25 Henry VIII. c. 20; 26 Henry VIII. c. 3; 25 Henry VIII. c. 16; 28 Henry VIII. c. 10.

sixteenth century, the State accepted as a fact, what
the Church affirmed ; that the work to be done, by the
co-operation of the civil and ecclesiastical authorities
in England, was not the displacing of the old Church,
and the supplanting of it by some new sect; but the
gradual reformation of that old Catholic Church;* which

* The word Catholic was originally employed to distinguish the
Church after our Lord's coming, when it was open to all mankind
who might seek admission by baptism, from the Church before our
Lord's coming, when it was confined to one nation—the Church
under the commission to preach the Gospel to every creature, from
the Church enjoined to keep itself separate from all the rest of mankind—the Church preparing for the second coming of our Lord,
from the Church preparing for His first coming. When Christians divided themselves into sects, it was used, as a word of the
second intention, to distinguish from the sects that Church in which
the apostolical succession was preserved ; and when Christians became separated by doctrine, it was used to distinguish those who
deferred to the creeds and formularies of the Church from heretics,
those who, as their name denotes, relied upon their private judgment, without extraneous help. It came to mean, by degrees, the
real Church in any locality, implying that those who seceded from
it were schismatical, even when not absolutely heretical. Hence
Mr. Coleridge, with his usual clearness of expression, remarks,
" The present adherents of the Church of Rome are not, in my judgment, Catholics. We are Catholics. We can prove that we held
the doctrine of the primitive Church for the first three hundred
years. The Council of Trent made the Papists what they are."—
Table Talk, p. 31. " The adherents of the Church of Rome, I
repeat, are not Catholics. If they are, it follows that we are heretics and schismatics."—*Table Talk*, p. 32. Although for party
purposes the Romanists are permitted very frequently to assume a
title which conveys an argument, what is here stated by Coleridge
is well known to every student of English history. A late decision
in the Court of Queen's Bench may be cited as showing what our
law is on the subject treated above. A clergyman desired to establish his claim to certain marriage fees. He would have gained his
suit if he could have proved that his predecessors in the time of
Richard I. had received the payment ; and failing in that proof, he
was nonsuited. The whole process depended upon the sameness of
the Church before and after the Reformation.

had been established here in the first instance, by the joint labour and devotion of Augustine, the first Archbishop of Canterbury, and Ethelbert, King of Kent, the Bretwalda.

In the preamble of the statute of 1532, it is expressly stated, that the act had reference to the body spiritual, usually called the English Church; that this Church had power when any cause of the law divine happened to come in question or of spiritual learning; and is meet of itself, without the intermeddling of any exterior person or persons, to declare all such doubts and to administer all such offices and duties as to their rooms spiritual appertain; that to keep them from corruption and sinister affection the king's most noble progenitors, and the antecessors of the nobles of the realm, had sufficiently endowed the said Church with honour and possessions.[*]

In an act passed in the following year, for abolishing the payment of Peter-pence to Rome, there is a proviso, that nothing, in that act contained, shall be hereafter interpreted or expounded, "that your grace, your nobles, and subjects intend by the same to decline or vary from the congregation of Christ's Church, in anything concerning the Catholic faith of Christendom."

Henry VIII. in a letter, which he caused to be addressed in his name to Cardinal Pole, speaks thus:—
"In all your book, your purpose is to bring the king's grace by penance home into the Church again, as a man clearly *separate* from the same already. And his recess from the Church ye prove not otherwise, than by the fame and common opinion of those parties who be far from the knowledge of the truth of our affairs here," &c. . . . . "Ye presuppose for a ground the king's grace to be *severed* from the *unity* of Christ's Church,

[*] 24 Henry VIII. c. 12; Statutes of the Realm, II. 427.

and that, in taking upon him the title of supreme head of the Church of England, he intendeth to *separate his Church of England from the unity of the whole body of Christendom*, taking upon him the office, belonging unto spiritual men grounded in the Scripture, of immediate cure of souls; and attribute to himself that which belongeth to priesthood, as to preach and teach the word of God, and to minister the sacraments; and that he doth not know what belongeth to a Christian king's office, and what unto priesthood; wherein surely both you and all others, so thinking of him, do err too far," &c. . . . "His full purpose and intent is, to see the laws of Almighty God purely and sincerely preached and taught, and Christ's faith without blot kept and observed in his realm; *and not to separate himself or his realm anywise from the unity of Christ's Catholic Church, but inviolably at all times to keep and observe the same*, and to redeem his Church of England out of all captivity of foreign powers heretofore *usurped* therein, into the Christian state that all Churches of all realms were in at the *beginning*; and to abolish and clearly put away such *usurpations* as heretofore in this realm the Bishops of Rome have, by many undue means, increased to their great advantage," &c. . . .

"Wherefore, since the king's grace goeth about to reform his realm, and reduce the Church of England into that state, that both this realm and all others were in at the beginning of the faith, and many hundred years after; *if any prince or realm will not follow him, let them do as they list:* he doth nothing but stablisheth such laws as were in the beginning, and such as the Bishop of Rome professeth to observe. *Wherefore neither the Bishop of Rome himself nor other prince ought of reason to be miscontent herewith.*"[*]

[*] Burnet, III., Records 52.

How carefully this principle was observed, throughout the reign of Queen Elizabeth, the student of history is well aware. If, during the reigns of James I. and his successor, an Erastian tone insinuated itself into the writings, even of some of our great divines, yet they still asserted, in the words of one of the most distinguished among those eminent men: " I make not the least doubt in the world, but that the Church of England before the Reformation and the Church of England after the Reformation are as much the same Church as a garden before it is weeded and after it is weeded is the same garden; or a vine before it be pruned and after it is pruned and freed from the luxuriant branches is one and the same vine." *

CHAP.
I.
Introductory.

The representatives in England of the Church of Rome are, at the present time, as much a dissenting sect as any Protestant nonconformists. We can indeed give the date when the Romanists formed themselves into a separate community. We all know, that it was only within the last few years, that they established a hierarchy in England—tracing that hierarchy not to Augustine, but to Pope Pius IX. the reigning pontiff. Their position in England is symbolized in their establishment at York. In that city we, the reformed English Catholics, have inherited the cathedral erected by our forefathers. It is our inheritance, just as an estate pertains to some ancient family in right of its being the representative of the family to which the property was originally granted. Close by the side of the ancient cathedral, the Romish nonconformists have erected, with questionable taste, what they call a pro-cathedral. It is as like a foreign cathedral as a building can be, which, in the absence

* Bramhall, i. 113.

of that which constitutes a cathedral, the Cathedra of the diocesan, can only be a cathedral nominally.

They may retort the charge on foreign Protestants; for the Lutherans, driven out of the Church, were under the necessity of forming a sect. Their sect was made to resemble the ancient Church as nearly as was consistent with their protest against those corruptions which, if they took the Bible for their guide, rendered their conformity to the ancient Church in their country, a thing impossible.

The Church of England, on the contrary, stood like an old cathedral. We were Catholic and Anglican; and when, with the Bible in our hands, we looked around us, we found " our holy and beautiful house, the place where our fathers worshipped," filled with graven images, which we displaced. We found only a few, comparatively speaking, kneeling at the altar of our Lord our Saviour and our God; while multitudes were prostrate before the image of the Virgin Mary. That image became to us Nehushtan; and, explaining to men the nature of idolatry, we bade them do service, by worshipping, to God, and to God only. The walls were daubed with untempered mortar, and on them were painted the history of saints, either wholly imaginary, or whose legends, we are told by an hagiographer, were intended to relate not what they really did, but what they might have done, because to do so was part of the saintly character. The bats and birds were occupying portions of the building, and other portions were beslimed with filth. We did away at once with that which was absolutely wrong; and we prepared to set in order that which, though right, was out of place. The papal arms were demolished; but the bishop's throne remained, the marble chair in which Augustine sat. The tawdry vestments in which the clergy were arrayed or the sanctuary decorated, were rendered conformable to a better taste, than that by which they were overlaid in the middle ages. The pulpit remained ; but the preacher was required to ground his discourses on the Bible, and the Bible only, which he was to interpret by the light afforded from the primitive Church. The Holy Table still continued an altar, at which communicants might offer themselves with the Church militant and triumphant, their souls and bodies to be a reasonable, holy and lively sacrifice to our heavenly Father ; but the sacrifice of the Mass—the re-offering of Christ as a sacrifice for the living and the dead—was repudiated and condemned.

The Church of England being one and the same Church before and after the Reformation, our Reformers accepted the doctrine and followed the usages handed down to them from our forefathers. But, by the intellectual hurricane which was convulsing European society, they were made sensible that, although the foundation was secure, there was much in the superstructure which it could not sustain. Like the Lutherans and Zuinglians, they were ready to bring the doctrines transmitted to them, whenever their meaning was disputed, to the test of Scripture ; and, when the dispute extended further as to the meaning of Scripture, they were prepared to yield to the decisions of the first four general councils. These councils were distinguished from all others ; they were convened not to record the opinions of the fathers, but to bear testimony to the tradition of apostolic doctrine, preserved in the primitive Churches, over which those fathers respectively presided. Our Reformers received the doctrines of the Church as they found them, assuming, that their existence was a *primâ facie* evidence in their favour. They did not reject anything *because* it was mediæval; but when anything mediæval was of a questionable character, they then sought for guidance from Scripture; and if the Scripture was not clear,—if, when two parties were at variance, both of them claimed Scripture as being on their side,—they then yielded to the decisions of the primitive councils or to the evidence of the primitive writers. They did not do as the Romanists, who professed to yield to the authority of the fathers, but interpreted the fathers by the tenets and practices of the existing Church; but if at any time they found an existing dogma contrary to the patristic theology, then they made an alteration; the modern yielded to the ancient. They fully understood, that "antiquity ought to attend as the handmaid of Scripture, to wait upon her as her mistress, and to observe her; to keep off intruders from making too bold with her, and to discourage strangers from misrepresenting her." For as Dr. Waterland observes: "Those who lived in or near to the apostolic times, might retain in memory what the Apostles themselves, or their immediate successors, thought or said upon such and such points; and though there is no trusting in such case to *oral* tradition as distinct from Scripture, nor to *written* disagreeing with Scripture, yet written accounts, consonant to Scripture, are of use to confirm and strengthen Scripture, and to ascertain its true meaning." They held that if " what appears but *probably* to be taught in Scripture itself, appears certainly to have been taught by the Primitive and Catholic Church, such probability so confirmed and strengthened carries with it the force of demonstration." *

But although this principle was strictly observed throughout our Reformation,—from the primacy of

* Waterland's Works, v. 261, ii. 8.

Warham and the reign of Henry VIII. to the primacy of Juxon and the reign of Charles II.—it was applied gradually and according to circumstances. Our Reformation was a practical movement throughout. We had no fine-spun theories, no speculations among our divines, no original thinkers, such as Luther, Melancthon, or Calvin; as we are not now, so we never have been a theorizing people. A grievance was complained of, admitted, and redressed. Abuses were pointed out, examined, and removed. There was no desire to innovate from the mere love of innovation; there was an instinctive feeling that the present was connected with the past, and a reverence for antiquity was the result. For every step taken a precedent was sought. The first decided measure towards the Reformation of our Church was the resumption of the royal supremacy; and no point can be produced more fully calculated to establish the statement now made. On this subject Professor Brewer justly observes: "The notions that the royal supremacy leapt full armed from the brain of Henry VIII.; that the clergy were irresponsible even in spiritual matters, or that the Pope could dictate from Rome to the sovereigns of this country, at least to Henry VII. or Henry VIII. beyond what those princes were willing to allow—still more, that on the papal fiat depended the abstract right or wrong of any question in the minds of the people—are idle phantoms. The canon law had grown up side by side with the laws of the realm. In the weakness and imperfection of other laws, it seemed no more than fitting, that the clergy, as a spiritual body, should be governed by spiritual laws; the encroachments of those laws, and the difficulty of adjusting them with the temporal laws, provoked frequent disputes; but then it remained with the king to decide how far those spiritual laws should be operative.

Antecedently to the Reformation, Convocation could pass no canons without the king's consent; no bull or ecclesiastical constitution could be published in this country without his sanction; no bishop, no abbot, no prior could assume their several offices without the royal permission. As a right, though not always as a fact, the supremacy of the king had continued from time immemorial :—the usurpations upon that right were resisted and modified by the energy and will of the sovereign." [*]

With the truth of this statement the reader of the present work is already familiar; but, if he desires to see the fact more fully established, he may be referred to Sir Edward Coke's reports, " On the case of Caudrey, Parson of South Lufnam." He shows, by historical references, that the Act of Supremacy was not a statute introducing a new law, but that it was merely declaratory of the old. He proves, that the royal supremacy was in theory always held. Although it was frequently the interest of the crown to make common cause with the pope against the English bishops and other clergy, yet, when the prerogatives of the crown, at any time, came into collision with the assumed power of the papacy, the supremacy of the king over all causes and all persons, ecclesiastical as well as civil, was regarded as an indisputable fact of the constitution.

The reader will remember that from the Conquest to the Reformation, the kings of England were, at their coronation, required to make oath, that they would observe and do the laws of good King Edward. Edward the Confessor was acknowleged by all to be a nursing father of the Church; but touching the royal supremacy he thus declared the law : " The king, who is the vicar of the Highest King, is ordained to this end, that he

---

[*] Preface to Letters and Papers, Henry VIII. vol. ii.

shall govern and rule the earthly kingdom and people of the Lord, and above all things the Holy Church, and that he defend the same from wrongdoers, and pluck up destroy and root out workers of mischief." *

When we remember, that William the Norman invaded England under the papal benediction; the enforcement of this law, as soon as the conquered English regained their ascendency, is peculiarly significant.

To Coke's statements, additions might be easily made; although he is sufficiently copious for the complete establishment of his case. He shows, that the bishoprics in England having been founded by the king's progenitors, the advowsons belonged of right to the crown; that they were at first donatives, as is the case at the present time in Ireland and the colonies; and that the privilege of election was a concession made to chapters by the king, whose *congé d'élire* was therefore necessary. Long before the Reformation, the king could exempt from the dominion of the ordinary; and grant, not episcopal orders of course, but episcopal jurisdiction. All religious houses of royal foundation were by the king exempted from episcopal jurisdiction, and he constituted himself the visitor, discharging the office by a royal commission appointed for the service. He could convert seculars into regulars,† and exonerate—which the pope could not—Cistercians and other orders from

---

* *Rex autem qui Vicarius summi Regis est, ad hoc est constitutus ut regnum terrenum et populum Domini et super omnia sanctam veneretur ecclesiam ejus, et regat et ab injuriosis defendat, et maleficos ab ea evellat, et destruat et penitus desperdat.* See K. Edw. Laws, c. 19, Spelm. Conc. tom. i. p. 62. The reader may also be referred to the preface to Collier's second volume, folio, the fourth of the octavo edition. See also Leges Eccles. Edw. Reg. et Confessor, cc. 15 et 5 ap. Spelman, Concil. i. tom i. 620, where the laws of the other Saxon kings referred to by Coke may be found. Cf. Bramhall, i. 141.

† 2 Hen. IV. c. 3.

the payment of tithes.* He could appropriate churches.†
Ten churches, for example, were appropriated to the
abbey of Croyland by the Saxon kings ; three churches
by the Conqueror to the abbey of Battle, and twenty
by Henry I. to the church of Salisbury. The disposition of preferments upon lapse, accrued to the king ;
and the king being lord paramount, he only could incur
no lapse,—" nullum tempus occurrit Regi." It was
death, or the forfeiture of all his goods, for any one to
publish the pope's bull without the king's permission ;
and, except with the royal licence, no papal legate
dared to place his foot on English ground.

Having introduced this subject by a quotation from
Professor Brewer, I shall sum it up in the powerful
language of Mr. Gladstone. "That the pope," he says,
"was the source of ecclesiastical jurisdiction in the
English Church before the Reformation, is an assertion
of the gravest import, which ought not to have been
thus taken for granted. It is one which I firmly believe
to be false in history, false in law — which in my
view, as an Englishman, is degrading to the nation, and
as a Christian, to the Church. . . . . The fact really is
this : a modern opinion, which by force of modern circumstances, has of late gained great favour in the Church
of Rome, is here dated back and fastened upon ages to
whose fixed principles it was unknown and alien ; and
the case of the Church of England is truly hard, when
the papal authority of the middle ages is exaggerated
far beyond its real and historical scope, with the effect
only of fastening that visionary exaggeration, through
the medium of another fictitious notion of wholesale
transfer of the papal privileges to the crown, upon us,
as the true and legal measure of royal supremacy."‡

* 2 Hen. IV. c. 4.   † 17th Edw. II. c. 8.
‡ Gladstone, Remarks on the Royal Supremacy, 17. Bishop

In the parliament holden at Carlisle in the year 1306, being the 35th of Edward I. the Church was spoken of in the same terms in which it would be spoken of at the present time. "The Holy Church of England was founded in the estate"—not of papacy but—"of prelacy; within the realm of England—not out of it—by the king and his progenitors with the earls, barons, and other nobles of the said realm and their ancestors; to inform the people in the law of God, and to keep hospitality, give alms, and do other works of charity, &c. And the said kings in times past, were wont to have their advice and counsel for the safeguard of the realm, when they had need of such prelates and clerks so advanced; the Bishop of Rome usurping the seignories of such benefices, did give and grant the same benefices to aliens which did never dwell in England, and to cardinals which might not dwell here, &c., in adnullation of the state of the Holy Church of England, disherison of the king, earls, barons, and other nobles of the realm, and in offence and destruction of the laws and rights of this realm, and against the good disposition and will of the first founders; it was enacted by the king,—

CHAP. I.

Introductory.

Gardyner wrote as follows:—"The question is now in everybody's mouth, whether the consent of the universal people of England rests on divine right, by which they declare and regard their illustrious king, Henry VIII. to be the supreme head on earth of the English Church; and by the free vote of this parliament, have invited him to use his right and call himself head of the English Church in name, as he is in fact. In which act," he continues, "no new thing was introduced; only they determined that a power which, of divine right, belongs to their prince, should be more clearly asserted, by adopting a more significant expression; and so much the rather in order to remove the cloud from the eyes of the vulgar, with which the falsely pretended power of the Bishop of Rome has now for some ages overshadowed them."—Steph. Gardineri, *De Vera Obedientia*, Fasc. App. p. 108.

Edward I.—with assent of all the lords and commonalty in full parliament, that the said oppressions, grievances and damage in this realm from thenceforth should not be suffered." *

Of the Statutes of Provisors and Præmunire, having had occasion repeatedly to refer to them, we need only here remark, that they were passed to protect the clergy as well as the laity—or the clergy more than the laity—of the Church of England, from papal aggression ; and that they are based on the royal supremacy. In the Statute of Provisors it is declared, " Our sovereign lord the king and his heirs shall have and enjoy for the time the collations to the archbishops and other dignities elective which be of his advowry ; such as his progenitors had before free election was granted : sith the first elections were granted by the king's progenitors upon a certain form and condition, as, namely, to demand license of the king to choose, and, after choice made, to have his royal assent . . . which condition not being kept, the thing ought by reason to return to its first nature." Further, by the same Statute of Provisors, it is declaratively enacted, that it is the right of the crown of England, and the law of the realm, that upon such mischiefs and damages happening to the realm (by the encroachments and oppressions of the court of Rome, mentioned in the body of that law), the king ought and is bound by his oath, with the accord of his people in parliament, to make remedy and law for the removing of such mischiefs. We find," says Bramhall, " at least seven or eight such statutes made in the reigns of several kings against papal provisions, reservations, and collations, and the mischiefs that flowed from thence." †

* Coke's Reports, i. 14. Gibson's Codex, tit. iii. cc. 1, 2.
† Bramhall, ed. Haddan, i. 147.

In the Statute of Præmunire it is asserted, that "the crown of England hath been so free at all times, that it hath been in no earthly subjection, but immediately subjected to God in all things touching its regality, and to no other; and ought not to be submitted to the pope." *

That such a Church had power to reform itself is at once apparent, and we may be inclined to applaud the wisdom of the sixteenth century; when our ancestors, no longer content with damming up the stream, as their predecessors had done, stopped up the very fountain of papal tyranny.

As the subject of royal supremacy will come frequently before us in the present book, it has been judged expedient to enter upon it thus fully; but the whole question relating to the royal prerogative has been complicated and obscured by a neglect, which not unfrequently occurs, of distinguishing between the royal and the sacerdotal powers. Both Henry VIII. and Queen Elizabeth clearly perceived, and, in theory admitted, the distinction. They could discern the boundaries between the two; although, by their despotic tempers, they were continually involved in inconsistencies and contradictions.† The distinction itself was totally disregarded by Crumwell and the unprincipled men who formed the government of Edward VI.; and the royal supremacy was too often permitted to encroach on the sacerdotal powers through the weakness, the servility, and want of fixed prin-

* 16th Ric. II. c. 5, s. 1, Statute of Præmunire.

† Mr. Gladstone having entered into a full explanation of this subject, refers to the authentic explanation of the Royal Prerogative, issued by Queen Elizabeth in the year 1559. In these she claims "no other authority, than, under God, to have the sovereignty over all manner of persons, ecclesiastical or temporal, so as no foreign power shall or ought to have any superiority over them."

ciples on the part of Archbishop Cranmer. Much injury was done to the cause of the Church through the mistaken policy of our leading ecclesiastics, under the unfortunate dynasty of the Stuarts. To strengthen their position against the Romish nonconformists on the one hand, and the Puritan nonconformists on the other, they first exaggerated the royal prerogative, and then applied it for the annihilation or depression of their opponents. A deviation from right principle exposes those who are guilty of it to a recoil; and, at the present time, Romanist, Puritan, and Infidel unite with party politicians, and, in parliament or through the press, call for a tyrannical and despotic exertion of the royal supremacy, for the purpose of damaging the Church itself.

On the 31st of March, 1534, the Convocation of Canterbury, and on the 5th of May the Convocation of York, declared, that "the pope of Rome hath no greater jurisdiction conferred on him by God in Holy Scripture, in this kingdom of England, than any other foreign bishop."* Thus spoke the clergy first, and their decree was, though not till after the lapse of some time, ratified by the laity in parliament.

It was at the same time admitted, that the sacerdotal power, controlled as we have seen by the royal supremacy, devolved upon the primate of all England. When the title of "supreme head," subsequently dropped by his successors, was for a season assumed by Henry, Tunstal, bishop of Durham, a good and learned man, objected that, although the title had an inoffensive appearance at first view, he nevertheless thought, that this recognition of the ancient royal prerogative ought to be couched in more discriminating terms. The position in which Convocation was left at the Reformation, and the royal authority as admitted by the act of sub-

* Wilkins, iii. 767.

scription, are so generally misunderstood, and the whole subject is so forcibly expressed by Mr. Gladstone, that, long as the passage is in which he treats the subject, I shall present it to the reader. "The Reformation statutes," he says, "did not leave the Convocation in the same condition relatively to the crown as the parliament. It was under more control: but its inherent and independent power was thereby more directly recognised. The king was not the head of Convocation; it was not merely his council. The archbishop was its head, and summoned and prorogued it. It was not power, but leave, that this body had to seek from the crown, in order to make canons. A canon without the royal assent was already a canon, though without the force of law; but a bill which has passed the two houses is without a force of any kind, until that assent is given. Again, the royal assent is given to canons in the gross, to bills one by one; which well illustrates the difference between the control in the one case and the actuating and moving power in the other. But the language of these instruments respectively affords the clearest and the highest proof. In the canons (Canon 1) we find the words, 'We decree and ordain;' that is, we the members of the two Houses of Convocation. But in our laws, 'Be it enacted by the king's most excellent majesty, with the advice and consent of the lords spiritual and temporal, and commons.' Whereas in the canons the king does everything except enacting: with a remarkable accumulation of operative words he assents, ratifies, confirms and establishes, propounds, publishes, and enjoins and commands to be kept. Every one of these words recognises that the canon has a certain force of its own, while it purports to convey, and does convey, another force. In the one case the crown is the fountain of the whole authority of the law; the lords and commons are its advisers. In the other, the Convocation decrees and ordains; the king gives legal sanction and currency to that which, without such sanction, would have remained a simple appeal to conscience. In statutes, the king enacts with the advice and assent of parliament; in canons, the Convocation enacts, with the licence and assent of the crown. I now speak not of what is desirable or otherwise, but simply of the matter of fact: from which it appears that the idea of a separate spiritual power for legislative purposes was much more carefully preserved (and with good reason) by the statutes of Henry VIII. than it had been when Church law went forth in the Capitularies of Charlemagne, or the Code and Novels of Justinian, undistinguished as to the form of its authority from laws purely civil.

"Let it be seriously considered whether, so far as the essence of the principles of the Church is concerned, there was any violation of them in this submission and promise of the clergy, more than in the *placitum regium,* which the see of Rome itself, with however bad a grace, has been obliged to endure, and which the whole Gallican Church, the most learned and illustrious of all the daughters of the Roman see, and with it the entire Cisalpine school, cordially received. This *Placitum,* says Van Espen, comes to exist in consideration of the necessary impact of ecclesiastical laws upon the civil rights and secular interests of men. It cannot be restricted to any class of subjects. It reaches even to those bulls of the pope which are dogmatical. '*Ex hactenus dictis concluditur, placitum regium æque requiri ante publicationem bullarum dogmaticarum, quam cæterorum rescriptorum.*' And he quotes an author much more favourable than himself to the papal power, who nevertheless holds it

allowable—'*Potestatem sæcularem mandare aut con-
stituere, ut sine suo beneplacito et examine nemo
pareat hujusmodi litteris, vel executioni mandet
easdem.*'"*

Against the resumption of the royal supremacy,
which for the last hundred years had been scarcely
recognised, objections were urged by other persons
besides Tunstal. Whenever Henry could lend his
mind calmly to the consideration of the subject, his
skill in argument was such as to command attention;
he contends, that it pertains to the prerogative of the
crown to legislate even in things spiritual when they
bear upon life, liberty, or property. He admits, what
nobody at that time, as the king asserts, would deny;
that preaching and administering the sacraments pertain to the sacerdotal function; and that our Lord and
Saviour gave to the bishops a commission for that purpose. But he adds, our Lord Himself, though possessing a sacerdotal character, nevertheless submitted to
Pilate's jurisdiction; and St. Paul, he observes, though
a priest of apostolical distinction, made no scruple to say,
" I stand at Cæsar's judgment seat, where I ought to be
judged." The king refers to the laws of Justinian, and
asks, with what conscience could that emperor have
made laws touching the regulation of the Church, if he
did not believe that spiritual society to have been part
of his charge? " It is true," he said, " princes are sons
of the Church, but this does not hinder them from being supreme heads of Christian men." " We grant," he
continues, "that the sacraments,—those conveyances of
grace—are to be ministered only by the clergy invested
with spiritual power; but then, if in their function
they misbehave themselves to a degree of scandal, the
civil magistrate may try the cause and punish the

* Gladstone, Remarks on the Royal Supremacy, 31.

crime. And then as to the spiritual character : since the prince's permission is required, before they can discharge the functions of their office, why should they scruple to call him head, with respect to that power which they derive from him ? At the same time, he remarks that to avoid calumny a restriction is added by the Convocation—*quantum per Christi legem licet.*" *

The arguments of the king had their full weight on the mind of Bishop Tunstal. The bishop consented in 1535, to swear to the royal supremacy ; and in 1536, when Henry was attacked by Reginald Pole in his *De Unitate Ecclesiasticâ,* Tunstal came forward in the king's defence. He indignantly, as we have shown in a preceding quotation, repudiated the calumny brought against the king of a defection from the Catholic Church, and justified him against the absurd charge of confounding the royal and the priestly offices. "It is true the king hath rescued the English Church from the encroachments of the court of Rome, and if this be a singularity, he deserves praise. For the king has only reduced matters to their original state, and helped the Church of England to her ancient freedom." He boldly asserts, that the conduct of the king was in accordance with the wish of the nation ; and that, if he should change his mind and be willing to concede to the Bishop of Rome a right to exercise the powers, which he had latterly usurped and had long since claimed, he would find it difficult to obtain the consent of his people through an act of parliament. So united were all parties upon this subject at this time, that both Gardyner and Bonner reiterated the same assertion ; the first in his book *De*

---

* Herbert, 320 ; Collier, iv. 180. The letter is printed in the second part of the Cabala, i. 127. This passage shows that to the proviso introduced in convocation the king was not opposed.

Verâ Obedientiâ, and the second in the introduction he prefixed to that celebrated work. Bishop Gardyner declares that, on the resumption of the royal supremacy, the king acted with the consent of " the most excellent and learned bishops, and of the nobles and whole people of England." He states, " that no new thing was introduced when the king was declared to be the supreme head; only the bishops, nobles, and clergy of England determined that a power which of divine right belongs to their prince, should be more clearly asserted by adopting a more significant expression.*"

It has been acutely observed, that a further and very important mitigation of the supremacy existed in the fact, that it was claimed even by Henry VIII. not as an accession to his prerogative, but as an inheritance of which the crown had been of late years defrauded.

Queen Elizabeth, with a temper as despotic as that of her father, and with less command over her tongue when her angry passions were aroused, was equally clear-sighted when she approached the subject of the supremacy as a legislator rather than as an administrator. Her admonitions were issued in 1559. She complains of " simple men deceived by the malicious;" and solemnly declares, that she had no intention or desire to claim in things spiritual any other authority than that " *which is, and was of ancient time, due* to the imperial crown of this realm."

In 1569, on the suppression of the northern rebellion, she published a proclamation, in which she says that " she claimed no other ecclesiastical authority than had been due to her predecessor; that she pretended no right to define articles of faith, to change ancient ceremonies formerly adopted by the Catholic

* Steph. Gard. *De Verâ Obedientiâ,* Fasc. App. 108.

and Apostolic Church, or to minister the word or the sacraments of God; but that she conceived it her duty to take care that all estates, under her rule, should live in the faith and obedience of the Christian religion; to see all laws, ordained for that end, duly observed; and to provide, that the Church be governed and taught by archbishops, bishops, and ministers, *i.e.* deacons." She assured her people, that she meant not to molest them for their religious opinions, provided they did not gainsay the Scriptures, or the Creeds Apostolic and Catholic; nor for matters of religious ceremony, as long as they should outwardly conform to the laws of the realm, which enforced the frequentation of divine service in the ordinary churches.

Her sentiments may, in fact, be found in the well-known letter from Bishop Jewel to Bullinger, in which he says:—"The queen will not endure the style of Head of the Church of England. She is altogether of opinion, that the title is too big for any mortal, and ought to be given to none but our blessed Saviour."[*] The whole subject is summed up in our Thirty-seventh Article. "The queen's majesty hath the chief power in this realm of *England* and other her dominions, unto whom the chief government of all estates of this realm, whether they be ecclesiastical or civil, in all causes doth appertain; and is not, nor ought to be, subject to any foreign jurisdiction. Where we attribute to the queen's majesty the chief government, by which titles we understand the minds of some slanderous folks to be offended; we give not to our princes the ministering either of God's word or of the sacraments, the which thing the injunctions also lately set forth by *Elizabeth* our queen do most plainly testify; but that only prerogative which we see to

[*] Collier, vi. 244.

have been given always to all godly princes in Holy Scripture by God Himself; that is, that they should rule all states and degrees committed to their charge by God, whether they be ecclesiastical or temporal; and restrain with the civil sword, the stubborn and evil doers. The Bishop of *Rome* hath no jurisdiction in this realm of *England*."*

When Henry had determined, for reasons which will presently appear, to appropriate the title of Supreme Head to himself, he acted, under the influence of Crumwell, with adroitness and a sound judgment. He was not disposed to seek a favour from the clergy, or to require at their hands, any accession to his dignity or prerogative. It was not his intention—nothing could be further from it—to establish a new sect. He was a Catholic king, resuming in the national Church, rights and authority which his Catholic ancestors had claimed, if they had not always enjoyed, from

---

* The title adopted by Henry VIII. in 1534, was " In terris" or " terra, Ecclesiæ Anglicanæ et Hibernicæ Supremum Caput."—Stat. 26 Henry VIH. c. 1; see also 35 Henry VIII. c. 3, and 37 Henry VIII. c. 17. It was continued by Edward VI, 1 Edward VI. c. 12, sec. 6. In the beginning of her reign it was assumed by Queen Mary, but was dropped on her marriage with Philip of Spain. 1 and 2 Philip and Mary, c. 8, sec. 23. It was rejected by Queen Elizabeth, or rather exchanged for that of " supreme governor as well in all spiritual and ecclesiastical causes," &c. (Oath of Supremacy, Stat. 1, Eliz. c. 1), and has never since been resumed (Coke upon Littleton, 7 b). It is sometimes given to the sovereign in ignorance or in malignity. Mr. Gladstone, alluding to its being supposed by ignorant people to be in force, says : " This allegation, however, appears to be quite erroneous. The note on the act in the statutes at large, directs our attention to the circumstances, that the act was repealed by the 1 and 2 Phil. and Mary, c. 8, and that, when the repealing act was itself repealed, the repealing parts of it were saved, in the 1 Eliz. c. 1, except as to certain of the rescinded acts therein particularized, among which this is not contained. (See 1 Eliz. c. 1, sects. 2, 13.)"—Remarks on the Royal Supremacy, 11.

time immemorial—rights which had only been of late
years violated or denied.   As for the clergy, from their
proceedings in this very convocation, — when two
months afterwards they declared that "the pope of
Rome hath no greater jurisdiction conferred upon him
by God in Holy Scriptures, in this kingdom of England,
than any other foreign bishop," *—we know that they
were prepared to reject the papal jurisdiction.   They
were aware of the royal prerogative, for it was a question
which had been under discussion for several years ; but,
after what had lately occurred, they were certainly justified in regarding with suspicion every step taken by the
king.   There was no disinclination to acknowledge his
regal powers to their full extent, or to increase them if the
exigencies of the time required it.   But this precise
title, why was it adopted, and adopted at this crisis ?
This, at all events, was a novelty.   Did the king, who
had compelled them to tax themselves to such an
enormous extent, intend to claim a right to all their
property ?   Was there not some unconstitutional power
clandestinely claimed under a title new to the constitution ?   These were questions which might fairly
be asked ; and if the title was offensive to Queen
Elizabeth, if it is still only used by persons who desire
to see the prerogatives of the crown exercised tyrannically against the Church ; it cannot surprise us to hear
that, after a long debate, on the 7th of February the
Convocation adjourned without coming to a decision
upon the subject ; that the debate was by adjourn-
ments continued on the 8th, 9th, and 10th of the
month ; that a conference was at last had with the
king,† and that the title was finally conceded in only

* Wilkins, iii. 725.

† It was carefully explained to the king, that there was no wish
to interfere with his rights ; but that the title was objected to

a modified form. On the 11th of February, Archbishop Warham introduced into Convocation a form
which appeared to him to be inoffensive, and which
the king was willing to accept. The terms of it ran
thus : " Of the English Church and clergy, of which
we recognise his majesty as the singular protector, the
only supreme governor, and, so far as the law of Christ
permits, the supreme head." *

*ne forte post longævi temporis tractum termini in eodem articulo
generaliter positi in sensum improbum traherentur.* Att. Rights, 82.
Ex actis MSS.

    * Wilkins, 723. Plain as the historical statement really is, it
has been so often wilfully mis-stated, or is so ignorantly misunderstood, that I am induced to add another note from Mr. Gladstone.
His statement is accordant with that which is given above. He says :
" It is utterly vain to argue that the threat of civil consequences which
was held over the Convocation of 1531, as the alternative to follow
upon their resistance to the claim of the crown, could destroy the
validity of their formal act. For in the first place, it does not
appear that the bishops, with whom the final authority must, on
Catholic principles, be held to lie, were under the influence of these
menaces. Fisher himself was one of those who were present in the
Convocation of 1531, and agreed to the petition of that year. The
spiritual lords constituted an actual majority of the Upper House of
Parliament when the act of 1534 was passed, and do not appear in
any way to have resisted it. The whole of the bishops swore to
the royal supremacy in 1535, Fisher having then been already deprived for refusing to take the oath of the succession. Collier says :
' Many of the bishops who had consulted the records and examined
the practice of the earliest ages, were not disinclined to this change.'
Of the most prominent persons among them, Gardiner, Bonner, and
Tunstal had actually written in favour of it. There is, therefore, no
reason to believe, that the act was one at variance with the conscientious persuasion of the then governors of the Church,—and
Lord Clarendon states in reference to this crisis, with strict historic
truth, that Henry ' applied his own laws to the government of his
own people, and this by consent of his Catholic clergy and Catholic
people.' Further, it does not appear that the reluctance which was
manifested by the clergy to the title of headship had any reference
to their regard for the papal claims ; but, on the contrary, that it

· In 1531, the royal headship was admitted by the clergy of the Church of England as represented in the two Convocations of Canterbury and York. It was not till the year 1534, that this title was conceded to the king by parliament. The parliament had before this legislated in Church matters,—having followed the precedents set in former times and especially in the Statutes of Provisors and Præmunire,—to pass in 1532 an act against the payment of *annates,* and, in 1533, an act againt appeals to Rome. In the year 1534, when the parliament confirmed the act of Convocation and acknowledged the supremacy of the king, it declared at the same time the adherence of the nation to the

was founded upon an apprehension they reasonably entertained, that it might seem to detract from the prerogatives of the Redeemer. Of the qualification itself, *quantum per Christi legem licet,* it has been alleged that it nullified the grant ; but on the other hand it might be urged, with at least equal fairness, that the admission of the headship is unquestionable, from the very fact that it was thus limited and defined. It is, however, more material to remark that these qualifying words only apply to the term 'head ;' and that if the clause in which they are found be removed altogether, the document remains as obviously fatal to the papal pretensions as if the headship had been asserted in the ·most absolute form. For the Convocation, without any scruple or resistance, as we have seen, acknowledged the king to be 'of the Church and clergy not only 'the chief protector,' but likewise 'the only supreme lord.' And, indeed, there is the most direct evidence upon this subject. The Convocation of the Province of York stated in writing to the king the objections which they entertained ; and, according to Burnet it appeared by the king's answer to them, that they chiefly contended that the term 'head' was an improper one, and such as could not agree to any but Christ alone. And we shall observe that the phrase 'supreme and only lord,' which appears to have passed wholly without opposition, is in itself a much higher title than that now ascribed by our law to the sovereign of these realms. So much for the regularity and sufficiency of the judgment of our national synod against the papal supremacy."— Gladstone, ii. 109.

articles of the Catholic faith of Christendom. "Thus," says Mr. Gladstone, " we have before us the judgments by which the papal supremacy was ecclesiastically abolished, and likewise upon which external and legal effect was given by the law to that sentence of the native Church."*

To the proceedings which led immediately to the resumption of the royal authority we shall have occasion hereafter to revert. The subject has been mentioned in this place from its connexion with the dissolution of the monasteries and the history of Crumwell.

The same historical investigations which had enabled Henry to claim the royal supremacy, as an inheritance of his crown, were equally of avail, to prove, to the satisfaction of Convocation and of Parliament, that, in this prerogative, was involved a right of visitation extending to all collegiate and monastic institutions. Independently of precedent, it was reasonable, that the supreme authority in the state, should have intrinsically a right to ascertain, whether in any institution lay or clerical, the members were acting in accordance with the will of their founder, and in obedience to statutes which they had pledged themselves to observe; whether the estates had been judiciously managed or illegally squandered; and whether by being taken out of mortmain they could not be rendered more

---

* The State in its Relations to the Church, 108. I have quoted Mr. Gladstone, because the principles of the Church are expressed by him with his usual force and happy command of words; and because I am happy to show that the holding of what are called liberal political opinions is not inconsistent with the highest view of Church doctrine and discipline. My American friends will remember, that their Bishop Hobart, to whom the whole Church is so deeply indebted, was the most zealous republican.

conducive to ends for the promotion of which they were originally granted.

The precedents produced from the history of the country and the conduct of preceding monarchs established a further right, frequently though not consistently, called into action. When an institution had outlived its usefulness, or ceased to meet the requirements of the age, it might be legally suppressed; and its property, on the principle of *cy prés*, applied to the promotion of other though cognate works of public utility.

It has been shown in the preceding book—and the fact cannot be too often impressed upon the reader's mind—that popery, as approaching to the modern notion of ultramontanism, obtained its footing in England during the Wars of the Roses; and yet, even in the unfortunate reign of Henry VI., a commission was granted by the crown for the visitation of the Cistercian monasteries.[*] In this king's reign also, certain manors and estates of the alien priories, which had been forfeited to the crown, were assigned to a commission, partly lay, partly clerical, in trust for his school and college. In the fourth year of Henry V. an act of parliament was obtained by which the alien priories were suppressed; and—which was much to Crumwell's purpose—the estates were vested in the crown. The whole history of the alien priories strengthened the position of Henry VIII. and his minister; and the case of these priories had certainly been hard. Originally filiations of foreign abbeys, their dependance on the continental monasteries was, in the time of Henry V, little more than nominal. The monks of those establishments had become, in process of time, absolute proprietors of their own estates, and lived

* Fœdera, x. 802.

under priors elected by themselves. No special charges
of immorality were brought against them ; but it had
always been assumed, that they must be in the interest
of the enemies of their country ; and their estates were
generally confiscated when there was a war between
England and France. Eighty-one of these priories
had been sequestered by King John ; and, if their
property was restored by Henry III. this only shows,
the more strongly, the right claimed by the civil
authority to deal with those endowments whenever an
emergency arose. Such a confiscation of their property
took place under Edward III. when the property of at
least thirty of those establishments was alienated. In
the first year of Henry IV. they were restored ; but
only to be again suspended in the eighth year of that
king's reign. Acting under the advice of his privy
council, he seized the property of a certain number of
those houses for the support of his own household.*
How they were finally extinguished by his son has
been already related ; and we may add, that Henry V.
in the last year of his reign issued injunctions for the
reformation of monasteries. The necessity of such a
reformation had been admitted by a general chapter of
the Benedictines, at which certain reforms were introduced.† But to the practical mind of Henry V. it was
apparent, that the unsympathizing sternness of the
royal prerogative was required to remedy evils, which
monastic tenderness might overlook.

Perhaps a much stronger precedent was to be found
in the suppression of the order of the Knights
Templars at the beginning of the fourteenth century.
The opponents of the Templars set an example which
Crumwell and Henry were too ready to follow. Resort

* Fœdera, viii. 101, 510.
† Chron. Croydon Contin. 567.

was had in the fourteenth, as afterwards in the sixteenth century, not only to legal murders; but also
to that moral persecution to which we still are subject,
and which consists of evil speaking, lying, and slan-
dering. But, however much we may discredit the
exaggerated charges brought against a whole society,
facts will not permit us to doubt, that the knights in
the one instance and the monks in the other afforded,
unfortunately, strong grounds for some portion of the
accusations to which they were exposed.

But, after all, the strongest and most damaging
attack made upon the monasteries was made by the
Church, or rather by Churchmen, in the middle ages;
by men whose names are, to the present hour, gratefully remembered by beneficiaries still profiting by
their munificent wisdom.

In the prevailing ignorance of history in the nineteenth century, particularly of what relates to ecclesiastical history, the sarcastic ignoramus is permitted,
unrebuked, to speak of our colleges and public schools
as monastic institutions. But from the days of Walter
de Merton colleges and schools were founded in direct
opposition to monasteries; or certainly for the purposes
of depriving the regulars of the monopoly in education which they had hitherto possessed. It is remarkable, that the few schools and colleges which form an
exception to this rule were themselves, at the dissolution of the monasteries, suppressed. It was with the
forfeited estates of alien priories and of other monasteries granted by, or purchased from, the crown,
that William of Wykeham endowed his two St. Mary
Winton colleges, the one at Winchester and the other
at Oxford. He is the father of the public school system. We have seen in these pages, that his example
was followed by Archbishop Chicheley and William

of Waynflete. All Souls' College and Magdalene are
enriched by the spoils of monasteries. The royal
founder of King's College, Cambridge, and of Eton—

"Where grateful science still adores
Her Henry's holy shade,"

only carried out an intention of his illustrious father.
Henry V. had expressed his intention thus to dedicate to
the purposes of education, the wealth that flowed into the
royal treasury from the dissolution of the alien priories.

These illustrious personages maintained, that the property had been devised for educational purposes and
pious uses ; and, they contended, in the fourteenth
century, as ever since, that the end which the founders
had in view, could be better accomplished by schools
and colleges than by monasteries ; ill-conducted as too
many monasteries had, before that time, become.

Their example had been followed by Cardinal Wolsey
when he planned

"Those twin sisters of learning raised in you,
Ipswich and Oxford."

This great statesman surpassed his predecessors in
the splendour of his conceptions ; and no college in
either University, or in any University in Europe,
would have been able to compete with his, had he
been permitted to accomplish his design. He used
his influence with the crown, to attach to his college
at Oxford the property of twenty-four monasteries,
together with sixty-nine benefices. The same system
of utilizing the property of decayed monasteries was
adopted by a contemporary of Wolsey, not his equal
in genius, but far superior to him in that piety which
enabled him to serve his God with more than half
the zeal he served his king ; and to win an incor-
ruptible crown there, "where the wicked cease from

troubling and the weary are at rest,"—Bishop Fisher.
He was the spiritual adviser of Margaret, countess of
Richmond, the grandmother of Henry VIII, and she,
acting under his advice, obtained the dissolution of
certain monasteries, on the ground of the immorality
of their inmates. She devoted the property to the
support of colleges and professorships, in the two
Universities of Oxford and Cambridge.

It must not be forgotten, that the dissolution of the
Hospital of St. John was advised by Bishop Fisher,
because the brethren had entirely neglected the Divine
Service and their other duties; while of the Nunnery
of St. Rhadegund at Cambridge it was said, that the
inmates had become notoriously profligate. Similar
charges were brought against the nunneries of Higham
and Bromhall to justify the confiscation of their houses
and lands.*

The notion of the sacredness of monastic property
did not spring up, till a later period of our history.
There was no sentiment upon the subject in the fifteenth
or the immediately preceding centuries; nor did any
superstitious fears arise, such as were afterwards encouraged, that a curse would attach to the family
of any one who, when the monastic property was
in the market, became a purchaser. At the time
of the Reformation, the greatest care was taken to
distinguish between Church property and monastic
property. The former as a rule remained untouched,
unless we regard chantry lands as property belonging
to the Church; and, if we regard it in that light, we
shall presently see, that this formed a legitimate
exception to what was in general regarded as a rule.
The Church property has come down to us as the
original donors, before the Reformation bequeathed it

* Hymer's Account of Lady Margaret, p. 13.

to us, except where it had been first absorbed and appropriated by the monasteries; for the titles were lost by the appropriation; but whatever belonged to a monastery was confiscated, because the monasteries, although connected with the Church, were, nevertheless, as distinct from the Church itself, as are now the colleges of our two Universities. They stood to the Church in the same relation. So distinct were the two properties regarded, that, until the reign of Queen Victoria, the cathedrals of the old foundation—as they are called,—retained the property of which they had been in possession from the earliest times. The cathedrals in which the chapters consisted of secular clergy were unmolested. Those cathedrals from which, through the influence, first of Dunstan and then of Lanfranc, the secular clergy were driven, to make way for the regulars, were, on the restoration of the seculars under Henry VIII. subjected to the same treatment as other monastic establishments, and became new foundations. Moreover, by a short-sighted and selfish policy, the monks of the larger convents had been unintentionally preparing the way for the dissolution of the monastic institute. There are certain animals who fatten themselves by making inferior animals of their own species their prey. In like manner the lesser monasteries had been very frequently absorbed by the larger abbeys. The distinction between the two classes, the greater and the lesser monasteries, was not made for the first time by Crumwell; nor was it he who, in the first instance, disparaged the conduct of the lesser monasteries, contrasting their immoralities with the decorum observed in the larger establishments. The abbots had themselves brought the charge against brethren living in distant cells. That the inmates of the latter might

be rendered amenable to discipline they were summoned to the parent institution; their own buildings
were desecrated or demolished. In a detachment of
a regiment of soldiers, discipline is more relaxed than
at head-quarters; and this may have been the case,
when monks were quartered at some remote place,
beyond the reach of the abbot's eye, or the public
opinion of their brethren. But for the dealings of
the wealthier communities with smaller monasteries
of an independent foundation we cannot advance the
same apology. We must attribute to other motives,
their purchase of the small monasteries, when the
necessities of the inmates compelled them to sell their
property cheap to purchasers, who held over them a
threat of prosecution or of exposure for offences, which
might, if proved, lead to their confiscation. Whatever the motives, the result was the same. Monastic
property was brought into the market; among the
buyers and sellers were the monks themselves.

There was not, at this period, that extreme reverence
for consecrated buildings which is at present peculiar
to England. A house dedicated to God was open to any
purpose by which God's glory might be promoted,—
for schools, for public councils, for convocations, for
parliaments, even for the religious drama. Nevertheless, common sense would suggest the prescription of
certain limits, which good taste,—the instinct of correct
feeling,—would prevent us from transgressing. At all
events, an *ex post facto* judgment would pronounce
upon the bad policy, if we call it by no other name,
of habituating the public eye to gaze without winking,
on dilapidated churches converted by monks themselves
into Benedictine barns or Cistercian sheep-folds.

There was a general impression, that the monastic
institute had done its work. The ascetic preferred his

solitary hermitage, to a cell where he might be disturbed by indevout revelry, in the vicinity. The enthusiast denounced the somnolent decorum of the best regulated monasteries. With closed doors he was studying Wiclif's Bible : he whispered, that "stolen waters were sweet, and that bread eaten in secret is pleasant;" and as his ancestor drew his sword in the crusades, so was he ready to do battle against the papist. The student was at the university. The art of printing had placed in his hands the books which, at one time, could only be found in the monastic library. The traveller passed by the abbey, that he might take his ease at his inn. The lord abbot and the superior monks were in the position of a provincial aristocracy, and were disliked by the less refined nobles ; the inferior monks were not to be distinguished from the farmers in the market-place ; the land in mortmain, carelessly farmed, was less productive, than the merchant adventurer, now become a country gentleman, opined that, if in his hands, he could make it. The profligate man of the world suspected evil in the convent, and exaggerated it, if detected ; because, in the evil doings of the monks, he thought to palliate his own misdeeds. The monasteries suffered in repute by the very charity they displayed in the civil wars. They received, pitied, and entertained the weary and the wounded among the combatants on either side ; when a soldier wanted a meal he knew where to find it. But this led to much rioting and wantonness : soldiers, without discipline, associated with monks, at a time when monastic discipline could not be enforced. The monks were corrupted and the soldiers not reformed ; the question arose whether monasteries were now answering the purpose for which they had been designed.

The monasteries had done nothing to retrieve their

character. At one period, we find our kings and pre-lates having recourse to the monasteries, for the supply of men, whenever the services of a statesman, a lawyer, or a divine were required for a special or a delicate duty. The monasteries had been the nurseries of all that was great and good for Church and State; but it is a remark-able fact that, for a long period before the final dissolu-tion of monasteries in England, these institutions had scarcely produced any personage eminent, either as an ecclesiastic, a scholar, or a statesman. The secular clergy maintained their position throughout the reign of Henry VII.; and with Wolsey at their head, during the early part of his son's reign. The regulars had forfeited the respect and esteem of the public.

The public opinion was expressed by Hugh Oldham, bishop of Exeter. When Richard Fox, bishop of Winchester, had determined upon the erection of Cor-pus Christi College at Oxford, his intention at first was to make it a monastery—a school to be conducted by the religious. He was dissuaded by Oldham, who said, "What, my Lord, shall we, the secular clergy, build houses and provide livelihoods for a company of buzzing monks, whose end and fall we ourselves may live to see? No, no; it is more meet a great deal, that we should have care to provide for the exercise of learn-ing, and for such as by their learning shall do good to the Church and commonwealth." * One of the reasons given by Wolsey for the diversion of monastic property from the support of convents was, that the prejudice was so great against placing more land in mortmain, that to obtain new endowments would be impossible. This brings us on to the remark, that the monasteries

---

* Holinshed, iii, 117. Bishop Oldham was a native of Man-chester. This was said as early as the year 1518.

had no one to defend their cause; every man's hand was against them. They had hitherto, under all their difficulties and dangers, relied for protection and support upon the pope; but in Crumwell's time, to utter the pope's name, except to anathematize it; or indeed to style the pope anything but Bishop of Rome, would have subjected the offender to a prosecution which might end in proving him guilty of high treason. The king now claimed to be their visitor; and from his decision there could be no appeal.

The bishops and parochial clergy were not likely to take the part of monks or monasteries. Between the clergy and the monks there had never been a good understanding. We might as well expect the bishops and clergy of the present day to undertake the defence of the Nonconformists as to suppose, as some persons do, that the bishops and clergy of the sixteenth century would plead the cause of the monks. Scarcely a word was uttered in their favour by any of the clergy. To exempt themselves from episcopal jurisdiction had been, for many years, the object of ambition to the monasteries, for which they wasted much of the money, the energy, and the time, that might have been more profitably employed. A kind of chronic controversy* had long existed between the seculars and the regulars; and if active hostility had of late years ceased, the altered feeling only went so far as to prevent the seculars from taking an active part in the proceedings against the monasteries; on the dissolution of which they looked with feelings of indifference.

The apathy evinced by the abbots is, however, more surprising, and remains to be accounted for. With a very few brilliant exceptions, they yielded without re-

* See Reynolds's Historical Essay, c. iii. for some proceedings of the secular clergy against the regular.

sistance, almost without a murmur, to the pressure of the times. This is the more remarkable, when we bear in mind that the abbots were largely represented in the House of Peers, and many of them sat with the bishops as spiritual lords, forming a majority of the Upper House.

The condition of the monasteries and the policy of the Government must be taken into consideration.

The truth is, that in the fifteenth and sixteenth centuries the leading men in the monastic establishments were not reclining on a bed of roses; they were not enjoying that luxurious ease which is presented to the readers of historical romances in the nineteenth century. We have remarked, that, during this period, we seldom find the English monks engaged as heretofore, in the public affairs of the country; they were too much occupied with the intricate but petty business of their respective establishments. That the heads of the larger monasteries were successful in sustaining a moral tone in their houses, we have the positive assertion of parliament, opposed to the *ipse dixit* of King Henry VIII, who coincided in the judgment of his parliament, until it became his interest to make the opposite statement. It could have been no easy task, and it required considerable ability, to keep anything like discipline and order in monasteries, which had become such as we have represented them during the Wars of the Roses. We may here add, that the corrupting influence occasioned by the admission of strangers to share the hospitality of monasteries, was not of a temporary nature. In the very constitution of a monastery, there was an arrangement which rendered discipline difficult, when piety ceased to be an enthusiasm and was only partially a principle. There were many who, not monks themselves, claimed an interest in the endowments, the nature of whose claim was not very clearly defined. The representatives of a founder's family retained the right of granting corrodies, a privilege of nominating a certain number of persons, younger brothers, or decayed servants, who were billeted upon the house. The head of the family required frequent donations to secure his interest at court; the younger brothers, having failed in court and camp, presented themselves daily in the hall; they demanded the best cheer, and, under the sweet-smelling savour of the repast, the monks themselves were tempted to become epicures. If the abbot did not control the licence which ensued, the monastery was noted as corrupt; if he exerted himself to restore discipline, he raised a faction against himself; and his enemies were ready to represent him as guilty of the very vices which he had sought to repress. In most monasteries there arose two sets: what would now be called "the fast set," would bring against the strict set the accusation, so easy to make, and so difficult to disprove, of hypocrisy; the strict set would retaliate by indisputable facts charged upon their opponents; and afterwards, by setting one faction against another, the emissaries of Crumwell were able to make out their case, and to involve the whole body in the disgrace, which literally attached to only a few of its members.

For the preservation of discipline a corrody was frequently commuted for a money payment. Where the monastery had the honour of having a royal foundation, the king would forget the number of corrodies he had a right to grant; and it was not for the loyal monks to resist or to set limits to the royal will. Among the State Papers we find the grant of some corrodies which evince recklessness on the part of the crown in yielding to the petition of courtiers and the

CHAP.
I.

Introductory.

hangers-on of a court. Complaint could not be made when a large sum was demanded to support a student in one of the universities; and the monastery of St. Frideswide may have felt itself honoured, when it was directed to contribute towards the education at Oxford, of a royal youth of great promise,—Reginald Pole. But murmurs were assuredly whispered when corrodies were granted under the Privy Seal to Yeoman Ushers of the Wardrobe and the Chambers; to secretaries of the queen, and to Clerks of the Sewers. The table kept at the monasteries was not always so splendid as that which presents itself to modern imagination. The funds of a monastery were eked out by taking boarders. Some monasteries became large boarding houses; and discretion was required in the selection of a temporary domicile in one of these houses. Andrew Ammonius, in writing to Erasmus, states that the monastery in which he was himself lodged was crammed, and that they kept a poor table. He remarked, that there was a college of certain doctors near St. Paul's, who lived comfortably, but it was a stinking place. He thought that there were no Augustinians with whom Erasmus could chamber, and the Franciscans were wretchedly poor.*

The poverty of many monasteries, through the mismanagement of their property, was one of the complaints brought against them. If their property was well managed, it was said, they would have plenty themselves, and, at the same time, enough for the king. How to meet the heavy demands upon them, however inadequately, must have been a cause of much anxiety to heads of houses and their bursars.

There was scarcely a monastery, at this time, which was not involved in debt. This appears from the

* State Papers. See especially Nos. 1235, 1360, 4190, 930, 60, 106, 5198.

statements made in contemporary letters bearing upon
the subject of the monasteries. When living to the
full extent of their incomes, the monks would be
thrown into consternation by a sudden demand from
the king, not only for the subsidy which they were prepared to pay, but for a benevolence. Whatever was the
condition of the conventual treasury this demand was
to be met at once. The house might probably be, at
the same time, involved· in a lawsuit; and, with so
many claims upon them, lawsuits could hardly be
avoided. Lawless neighbours would occasionally render
an application for the royal protection necessary. Such
protection could not be obtained without a bribe to the
courtiers and a *douceur* to the king. Other circumstances were continually occurring, implying an
expenditure which it was impossible antecedently to
calculate. These demands and expenses could only be
met or defrayed by incurring a debt. There were
times when money could only be borrowed at a rate
of 50 per cent. interest

We are not surprised, therefore, at the result to which
allusion has just been made; that there was scarcely a
monastery in England that was not involved in debt.
There were instances in which the creditors took possession of the monastic buildings, and, having ousted the
monks, resided in them with their wives and children.

Such was the condition of the monasteries, when to
the abbots and the superior monks the offer was made
by the Government of a handsome pension, on condition of their surrendering their establishments into
the hands of the king. Most liberal pensions were
offered, and all accounts agree in stating, that they
were regularly and scrupulously paid. The debt was
like a millstone round the neck of the abbot. When
almost in despair, he saw no way of extricating himself

or the establishment, ease and comparative wealth were offered to him. He would lose the importance attached to high station; but he would find a compensation in his freedom from care. If we add, that the pensions were granted subject to the condition of its termination when the pensioner obtained any ecclesiastical preferment of proportionate value, we have in the two facts a proof, that either the Government was extremely corrupt, or, that the charges brought against the monasteries were greatly exaggerated. The policy of the Government did not end here: it extended to the appointment of abbots known to be subservient to the king. The abbots were nominated by the king; and the later appointments were made with the understanding, that, when the king attacked their establishments, they were at once to capitulate, and accept a pension such as a generous sovereign was sure to concede to the friends who served him faithfully.

This was the state of things, when an attack upon the monasteries was finally resolved upon. In the year 1535, Thomas Crumwell having been appointed vicar-general of the king,* was authorized, in the king's name, to hold a visitation of the monasteries, with liberty to appoint assistant-commissioners or deputies. Although Crumwell proceeded, at first, with caution, and evinced considerable discretion in the measures he proposed; yet we may date, from this time, the commencement of that reign of terror which lasted throughout his entire administration. What was at first proposed met with general acquiescence, if not with approbation. It was the suggestion of a measure very similar to that which was effected by

* He was also called Lord Vicegerent. Collier shows from his commission that these are only two names to describe the same thing, and not two distinct offices. Vol. iv. 296.

Sir Robert Peel, with reference to the estates attached
to the prebendaries of our cathedrals and the capitular
bodies.   Where monasteries had, in the lapse of ages,
become useless to the ends, for the furtherance of
which they were endowed, they were to be disincor-
porated and dissolved.   Where the estates had been
let on fines too favourable to the tenant, they were to
be subjected to certain regulations; which, without
injury to the convent, would be productive of a surplus applicable to other religious and public objects.

The visitation commenced in the October of 1535.
Several religious houses immediately surrendered.   We
may presume, that these were the monasteries which
had become notorious for that immorality and profligacy which the visitors predicated of the whole
class.*

* The Report was made to Parliament in what was called the
Black Book, and is said to have horrified the hearers.   This report
has not been preserved, or has not been discovered.   We are therefore dependent for our information on the subject of the dissolution
of the monasteries, on two series of letters.   The Camden Society
published, under the editorship of Mr. Wright, "Three Chapters of
Letters relating to the Suppression of Monasteries."   They have
been printed from a volume in the Cottonian Library in the British
Museum (MS. Cotton. Cleopatra E. IV.), composed of letters and
documents which appear to the editor to have been selected from
the Crumwell Papers so long preserved in the Chapter House of
Westminster, and now lodged in the Record Office.   He has added
a few documents from other collections in our national repository,
and more especially from the Scudamore Papers.   The other series
of letters are published by Sir Henry Ellis in his "Original Letters
illustrative of English History."   An advocate on either side might
establish his case by attending to one of these series of letters to
the exclusion of the other, and this has been too often the case.
The series of letters first mentioned are, in fact, the private reports,
made from time to time, by the commissioners in the employment
of Crumwell.   They knew what was expected at their hands; and
that they did not deceive the expectations of their employer we infer

The commissioners were ready with their report when parliament met in the following February.   The

from certain documents which have lately been discovered in the Record Office.   In 1536, a commission was issued to certain country gentlemen, in conjunction with nominees of the court, and they were required to report on the condition of the smaller monasteries.   The reports from the three counties of Leicester, Warwick, and Rutland are the reports which have been lately brought to light.   These commissioners enter fully into a detailed statement, both of the state of each monastery they visited, and of the character sustained by its members, including servants and pensioners.   We find that almost all were in debt, that in many the houses were ruinous, that in some the inmates were desirous of being secularized; but out of nineteen houses visited there is only one in which these country gentlemen, assisted by the nominees of the court, found the existence of any moral delinquency.   We ought, certainly, to take this into account, when we consider the subject, and we cannot fail to be suspicious of unfair play, when we find this commission dropped; and commissioners appointed, of whom we must say that there seems to be no one of a serious and religious turn of mind, while charges of immorality were brought against all, and in one case fully established.   Although it cannot be proved that Dr. London violated the nuns at Godstowe, although he was, probably, not guilty of this offence, yet such a report could be believed of him; and it is certain that he was afterwards obliged to do open penance for an incestuous connexion; that he was convicted of perjury; that he was condemned to ride with his face to the horse's tail at Windsor and at Ockingham.   No one was more zealous than he, in punishing the suspected monks by turning them adrift into the world, seizing their houses, and confiscating their property.   The correspondence of Legh and Layton bears out the charge brought against them by the Pilgrimage of Grace, when the king was petitioned to prosecute them and the other visitors or inquisitors for bribery and extortion and other abominable acts.   We are not on this account, to reject their reports as entirely untrue; but we are inclined to attach more weight to the letters in Sir Henry Ellis's series, which were written by men of higher position in society and of better character, and these letters are generally favourable to the monasteries.   We must add that even Crumwell's commissioners made strong appeals in favour of some monasteries, and were rebuked.   Henry himself accused them of being bribed, principal act of the session was an act grounded on the report. The preamble is important, as showing what was the impression which the king and his minister desired, at this time, to make on the public mind. It asserts, that manifest sin, vicious, carnal, and abominable living, was daily used and commonly committed in the religious houses of monks and nuns, when the congregation of such religious persons was under the number of twelve; and that the property, goods, and chattels of such houses were spoilt, destroyed, consumed, and utterly wasted. It is observed that, although these houses had been subjected to continual visitations for the space of two hundred years and more, yet there was little or no amendment. It was thus impossible to apply any remedy except that of suppression. On the suppression of the smaller monasteries, religious persons, their inmates, would be committed to *great and honourable monasteries of religion in this realm*, where they would be compelled to live religiously, for the reformation of their lives. The king solemnly returns thanks to Almighty God, for that, in the great and solemn monasteries of this realm, religion is right well kept and observed.* But he remarks, that they were generally destitute of such full number of religious persons as they ought to keep; it was therefore no hardship upon them to have the monks of dissolved monasteries quartered upon them.

when they asked for mercy to be shown to the little monastery of Catesby, against which no accusation could be substantiated. The whole case is stated with great fairness by a Protestant writer in the Home and Foreign Review, whose name I am not at liberty to mention; to whom I desire to express my obligations.

* If the king spoke truly now, he spoke falsely afterwards. If he knew now that the larger monasteries were corrupt, then he thanked God for what he must have believed to be the work of the enemy of God and man.

Upon this, the Lords and Commons "by a great de-liberation" finally resolved, that all the monasteries which had not land or other hereditaments above the clear yearly value of two hundred pounds; with their lands and other hereditaments and their ornaments, jewels, goods, chattels, and debts, should be given to the king, his heirs and assigns for ever, to do and to use therewith of his and their own wills, to the pleasure of Almighty God, and to the honour and profit of the realm."

For reasons already expressed, there was no opposition to this measure.* That Crumwell from the beginning was prepared to proceed further, we may fairly conjecture; when we observe with what ability and craft he made provision against certain contingencies, of which he afterwards availed himself. To the king himself it is due to observe that, from documents which have lately been brought to light, we are justified in crediting him with a desire, at this time, of acting up to the spirit of the statute. Through the surplus revenue he expected so to replenish his treasury as not to subject his people to further taxation: at the same time he designed to carry into effect some public works for the benefit both of the country and of the Church.

The king devised several projects in his mind. It occurred to him that an increase in the episcopate was the most proper mode of expending the surplus revenue. For want of episcopal superintendence, the monasteries had fallen into disrepute, and by an increase of the

---

* A troublesome opposition might have been offered at this period to the proposed measure; for when this parliament, in which had been passed so many Acts for the Reformation of the Church, was first called, the House of Lords consisted of forty-six temporal peers, two archbishops, sixteen bishops, two guardians of spiritualties, twenty-six abbots, and two priors. Twenty-five temporal peers sat for the first time.

episcopate it was hoped that the discipline of the clergy would be more efficiently increased.

There is in the Cottonian Library a list of the "Byshop-prychys to be new made;" * from which we discover, that the project was entertained of forming episcopal sees in Essex and Hertfordshire, Bedfordshire and Buckinghamshire, Oxfordshire and Berkshire, Northamptonshire and Huntingdonshire, Middlesex, Leicestershire and Rutlandshire, Lancashire, Gloucestershire, Suffolk, Staffordshire and Salop, Nottinghamshire and Derbyshire, and lastly, Cornwall.

The project was nobly conceived, but it was very imperfectly carried out. The income which the king obtained from the confiscation of the monasteries was evidently less than had been expected by himself and his minister.† Besides, Henry was, like Catiline, if " alieni appetens," yet "sui profusus." This has become a proverbial expression; but we may apply to the case a still more homely proverb, and say, " What was got

* MS. Cotton. Cleop. E. IV. fol. 304. The list is printed in Strype, Burnet, and Collier. More credit is given to Henry than he deserves, for having established six new sees, Westminster in 1540, Chester, Gloucester, and Peterborough in 1541, Oxford and Bristol in 1542. These were old monastic establishments. Henry seized on a portion of their property, and left but a scanty provision for the new foundations when the monks or canons regular, were changed into prebendaries.

† People are apt to give full rein to their imaginations as regards the wealth of corporate bodies. Historians have repeated without examination the statement relating to monastic property made by Sprot, a chronicler of the time of Edward I. Wherever his statement has been examined, in any detail, his inaccuracy has been discovered; and I have little doubt, that the time will soon come, when what is said of the 28,000 knight's fees will be discarded as a fable. This does not interfere with the fact, that so much land was held in mortmain in the sixteenth century, that a confiscation of part of it was a political necessity. We may applaud the act, while we condemn the agents, their mode of action, and their motives.

on the devil's back was soon spent under his belly."
The income obtained from the suppression of three
hundred and seventy-six monasteries supplying the
exchequer with a revenue of 30,000*l.* a year, and
100,000*l.* in addition, as ready money, the value of
realized property confiscated,—all this was insufficient to meet the demands of a reckless expenditure, of a careless good nature, and of that which is
worse than the two daughters of the horse-leech, ever
saying, Give, give,—the gaming-table. That the stakes
were high may be gathered from one instance. It was
recounted that Jesus bells, hanging in a steeple not far
from St. Paul's, and renowned for their metal and their
tone, were lost to Sir Miles Partridge at one cast of the
royal dice.*

Crumwell had his own fortune to make, and was well
aware, that his very existence depended upon his successful management of the public finances. He could not
be contented with what the confiscation of the lesser
monasteries supplied. With the foresight and self-
possession of a powerful mind, he had already provided
against future contingencies, and was watching events.
At first, they involved him in difficulties, but to overcome difficulties is the pastime as well as the glory of
genius.

A reaction in the public mind soon took place. The
public, high and low, had some complaint against the
monks and friars ; they felt pleasure in the prospect of
"taking down their pride;" thoughtful persons saw the
importance of diminishing their possessions, and bringing some portion at least, of their estates into the market.

* Stow's Survey, 351. This Sir Miles Partridge, a man whom
Strype describes as a gamester and a ruffian, perished by the hands
of justice. The property was given to the king because of the
alleged immorality of the monks.

But the reform, easy and agreeable when viewed as a distant prospect, assumed another aspect when theory was reduced to practice. The monastery was destroyed; and the nobleman began to inquire what provision could be made for the younger son, whom he had destined to a stall in the ancestral abbey : and younger brothers, who had there been quartered as lay members, knew not where now to look for a dinner. While fresh demands were made upon them, heads of families found themselves poorer ; corrodies were stopped, and with them the means of pensioning a worn-out servant, or of assisting a tenant's son at the university. The school was closed, at which the surrounding gentry had thought to educate their boys ; and the medical adviser had been driven from the hospital where the sick had received medicine and advice. It was with sad and sorrowing hearts, that the pious of either sex heard of the demolition of the holy and beautiful house where their fathers had worshipped ; and mothers were seen weeping as they received back their unmarried daughters from nunneries, which had been to them a happy home. It was with feelings of indignant sympathy, that the people of a district saw turned adrift upon the world the holy women, who had been to them sisters of mercy.

The act stipulated for pensions and preferments for those who held high office in a monastery, but the inferior members received a priest's gown and forty shillings if they became seculars. No provision was made for the servants, who were thus deprived of the means of subsistence ; and we may form some notion of their comparative numbers by remarking, that in one monastery, where we find thirty monks, there were not fewer than one hundred and forty-four servants. To these must be added the many out-door labourers employed

on the farms, and now thrown out of work.   All these
were prepared to become sturdy beggars, at a time when
vagrancy was a capital crime.*   They were to be joined
by others not quite incapable of action, the dependants
on the doles and alms still given at the abbey gates.   I

* The punishment for vagrancy had been sufficiently cruel in
former reigns ; but the cruelty was increased by the act of the
27th of Henry VIII. an act called the king's own act against
vagrants, "rufflers, sturdy vagabonds, and valiant beggars," after
such time as any of them had been once whipped, and sent to any
place, "if they shall happen to wander, loiter, or idly use themselves, and play the vagabonds, or willingly absent themselves from
labour they have been appointed to," might be sentenced by a
justice of the peace, not only to be whipped again, but also to
have "*the upper part of the gristle of his right ear* clean cut off, so
that it may appear for a *perpetual token* after that time, that he
hath been *a contemner of the good order of the commonwealth.*"
Constables and the most substantial inhabitants of every parish
were to forfeit five marks for every time they refused, when ordered,
to whip, or cut off the gristle of an ear.   For the third act of
vagrancy committed by one "the gristle of whose ear had been cut
off clean," the punishment was *death* as a felon *and enemy of the
commonwealth ;* and, in order not to lose a chance of profit, however remote, the pauper was condemned to "forfeit *all* his *lands* and
goods."—Amos, 85.   By a statute passed in the 22d year of this king
"licences were grantable for begging within limits, with a provision
"that if any such *impotent* person do beg within any other place than
within such limits, then the justices, king's officers, and ministers,
shall, at their discretions, punish all such persons by imprisonment in
the stocks by the space of two days and two nights, giving them only
bread and water."   Impotent persons begging, without a licence,
were to be "stripped naked from the middle upwards," and to be
scourged.   "Men or *women*, being whole and mighty in body," who
were found vagrant, were subject "to be had to the next market
town, and there to be tied to the end of a cart, naked, and to be
beaten with whips throughout the same town till his body be
bloody by reason of such whipping."—Amos, 84.   The age was
cruel ; and this should be borne in mind when we read of the little
compunction with which victim after victim was sent to the block,
whether offending politically or as religionists, or as having incurred
the king's displeasure.

am aware that, passing from one extreme to another, modern historians treat as mythical the stories told of the charity displayed by the monks. But it is scarcely possible for a large establishment, conducted by Christian men or women, to exist, without an exhibition of charity to various hangers-on ; and this must have been particularly the case in establishments, where the cultivation of an eleemosynary spirit was encouraged as a merit.

All these circumstances combined to induce a reaction in the public mind, and this reaction was proved by two formidable insurrections. The first broke out at Louth, in Lincolnshire, on the 2d of October, 1536. It was headed by the Prior of Barlings, Dr. Mackerel, Bishop of Chalcedon, *in partibus*, in conjunction with another leader, who assumed the name of Captain Cobler. The second, of a more formidable character, broke out early in 1537, in Cumberland, and directed by Robert Aske, of Howden in Yorkshire, is known in history and in poetry, as " the Pilgrimage of Grace." We see from the correspondence of Henry in the State Papers, how alarmed the Government was at this crisis ; how vigorous and self-possessed the king was ; and how, as usual, the insurgents, under the marvellous influence of that spirit of loyalty, which seems to be characteristic of Englishmen, abstained from censuring the king, while they vowed vengeance against his ministers.

The reader is aware, that these insurrections were quelled not by force of arms, but by diplomacy—in plain English, the victory was won not by fighting but by lying. The insurgents in Lincolnshire were disarmed by an amnesty, which the king broke ; and the insurgents in the north were dispersed by promises which the king neither kept nor designed to keep. We gather from the State Papers, that Henry had been alarmed. He had acted with firmness and promptitude, and was triumphant. He retired from the contest an impassioned man; and neither he nor his minister was likely to overlook the fact, that by nothing are the hands of a Government so much strengthened as by unsuccessful resistance. Henry now lent a ready ear to the suggestion of Crumwell, that his throne would not be secure so long as a single monastic establishment remained in the land. The monasteries, it was urged, stood opposed to the king; they were a burden to the Church; they were an expense to the country, and they owed allegiance neither to the king nor yet to the Church, but only to that foreign prince and potentate, the Bishop of Rome. And then came, as a climax, the strongest of the strong arguments to be addressed to the royal mind—money was wanted. The insurrection was not quelled without expense; the treasures accumulated from the confiscation of the property of the lesser monasteries had been consumed: of one thing only the people were impatient, and that was taxation. The property of the larger monasteries must be confiscated to the service of the crown. But there was a lion in the path. By the three estates of the realm it had been solemnly declared and proclaimed that in the larger houses "religion was well kept and observed;" and, in the fervour of his piety, the king had given God thanks for the fact.

The great statesman was equal to the crisis; he had foreseen and provided for the coming events. All things were ready, so far as he was concerned, to *compel* the abbots, by weapons, if not carnal, yet certainly not hallowed, to a *voluntary* surrender of their estates and property. The acts of parliament already obtained had a deeper meaning than those, who passed them, had suspected. They had been so framed as to arm the Executive with despotic power. It only remained now, to conciliate or to terrify the different parties in the state, if not into co-operation, at least into submission. The king,—Crumwell knew how to manage him. "They that rule about the king," said the people, and they spoke the truth, "make him great banquets and give him sweet wines, and make him drunk ; and then they bring him bills, and he putteth his sign to them, whereby they do what they wish, and no man may correct them." Crumwell supplied the king with the means of indulging his taste and appetites ; and, so long as he did this, and the people were kept in subjection, he might rule in the king's name ;* when he failed to do this, his administration came to an end, and with his administration, his life.

The nobility and gentry were to be propitiated; the first by grants from the crown out of the spoils of the monasteries ; "the merchant adventurers" and gentry, by being permitted to purchase land on favourable terms. Opponents were thus adroitly converted into allies.

Parliament was to be won not merely by that system of "packing" the House of Commons, of which we have several instances in the letters of the period; but by the rumours spread of a threatened invasion. It was re-

---

* We see from the State Papers, that, either from a sense of duty or from a love of business, Henry always attended to such details of business as it was necessary to bring before him ; but, more than any of his contemporaries, he yielded himself to the guidance of his ministers. For the glories of his reign he was indebted to that consummate statesman, Cardinal Wolsey ; for the commencement of the Reformation he was indebted to Crumwell. After Crumwell's death, there was no minister in whom he could place confidence. He was in fact his own minister, and under difficult circumstances he then showed himself a statesman of no mean ability.

ported, that Cardinal Pole was exciting a crusade against England, and that already a league against Henry had been formed by the Emperor and the French king. The thought of an insult offered to this country by France always fired the blood of Englishmen; and there was not a man in the country who would not have aided the king if he were to buckle on his armour for a French war; but where was the money to come from? A dread of imposing a tax, or raising a subsidy, was the besetting sin of the Parliament men of that age; and, instead of seeing how power went with the purseholder, they preferred an economical despotism to the purchase of their liberties by making the sovereign a pensioner of his Parliament. They again looked to the monasteries.

The insurrections had excited feelings of alarm in the breasts of that large body of peaceful subjects, who for the sake of a quiet life, would submit, readily, to a despotism like that of the Tudors; which was chiefly felt as an oppression to those who made themselves prominent either in religion or in politics. They form the great bulk of a nation, and, generally speaking, they would rather bear the ills they know, than fly to others that they know not of. In the days of which we are speaking, an insurrection was a more serious thing than it is even now. On either side, the belligerents would require free quarters; they demanded everything and paid for nothing; if the rebels could not force a man to take up arms with them, the king's generals might press him into the royal army. The War of the Roses was the bugbear of the age; to prevent a repetition of such a calamity the country was willing to permit the king to exercise despotic power, so long as he adhered to those forms of constitution, an attachment to which has been almost a

superstition among the English.*   Many lamented
the dissolution of the monasteries ; we have letters
which show how grieved they often were at witnessing
their spoliation ; at the same time, they would not move
a finger to prevent the king from taking possession of
property, which had been voted to him by parliament.

When the country was in this position, Crumwell
placed himself at the head of the reforming party.
He was certainly not a Protestant, so far as doctrine
was concerned.   In his last speech, after his condemnation, he professed opinions directly repugnant to what
was at that time regarded as Protestantism.   He is
generally supposed to have been a man of no religion
—a kind of religious tradesman, who supported the
party from which he could gain most ; or a statesman
to whom religion was a branch of politics.†   But the

---

* The Tudor Dynasty was not so firmly seated on the throne, as
to permit Henry VIII. to set at nought the feelings of the people.
The King of Spain, under an apprehension that Henry's succession
to the throne would be disputed, placed the Spanish army at his
disposal, and offered to head it.   It is important to note this, because it enables us to understand why Henry was so careful to
obtain an apparent legal sanction for his most despotic acts ; and
why also he prefixed long, elaborate, and often false preambles, ex-
planatory of his intentions and conduct, to the bills he caused to
be introduced into Parliament.

† In Cavendish's Life of Wolsey, he speaks of Crumwell at the
time of his master's fall.   "It chanced me upon All Allowne day
to come into the great chamber at Asher, where I found Mr.
Crumwell leaning on the great window with a primer in his hand,
saying Our Lady Matins—*which had been a strange sight in him
afore.*"   He was not wont to have recourse to his devotions ; and
now when he " thought he was like to lose all he had laboured for
all the days of his life," as a rare thing, he thought of prayer, and
was saying " Our Lady Matins." This his admirers have striven
to explain away, by altering the text ; but Mr. Maitland remarks ;
"that Crumwell before that time avowed infidel principles is beyond
a doubt."

extreme reformers rallied round him; and moderate reformers felt that they could not do without him. From
their letters we gather, that moderate reformers feared
rather than loved him, although almost every one was
under some obligation to him. To his supporters he was
wisely generous, and when they supported him in his
schemes of plunder they were sure to have a fair share
of the spoil. During the reign of Henry VIII. neither
Cranmer nor those who acted with him professed to be
Protestants, whether we apply the term to Lutherans
or to Zuinglians. They watched with interest the
Protestant movement on the Continent; and supported the minister, who warned the king that, if
he intended the Reformation of the Church to be
complete, his reform must extend from discipline to
doctrine. Of the pusillanimity of Cranmer in yielding to the insolence of Crumwell, and in not resenting
the insults offered to his office, we shall have to speak
hereafter. Cranmer was evidently willing to concede
much, under the conviction that Crumwell was a
sincere reformer. Crumwell, like Cranmer, under the
fear of death repudiated the doctrines which he had
previously patronized ; but, unlike Cranmer, he did not,
when death was certain, recant his recantation.

While Crumwell overruled the Reformers at home,
he sought to extend his influence yet further ; and in
foreign politics he took the line directly opposite to
that which had been pursued by his master, Wolsey.
Wolsey deferred to the pope ; Crumwell was willing to
make common cause with the Protestants of Germany.
Whenever a German or Swiss Protestant visited England, he found a friend and protector in Crumwell.
But after all, he had only one object in view,—to
enrich himself and his royal master by the entire
confiscation of the monastic property ; when that was

accomplished, he quietly acquiesced in the Act of the Six Articles. The measures to which he had recourse to intimidate the monks and their supporters were, some of them legitimate, while others were most iniquitous. He acted wisely and well, when he encouraged learned foreigners to visit England and enter into discussion with our own divines on the controversies of the day. He acted still better, when he persuaded the king to extend his patronage to those who had devoted their minds to the translation of the Scriptures into the vulgar tongue; and to permit throughout his dominions a free circulation of the sacred volume.* He wielded the lawful weapons of

* This may be a convenient place to make some remarks upon a subject upon which much idle declamation has been wasted, and to point out the different feelings with which a free circulation of Scripture has been regarded by men, who differing from one another on this and other important subjects, may fairly entertain their different opinions without being subjected to personal abuse. The study of Scripture, as a book of devotion, was encouraged, as we have had frequent occasion to show, in all ages of the Church by all classes of divines. From the time of Alfred, translations were made from time to time for the edification of those, who were unable to read their Bibles in the original. When Wiclif appeared he translated the Vulgate, and would probably have been unmolested in his holy work, if he had not proclaimed his object. The Church was corrupt. It was to be brought to the test of Scripture; "to the law and to the testimony." If the Church's teaching was not confirmed and corroborated by Scripture, the Church was in error, and required Reformation. He circulated the Scriptures, therefore, with the avowed purpose of making every one a reformer, and his version was eagerly sought by those who wished to bring an accusation against the Church, and to cause an ecclesiastical revolution. The heads of the Church may have been in error, when they opposed the circulation of Scripture for this purpose,—as a weapon of offence—but they do not deserve the hard names sometimes heaped upon them even by those who profess to be influenced by conservative feelings. Our reformers, in the sixteenth century, conceded the fact, and admitted the truism, that religious knowledge, like all

controversy in the cause of sincerity and truth, when
he exposed to the public gaze the impostures which
had been the disgrace of too many monasteries.   He
exhibited to the astonished multitude, the strings and
wires and pulleys by which the image, too long worshipped by an idolatrous people, was made to open its
eyes, to move its lips, to expand its mouth, and to perform other grimaces indicative of approbation when a
wealthy ignoramus made an offering of jewels or of
gold.   He did what was right when he condemned the
inanimate heretic to the flames.   He placed in men's
hands the crystal phial containing the blood, as it was
said, of a saint; which became visible to the money-
giving, and invisible to the niggardly beholder; he
showed how it was opaque on the one side, and
transparent on the other, and he dashed the lying
relic to the ground.   Men are never more indignant,
than when they find that they have been subjected to
delusion, and when by impious men, their holiest
feelings have been trifled with.

These tricks were played upon pilgrims by the

knowledge, is transmissive. They received it as a tradition,—but
then they desired to place the Bible in every man's hands, as the only
safeguard for preventing the Church from transmitting as an article
of faith what has never been revealed as such. The Church comes to
us, as St. Paul to the Bereans, and says, These things are so. We
accept what is handed down to us; and then, admitting it to be
probable, that those who have no object in deceiving us, have told
us the truth, we do, as the noble Bereans did, we search the
Scripture to see whether these things be so. The notion of making a
religion each man for himself out of the Bible is a modern notion, and
must stand for what it is worth. As the subject will frequently come
before us, the reader will probably agree with the author in thinking the protestant system the right one; but it does not follow,
that those who, at a revolutionary period, took another view of the
subject are deserving of the hard terms which Foxe and his
admirers heap upon them.

lowest class of persons in the monasteries, and were laughed at by some at the head of affairs. The indignation of all classes was directed against the abbots and priors, who having the power to put them down, had abstained from using it. So far they deserved their fate. They confounded credulity with faith, and forgot who is the father of lies.

It is with mitigated feelings of disgust, that we approach the shrines where were exhibited the relics, real or imaginary, of holy men of old. Men like Erasmus may have laughed ; men like Colet may have sighed, as they gazed at the wasted treasures of a bejewelled shrine ; but here there was not of necessity, as in the former case, conscious deceit on the part of the exhibitor. The deceivers were themselves often deceived ; and even when miracles appeared to be wrought, we know the power of the imagination too well, not to believe that cures were effected where cures were expected. But whatever may be said in palliation of the offence, the offence, in conjunction with other iniquities, was sufficient to create a vast number of conscientious iconoclasts. Their feelings were still further excited, when they compared the second commandment as taught in the Church, with the same commandment when printed in their Bibles. When the mysteries of the convent became revelations of its hidden pollutions, the doom of the monasteries was sealed.

Had Crumwell been contented with the legitimate modes of party warfare, he would have deserved only the gratitude of posterity. The exposure of a lie is a victory on the side of truth. But in his zeal to create a public opinion against the monasteries, he resorted to measures which, if they are regarded with feelings of approbation by any, must be so only by the mere partizans of religion, and not by persons, under the influence of a religion the characteristic virtue of which is charity.

A partizan of Protestantism was Foxe, the martyrologist. Describing Crumwell as a valiant soldier and captain of Christ, he informs us, that he had in his pay and kept near him " divers fresh and quick wits, by whose industry" (pious or profane, as the reader may think fit to regard it) the country was inundated "with pictures, jests, songs, interludes ;" of which some remain to exhibit to us what he regarded as wit ; and how wit might, in his estimation, be made subservient to religion, or at least to the propagation of what he regarded as such.

The stage plays and interludes, says Bishop Burnet, were acted, and the churches were too often the theatres. With a view of interesting men in the history of the Bible, sacred dramas had, in times past, been performed in consecrated buildings ; and, following this precedent, the buffoon, who formerly appeared as the arch enemy of man, amused the populace by his representation of a profligate monk or by the exhibition of such indecencies as convulsed the assembly with malignant laughter. Perhaps another place might have been more appropriately selected, when, advancing from men to things, the ordinances of the Church were burlesqued and things most sacred were turned into ridicule.* We have specimens of what was regarded as wit ; the consecrated oil was the Bishop of Rome's butter ; the holy water was

---

* Burnet apologizes for mentioning what he describes as the greatest blemish of the times ; but the sincerity of an historian, he says, obliges him to do so. "Surely," remarks Dr. Maitland, "a more quaint acknowledgment of party views was never made. A man need not set up for an historian at any time, but if he does, 'the greatest blemish of that time' cannot be passed over with any pretence to common honesty."

represented as something adapted to make sauce for a goose, or as medicine for a horse with a galled back; the tonsure was a mark of the whore of Babylon; the stole of a priest was the Bishop of Rome's rope; the sacrament of the altar was called the sacrament of the halter; it was spoken of as Jack in the box, or the round robin.

To the coarse ribaldry of the friars of old as directed against the secular clergy must be traced the relish for that which, whether regarded as piety or as blasphemy, was certainly repugnant to good taste and correct feeling. It is to the credit of the clergy that, when the weapons formerly directed against themselves were now pointed against the monks, the Convocation, through its prolocutor, remonstrated with the Government for encouraging that which was introducing " irreligion,—even atheism." Such, however, is the obtuseness of religious partizanship that, instead of seeing in the courage thus displayed in a reign of terror, something worthy of praise, Bishop Burnet can only express his surprise and indignation at the proceeding.*

In party warfare and in rationalistic argument, the puritan and the infidel are sometimes found to make common cause. It is so difficult to distinguish between what is to one man profane and another ludicrous, that we are not inclined to speak with undue severity upon what has been just described. But we have a sadder tale to tell; we have to pass from mental excruciation to the infliction of corporal punishment.

We have reminded the reader of the tumults, which had been caused by pity for the monks or by their success in the arts of insurrection. The probability of this had been foreseen by Crumwell. He had taken

* The reader who would investigate this painful subject may be referred to Dr. Maitland's Essays on the Reformation.

steps to terrify the abbots of the larger monasteries into the surrender of their houses, treasures, and estates. He had already taken steps to prevent further insurrections in their behalf. The master stroke of his Machiavellian policy—one of those wonderful acts of political foresight by which provision was made for a probable future—is to be found in the Treason Act; an act unostentatiously introduced as a mere rider to the Supremacy Act.

Convocation first, and the Parliament afterwards, in recognition of powers, from time immemorial attached to the prerogatives of the crown, conceded to Henry the title,—which he assumed, but which Queen Elizabeth repudiated,—of Supreme Head of the Church. Another bill was, towards the close of the session, introduced, in which it was enacted, that "if any person do maliciously wish, will, or desire, by words or in writing, or by craft, imagine, invent, practise, or attempt any bodily harm to be done or committed to the king's most royal person, or the queen's, or their heirs apparent, or to deprive them or any of them of their dignity, *title or name of their royal estates;* or slanderously and maliciously publish and pronounce, that the king our sovereign lord should be heretic, schismatic, tyrant, infidel, or usurper of the crown, every such person and their accessories shall be judged traitors."

This was not all. If an individual were obnoxious to the Government, if he were even accused, if he were suspected, to him the oath of supremacy might be tendered; and if he refused to take it he might be led to execution, as in the case of Sir Thomas More and Bishop Fisher for denying the royal title.

Thus was constituted an offence hitherto unheard of,—verbal treason; and terrible was the power with which it invested an unscrupulous sovereign and a yet more unscrupulous minister. Under legal forms, a despotism was tacitly established; some were interested in upholding it, no one was bold enough to resist.

Armed with this authority, and with manners most attractive, Crumwell caused his influence to be felt, even when not acknowledged, in every class of society.* The House of Commons was led by him, for, as we gather from his letters, by him the House was packed. In political trials, he dictated the verdict; for every juryman knew that if a verdict hostile to the Government should be returned, there was at the head of that government a man, who was generous when pleased, but was terrible in his anger. He exercised all the functions, and possessed all the powers, of a modern prime minister. He was a man of progress, who was urging the king to adopt yet stronger measures of reform; and to him therefore the discontented of all parties looked up as to a leader; all who, having nothing to lose, only desired a scramble, where something might be gained; all who, in disgust at the existing state of affairs, were ready to support the most extreme measures of reform; all who cared little for the building up, if they were permitted to pull down.

The immoralities of the powerful partizan of a religious faction are, by the expectants of his favour or the enthusiasts of his party, regarded as mere pecca-

* For the statements made with reference to Crumwell, I must express my obligations to Professor Brewer and to Mr. Duffus Hardy. In his preface to The Letters and Papers, Foreign and Domestic, of the reign of Henry VIII, Mr. Brewer has constituted himself the historian of that reign. I am indebted for much information on the subject to an article on the Royal Supremacy, published by him in the National Review. The whole has been authenticated by Mr. Hardy, to whose friendly criticisms these pages were submitted as they passed through the press.

dillos, or are discredited as inventions of the enemy.
We are not surprised, therefore, at finding men of
fervent piety and of earnest religious principle at-
tributing to Crumwell, virtues which he did not
possess; at the same time, we must admit, that he
himself did not seek through hypocrisy, the high
spiritual honours to which he attained. He was of
this world, thoroughly worldly. He simply accepted
what was thrust upon him; and he used the almost
boundless power, which caused him to be respected,
served and feared. In every county and village,
almost in every homestead, he had a secret force
of informers and spies. They depended for all they
possessed upon the patronage of the Vicegerent, who,
—generous and despotic,—could give as well as take
away. In the enthusiasm of their selfish loyalty,
they were on the watch for traitors; and in the well-
paid piety of their hearts, they had a terrible dread
of superstition. For a word uttered in argument, in
anger, or in jocularity, an offender might be summoned
before the magistrate and cross-examined. The accused was not permitted to see his accuser; each
case was decided by depositions, and the depositions
were sometimes garbled. If, for no assignable cause, a
man obnoxious to the Government was accused of disloyalty, and refused to acknowledge his guilt, the oath
of supremacy might be tendered to him; and the
officer who tendered it, would advert significantly to
the fate of Sir Thomas More and Bishop Fisher. If
further proof were wanted, the house of a suspected
person might be ransacked and his papers searched.
If this did not suffice to prove his guilt, the accused
might be sent to London to be there examined; and
that examination was sometimes conducted when the
prisoner was on the rack. Crumwell himself sometimes

superintended the torture.* When a clergyman was
suspected, his service-book might be examined, or even
a private manual of devotion might be searched. The
object of the search was to discover whether, in
obedience to a royal injunction, he had duly erased
the name of the pope and that of St. Thomas of
Canterbury. If this had not been done, the omission was a sufficient proof of his treason ; and his life
depended upon the caprice of Crumwell, or upon the

CHAP.
I.
Introduc-
tory.

* See particularly the case of Dr. Lush, Vicar of Aylesbury,
Ellis, 3d Series, iii. 70. At page 96 we find Robert Southwell
writing to Crumwell, then Lord Privy Seal, signifying the attainder
of two priests for denying the king's supremacy, and humbly
praying, that a day might be fixed for their execution. In a letter
from Crumwell to the king, concerning an Irish monk suspected
of treasonable practices, he says, "We cannot as yet get the pith of
his evidence, whereby I am advertised to-morrow to go to the
Tower, and see him set in the bracks, and by torment be compelled
to confess the truth."—Ellis, 2d Series, ii. 130. Sir Henry Ellis
informs us that the Brack or Brake was a species of rack. The very
instrument which Crumwell professes the intention of using, or a portion of the horrid machine, was till lately to be seen in the Tower.
It is engraved on wood in the Notes to Isaac Reed's Edition of
Shakspeare, vol. vi. p. 231. It is also mentioned by Judge Black-
stone in his Commentaries, vol. iv. ch. 25 ; he says, "The trial by
rack is utterly unknown to the law of England, though once when
the Dukes of Exeter and Suffolk and other Ministers of Henry VI.
had laid a design to introduce the civil law into this kingdom as
the rule of government, for a beginning thereof they erected a rack
for torture, which was called in derision, *The Duke of Exeter's
daughter*, and still remains in the Tower of London, where it was
occasionally used as an engine of State, not of law, more than
once in the reign of Elizabeth. In Mary's time it had been
frequently used." Among the unpublished papers of Crumwell
there are several references to the use of torture. For the statements given above, the reader is referred to the "Original Letters,"
published by Sir Henry Ellis, especially to the 3d Series, except
when other authorities are quoted. Numerous letters and documents relating to this period of Henry's reign are to be found
unpublished in the Record Office.

judicious administration of a bribe. The Franciscans were the persons who were most zealous in favour of the pope, and it may have been a political necessity to apprehend two hundred of these men in one day. This was a strong measure; but to stronger measures the court found it necessary to resort. Friar Forest was proclaimed a heretic and traitor for maintaining the cause of the Bishop of Rome, and as such he was hanged and burnt at Smithfield. Crumwell, Lord Privy Seal, accompanied by several of the courtiers of Henry, attended in great state on the occasion; and the preacher was no less a person than the Bishop of Worcester, Hugh Latimer.* We read of the execution, on another occasion, of eight poor men and of two women, for offences against the act of supremacy; the sermon was preached by the chaplain of Hugh

* Our admiration of Bishop Latimer, who himself died bravely for his opinions, must not make us blind to his faults. There is something offensively facetious and flippant in his letter to Crumwell, when the latter ordered him to preach at the burning of Forest: "And Sir, if it be your pleasure, as it is, that I shall play the fool in my customable manner, when Forest shall suffer, I should wish that my stage stood next unto Forest." It is due to the memory of a reformer, in many respects so justly admired, especially for his own martyrdom, to add that in another part of his letter he says, "If he would, in heart, return to his abjuration, I should wish his pardon, such is my foolishness." It was a sad time, when a bishop thought he should be accounted a fool, for pleading the cause of an innocent man. Much allowance must be made for the coarseness and cruelty of the age; but there is something revolting in the conduct of Bishop Latimer, as narrated by Sir Thomas More, when More was under trial for his life before Cranmer, at Lambeth. "I was in conclusion commanded to go down into the garden. And thereupon I tarried in the old burned chamber that looketh into the garden, and would not go down because of the heat. In that time saw I Master Doctor Latimer come into the garden, and there walked he with divers other doctors and chaplains of my lord of Canterbury. And very merry I saw him, for he laughed and took one or two about the neck so handsomely, that if they had been women, I should have went [weened] he hadd waxen wanton."

Latimer, Bishop of Worcester.　What was peculiarly hard, upon this occasion, was, the imprisonment of one Denison ; he expressed his disapprobation of the sermon, and called the preacher of it a foolish knave priest, " come to preach the new heresy which I set not by."

There was a poor woman of whom Sir Roger Townshend writes to Crumwell, that, " as far forth as his conscience and perceiving could lead him," was the originator of a report, that a miracle had been wrought by Our Lady of Walsingham.　The credulous old woman, a few years sooner, would have been honoured as a saint, but how she was treated in King Henry's time shall be given in the words of Sir Roger himself :—

"I committed her to the ward of the constables of Walsingham.　The next day after, being market day, there I caused her to be set in stocks in the morning, and about six of the clock, when the market was fullest of people, with a paper set about her head, written with these words upon the same, *A reporter of false tales*, was set in a cart and so carried about the market and other streets in the town, staying at divers places where most people assembled, young people and boys of the town casting snowballs at her.　This done and executed, was brought to the stocks again, and there set till the market was ended.　This was her penance, for I knew no law otherwise to punish her but by discretion ; trusting it shall be a warning to other light persons in such wise to order themselves.　Howbeit I cannot perceive, but the said image is not yet out of some of their heads.　I thought it convenient to advertise your Lordship of the truth of this matter, lest the report thereof coming into many men's mouths might be made otherwise than the truth was.　Therefore I have sent to your Lordship, by Richard Townshend, the said examination.　Thus I beseech Almighty Jesu evermore to have your good Lordship in His best preservation.　Written the 20th of January.[*]

Humbly at your commandment,

ROGER TOWNSHEND.

---

[*] Ellis, 3d Series, iii. 162.

What reward Sir Roger obtained or expected for his zeal, I am unable to say; but one other case must be mentioned, as it shows how completely the country was at this time governed, and felt itself to be governed, by Crumwell. He is the only minister who so completely identified himself with the king, that calumny against the minister was confounded, in the opinion even of educated men, with treason against the sovereign. The justices of Ludlow, eager to gain favour with the all-powerful Crumwell, informed him, that they had apprehended a priest for speaking words against Crumwell; that they had sealed his house; they had taken possession of his property; they had made an inventory of his goods, and had put his plate in trust for the use of the king. They had examined his papers to discover if there were "any untruth" to our lord the king. Although the inquisitors failed in their search, they were not to take all this trouble for nothing. Their expenses must be paid; to their delight they found a bag containing 76*l*. 16*s*.; they appropriated 20*l*. as a remuneration to themselves —a sum equivalent to about 200*l*. according to the present value of money; another sum amounting to half of this, they gave to the scrivener for endorsing the inventory; ten pounds were given to the fortunate messenger who was elected to convey this message to Crumwell.

To an Englishman, taught to regard his home as his castle, these acts of invasion upon property appear to be monstrous; our blood boils within us, when we learn, that by blending the act of supremacy with the treason act, the Protestant enthusiasts under Crumwell condemned to death not fewer than fifty-nine persons,*

* I give the numbers as I find them in Dodd. A general statement made by him in such a matter would be received with

—men who, however mistaken they may have been in their opinions, were as honest as Latimer, and more firm than Cranmer. Of the murders of Bishop Fisher and Sir Thomas More, the former the greatest patron of learning, the latter ranking with the most learned men that the age produced—both of them men of undoubted piety—the reader must not expect, in these pages, a justification or, even an attempt at palliation. We shall be as ready to accord the crown of martyrdom to the abbots of Reading and Glastonbury, and to the Prior of St. John's Colchester, when, rather than betray their trust, they died, as we are to place it on the heads of Cranmer, Ridley, and Latimer. Although the latter had the better cause, yet we must all admit, that, atrocious as were the proceedings under Mary and Bonner, the persecutions under Henry and Crumwell fill the mind with greater horror. Mary, however narrow her mind may have been, believed that, in sacrificing the lives of her fellow-creatures, she was maintaining the cause of truth; she thought that by their suffering in this world, the sufferers might be saved from eternal damnation. The persecutions under Henry originated in avarice; or in a desire to maintain the peace of the country, to the infraction of which the people were, at the same time, excited by lust of plunder on the part of the king and his minister.

The violence of Crumwell was surpassed by his venality. Whether controlling men's actions or obtaining the command of their purses, his prudence and forethought were equally conspicuous. The plebeian had determined to ennoble his family; and before he could ask for a coronet he required the means by which to

suspicion; but he gives a list of the names of the sufferers, and his statement is official.

support the honours of a peerage. He enabled his creatures to enrich themselves, and they knew that they were serving themselves when they brought grist to their patron's mill. Before Crumwell had determined on the steps to be taken with reference to the greater monasteries, he battened upon the hopes and fears of all, who were dependent for their livelihood on monastic property. Money flowed into his coffers from all who had favours to seek at court. The Abbess of Godstow appointed him steward of the estates belonging to the sisterhood; and he was a steward from whom a strict account would not be demanded. He had a retaining fee for the priory of Durham; which the prior thought it expedient to double in order that he might secure " a continuance of his favourable kindness." From Abbot Whiting the great man condescends to ask for the appointment of his nominee to be master of the game on the estates of the abbey. This with many similar appointments had not reference merely to field sports; Crumwell supported his household and retainers—a vast multitude—by the game he thus acquired. The abbot, more liberal than was expected, conferred on him a corrody and an advowson.* The Abbess of Shaftesbury offers five hundred marks to the king, and one hundred pounds to my Lord Privy Seal, to be allowed to remain " under any name or apparel" the king's bede woman, after the surrender of her nunnery. One noble lord places 40*l.* in Crumwell's hands if he will obtain for him the grant

---

* A corrody, says Fuller, a corradendo, eating together, consisted of the privilege retained by a founder, or granted to a benefactor, of sending a certain number of persons to be boarded at an abbey. Old servants were thus provided for; sometimes younger sons, when incapacitated for military service. Corrodies, in some well-regulated monasteries, were commuted for a fixed payment.

of a well-endowed monastery. In Crumwell's private memorandums, not yet published, there are continual references to grants made by the king of monastic estates, through the influence of the minister,—grants made after due consideration. Even the Bishop of Worcester, Hugh Latimer, when induced to intercede on behalf of the Prior of Great Malvern, would not venture to approach his friend and patron without a douceur. The prior, though *in* his diocese, was not *of* it,—it was an exempt monastery; but Latimer was suitor for the " foresaid house," because the prior was a good man, and willing to submit to the king's decree. The good prior himself offered five hundred marks to the king, and two hundred marks more, as an acknowledgment of his thanks, to the Lord Crumwell.* The money was accepted; the priory continued to exist for a few months; it was then dissolved.

The amount of property amassed by Crumwell, of which we can produce the accounts, would indeed be marvellous, even if we could not enlarge the list of bribes of which we have attempted to give a specimen. From a lady of rank he receives 20*l.*, if he will obtain for her the arrears of her salary. One of his inferior agents applies to him to stay proceedings between one Brooke and the Abbot of Bardney: " Hear me speak," says the constable, for such was the man's ostensible position in society, " ere you conclude, and it shall be in the way of two hundred marks." Archbishops and bishops found it their interest to retain him as their advocate. From Archbishop Cranmer he obtained 40*l.* a year, equivalent to 400*l.* according to the relative

* Strype, Memorials I. i. 399, and p. 407 we find Sir Thomas Elliot, in a sycophantic letter, promising Crumwell the first year's fruit of any lands from suppressed monasteries granted to him by the king through Crumwell's intercession.

value of money; from some other bishops 20*l.* and 10*l.*
by way of a new year's gift. From noblemen and
noble ladies, even from Queen Jane Seymour, from the
visitors of monasteries, and from all who looked for his
favour at court, he received certain pensions as retaining fees.   It might be said, that in receiving these presents, he was only doing, on a large scale, what every
man in power was accustomed to do; this excuse, however, his conduct does not permit us to make to its full
extent; we find from the entries in his steward's books,
that money was surreptitiously conveyed to him—to be
found in a pair of white gloves—"in a handkercher"—
in a black velvet purse—in a crimson satin purse—in
white paper—"in a glove under a cushion in the middle
window under the gallery."   Such secret presents, of
which we only mention a few by way of specimen,
must have been "secret-service money."   They occurred chiefly during that period, when to peer and
peasant the abbey lands appeared to be a mine of
wealth.

While Crumwell was enriching himself, he was, at
the same time, in his zeal against immorality, preparing
the way for the transfer of the property, so long mis-
applied by the monks, to the coffers of King Henry VIII.
He had appealed with such success, to the fears and
cupidity of the people, that when, in 1537, the visitation of the greater monasteries was ordered, the commissioners found that, in most instances, the terrified
monks were prepared, on receiving a compensation, to
surrender their houses into the king's hands.*   To avoid

* The pensions were sometimes considerable, and appear to have
been regularly paid. The last payment to an ex-monk was made
in the reign of James I. The hardship fell chiefly upon the inferior
members of a monastery and the dependants upon the several
establishments. At Athelney, the pliant abbot received a large

the odium of confiscating by main force the property of men, in whose favour the preceding commissioners, the king, and the three estates of the realm had borne honourable testimony, Crumwell offered every facility for a voluntary surrender.   To make the surrender voluntary, however, the inquisitors had recourse sometimes to measures which, though literally legal, were intrinsically unjust ; but which, to those who are not sufferers by the proceedings, suggest amusing ideas.

In most instances, the heads of houses, by bribes and promises, or by politic appointments, were prepared to surrender.   If there was any demur, the inquisitors added to the many difficulties in which, as we have previously shown, the monasteries were, through debt or discord, involved, by encouraging a factious spirit, and inducing one party to bring railing accusations against the other.   The testimony, on either side, was received without question, and a general bill of indictment was brought in against all.   The wearied prior was soon as ready as the terrified abbot to regard surrender as the only means of securing peace.

But though the abbot may have been gained, there were monks who, under the influence of conscientious motives, or because the offers made to them on their secularization were insufficient, exhibited signs of resistance.   Crumwell, though decided, was always cautious ; he knew full well, that his royal master, though he had armed himself with despotic power, was accustomed to act the tyrant, not by defying but by perverting the forms of law.   Nothing could be more in accordance with order, than the proceedings of the commission.   The

pension and was appointed to administer the estates.   At Evesham, the abbot had an annuity of 240l. and at St. Albans, 260l.   These sums must be multiplied by ten, to bring them to the present value of money.

members of it were empowered to institute, among other things, an inquiry as to the fact, whether the statutes of each monastery were rigidly observed; and whether the brethren acted strictly in conformity with the will of their founder.   On their arrival at a monastery, they were hospitably entertained by the brethren ; who had secured, as they supposed, the favourable regards of the vicegerent, and were aware, that they were well spoken of in the neighbourhood.   It did not, however, require much sagacity to discover that, even in the best ordered monasteries, the Benedictine rule had been relaxed; and that if an attempt were, in some places, made to observe the more stringent regulations of the Carthusians, these formed exceptional cases, and were of rare occurrence.   Although, therefore, the commissioners gave due weight to the favourable report of their entertainers, they would not be contented with the general respectability of the past ; their duty it was to enforce the statutes.   Obsolete they were represented to be; but the question was, whether every brother had not sworn to observe them.   The services in the chapel had been blended, so as to secure an undisturbed night's rest ; this, it was pointed out, was an evasion of the statute ; orders were given, that when the bell sounded in the early hours before day dawned, each brother should be found in his stall, prepared to take his part in the psalmody.·   At an early hour in the morning a divinity lecture was to be read; every inmate of the establishment was required to attend. After this, the abbot was to see, that every one was engaged in grammatical studies between the hours of devotion, except those whose business it was to labour in the field.   The fast days were to be strictly observed ; at meal times no attention was to be paid to the requirements of a fastidious appetite. The simplest fare was to be provided. With lay brethren the monks who were in holy orders were not allowed to hold intercourse ; and if, after a silent dinner, the lay brother thought to seek society in the neighbourhood, he found himself a prisoner in his own house ; it was notified to him, that it was not lawful for him to leave the precincts of the monastery without special permission; this permission it was not easy to obtain. To middle-aged gentlemen, accustomed to an innocent self-indulgence —if self-indulgence can ever be innocent—the enforcement of these and similar regulations was peculiarly irksome. It was as if the prebendaries composing the chapter of one of our cathedrals at the present time, were compelled to resign their livings by being called into perpetual residence ; or as if, at Cambridge, some "mute inglorious Milton" were ordered to the flogging form.

Among the younger men, some were found who wished to be released from their vows, and to return to the world. Others there were, who wept at the thought of leaving the home in which their youth was spent and educated, where they had whiled away their lives, and where they had hoped to repose in old age, until they should be laid in an honoured grave. The majority agreed that, if it were intended to enforce the statutes, and to compel them to live as veritable monks, it would be preferable to come to terms with the king, and to accept the pension the visitors were authorized to offer. With a heavy heart and an upbraiding conscience, many an abbot observed, that he was required to surrender what " it was not his to give ;" his scruples were silenced if not satisfied by the commissioners; the abbot, it was said, was only a tenant on the property, as the property itself had already been given by parliament to the king.*

We have an account of the surrender of one of these religious houses from the pen of Dr. Shire-brook, a writer nearly contemporary with the events; he wrote in the year 1591.† Comparing his statements with the letters and other documents of the period, we can represent to ourselves pretty accurately the usual process on such occasions. Before a surrender of the property to the king, Crumwell was careful to make his own private profit out of the hopes of the unfortunate monks. They paid him, from time to time, large sums to be " good lord " to them. Their good lord he was, until it was convenient to say, that the king's will must be done, and he could no longer befriend them. Another object he had in view, which was to make the surrender appear in the eyes of the public, a voluntary act on the part of the brethren. At the same time, he sought to conciliate or to intimidate the nobility and gentry of the neighbourhood. They were permitted to make cheap purchases of land and timber. He desired to keep the populace in good humour; to them the doors of the desecrated building, were opened, and they were permitted to scramble for what the robbers of a higher class had left.

The abbot and monks, having purchased the favour of Crumwell, were living in security under the vain imagination, that things would, at least, last their time.

* The letter of E. Horde, the prior of the Carthusian monastery at Honiton, to his brother Allen, expresses the feelings of a large portion of the heads of religious houses. It is to be found in Ellis, 2d Series, ii. 130.

† See a transcript of a MS. in Cole's collection in the British Museum, extracts from which have been published by Sir H. Ellis. It is attributed to Dr. Shirebrook, on the authority of Mr. Porter, the possessor of the original MS.

Suddenly it was announced to them, that the royal commissioners were at the abbey gate. The commissioners were accustomed to pounce upon their prey suddenly; they came when they were least expected, to render it impossible to secrete any large portion of the property. Arrived at the gate, the representatives of royalty demanded of the abbot and all the officer-bearers to deliver up their keys. They proceeded at once to business. Divided into sub-committees, they took an inventory of all the property within the house and in the offices without. The servants were sent into the pastures and to the granges, and the live stock were driven into the courtyard,—horses, cows, sheep. The brethren were summoned to attend in the hall, where the chief commissioner occupied the abbot's chair:

> " Quæsitor Minos urnam movet, ille silentum
> Conciliumque vocat, vitasque et crimina discit."

The silent monks heard for the first time that the property, formerly theirs, had been already sold. The special business of the commissioners was, in the king's name, to hand it over to the purchasers. An unconscious smile must have moved the lips of the commissioners, when they called upon the astonished monks to give " great thanks to the king, and to pray for him on their black beads, since he had been so gracious to them as to permit them to stay so long in a place, which parliament had taken from them and conferred upon the king." The condescending commissioners invited the grateful monks to partake, as guests, of the entertainment which, a few hours before, they had ordered as hosts. They took their places "with what appetite they might;" and were edified by discourses on the indulgence shown them by the king. But equal justice required that regard should be had to the interest of others besides the monks.   Before they rose from the table where they had been hospitably entertained by the king, it was signified to them, that it would be for the convenience of those who had now taken possession of the abbey, if the former inmates could leave the house that very night. As, according to their rule, they could possess no property beyond what they carried on their backs, it would not be difficult for them to find a lodging among their friends in the neighbourhood.   A few of them, anxious to see the last of their old home, obtained leave to remain in their cells for that one night longer, with the understanding that, when the morning bell should sound, it would not be for matins, but, simply to signify, that the time had come "when they really must go."   It was a sight, says our informant, to melt a heart of flint, and make it weep, to see the old men bidding a long and final farewell to the home of their youth ; and if there were, among the younger men, some who rejoiced in gaining their liberty, yet even they by their countenances showed that, if a leader could have been found, they would have worked vengeance on their persecutors.

As they went out by one door, the persons employed to dismantle the house, either for the king or for those to whom portions of the property were already sold, entered in by another door. They seemed to take pleasure in the work of demolition. The boards were plucked up, the spars were hurled down upon the floor; the marble floor itself was smashed by the lead poured down, through the fretted ceiling, from the roof. The stalls where the monks had prayed were rudely torn down ; and the painted windows were demolished. The shrines had been already rifled for the king; the tombs of the uncanonized were now thrown open to the mob.

From the fragments of the splintered marble, the brass was rent; from the skeleton, gold or jewel was torn. The rudeness of an hour annihilated the pious labour of ages; barbarism triumphed over superstition. The abbot's house, the dormitories, the cloisters, the libraries were pillaged. The vessels of silver and gold were seized, in the king's name, by the visitors; the timber, the pewter, and all else that was valuable, were conveyed to the dwellings of the neighbouring yeomen and gentry. When their servants had deposited the purchased property in the outhouses, for this purpose still regarded as sacred, they returned to the monastery. An astonished multitude found the doors demolished, or the locks and staples destroyed; they were invited or permitted to rush in and lay their hands upon whatever the royal plunderer, or the noble robbers had left. Broken lead, the window frames, the iron hooks which had supported the reredos or the altar, became their prey. Too often the splendid service books, unappreciated by their ignorant superiors in the art of robbing, when the jewels and the gold had been roughly torn from the boards, were seized for the sake of the vellum, and carried home to the housewife. The leaves were employed in scouring the jacks, in cleaning the candlesticks, or rubbing shoes, or sometimes in the stables "they were laid upon the waine-coppes to piece the same."

What created the special astonishment of our informant was, that they who, a few days before, were with apparent devoutness attending the matins and the masses, were now among the wildest of the intoxicated plunderers; they seemed to be possessed of the devil; for certainly what was yesterday the house of God, was now regarded by the self-same persons as the abode of Satan.

CHAP.
I.

Introductory.

It was Crumwell's order, that every place and thing which had been accounted holy should henceforth be desecrated. The church was turned into a malthouse or a stable,—the outhouses alone were to be religiously preserved, for in the housing of grain or the sheltering of cattle there could be no superstition. The father of Dr. Shirebrook, who lived in the neighbourhood of an abbey treated as we have described, had purchased a portion of the timber of the church, and all the wood-work in the steeple, with the bell frame. Of him his son demanded, thirty years after the suppression, whether he, the spoiler, "thought well of the religious persons and the religion they used. And he told me, 'Yea: for I did see no cause to the contrary.' 'Well,' said I, ' then how came it to pass you were so ready to destroy and spoil the thing you thought well of?' 'What should I do?' said he. 'Might I not as well as others have some spoil of the abbey? for I did see all would away, and therefore I did as others did.'" "Such a devil," remarks the piety of the son, " is covetousness and mammon!"

What is most to be deplored is, the demolition of some of the noblest libraries that the country possessed; the miserable martyrdom, as Fuller styles it, of innocent books. Works of inestimable value were sold, for next to nothing, to grocers and soap-sellers. Whole ship-loads were transported to the Continent, to become the possession of wiser foreigners. Bale knew of two noble libraries, the contents of which were sold for the paltry sum of forty shillings, to a merchant who used them as waste paper; and who, in ten years, had only consumed half.

It was a misfortune to the country, that Crumwell was an illiterate man: he was a man of the world who despised the learning which he did not possess.

·The enlightened mind of Henry was, at this time,
intoxicated by his various dissipations. Henry was,
with all his faults, always open and plain-spoken ; he
would have despised a recourse to artifice and deceit ;
and if his mind had been disengaged, he would not
have sanctioned conduct, on the part of Crumwell,
which has entitled that great minister to the title of
the Diabolus Monachorum.

Crumwell's great object being to effect the dissolu-
·tion of the monasteries, in a manner as unostentatious
as possible, he determined to deceive as well as to
terrify the public.   The inquisitors, the king, the
parliament, all having united in a declaration that,
·taking the greater monasteries as a whole, no charge
of immorality could be substantiated against them, it
became Crumwell's business to give the lie to a statement which, from a political motive, he had formerly
permitted to be made.   His mode of acting was
diabolical, and our authority for saying so is not
Sanders or any Romish partisan, but an honest blunt
partisan who would never wilfully deceive, however
much he might be deceived himself.   Fuller speaks
strongly and like a true-hearted Christian, when he describes, as a devilish damnable act, the system which
was adopted for the seduction or corruption of nuns, by
the very persons who were fiercely denouncing monastic
institutions on account of their presumed immorality.
Unprincipled young men were sent as visitors to a
nunnery : if any of them succeeded in winning the
affections of an unsuspecting girl, he sought Crumwell's favour by basely accusing her of incontinence.
Of their many repulses no mention was made ; though
by the confession of one diabolus, made in after life,
we know, that when men had sold themselves to the
father of lies, and had sworn allegiance to the accuser

of the brethren, innocence itself was no safeguard or protection. The tempter and another young man went to a nunnery, within twelve miles of Cambridge. They represented themselves as travellers, and their dress pointed them out as men of rank. Arriving late at night, they were not admitted within the walls of the convent, but were supplied with refreshment in one of the outhouses. Here they found straw sufficient for one night's rest to the travellers, and a supply of food. In the morning, they paid their respects to the lady abbess, and tendered their thanks for the cautious hospitality which had been accorded to them. They produced a forged document, by which it was made to appear, that they were appointed visitors of monasteries under a royal commission. To execute their commission in examining the accounts and taking note of the property, they were for several days partakers of the hospitalities of the house; they resorted to all the arts of fashionable life to corrupt the younger nuns. They entirely failed; but they had the baseness, after they had left the house, to make report " that nothing but their weariness bounded their wantonness." The conscience of one of these wretched beings reproaching him in his old age, he made a confession, too late to undo the evil of which he had been the cause, or to restore to society and peace of mind the unhappy victims of his calumny.

Among the falsehoods freely circulated, were those which related to the existence of underground passages leading from friaries to nunneries, for the clandestine convenience of those who hated the light because their deeds were evil. But this application of the sewers, which are found upon examination to have gone no further than the exigencies of drainage required, is now known to have originated in men who, whatever may have been their zeal against popery, had forgotten that, among deadly sins, falsehood is one, and that among Christian virtues, the charity which thinketh no evil is the first.

The charges brought against the larger monasteries will be received with greater caution when the treatment experienced by the monks of Christ Church, Canterbury, is brought incidentally under our notice. The reader will remember how the secular clergy were ousted from Canterbury Cathedral and supplanted by monks, through the strong measures first of Elfric and Dunstan and then of Lanfranc. With the monks of his cathedral Archbishop Cranmer did not live on very friendly terms; and, when it was expedient to attack the greater monasteries, against no monks were viler charges brought than against the monks of Canterbury. When, under Henry VIII, the regulars were in their turn displaced, and seculars were appointed to stalls in the metropolitan church, the prior was to be superseded by a dean, to be nominated by the crown, and the monks by prebendaries, to be appointed by the archbishop. The deanery was offered to the calumniated prior, who preferred the acceptance of a large pension; and Archbishop Cranmer selected for the first prebendaries of the new foundation the very monks who had been so foully traduced. It follows, that the infamous charges brought against them were, on examination, found to be without foundation; or else, that Cranmer was not only more worldly and time-serving than his admirers are prepared to admit, but that he was utterly regardless of religion and morality.

Of the monastic institution I do not profess to be an admirer. That the monasteries were, at one period, a blessing to barbarian Europe, no one who is acquainted

with the history of the Middle Age will deny; but
when, in the progress of civilization, the abodes erected
to protect virtue in its weakness, and to encourage
learning when it was despised, became the resort of
the idle and the stronghold of superstition, their reformation became a necessity, and their extinction an
event not to be deplored.

We admit and lament the increase of idleness, and its
daughter immorality, during several centuries, in some
of the monasteries,—and this on the showing of the
monks themselves. Such was the inevitable consequence
indeed of the celibacy to which they were vowed. By
aiming, not to perfect human nature, but to assimilate
the nature of men to the nature of those spiritual
beings who dwell there, where they neither marry nor
are given in marriage, the constrained celibacy of the
monks reduced them too often to the condition of the
fallen angels. But against that sweeping condemnation of the regulars in the time of Henry VIII, in
which popular or party historians indulge, historical
honesty must protest. While philanthropy mourns
over the fact of human corruption, it will receive with
suspicion charges of systematic immorality, brought
against thousands of our fellow-creatures. The suspicion of unfairness will be increased when it is found,.
that the avarice of the accusers was gratified by the
legal condemnation of the accused; and a fresh increase
of suspicion will arise, when we find that, as opposed to
the testimony of parliament in favour of the larger
monasteries, little is to be adduced but the *ipse dixit*
of such a man as Henry VIII. To party feeling, when
kept within bounds, there can be no objection; but party
spirit becomes licentious when it exaggerates the evil
and suppresses the good, when, without examination,
it circulates abusive libels, and, at the same time, with-

holds, as unworthy of credit, the testimony producible
to the merit of those who, after all, were human beings,
not demons in human form.

Party spirit can do great things; but perhaps its
most wonderful feat is the conversion of Thomas Crumwell into a saint.   Protestants are so unreasonably
vehement in their condemnation of what Latimer called
monkery, that they not only believe every tale that can
be told against a monk, but the Diabolus Monachorum
himself they have canonized.

The life of Crumwell from the pen of Foxe is found,
upon investigation, to be little better than a romance.
Whenever his life shall be selected as the subject
of a monograph, the author will find almost an auto-
biography of the great statesman in the numerous notes
and memorandums which, never intended for any eye
but his own, are now preserved in the Public Record
Office.   He was in the habit of drawing up short notes
or remembrances to guide his memory, when he attended
the king or council.   An historian who has the merit of
having consulted these documents, Mr. Tytler, does not
hesitate to say, that they exhibit Crumwell as "equally
tyrannical and unjust, despising the authority of the
law, and unscrupulous in the use of torture."

The eulogists of Crumwell have availed themselves
of the obscurity which covers his origin, to exalt
his merit by exaggerating the poverty with which in
early life he had to contend.   That he was born in
humble circumstances is certain, and he was nobly
proud of the honour of being a *novus homo*; the first
of a family to be ennobled by himself.*   But of his

---

* According to Foxe, he was born at Putney, *or thereabouts*, and
was the son of a smith.   His mother afterwards married a "shear-
man," *i.e.* a cloth shearer.   Pole, with aristocratic superciliousness,
says: "Si tale nomen quæratur, Crumvellum eum appellant; si
genus, de nullo quidem ante eum, qui id nomen gereret, audivi.

extreme poverty no proof exists. On the contrary, we find him, at an early period of life, in the service of Cecily, marchioness of Dorset; the servant of the Marchioness of Dorset could not have been a "shoeless vagabond;" or, at all events, if he was "a poor object," he was soon raised from his dunghill. Foxe, to whom we are indebted for these expressions, informs us, that Crumwell, when he was in Italy, learned Erasmus's Latin translation of the New Testament by heart, and his statement is repeated by those historians who accept him as an authority. This story is improbable; but if it be true, it is inconsistent with the statement which represents his poverty in early life as extreme. It was not customary for "young vagabonds" to learn Latin; it was an accomplishment reserved for young ecclesiastics, or for persons educated at the universities; and a university education Crumwell certainly did not receive. No other time can be found in his busy, and for a long period disreputable, life, in which he could master the Latin language; it is more than doubtful whether he ever understood Latin at all. He told Cranmer that he had been at one time "a ruffian;" and all authorities agree, in mentioning the tradition that he served in Italy as a common soldier. There is a difficulty in fixing the time when this took place. He could not have been "a trooper of the Constable of Bourbon" at the sacking of Rome;* before that event took place, he was in the service of Cardinal Wolsey.†

Dicunt tamen viculum esse, prope Londinum, ubi natus erat, et ubi pater ejus pannis verrendis victum quæritabat; sed de hoc parum refert."—*Poli Apolog. ad Car. V. Imperat.* 126.

* Maitland's conjecture is, that if he was there, he was present as an accredited agent of Cardinal Wolsey.

† Hitherto it has been uncertain when he first entered into the service of Wolsey. But among Wolsey's miscellaneous papers preserved in the Record Office, we find a letter from Wolsey to Sir

We shall, therefore, be probably correct in placing his military career at an early period of life, when, according to Foxe, "it came into his mind to see the world abroad, and to learn experience." He undoubtedly mastered the Italian language; he was so captivated by the manners and tone of feeling in Italy, that he returned to England with something like a contempt for his native country. He was put to many shifts to support himself when he was abroad; but it is certain that he obtained admission into a merchant's house at Venice, of which he was for a time commercial agent. He is said to have been employed as clerk to a mercantile firm at Antwerp; he established so high a character, that, on his return home, he was employed by the authorities at Boston as their agent, to procure for them certain privileges from Rome. All the statements relating to his early life are involved in obscurity, perhaps designedly by himself; and we must trace his career by reference to the documents of which mention has just been made.

From his own correspondence we discover, that, in 1512, he was a thriving merchant at Middleborough; and this is perhaps the first indisputable notice of him in history. He was not as yet a landed proprietor; but his personalty was so considerable and increasing, that he employed a correspondent at Antwerp to procure for him an iron chest in which to keep it; for this the price demanded was, according to the present value of money, not less than eighty pounds. He was a factor

Thomas More, in the handwriting of Crumwell, corrected by the Cardinal. The date of the letter is 1526; the attack upon Rome was in 1527; and, independently of what has been said, we have evidence under Crumwell's own hand, that he was, at this time, advancing large sums of money, as a money-lender, to the younger members of aristocratic families in England.

or general merchant, engaged in a variety of mercantile speculations, until the year 1520. His correspondent, Steven Vaughan, in 1512, addressing him with respect as "Right Worshipful Sir," and evidently regarding him as a person of some influence among the commercial aristocracy, says in a postscript to the letter just referred to, "If you could help to get a licence for cheese, I could get both you and me much money."[*] He was more particularly engaged in the cloth trade. That he was not a needy man in 1512, is certain ; it is equally certain, that he was a thriving man in 1520. He may, in the interval, have been unfortunate in some of his transactions ; but it is very improbable, that he was reduced to beggary. On the contrary, he was, during that period, enjoying the comforts of domestic life. In 1528 or 1529, Crumwell was in Wolsey's service. At this period, he sent his son Gregory to Cambridge. Young men, at that time, went to the university at an earlier age than they do at present ; but Gregory Crumwell must have been not less than fourteen or fifteen years of age. He was therefore born in the year 1515 or 1516. This historical statement— for which I am chiefly indebted to the researches of Mr. Brewer—is of value, since it discredits the story which Foxe gives us from a novel of Bandello; according to which the prosperous English merchant was, at this time, a poverty-stricken wanderer in Italy, dependent upon the charity of Francis Frescobaldi, whom he gratefully rewarded when Frescobaldi was in want and Crumwell in his grandeur. There are other stories relating to obligations, incurred by Crumwell at one

* Tytler, Henry VIII. 425. Ample use has been made of these materials by Sir Henry Ellis, whose notes prefixed to the "Original Letters" are valuable fragments of history made by a profound scholar.

period of his life and generously repaid at another. But it is very difficult, to discover the period of his life when his poverty was such as, in these stories, it is assumed to have been.

Although we may be compelled to reject as fabulous some of the anecdotes invented or advanced, to surround with a romantic interest a very prosaic personage, it is not necessary to doubt, that there was much of generosity in the character of Crumwell, or that he was one of those whose sympathetic nature can rejoice with them that do rejoice; although we dare not assert, that one who could witness the application of torture could without hypocrisy weep with them that weep. No one could have had such devoted adherents, eager to advance his interests, as Crumwell had, if there were not a conviction, on the part of his *employés*, that he desired the promotion of their fortune as well as his own. He rewarded liberally, and indulged the sympathies of his nature in requiting past kindnesses. It was the universal tradition that, although ungainly in person, his manners were prepossessing; and that he could add to the value of a favour by the grace with which he conferred it. He merely required in return that deference and respect, which are peculiarly dear to a self-raised plebeian. All this we may gather from his correspondence; and without these advantages we know not how a man, circumstanced as Crumwell was, could have reached the elevation to which he was raised when he became the second man of this realm —the *alter ego* of the king.

Before the year 1520, Crumwell had added to his other avocations that of a lawyer; he became a scrivener or attorney. He had a sufficient command of money to be able to advance, on loan, considerable sums to the younger members of the aristocracy, who, to maintain their position in the splendid court of Henry VIII, were frequently involved in difficulties. Crumwell was of sufficient importance to be elected a member of the parliament of 1523. There is extant a humorous letter of his, to his " especial and entirely beloved friend John Cheke, then residing at Bilbowe in Biscay," in which he describes what he had to endure in a session of seventeen weeks. He did not take any prominent part in the debates ; but the parliament met the demand of the cardinal, by granting to the king a larger subsidy than ever before was voted in this realm. It is not improbable that Crumwell made himself useful to the Government on this occasion ; and as we find Lord Henry Percy, the unfortunate suitor of Anne Boleyn, among those who had applied to Crumwell for pecuniary assistance, we may presume that the thriving attorney was brought under the notice of the cardinal by the young noblemen who formed the court of the lord legate,—a court as expensive as that of the king.

Crumwell was appointed attorney to Cardinal Wolsey. The cardinal was, at the time of this appointment, engaged in the suppression of certain smaller monasteries, and in the transfer of the property to his two colleges, the one at Ipswich and the other at Oxford. He required in his solicitor, a man of the world, skilled in understanding the value of property, learned in the law, and able to surmount all legal difficulties, not very scrupulous as to the means to be employed in the furtherance of a great end, conciliatory in manner, and firm of purpose. Such a man he found in Crumwell ; and how busily the solicitor was employed, the drafts of leases and agreements in his handwriting preserved in the Record Office remain to attest.

Crumwell was not at this time a Protestant. It is

quite certain that a Protestant would not be employed in Wolsey's service. At this period, he was far from being a religious man. A mark of religion, at this period, was an attention to the offices of the Church. Although a member of a churchman's family, these he neglected. We know that a man may be an infidel, so far as the facts of Christianity are concerned, and yet be a superstitious man, and of Crumwell's superstition we have proof.*

His political opinions were in advance of his age; and he gave free utterance to them, when conversing with the young nobles, who were learning statecraft in the household of the cardinal. The difficulty which presented itself to the cardinal's mind at this time, was how to reconcile his duty, or what he thought to be such, to his country and his Church with the wishes of the king. It may seem to some, that the question really related to a contest between his own interest and that of his master; but self-deception enabled Wolsey to

---

* Of his religion we have spoken before. Of his superstition, or certainly of the absence of Protestant principle on his part, at a time when he was at the head of the ultra-Protestant party, we have proof from his will. The first draft of his will is dated in June, 1529; in it he leaves twenty shillings to each of the five orders of friars within the city of London, to pray for his soul. He directs his executors "to engage a priest" to sing for his soul three years next after his death, and to pay him for the same twenty pounds. Five or six years afterwards he had occasion to correct his will, when the bequests for prayers to be made for his soul were retained; and it is proved that this was not an oversight, for, as regarded the priest who was to pray for the dead, he desired him to continue his services for seven years, and he increased his stipend from 20*l.* to 46*l.* 12*s.* 6*d.* His partisans considered as not authentic the report which was circulated of his last dying speech and confession, but the will must make their labour vain. What religion he had, would appear to be superstition, and the superstition of an irreligious man induces him to seek the advantages while he avoids the responsibilities of religion.

put it under the former aspect to his own conscience ; and from this point of view it was discussed by his friends. In conversation, on the subject, with Reginald Pole, then a young man, Crumwell did not hesitate to declare the principles upon which he thought every wise politician should act. Pole contended, that the counsellor of the king should have a single eye to the honour and real interests of his master ; he discoursed learnedly on the subject, enforcing his view by an appeal to the law of nature and to the writings of the learned and pious. Crumwell scouted the notion, as adapted exclusively to obtain applause, when propounded in the schools or declaimed from the pulpit. He contended, that these antiquated notions would be met by ridicule in the secret counsels of princes; that the business of a wise counsellor is, first to discover what are the secret wishes of his king, and then, in carrying them into effect, to make them appear by specious argument to be consistent with the dictates and requirements of morality and religion. Instead of devoting himself to the old-fashioned schoolmen, he advised Pole to study the writings of a distinguished modern, and to read Machiavelli.[*]

The statement is of importance to those, who would

---

[*] Pole's veracity in making this statement has been questioned. Except on the principle of rejecting every historical fact, which does not coincide with our preconceived opinions, one can scarcely understand why. If the reader will peruse the "Apologia Reginaldi Poli ad Carolum V. Cæsarem," he will find it a dull, dry book ; but he will not suspect the writer of that wilful misrepresentation which the description of the conversation with Crumwell must be considered, if it did not take place. He might occasionally mistake or misunderstand, or even colour a fact, but he would not deliberately invent a conversation. Nor is there any reason why Crumwell should not recommend Machiavelli. Machiavelli was, at this time, rather famous than infamous. The worldly wisdom would be the more attractive to a worldly man like Crumwell, from its novelty.

form a correct estimate of Crumwell's character. He was influenced by policy, and not by principle. He was not singular.

Crumwell was not a man to lose the splendid opportunities of making his fortune, when he had obtained a footing in the cardinal's court. Upon Crumwell, as upon his man of business, Wolsey placed extraordinary reliance; and the proud cardinal, on his fall, humbled himself before his dependant, under whose obsequious manners he was not slow to discover an indomitable pride. It strikes one as extraordinary, to find Wolsey, who was accused of haughtiness to his equals and even to his superiors, addressing his low-born solicitor as "his own entirely beloved Crumwell;" "My own aider in this my intolerable anxiety and heaviness;" "My own trusted and most assured refuge in this my calamity;" "My only refuge and aid." We are compelled, however, on reading the letters, to come to the conclusion, that the endearing terms were used, not out of gratitude for kindness already shown; but from an earnest desire to retain the services of a sagacious man, whom the cardinal distrusted, but was obliged to employ.

The king was, at one time, prejudiced against Crumwell to such an extent, that it was generally supposed that, for malpractices in the suppression of the monasteries, when Wolsey was disgraced, Crumwell would be hanged; a change of ministry too frequently implied the execution of the minister and his immediate partisans. But Crumwell found powerful friends at court. Sir Christopher Hales, who afterwards became Master of the Rolls, "a mighty Papist," as Foxe styles him, mentioned Crumwell to the king, as one likely to be of good service in his controversy with the pope. The Earl of Bedford also extended to him his protection: and introduced him to the king, as one who had been instrumental in saving the earl's life when, in Italy, he was engaged in the king's service. The king was made aware of the fact, that he was bound as a lawyer to plead the cause of the cardinal, and he liked him none the less for that. The king's heart often relented, and would have spared his old and faithful servant, had it not been for the interference of Anne Boleyn.

At all events, I gather, from Wolsey's correspondence, that Crumwell had already secured for himself the patronage of several powerful persons, who were willing to promote his interest at court. So deeply was Wolsey impressed by an opinion of Crumwell's ability, and of his power of influencing others, that to him the once proud cardinal became, at last, a supplicant for protection. Wolsey received with humility a letter of admonition and advice from Crumwell; which, considering the relative position of the respective parties, we must regard as insolent. I have read with attention the letters addressed to Crumwell by Wolsey, and I think, that any one who does so, will come to the conclusion, that Wolsey had no confidence in Crumwell's sincerity; and that Crumwell, on the other hand, did not treat his fallen master with consideration and kindness. He was obliged to defend him, for he had no other course to pursue; but he was in a state of the greatest alarm for his own safety. He heard it rumoured, that he was himself to share his master's prison. The cardinal, in one letter, entreats him, as one who had neglected to come to him when he had been expected—to repair to him, " as soon as parliament was broken up." He entices him to come by saying, that he has things to say to him concerning his own self—as if he knew the selfishness of the man. In another letter, he says, "There are few things, since my trouble, that more grieveth me than your not coming hither at this time;" in another, "The ferdoying and putting over of your coming hither hath so increased my sorrow, and put me in such anxiety of mind, that this night my breath and wind, by sighing, was so short, that I was, by the space of three hours, as one that should have died." Other passages to the same purpose might be produced. There is one which is almost affecting: "Mine only comfort,—At the reverence of God leave me not now; for if ye do, I shall not long live in this wretched world." Owing to the solicitor's not having come to him, as he had promised, the preceding night, the great cardinal adds: " I fear much the sending of Mr. Bonner with the deed hath put you in some displeasure; so God be my judge and save my soul, I meant no hurt therein. If he for lack of wit and experience hath not, as I fear me, done well, let me not perish for the same."

For the exquisitely pathetic scene in Shakespeare, we certainly have not the authority of Wolsey's biographer, George Cavendish. Shakespeare represents the reluctant Crumwell exhorted by Wolsey to provide for his own safety, by seeking service under the king. But according to Cavendish, Crumwell required no prompting. The scheme of passing from the service of the cardinal to that of the king was entirely his own. He had been preparing the way. He complained to Cavendish—" I never had promotion by my lord to the increase of my living;" and he added, "Thus much will I say to you, that I intend, God willing, this afternoon, when my lord hath dined, to ride to London, and so to the court, where I will either make or mar ere I come again."

The next day, Crumwell had passed from Wolsey's service; he had been accepted as the servant of the king. When he left the cardinal's house, he sought

CHAP.
I.

Introductory.

and obtained an audience of the king.　Pole, who had the information from those who were present, informs us, that the servant of Wolsey now suggested to the king that he should overcome the pope's opposition to the divorce, by an exertion of his supremacy.*　What further ensued we know not. With the one exception of his being the bearer to the cardinal of the thousand pounds, which the king had granted him to pay his expenses to Yorkshire, the name of Crumwell is no longer connected with that of Wolsey.　He was not with him when Wolsey journeyed into Yorkshire; he was not with him at his last moments.　Crumwell was, at that time, making the fortune which had first been made and then nearly marred, when he was in the service of Wolsey.　We only know, without being able to account for the fact, his wonderful and rapid rise.　In the Michaelmas term of 1531, we find him addressed as "the king's trusty counsellor."　In 1532 he was Master of the Jewels, and Clerk of the Hanaper.　In 1533, he was appointed Chancellor of the Exchequer for life; he was knighted, and was probably now appointed Vice-Chamberlain.　In 1534, he was Master of the Rolls, Vicar-General, and Secretary of State, an office he retained till 1539.　About the same time, he was made Justice of the Forests north of the Trent.　He was appointed Lord Privy Seal on the 2nd of July, 1536, and was created a peer on the 9th of July.　In the same year, 1536, his ecclesiastical title was changed, without any change in the office, to Vicegerent in Ecclesiastical Causes.　In 1537, as there was no Act

---

* What he really did was probably to urge the king to act upon the suggestion already made by Cranmer.　Could anything, asks Sir Henry Ellis, have more completely sealed the ruin of Wolsey's fortunes than this suggestion?

of Uniformity, he, though a layman, became Dean of
Wells. In 1539, he was appointed Great Chamber-
lain. On the 17th of April, 1540, Thomas Crumwell
became Earl of Essex.

Such was the remuneration, cheap to the king but
highly prized by the minister, by which Henry VIII.
requited the industry of Crumwell; insulted, through
his elevation, the proud remnant of the ancient nobility; and taught the new aristocracy, that it was not
by an assumption of the traditionary rights of an
obsolete feudalism, but by subservience to the crown,
that wealth and power were to be acquired in the
English Court. The feudal notion, indeed, by which
the king amidst his nobles was only *primus inter pares*,
was exploded; the modern notion of sovereignty was
introduced, leading, under the vigour of the Tudors,
to despotism, and terminating in the extinction of a
dynasty through the weakness and vanity of the Stuarts.

From the endowments of the Church the great
officers of state had derived their income, when the
duties of the government devolved upon ecclesiastics.
When the temporal lords became aware, that other
duties pertained to their high station, beyond that of
maintaining the liberty of the subject, they could
serve the crown without being a burden on the
sovereign to any great extent. But when the Tudors
determined to be served not by rank but by talent,
and when the spirit of the age required the clergy
to attend to their long neglected clerical duties, we
find complaint frequently made by diplomatists, that
the service of the crown was ruin to their families.
The crown commanded their services, but paid little
attention to their salaries.

In this state of things we have the explanation of,
if not the apology for, the avarice of Crumwell. He

was determined to become an earl and to found a family; but the profits of office were not sufficient to support its dignity. While destroying, therefore, the hen, by which the golden eggs had been laid, for his predecessors in public office, he appropriated for his own use what he found in the nest. His family he enriched by obtaining from the crown a grant of not fewer than thirty manors out of the confiscated monastic estates; we have seen how he obtained ready money by the acceptance of bribes, and by recourse to various measures of extortion. He was accused of peculation; and there can be no doubt that much which ought to have found its way into the royal treasury, remained, unaccounted for, in the coffers of the minister. His expenses were enormous, for he knew the importance of purchasing the favour of the great by princely donations; we have a list of his frequent presents to royal and noble personages. His tastes, also, were expensive: he provided theatrical entertainments for the court;* he encouraged the drama among the boys at Eton; he found time to indulge in play; we find him losing at cards and dice various sums from twenty shillings to thirty pounds. His establishment was conducted on a suitable scale, and he delighted in hawks and hounds. On the 19th of November, 1538, he indulged his taste, and at the same time made a good investment, by paying two thousand pounds for a diamond and a ruby. Like most "new men," he was, to adopt a homely phrase still used in the north of England, "house-proud;" he fell into the extravagance in building, against which he had warned Car-

---

* In 1539 he went to great expense in exhibiting a masque; among the items is one of twenty-one shillings and two pence "paid for the hiring of Divine Providence, when she played before the king."

dinal Wolsey. Besides his official residence at the Rolls, he had establishments at Austin Friars, at Hackney, at Stepney, at Mortlake, and at Ewhurst. Of these Stepney was probably his favourite abode, as from thence many of his letters are written. While extensive works were carried on at all these places, as if their owner were reckless of expense, we sometimes see the economy of the thrifty merchant making itself apparent. To save the purchase of mutton, his steward is directed, on one occasion, " to find the household with venison ;" from all quarters the great man was complimented by presents of game.

We have seen how he caused his despotism to be felt in every part of the country ; one would have supposed that for gambling, plays, and field sports he would have little time. As is the case with all really great men, he could descend from the administration of a case on which the life of man depended, to the direction of the most minute details. Among the Cottonian manuscripts there are certain memorandums in Crumwell's handwriting, which are called by him "Remembrances ;" they were notes intended to remind him of what he was to do or say, when waiting upon the king, or attending in his place at parliament or convocation. Their miscellaneous character renders them extremely interesting and valuable. They show how he had brought his mind to disregard sentiment, and to look upon everything from a business point of view. We are amused when we discover the great minister making an especial note, that he may not fail to exhibit to the king " the patterns of the embroidery for the queen ;" and "in the king's name to demand from my Lord of Canterbury the best mitre of his predecessor." It is only what we should expect, when we find him making a memorandum to have the goods of Castell-acre valued "for my part thereof;" though perhaps it may surprise us as a work of supere- rogation, when, in apportioning some monastic estates to certain of his friends, he found it necessary to add " myselfe for launde." We are pleased with his judi- cious piety or policy in reminding himself to appoint preachers, to go throughout the realm to preach the Gospel and the true word of God; but it is not pleasant to read the following: " Item—the Abbot of Reading to be sent down to be tried and executed at Reading; Item—to see that the evidence is well sorted, and the indictments well drawn against the said abbots"—of Glastonbury and Reading—" and their employers." This is not, in modern times, the business of a judge. " Item—to advertise the king of the order- ing of Master (Bishop) Fisher, and to show him of the indenture, which I have delivered to his solicitors. Item—to know his pleasure touching Master More. Item—when Master Fisher shall go to his execution, and also the other." Modern notions will be especially shocked at another item : " To send Gendon to the Tower to be racked, and to send Mr. Bellesys, Mr. Lee, and Mr. Petre to assist Mr. Lieutenant in the examination,"—i.e. the torturing of the poor victim. We are tempted to inquire into the meaning of another item : " Certain persons to be sent to the Tower for the further examination of the abbot of Glaston."

Thus, within six years, the scrivener, who had trem- bled lest in the vortex in which his great master sank, he should be involved, became the foremost man in England. To a similar amount of power no other minister ever reached, before his time or after. He was the confidential adviser of the king; and, though he had to act with caution, yet, in relation both to foreign and home affairs, his own will became that of Henry;

he ruled the monasteries before he dissolved them;
and had the disposal of all preferments in Church and
State; he corrupted or cajoled the parliament, and
packed the House of Commons; he domineered over
Convocation; he terrified into silence those whom he
could not persuade by his eloquence; he intimidated
juries; he rendered his master despotic, that he might
himself rule as a tyrant.

We have seen how he brought this power to bear
upon the destruction of the monastic institute. To
destroy what had been blended with the institutions
of the land, the habits, and at one time the affections
of the people, could not have been effected by any one
less determined to act up to the fulness of his powers,
and whose powers had become exorbitant through the
astounding weakness of his opponents, and his own
legal sagacity and administrative industry. His
further proceedings, both as minister of the crown
and as vicegerent of the king in spiritual matters,
will force themselves upon our notice, when we are
treating of the life of Archbishop Cranmer. We shall
only here remark that, as we read the life of Crumwell
in the ordinary history of the period, his fall seems to
have been as unexpected, and almost as rapid, as his
rise. We seem to be reading some fictitious narrative
in an Oriental tale. The destruction or dishonest
manipulation of public documents to which we have
alluded before, excludes the hope of throwing light
upon the fall of Crumwell from any records we possess.
We may partially account for it by looking at the
state of the case and the character of the king.
Henry judged of a man's merits by his success.
When he had decided upon a line of policy, he confided the conduct of it to the minister by whom it had
been suggested; he only so far interfered with the

details, as to cause it to be felt that he was actually
the master. When the measures of a minister became unpopular, the king—whose desire for popularity was a passion, only checked under the predominance of some more powerful feeling—sought
to save himself by casting his servant upon the
troubled waters; he sometimes looked after him with
a transient sigh of pity, but he never stretched forth
his hand to save him.

Crumwell had failed in every promise he had made
to the king, except in the suppression of the monasteries. Even here, in the king's view of the subject,
he had failed. Henry had no antipathy to monasteries
on religious grounds; his conscientious and even his
religious principles would have led him to reform, and
not to destroy. But he suffered himself to be inflamed
against the monks by the representations he received
of their disloyalty; and his revenge was quickened by
the belief, that, through the confiscation of their property, he would be independent of parliament. The
lamentation and outcry, sure to be occasioned by the
overthrow of an ancient institution even when the
revolution is necessary, had reached the royal ear, and
what was the result? The policy of Crumwell had
been too refined. To prevent disturbance, he had enlisted nobles, country gentlemen, and the populace, as
his allies in the attack upon the monasteries; he had
invited them to a participation of the plunder. For
a time, all went on well: the king had money for his
pleasures; the courtiers were enriched to meet him
at the gaming-table; the abbots and leading monks
were satisfied with their pensions;—but the treasury
was exhausted. The monastic property had gone no
one knew where or how. King and parliament had
been cajoled into the expectation, that taxation would

henceforth cease. The king was humiliated and the people were exasperated, when a larger subsidy was required, demanded, and reluctantly granted, than the people had conceded or the king had asked in any preceding year.

While he was bribing the superiors of the monasteries to betray their trust, it may have been good policy for Crumwell to have had recourse to a system in which he has had, in every age, too many followers; that of turning the religious party to which he was opposed into ridicule. He forgot, or never understood, that the religion of the monks was Christianity, though Christianity under a corrupt form; and in point of fact, when laughing at monkery, the playwrights who found in Crumwell a patron, were advocating— perhaps unintentionally—the cause of irreligion; and as Convocation expressed it, of atheism. Convocation petitioned for protection, not, as it was said, from the love of papacy; for it was the Convocation which had denounced the pope as having no authority in England; but because all the piety in England, except when pious men were blinded by their party zeal, had been disgusted and shocked.*

The Act of Six Articles, of which we shall have occasion to speak at greater length hereafter, was introduced for the protection of religion. It was, as were all the measures of Henry, violent and unjust, though it was only partially enforced; but Crumwell acquiesced in the policy, from a conviction probably that he had gone too far.

Crumwell had engaged to humble the clergy as well as to make free with their money, and to annihilate the power of the pope; but he had suffered himself to be the fautor of heretics, and so to stultify the king,

* Wilkins, iii. 850, 863.

whose boast it was, that it was on Catholic principles only,—and on Catholic as distinguished from Protestant principles,—that he rejected the pope.

Crumwell had promised to restore the country to peace. He had, for a season, established a reign of terror. For a time, he appeared to be successful; but the excited state of London, apparently on the eve of insurrection, at length convinced the king, that a change of measures was not sufficient. The minister must be himself dismissed. Crumwell's Irish policy had been a failure. He had there attempted to purchase peace by bribing those who threatened to break it; and by heaping rewards upon the supporters of Government. The money was taken, but the rebellious spirit was unsubdued; it only waited for an opportunity to burst into a blaze. Crumwell was equally unsuccessful in his foreign policy. Instead of treading in the steps of his illustrious predecessor, his desire had been to form an alliance with the Protestants of Germany; at the head of this alliance he designed to place the King of England. It would appear, that instead of propounding his policy to Henry he endeavoured to entrap him; to make the king the foremost man in Europe, but to keep him ignorant of his intentions, until the king should find that accomplished, to the means of accomplishing which he might have objected. Such a man as Henry would never forgive the minister, among whose papers was discovered a clandestine correspondence with the German princes. Although the correspondence may not have been discovered until after his fall, it was probably notified to the king before his arrest. This conjecture enables us to account for the report that Ann of Cleves was the cause of Crumwell's disgrace. If this be stated, as an isolated fact, it is, as Burnet observes, contradicted by the favours which, after the arrival of Ann of Cleves, the minister still received from the hands of the king. It was after her arrival, that Crumwell received his earldom. The king's conduct to Ann of Cleves was offensive, disgusting, and unmanly ; it proved, as is too often found to be the case with princes, that he had not the common feelings of a gentleman ; but, instead of venting his anger upon Crumwell, he confided to him his disappointment, and consulted him as to the means by which he might extricate himself from his contract.* But when that marriage contract was found to be an item in those clandestine communications which Crumwell had conducted with the German princes, the indignation of the haughty sovereign knew no bounds.

There is a letter extant among the Cottonian MSS. from the wife of Gregory Crumwell addressed to the king, in which she alludes, not to one act of treason, but to "the heinous trespasses and grievous offences of my father-in-law."

It is said by Foxe, that Crumwell had foreseen his fall ; and that two years before the event, he had prepared for its occurrence, by making provision for his servants. He knew the uncertain tenure of office ; and that, in those days, a change of ministry implied the almost certain death of the minister. His affection for his family was great, and his kindness towards his dependants is praiseworthy. He desired to disconnect their fortunes from his own ; he remembered the inconveniences to which he had been himself exposed on the death of Wolsey. But this exercise of his usual forethought did not imply that he expected what he accepted as a possibility. He evidently intended by his lavish expenditure upon his various houses, when a

---

* This appears from Crumwell's letter to Henry from his prison in the Tower.

fitting time should have come, to retire from public life, and to enjoy his *otium cum dignitate*. The blow, when it came, was as a flash of lightning; and the very pusillanimity which he displayed in his letters to the king, written after his arrest, are sufficient to show, that the precautions he had taken did not imply more of fear than that which is entertained by a man when he insures his house. The destruction *may* come, but he fully expects that, by proper care, it may be averted.

He was arrested in the council chamber, on the 10th of June, 1540, on a charge of high treason. The act of the king was ratified by the tumultuous applause of the Londoners; the only drawback to the joy of the splenetic and hypochondriacal, was the fear, that although imprisoned, the criminal might nevertheless escape.

It was determined to proceed against him by bill of attainder; we may therefore infer, that no specific act of treason could be substantiated against him; or that there were political reasons why the real cause of his condemnation should remain unknown to the public.[*] Careless as he had been of the life of others, he pleaded for his own with so much pathos and vehemence as to bring a tear to the eye of Henry. The king nevertheless did what he called his duty by his country.

[*] A bill of attainder was introduced when there was a moral certainty of the guilt of the person accused, without sufficient evidence to secure his conviction by an ordinary process in a court of justice. It is a mistake to say that bills of attainder were an invention of Crumwell. In the reign of Edward III. it was by bill of attainder Roger Mortimer and Edward Earl of Arundel were condemned. The principle was a simple one: "We cannot prove you to be guilty, nevertheless we will vote you a traitor, and you shall die as such." It was a fearful instrument of cruelty and injustice in the reign of Henry VIII. Against the mode of proceeding, as exercised against himself, Crumwell protested in his letters to the king.

This he was wont to do, when that duty accorded with his inclination, his interests, or his caprice.

On the 28th of July, 1540, Thomas Crumwell, earl of Essex, was beheaded on Tower Hill. From internal evidence we reject both the speech and the prayer as they are presented to us in the pages of Foxe. They were evidently manipulated, if not originally composed, to answer the purposes of party. The work was not well executed. In later times the Romanists claim him on account of the speech; the Protestants on account of the prayer. It is probable that the large sums he bequeathed to a priest, who should for seven years sing masses for his soul, were never paid. His daughter-in-law, in a letter to the king, complained of "the extreme indigence and poverty in which, through her father-in-law's most detestable offences, the family was involved."[*]

In accordance with the plan of the present work, a detailed account has been given of the dissolution of the monasteries, and a brief review has been taken of the life and character of Thomas Crumwell.[†]

By prefixing introductory chapters to the several books, I have sought to avoid the digressions or dis-

---

[*] Gregory Crumwell married Elizabeth, daughter of Sir John Seymour, of Wolfhall, in the county of Wilts, sister to Edward duke of Somerset, and widow of Sir Anthony Oughtred. By her he had three sons and two daughters. About five months after his father's death, he was created Baron Crumwell. His descendant, Thomas Crumwell, was created Viscount Lecale and Earl of Ardglass in Ireland. The family became extinct in 1687.—Dugdale; Nicolas.

[†] The name is spelt both Cromwell and Crumwell, and in the uncertain orthography of the age it is difficult to decide which is correct. Having the choice, I have adopted the spelling which enables us at once to distinguish between the minister of Henry VIII. and the Protector. It is on the same principle, and on similar authority, to mark the man, that I write Gardyner instead of Gardiner, and Foxe instead of Fox.

sertations, which would have interrupted the narrative;
and I have evaded the tediousness of a twice-told tale,
when, in one and the same public transaction, two
primates of this nation have been concerned. Hitherto
the relations of Church and State have been so intimate
that in writing the life of an archbishop, I have found
myself composing the life of a statesman; and when I
undertook to be a biographer I have become an historian.
In the last book especially I have availed myself of the
fresh sources of information laid open to the public
under the auspices of the Master of the Rolls, to throw
new light upon that progressive though tumultuous
portion of our history, which relates to the Wars of
the Roses. I have, however, confined myself to those
political events in which the primates were immediately
concerned.

From the commencement of the Reformation period,
we shall find our primates and their suffragans gradually withdrawing from political life; but this has rendered it the more necessary to advert to the civil history
of our country in an introductory chapter. In order to
appreciate properly the character of an individual who
has occupied a prominent position in society, it is
necessary to take into consideration the circumstances
under which he received his training, through which he
has fought his way to eminence, or to which he has
succumbed; as well as the idiosyncrasies which have
rendered him singular in his greatness or goodness.

In the overthrow of the monasteries the Church
concurred, but took no part; the narrative of this
event belongs, therefore, to the civil history of the
country. But the leading Reformers—Cranmer and
Latimer especially—approved of the suppression of the
monasteries; and we must pay minute attention to
the history of that event, in order that we may account

for the fact, that while the dissolution received their
sanction, they abstained from co-operation with Crumwell. Crumwell's own history is, though circuitous,
closely connected with that of Cranmer. The accounts given of the dissolution are generally one-sided;
I have thought it right therefore to place both sides
of the case before the reader. The papers found in
the Record Office throw fresh light on the history
of Crumwell. Of these subjects I have therefore
treated at some length.

On the other hand, a separate consideration of the
measures, which were gradually adopted to educe a
book of Common Prayer from "the Use of Sarum" and
the other rituals of the English Church, would create
the inconvenience which an introductory chapter is
designed to avoid. The labours of our primates and
their clergy, during the reigns of Henry, Edward,
Elizabeth, James I. and Charles II, in committees, in
convocation, and in parliament, are inseparably inter-
woven with their biographies. A digression upon this
subject is part of their history.

Again, in the rise, the progress, the proceedings, and
the aims of Puritanism, the statements of the civil and
ecclesiastical historian are so interlaced, that it is
impossible to trace the history in detached threads;
it must be considered as a whole. The archbishops,
sometimes as partial supporters, more frequently as
decided opponents, are continually employed in the
refutation or the propagation of Puritan as distinguished from Catholic principles; and, whether agreeing
in the principles or not, are in hostility to the Puritan
party, when considered in its party combinations.

The Reformation period commences in the reign of
Henry VIII. and in the primacy of Warham; it ter-
minates in the reign of Charles II. and in the primacy

of Juxon. When we speak, however, of the termination of the Reformation in 1662, what is meant is only
this; that we refer to that year as to the period of that
ecclesiastical settlement devised in convocation and
confirmed by parliament, on which we have rested,
during the last two hundred years and more. We do
not rest on any reformation carried on in the reign of
Henry VIII. or Edward VI.* What was then done was
partially repealed in Queen Mary's time, and only
partially re-enacted under Queen Elizabeth. We do
not say, that any further reformation is impossible.
We merely affirm, as a matter of fact, that the Act of
Uniformity binding upon us now, is not the act of
Elizabeth, but the act of Charles II. The Prayer-
book to which that Act refers is not the first or the
second of Edward VI. or the Prayer-book of Queen
Elizabeth ; it is the Prayer-book which was adopted
by the Houses of Convocation, in the two provinces of
the English Church in the year just mentioned.†

* In showing that we are in no way concerned with the particular
measures of reformation adopted in the time of Henry and Edward,
Mr. Gladstone observes : "The Bishop's Book, the King's Book,
the first and second Liturgy of Edward VI. with the Forty-two
Articles, *are to us as though they had never been,* so far as respects
any bearing upon the ecclesiastical title of our present settlement.
Had Cranmer and Ridley promulgated a Socinian Liturgy and
Articles, the circumstance need not in the slightest degree have
affected the basis on which the acts of the subsequent reign were
founded."—*State in Relation to the Church,* ii. 117.

† On the 29th of May, 1661, Archbishop Juxon issued his
mandate for the assembling of a convocation, with a view to the
further reformation of the Church. The work of reformation commenced in the formation of a committee, and the members were
guided by the principles invariably acted upon since the reign of
Henry VIII. Everything was to be brought to the test of Scripture, and of the primitive as distinguished from the mediæval
Church. On the 20th of December, 1661, the reformed Book of
Common Prayer—the last version of the "Use of Sarum," and the

In writing the lives of the English primates during this period, we are encountered by the difficulty, that of this period we do not possess an impartial history containing a simple assertion of facts as they really existed. Every writer will have his bias, for which, as in a game of bowls, every judicious reader will make due allowance. But this is a very different thing from a wilful and conscious suppression of unpalatable truth; from a sarcastic suggestion of a profitable falsehood; from a colouring of facts, so as to force them to throw a false light upon a foregone conclusion. A work so composed may amuse or exasperate the reader, but can scarcely be called a history. The honest mind is equally offended, when an author is seen defending, on one side, a course of conduct which, when pursued by a person attached to the opposite faction, is subjected to the severest censure; when a bad action is justified, because the doer of it is a reputed saint; and when a good action is almost condemned, because it is assumed, that a political or religious opponent must be in league with the spirits of darkness.

Of the Reformation, the history has been written by Puritans, by Roman Catholics, by infidels under the garb of philosophers. These all profess to be one-sided; and for one-sided publications the demand in the literary market is met because it is made. It is well known, that a Protestant will not, as a general rule, read a history of the Reformation written by a Roman Catholic; nor

CHAP.
I.

Introduc-
tory.

other ancient Uses of the English Church—was adopted and sub-scribed by the clergy of both Houses of Convocation, and of both provinces of the Church. A copy of the new Prayer-book, with the Great Seal attached, was delivered, with a royal message, to Parliament on the 25th of February, 1662. The Bill of Uniformity having passed the Lords on the 9th of April, received the royal assent on the 19th of May, and thus became part of the law of the land.—*Kennet's Register*, 584, 585; *Syn. Ang.* 94, 96.

will a Roman Catholic read a history written by a Protestant.   The history of an avowed unbeliever,—of
Hume for instance,—may be sometimes read, under
the notion, that he who disbelieves all religion must
be partial to none; but we find that, from the days of
Julian to the present hour, no fanaticism can, in its
calm malignity, equal the fanaticism of infidelity.

The difficulty, indeed, of attempting to write a history of the Reformation in the reign of Henry VIII. is
peculiarly great from the want of materials.   A laudable
diligence has been shown by Collier, Burnet, and Strype,
in collecting records and other public documents; much,
however, in this direction, remains to be accomplished.
But when all shall have been done, the difficulty will
not be surmounted in what relates to this reign, until
further light shall have been thrown upon its history,
by revelations to be made from the private correspondence of foreign ambassadors to their several courts.
Much important information has been obtained from
the Simancas papers, deciphered by the incredible
industry, and illustrated by the learned sagacity, of
Mr. Bergenroth.   The difficulty of doing justice to all
persons and parties in this reign is enhanced by that
wilful destruction of papers of deep historical import-
tance, of which mention has been made before.

Much is left open to conjecture, when we would
seek to account for actions thus purposely involved in
mystery; the removal of the mystery would involve the
king and government in disgrace.   We are dependent,
too often, on the inconclusive arguments of partisans
on either side.   Each arrives at the conclusion he has
previously determined to deduce, by adding his surmises
to the few indisputable facts of which we are in possession.   The documents and accounts, moreover, which
are not destroyed have received a treatment with which

modern dishonesty has made us familiar, and which is described by an inelegant but expressive term, when we venture to speak of them as having been " cooked." The preambles to acts of parliament were dictated by Henry himself, who, in the spirit of Augustus, desired to rule as a despot, under the forms of a free constitution. Henry VIII. would indulge his passions, his avarice, or his lust, under the semblance of designing what was right. In an uncritical age, the spirit of the constitution might be violated with impunity, if the letter of the law was observed ; and through the letter of the law every man's liberty was subjected to the caprice of the king. Although Burnet and Strype as well as Collier supply a large mass of materials for history, yet Strype is often inaccurate in his transcriptions ; and Burnet seems very frequently not to have read what his secretary was directed to transcribe. Bale and Foxe were accepted by them as primary authorities ; and instead of correcting these writers by the public records, they too generally adopted their statements without further investigation ; they passed over with a slight notice, or with no notice at all, the documents which would, if duly examined, have convicted them of misrepresentation.* The statements of Foxe and Bale have become the basis of Protestant historians of this period ; for to all the writers with whom I am acquainted, Burnet is the chief authority.

CHAP.
I.

Introductory.

* Burnet has found an editor in Mr. Pocock, whose superiority to the bishop has rendered his acceptance of the editor's office a condescension. He has been careful not to do injustice to Burnet ; but has corrected many of his errors in point of learning. Strype's works have been reprinted at the University of Oxford, but it can scarcely be said, that they have been edited. To him the grateful acknowledgments of every student of history are due. No one ever laboured more diligently to collect the material for history ; he was a collector of records, not an historian.

L 2

Protestants complain with justice of Sanders, who stands in the same relation to the Roman Catholic writers, as Foxe does to the Protestant. Sanders was the purveyor of the filthy scandals of the age, and it is not too much to say, that of some he was the author. Of him it was said, " he lied, and he knew that he lied." But they who would throw the stone at Sanders, must not forget the amount of glass of which their own house is composed. For the character of Foxe I will refer not to a Roman Catholic, but to the scholar most competent, from his deep researches into the public records, to form an opinion upon the subject. " Had the Matyrologist," says Professor Brewer, " been an honest man, his carelessness and credulity would have incapacitated him from being a trustworthy historian. Unfortunately he was not honest. He tampered with the documents that came to his hands, and freely indulged in those very faults of suppression for which he condemned his opponents."*

Of the other great authority of Burnet and his followers, Bishop Bale, Henry Wharton said : " I know Bale to have been such a liar, that I am unwilling to take anything on his credit."

The case is scarcely improved when, proceeding to the next century, we have to consider the struggle between the Church and Puritanism for supremacy. It seems, that an unimpassioned history of the Great

* Pref. to Letters and Papers, Henry VIII. p. 30. Some years ago I had occasion to consult the Rev. Dr. Maitland, the learned librarian of Lambeth, on the amount of credit I might give to a statement made by Foxe. His answer was, " You may regard Foxe as being about as trustworthy as the *Record* newspaper. You must not believe either, when they speak of an opponent ; for, though professing Protestantism, they are innocent of Christian charity. You may accept the documents they print; but certainly not without collation. Foxe forgot, if he ever knew, who is the father of lies."

Rebellion, as it is called, cannot even yet be expected from an English pen. Those who pretend to impartiality are swayed, unconsciously, to the one side or the other by the current of public opinion. At one period, too much evil could not be said against the Protector; and Charles I, with all his faults, was regarded as a saint. In an age when republican sentiments are predominant, the faults of the Protector are forgotten or explained away, and he is canonized; while the enthusiasm of loyalty having become faint, the virtues of Charles are no longer permitted to excite compassion for his sufferings. The enthusiasm of the present generation is easily excited in behalf of those who contended for the liberty of the subject; but the prejudices are not to be despised of the gallant spirits who fought for the royal prerogative. Both were right, and both were wrong; between the struggles of the two, liberty was prevented from degenerating into licence; and a warning, as well as an example, is set to those who rightly hold the great truth, that governments are to be so administered as to produce the greatest amount of good to the greatest number of persons,—real good being always in close contact with the laws of God.

The only author between the reigns of Henry VIII. and Charles II. who has really laboured to deal equal justice to all parties, is Jeremy Collier, the Nonjuring Bishop. But indebted as we are, for his researches, to Collier, we must admit, that he was more laborious in collecting than skilful in arranging his materials; he lived in an uncritical age, and his quotations must be compared with their context before we can, at all times, subscribe to his conclusions. Without any tendency to Romanism, Collier laboured to do justice to the opponents as well as to the advocates of reformation.

He has avoided one great error of Protestant historians, especially of those who have written in the interests of the Church of England. Among such persons, there is apparent an eagerness, which is sometimes amusing, to select some one or more of the personages connected with the Reformation, in order to canonize him as a saint, or to immortalize as a hero. It must be admitted, that in their attempts they have miserably failed. In vain do we look in the annals of our country for a hero like Martin Luther, full of earnestness, fervour, enthusiasm, courage; dauntless, decided, resolute; the man of the people. We look in vain for a theologian like John Calvin; systematic, accurate, severe; whose mighty mind, fired by contact with the spirit of St. Augustine, has left its impress on the Protestant world; and has compelled men, unconsciously, to accept and to propagate, in essentials, much of the scholastic doctrine. We cannot even point to any one who approaches to Melancthon or Zuingle, the man of deep thought, and the man of wild enthusiasm.

In the writings of our early Reformers, which have lately been published, we search in vain for

"Thoughts that breathe, and words that burn."

We desiderate in all the *fervida vis* of genius. As regards their learning, it is chiefly that which, in the exigencies of a controversy and for the maintenance of a cause, they were obliged to acquire.[*]

* A few years ago, for party purposes, the writings of those who took an active part in the early reformation of the Church of England were published by the Parker Society; and, for the most part, they were carefully edited. But if the object was to magnify the

Our early Reformers were men of sound common sense, pious, judicious; as reformers, they were cautious almost to timidity; they felt their way step by step; now advancing, then receding, and at last making firm their position. They were true-hearted Englishmen, attached to our constitution in Church or State. Seeing that both required a reformation, they commenced with the Church; a reformation of the Church was sanctioned by the king; it would have been death to deal with state affairs.   As was natural, they were not uninfluenced by the spirit of the age; and—from a deference, natural but to be lamented also, to the illustrious men who were revolutionizing religion in Germany and Switzerland,—they were led occasionally into inconsistencies. They were, however, soon brought back to common sense by the master minds and stern resolve of Henry and of Elizabeth. These monarchs, with all their faults, were patriots loyal to their country; they determined that England should lead, and not be led. To Henry and Elizabeth the Church of England is deeply indebted; for they compelled our reforming divines to conduct the Reformation on those principles by which the English have ever been distinguished and

---

Reformers, the result has been a failure.   It has been well observed, that none of these writers would now be quoted as an authority in any great question of philology, of philosophy, of ecclesiastical history, or even of theology, except Archbishop Parker's Antiquitates, which, on the principle of the play of Hamlet with the character of Hamlet omitted, the Parker Society did not publish. The works of Cranmer have been separately printed, and are of great value to those who study the progress of our Reformation. But Cranmer was a lawyer rather than a theologian.   He decided by common sense, and then looked out for precedents to silence opponents.   The works are never interesting of a man who has to read *up* to his subject.   The well-fraught mind comes *down* upon its subject, and makes even its unconscious plagiarisms its own, by the genius it has infused into them.

guided. We know that miraculous inspiration has ceased. Nevertheless, under the ordinary operations of Providence, we speak of men being inspired; as society is only an aggregate of individuals we may therefore, without presumption, trace to the merciful ordering of God that strong common sense, which has induced the English people, at all times, to postpone the theoretical to the practical. Like the attractions and repulsions in electricity, there have been, throughout our history, two principles, co-operating though opposing; and productive, in their joint operation, of motion and powerful action. We have ever moved on by concessions and compromises made to the principle of progress by the conservative principle; and by similar concessions to the conservative principle by those who are animated to enthusiasm by theoretical notions of perfection. There is something conservative in our man of progress; there is a desire of progress in our most timid conservative. The one is applauded when he says " Festina ;" the other is not unheeded when he adds " Lentè."

Occasionally the rupture has been serious, prolonged and violent; and, by a spirit of unchecked intolerance and persecution, either party has been disgraced. When the passions have yielded to reason, it has been seen that the practical man will aim not at the best, considered abstractly, but at the best according to circumstances.

The practical aim was that which our Reformers proposed; they were opposed by the Puritans, the men of theory. The Puritans, taking the great Reformers of the Continent for their masters, and adverting to their systems as models, nobly sought, as their name denotes, the highest theoretical perfection. They sought in a sect, what they could not realize in a Church; and, when toleration was unknown, their endeavour was to displace the old Church and to establish Calvinism.

This is not the place to attack, to defend, or to palliate the proceedings or the tenets of this great and influential party. Among the Puritans were men of piety equal to that of our own divines; eminent for their learning and their devotion to the service of their Saviour and their God. To them, to their exertions, and to their sufferings, the country is indebted for many enduring benefits. But while we give to them the honour which is their due, we may be permitted to regard with complacency, the position of the English Church. That Church is to us an inheritance which we cherish, and a blessing for which we are devoutly grateful. We sympathise with the mighty men of genius who manfully contended on the Continent, against the superstitions of the Church, and the corruptions of their age; but, when we compare results, to the fire of genius we prefer the sober-mindedness, the sound judgment, the wise caution, by which our own divines were enabled to retain what they had received, and to hand down to us what was transmitted to them—the Church of Augustine and even of the ancient Britons before him; not made new, but reformed. We admit the weakness of the agents, only that we may adore with gratitude, the mighty hand and the outstretched arm of Jehovah :—

> "Pater amisso fluitantem errare magistro
> Sensit, et ipse ratem nocturnis rexit in undis."

To the Lutherans Luther is an authority; and if they differ from his doctrine, Lutherans they cease to be. The Calvinist forfeits the title of which he is proud, if to the conclusions of his master's great mind he demurs. Of our Church the foundation was laid, not by any Reformer, but by Augustine. Our Reformation was not a beginning, it was a turning-point in the history of the Church of England.* We have a Church reformed by the joint action of the Convocation, the Crown, and the Parliament. By the co-operation of these still existing authorities, the work of 1662 may be resumed; and measures may be adopted, if need shall be, to meet the requirements of a new generation and the exigencies of an altered age. The Church is like a ship at anchor; to the full length of the cable the vessel may swing with the tide. A certain latitude is allowed in the Church to opinions and practices, so long as it continues anchored to the Rock of Ages. We assert, that further improvements may, from time to time, be necessary; we only say, that they must be conformable to the principles of the Church universal. To deny this right of reform is to convert the Church into a sect.

* It is thus that Mr. Freeman, from whom I borrow the expression, describes the Norman Invasion, in a work which we hope to see developed into a complete History of England.

CHAPTER II.

WILLIAM WARHAM.

Educated a Wykehamist at Winchester and at New College.—His Career at Oxford.—A Student of Law.—Practises in the Court of Arches.—Diplomatic Employments.—An Account of Perkin Warbeck.—Warham attached to the Embassy to the Duke of Burgundy.—Principal of St. Edmund's College, Oxford.—Consecrated Bishop of London.—Translation to Canterbury.—Appointed Lord Chancellor.—Splendour of the Enthronization. — Enthronization Feast at Oxford.—Appointed Lord High Chancellor.—In favour with Henry VII.—Question relating to the Marriage of Prince Henry with the Princess Katherine.—Light thrown on the subject by the Simancas Papers.—Death of Henry VII.—Warham officiates at the Marriage of Henry VIII. and the Lady Katherine.—Sponsor to their first Child.—His parliamentary Career.—Corruption of the Church.—Condition of the Clergy.—Iniquities of the Ecclesiastical Courts.—Warham's Attempts at Reform.—Warham assists to aid Henry VIII.—Labours to effect Wolsey's Appointment as Cardinal and Legate *a latere.*—Amicable Relations between Warham and Wolsey.—Their occasional Misunderstandings.—Warham's Retirement from Public Life.—His Patronage of the Reformers before the Reformation.—His Conduct as Chancellor of Oxford.—The Reforms introduced at the University.—An Account of the leading Literary Men of the Day, Friends of Warham.—Warham the Patron and Protector of Colet.—The intimate Friend of Erasmus.—Erasmus in England.—Erasmus speaks of Warham as a married Man. —Question of Warham's Marriage considered. — Royal Divorce.—Wolsey sounds Warham on the Subject.—Warham inclined, though passive, to side with the King.—The Public first in favour of a Divorce.—Indignation and Discontent when Announcement was made of the King's intended Marriage with Anne Boleyn.—Wolsey in Disgrace.—Cranmer and Crumwell secret Advisers of the King.—Royal Supremacy mooted.—Account of Dr. Standish.—Matronage of England insulted by the King's proposed Marriage with his Mistress.—Clergy vehement in their Denunciation of the Marriage.—Pulpits silenced. — Henry determined to punish the Clergy.—Parliament of 1529.—Bills affecting the Clergy.—Clergy involved in the Penalties of Præmunire.—Convocation of Canterbury.—Latimer's Recantation.—House of Commons attack the Ordinaries. — Ordinaries as distinguished from Bishops.— Gardyner's

Reply.—Royal Supremacy admitted by Convocation long before it was asserted by Parliament.—Discussions on this Subject.—Warham's View of it.—Submission of the Clergy.—Opposition in Convocation.—Concessions on both sides.—Warham in favour with the King.—Prepares for Death.—Last Illness.—His Disregard of Money.—Dies poor.—Obsequies.—Benefactions.

THE family of Warham had, in the fifteenth century, been long settled at Walsanger, in the parish of Church Oakley, in the county of Southampton. In this parish, and we may presume at Walsanger, William, the future Archbishop of Canterbury, was born about the year 1450.*

At an early age he was sent to Winchester, and became a Wykehamist. At this school, where Chicheley had studied, and Waynflete had taught, there was no deficiency, at that early period, of the prestige which, attached to an educational institution, tends to the creation of a sentiment, of which in the

Authorities—Warham's Register at Lambeth. This register is extremely well represented in Burnet and Wilkins. It is in itself the worst kept of all the Lambeth Registers. Lord Calthorpe has a volume written by the Registrar of Warham, and including several documents that ought to be in Warham's and in Cranmer's Registers, especially some valuable extracts from the lost records of Convocation. Bacon's Henry VII.; Herbert's Henry VIII.; Hall; Holinshed; Fabyan; Erasmi Opera; Letters and Papers of the Reigns of Richard III. and Henry VII. in the Record Office, ed. Gairdner; Calendar of State Papers, Henry VIII, ed. Brewer; State Papers, ed. Lemon; Calendar of State Papers in the Archives of Simancas and elsewhere, ed. Bergenroth; Collections in Append. to Fiddes' Life of Wolsey; Original Letters published by Sir Henry Ellis, reprinted with additions in the Archæol. Cantiana.

* In a letter of Erasmus, Jortin, i. 492, it is stated that Warham was fourscore years old in 1530. He is described in a letter of Henry VII. of 1531, "as being above fourscore years." State Papers, vii. 311. According to Wood, his father's name was Robert. Athenæ, iii. 738.

formation of character, Dr. Arnold, himself a Wykehamist, asserted the importance. In choosing a site
for his new foundation, William of Wykeham had
selected a spot in which the youthful Wykehamist
would make a boast that no less a personage than
King Alfred had pursued his studies; and, under the
influence of the Renaissance, young Warham may
have contended, that, in the time of the Romans, here
stood a temple of Apollo.

From Winchester, Warham was elected to a scholarship at New College, where in due course he became
a fellow in 1475. To the rules of his college he
steadily adhered. He kept neither ferrets, nor hawks,
nor dogs of chase. He was never seen with a sling,
with darts, or with bow and arrow in his hand.
These things were not permitted; he was prohibited,
indeed, from carrying a sword or knife, or any weapon
whatever of offence or defence. He refused to play at
games of hazard. In cold weather he availed himself
of the permission given by the founder to wear a cloak
or surcoat, or even a military coat, so long as attention
was paid to what was decent and decorous. No particular college dress was at this time adopted; each
student was permitted, according to his taste or convenience, to wear a cape, or a chimere, or any long
mantle reaching to the feet. He was, however, warned
against foppery; and the wearing of green or red
boots, or "pick-toed shoes," or knotted hoods, was
expressly forbidden. The scholars of New College
were also warned against pedantry; they were indeed
to converse among themselves in the Latin language,
but among strangers they were to use the vernacular.
Then, as now, the tutorial system prevailed in the
colleges; but young men were expected to remain
longer at the University, in order that they might
profit by the public lectures delivered for the instruc-

tion of advanced scholars by the professors in the several faculties. The students were chiefly confined to college lectures during the first two years of their residence at the University, and the lectures given in New College were a continuation of the lessons to which Warham had been accustomed at Winchester. The trivium remained as the basis of primary instruction; but it was a basis much enlarged by the altered circumstances of the times. Grammar, rhetoric, and dialectics were the three arts of the trivium. But grammar had now an extended reference to philology in general, and to the Humaniores Literæ. The Renaissance had inspired a taste for classical literature; and if Greek were not yet regarded as a *sine quâ non* in the University examinations, it was certainly required at New College, and we may presume at King's College, Cambridge. It is especially stated that at New College, Greek was taught daily.* Both at Winchester and Eton it was studied, and these, the only Public schools then in existence, adopted the same grammar.

To perfect the boys in Latin grammar, practice in versification had been already adopted; but this, together with the study of poetry and history, was regarded as connected with lectures in rhetoric. Dialectic branched out into the whole of philosophy, and thus enabled the trivium to merge imperceptibly into the quadrivium, which embraced arith-

---

* Of the studies of the Universities I shall have occasion to speak hereafter. I will only here remark, that William of Wykeham required the study of the three languages, Latin, Greek, and Hebrew, at his school, foreseeing that education by language would supersede education by philosophy. Greek, however, did not enter into the curriculum of the studies of the Universities until the sixteenth century. It was, as Hebrew is now, an optional study.

metic, geometry, astronomy, and music regarded as a science.

Warham was expected to rise at five, when the chapel bell summoned him to prayer. The morning was devoted to study. He dined in the common hall; and during dinner a portion of Scripture was read by the Bible clerk. The afternoon was given to recreation, until the college bell sounded, at nine in summer and at eight in winter. The gates were then closed, and the studious resumed their labours.*

At the expiration of two years, Warham passed from the tutor's room to the hall of the public professor. Having devoted himself to the course marked out in the quadrivium, and to the studies of the University, he presented himself, in the chivalrous spirit which was now expiring, as a candidate for literary knighthood, by appearing in the public schools, there to defend certain theses against all comers. He maintained his position, and became a Bachelor of Arts—a Bas-chevalier, or knight of low degree.

A Master of Arts having received gratuitous instruction at New College, was expected to repay the benevolence of the founder by remaining for some years at the University, there to act as the gratuitous instructor of others. This indeed had been, as in a former volume we had occasion to show, the duty originally of every graduate. As a Master of Arts, his instructions were confined to the University; but upon receiving his doctor's degree, conferred after examina-

* These statements are made on the authority of Pits *de rebus Anglicis*, and more particularly of some valuable documents preserved in Winchester College, of which a judicious selection was made and arranged, with his usual sound judgment, by the late Mr. Gunner, and printed in the Archæological Journal. See also *Wykeham and his Colleges*, by Mr. Mackenzie Walcott.

tion, he had a licence to teach anywhere. Warham is said to have lectured two years on philosophy, on Aristotle, and on St. Augustine. There were translations of Aristotle as well as of Plato, but the study of Greek literature was not so far advanced as to justify us in supposing that by lecturing on Aristotle we are to understand more than lectures on the great Commentary of Averroes—or Aristotle diluted through his Arabian commentator, until almost everything Aristotelian was lost.

William Warham was sensible of the advantages he derived from the wise benevolence of William of Wykeham; and in after life he proved his gratitude by liberal benefactions to the two St. Mary Winton Colleges.*

While he was yet at Oxford, Warham commenced the study of law, and having become a Doctor of Laws, he repaired to London in 1488. He practised with considerable ability as a lawyer in the Court of Arches; but at the same time he continued to take a lively interest in all that related to the affairs of the University.

The date of Warham's ordination is uncertain. Among the names of persons ordained by Bishop Smyth, at Lichfield, September 21, 1493, that of William Warram occurs, as having been ordained subdeacon under letters of dimission from the Bishop of

---

* To Winchester he gave hangings for the hall; and the arras in the Audit Room emblazoned with arms and sacred emblems. The doorways and the screen in the Refectory at New College were also his gift. He presented the College with silver plate, weighing 144 ounces; and a messuage or land in King's Clere. At his death he bequeathed his theological books to All Souls College; his books on Church music to Winchester; and his collections on civil and canon law, together with the Greek works which he had purchased from the Greek refugees, who on flying from Constantinople had found a refuge in England.

Hereford.* Mr. Churton, with some hesitation, identifies this person with our Archbishop. All that can be said is, that this is not inconsistent with the known dates of Warham's preferments. It is said that before he vacated his fellowship, he had accepted a living from his college, and was incumbent of Horwood Magna, in the county of Lincoln.

He certainly held the rectory of Barley, in Hertfordshire ; but there is considerable difficulty in assigning the proper dates to his early preferments. He was non-resident, but he met the claims upon his purse with liberality, and occasionally visited his parishioners. So long as he was represented by a pious curate, the people did not complain, the duty was duly performed, and, through the increasing wealth of their rector and his interest in high quarters, the parishioners were benefited and enriched.†

The abilities of the young lawyer attracted the notice of Archbishop Morton ; and through Morton the merits of his *protégé* became known to Henry VII. Learned, accomplished, discreet, and active, Warham was the kind of man whom Henry VII. delighted to honour and employ. He was one of that large class of persons who, in quiet times, rise to eminence, not on account

---

* Life of Smyth, p. 217.

† We are informed by Weever, 547, that in his time, the early part of the 17th century, there was a window in the church of Barley in which was visible the following inscription :—*Orate pro salubri statu Domini Willelmi Warham, Legum Doctoris et Pauli London Canonici, Magistri Rotulorum, Cancellarii Regis et Rectoris de Barley.* He was Master of the Rolls from the 13th of February, 1494, to 1502. See also Hasted, 343, and Wood, Athenæ, ii. 740. Hasted mentions Warham as Chancellor of Wells, in 1493. His name appears in Le Neve, not as Chancellor but as Præcentor. Hardy's Le Neve, i. 171. There is no tradition of Warham in the parish of Barley, and I am informed by the present Rector, the Rev. Robert Gordon, that of the window mentioned by Weever no trace remains.

of any transcendent merits, but from an absence of dis-qualifications and faults.   Warham did nothing great; but he was never known to do anything conspicuously wrong.   He was moderate in all things, whether we look to his intellectual or his moral character.   If he had not genius to originate a wise measure, he had sagacity to see and to applaud its wisdom, when it was once proposed.

It was the policy of Henry VII. to restrain, while employing, the energy of genius.   He was accustomed to associate the impetuous man of action with a coun-sellor sympathising but cautious.   When, in 1493, Sir Henry Poynings was sent to Ireland, he was attended by Bishop Dean.   When the same ambassador was accredited to the Court of Burgundy, Dr. Warham was his legal adviser.   While, through Poynings, it was made evident that the King of England was not to be trifled with; it was shown by Dr. Warham that their royal master was amenable to reason.

The embassy on which Warham was now engaged had reference to one of the most extraordinary of events or impostures that has ever appeared on the page of history.   By the historians of the last century Perkin Warbeck was regarded as a vulgar impostor; and that he was an impostor is the general opinion at the present time.   In the fifteenth century, however, an opinion was more generally prevalent than openly avowed, that Perkin Warbeck was what he pretended to be—the Duke of York; who, when his brother, King Edward V, was murdered in the Tower, con-trived to make his escape.   The vulgar and uneducated are always willing to believe the tale of an impostor, who represents himself as deprived of his rights ; and the arguments on the opposite side are met with this sage assertion, that the weakest always goes to the wall.   But in the case of Warbeck, his supporters were to be found in the upper classes of society; among those who are least likely to tolerate an intruder into their ranks. While statesmen hostile to Henry were searching in vain for facts and documents to substantiate Warbeck's claim to the English crown, he was winning the courtiers by his royal bearing, and fascinating the ladies by his agreeable manners. To those who had never seen a prince he appeared exactly what a prince ought to be; to the imagination he was "every inch a king." His moral character, barring the fact of his being a living lie, was irreproachable; and this is the more creditable, as he was placed in those circumstances of peculiar temptation, under which kings and princes too generally fail. There is a love letter among the archives of Simancas which is said to be his, and which it is scarcely possible to attribute to any one else; and after its perusal we cease to wonder at the statement, that the Lady Katherine Gordon gave to him not only her hand but her heart, and was ready to follow him to prison or to death. We can understand how the writer of such a letter, thrown into the society of James IV. of Scotland, should have kindled into enthusiasm the friendship with which the king had honoured him, and which induced him, in maintaining his cause, to set all political considerations aside. Among his contemporaries, James was not likely to find a disposition as refined and chivalrous, as that by which Perkin Warbeck was distinguished. There can be little doubt, indeed, that, besides the King of Scotland,—the Pope, the King of the Romans, the King of France, the Archduke Philip, the Duke of Savoy, and the King of Denmark, all believed, though they were not all prepared to assert, that Perkin Warbeck was the veritable Duke of York. From the secret documents discovered at Simancas, and

M 2

on the authority of which these statements have been made, it is plain that even Ferdinand and Isabella, when they refused to recognise him as the son of King Edward IV, were influenced, not by their convictions, but by political considerations and for the furtherance of their private ends. Under these circumstances, we are not surprised to find that, at the present time, there are learned men who, without any peculiar inclination to paradox, are disposed to regard Perkin Warbeck as anything but an impostor. Suspicion, however, must always attach to the statements of one, whose antecedents being unknown, makes his appearance abruptly in history, at the precise time when his appearance is, for political intrigue, peculiarly opportune. By most persons the case will be decided against Warbeck from the fact, that of his early life we possess no history, except the very probable story which, in his confession, he himself gives,—and which is, in fact, his condemnation. If the Duke of York escaped from the Tower, it would have been under circumstances which would give the escape all the interest of romance; and if he could not himself remember the details, yet his deliverer would hardly have been silent. It remained for the advocates of Perkin Warbeck, by stating the circumstances of his early protection and education, to contradict the statement on the subject which, in his confession to Henry VII, was made by Perkin himself. It was not sufficient to say he confessed under intimidation, but a counter-statement, such as would have borne investigation, ought to have been made. Those who, at the peril of their lives, had offered an asylum to the pretender to the throne of England, were not likely to have been silent spectators of the royal honours of their *protégé*; but in the patronage which royalty extended to Warbeck, they would have expected to have their share; yet of those who, at the peril of their own lives, saved that of the supposititious Duke of York, no mention is made.

Perkin Warbeck had certainly been an apt scholar of Margaret, duchess dowager of Burgundy; and she was his partisan, not from love of the youth himself, but out of intense hatred of the house of Tudor. Other princes pitied him, and sometimes, in secret, assisted him, under the impression that, although they were unwilling or unable to support his cause, he was a poor and persecuted prince. The Duchess Margaret must have known the circumstances of Warbeck's early life. He must have told her what he afterwards confessed to Henry; and the prudence which dictated silence, if it practically answered her purpose among her contemporaries, has eventually become his condemnation. At the time of Warham's mission to the court of Burgundy she was intriguing in Warbeck's behalf.

Perkin Warbeck had been received by the court of France with the honours due to the Duke of York; but, in the treaty between the English and French kings in 1492, it had been stipulated, that the adventurer should be extruded from the French territory. Warbeck then found a home with his reputed aunt, the duchess dowager of Burgundy. The duchess, through her political intrigues with the Archduke of Austria, and with Maximilian, king of the Romans, obtained their secret connivance at the measures taken by Warbeck to raise an army for the invasion of England; and he was permitted to make Flanders the rendezvous. Through the merchants of Flanders, she opened communications with the merchants of London, among whom pleasant memories still lingered of Edward IV. These proceedings did not escape the vigilance of

Henry VII, who was firm, politic, and cautious.
The party in England favourable to Warbeck was,
as we have before remarked, always small. The
rising middle class were not willing to be engaged
again in a dynastic war. The few individuals among
the merchants who might show symptoms of discontent were, without a leader, powerless. To prevent any ambitious nobleman from appearing on the
stage at this crisis, Henry, through his treatment of
Sir William Stanley, warned the aristocracy, that
the slightest indication of sympathy with Warbeck
would obliterate the remembrance of all past services
from the stony heart of a Tudor.* To the merchants
of Flanders a significant hint was to be given: so
far as they were concerned, subservience to the
court of the duchess would be ruin to the warehouse.
To the court of the reigning duke the embassy was
despatched, which has rendered it necessary to re-
call these facts to the memory of the reader. The
government was to be addressed ; but it was upon the
merchants that the arguments were to be made to tell.
Warham was to be the spokesman, and he is thus
described by Hall, " Sir William Warram, doctor of
laws, a man of great learning, modesty, and gravity."
A better description could not have been given of a
clever man of second-rate abilities ; a man not, of
course, to be compared with Wolsey, but one of the
most acute of those whose talents are at the command
of a master mind, and able to do its will.

When an audience was granted to the embassy by
the reigning duke, a speech was made by Warham.
Whether the speech which has been handed down to

---

* I have not discovered any document which throws light on
the extraordinary conduct of Henry VII. to this nobleman, to whom
he was under such deep obligations. Something must have occurred
which remains to be discovered.

us by Lord Bacon, as delivered by Warham, is the speech that he actually made is more than doubtful; but it can scarcely be doubted, that it was manipulated into its present form from arguments which Warham adduced on the occasion. He argues on the absurdity of supposing Duke Perkin, as he calls him, to be the veritable Duke of York. He might produce documents to prove the certainty of the duke's death; but as these documents would be supplied by the King of England, his master, they might be regarded with suspicion. Without relying upon them, therefore he would argue the case. His argument chiefly rests on the absurdity of supposing that, when King Richard determined to murder his nephews, he should employ men whom he could not trust; or that men entrusted with the horrible work should leave their work half done. The only remarkable point is the conclusion, and this is remarkable for the coarseness of the wit, evincing the coarseness of the age. "Admit," he says, "that the agents of Richard had saved the Duke of York: what could they have done? If they turned him out into the streets of London, any watchman, or the passers-by, would have taken him before a magistrate, and all would have been known. To have concealed him would have required an amount of caution and care of which it would be easy to adduce the proof, if proof there were." He represented the whole story as a romance, and said that the king would supply the materials if any poet were willing to sing the adventures of the youth. Then he traced the whole plot to the malice of the Lady Margaret, and, accusing her of having abetted Lambert Simnel, he says that "it is the strangest thing in the world that she, now stricken in years, should bring forth two such monsters, being not a birth of nine or ten months, but of many years. And whereas other natural mothers bring forth children weak, and not able to help themselves; she bringeth forth tall striplings, able, soon after their coming into the world, to give battle to mighty kings." "My lords, we stay unwillingly upon this part. We would to God that lady would once taste the joys which God Almighty doth serve up unto her, in beholding her niece to reign in such honour, and with so much royal issue which she might be pleased to account as her own. The king's request unto the archduke and your lordships might be, that, according to the example of King Charles, who hath already discarded him, you would banish this unworthy fellow out of your dominions. But because the king may justly expect more from an ancient confederate than from a new reconciled enemy, he maketh his request unto you to deliver him up into his hands; pirates and impostors of this sort were fit to be accounted the common enemies of mankind, and no ways to be protected by the laws of nations."*

This is what Hall denominates a pleasant and luculent oration. It certainly gave satisfaction to Henry VII. Although the negotiations with the Burgundians were so far a failure, that it became necessary to have recourse to measures more stringent, yet from this time to the end of the reign of Henry VII. Warham retained the king's favour, and was frequently employed.

Warham obtained the precentorship of Wells on the 2d of November, 1493. He was already a statesman and lawyer; he was soon to be a judge. When not engaged on foreign missions, his attendance at the Council board was necessary, and he could not therefore discharge the duties of the precentor's office, which had now become, what it was destined

* Lord Bacon's Life of Henry VII.; Kennet, ii. 609; and Hall's Chronicle, 465, 466. Hall gives the substance of the speech, which accords with Bacon's more elaborate report.

to remain, a sinecure. It was a benefice some-times highly endowed; but the duties were per-formed by a succentor appointed by the chapter under whose direction the choir remained. On the 13th of February, Warham became Master of the Rolls, and the duties of this high office he continued to discharge for eight years. He had at the same time a seat at the Council board. On the 28th of April, 1496, he was collated to the Archdeaconry of Huntingdon. Here again, the duties of an archdeacon being at that time chiefly judicial, he must have dis-charged them by deputy. We are not, however, to judge of him by modern notions. The feeling was still what we have seen it to be before, that the claim upon the beneficiary was not of necessity to perform the duties of the office himself; but to take care that the duties were well performed by a competent deputy, while the income enabled the dignitary to serve the Church, or the king, in some other office of a higher though less remunerative character. He was now engaged in various diplomatic employments. I trace him, indeed, in most of the important State papers of the time, though bearing a subordinate part. On the 5th of March, 1496, he is named as one of the commis-sioners empowered to treat with De Puebla about the marriage between Prince Arthur and Katherine of Arragon.* In 1499, he was at Calais with the Bishop of Rochester (Fitz James) and Sir R. Hatton, negotiat-ing a treaty with the Archduke Philip, relating to the export of wool.† In 1501, he was associated with Sir Charles Somerset, vice-chamberlain to the king, in a mission to Maximilian, king of the Romans, which had for its object a renewal of a league with England, and the banishment of English rebels from the im-

CHAP.
II.

William
Warham.
1503-32.

* Calendar of State Papers at Simancas and elsewhere, 187.
† Letters of Henry VII. i. 425.

perial dominions. In the account of the proceedings
it is stated, that, in testimony of renewed good will
on the part of the King of the Romans towards the
King of England, the former would consent to wear
the Garter, as formerly, on condition, that Henry and
his son the Prince of Wales would undertake to wear
the Toison d'Or. Although King Henry had refused
to grant any collection of money to be made in
England in favour of a crusade, when the request
was made by the pope; yet it was now intimated, that
perhaps he might accede to the request if it were urged
by Maximilian. With respect to the undertaking not
to harbour rebels, Maximilian was willing to bind
himself and the lands of his inheritance; but he
affirmed that he had no power to bind the empire.
For the unfortunate Edmund de la Pole, the imperial
commissioners were directed to intercede.*

In another attempt to bring Maximilian to terms
with the English Government, Warham was again, in
the year 1502, associated with Somerset. The ambassadors were detained five weeks at Antwerp, where
they were not treated with much courtesy by the
imperial commissioners; neither did they come to
satisfactory agreement.†

In proof that the system of acting by deputy, when
a principal was conscientious, did not always, or of
necessity, prove detrimental to the Church, we have
an instance in the history of Warham. He had
been appointed, as we have been reminded, principal or moderator of a hall, called St. Edward's or
Civil Law Hall; and this hall soon ranked first

* Letters and Papers of the Reigns of Richard III. and Henry
VII. i. 152, 161, 167, 169, 176. To the historian these two
papers, the instructions given to Somerset and Warham, are full
of deep interest.

† Letters of Henry VII. ii. 106.

among the colleges of Oxford. This was effected by Warham through a judicious selection of deputies, or, as we should now style them, tutors, and by a system of inspection which involved all oversight of the instruction and an examination of the pupils. How much the hall was indebted to Warham is proved by the fact that, when he resigned the office of principal, the hall was deserted, and soon dwindled into insignificance.[*]

The resignation of Dr. Warham was occasioned by his nomination and election to the see of London, rendered vacant by the translation of Dr. Savage to the archbishopric of York.[†] The election took place in October, 1501 ; he was not consecrated till the 25th of September, 1502.[‡] The delay was owing probably to his absence on the embassy. Even then there was some delay before he was settled in the

---

[*] Wood, Annals, i. 601.

[†] Thomas Savage was born at Macclesfield, of a knightly family, the son of Sir John Savage, of Clifton. He was educated at Cambridge, where he became Doctor of Laws. He was not a scholar or a divine, but a courtier. It is stated that he was Canon of York and Dean of the Chapel Royal. But I do not find the appointments in Le Neve or Hardy. He was engaged in temporal affairs under Henry VII, but his chief delight was "in the sound of the huntsman's horn and the braying of his hounds." He neglected his episcopal duties, but according to Stowe, he lived in a splendid style, having many tall yeomen to form his body guard. On the 28th of April, 1493, he was consecrated to the see of Rochester. On the 27th of October, 1496, he was translated to London, and in February, 1501, he was translated to York. He presented a contrast to Archbishop Warham, whose enthronization and subsequent feast were of a most sumptuous description, whereas Savage was enthroned by deputy, and for the first time broke through the old custom of giving a feast. He died at Cawood, on the 2d of September, 1507, and was buried in the cathedral. According to Godwin, he directed that his heart should be buried at Macclesfield. —Godwin; Drake; Le Neve; Hardy; Stubbs.

[‡] Stubbs, Reg. Sac. Anglic. 74.

see, for he did not receive the temporalities until the October of the last-mentioned year.*

Honours and emoluments now flowed in rapidly and abundantly on William Warham. He was himself aware, that his talents were overrated, and one of the causes of his success in life was the care which he took not to undertake more than he was able respectably to perform. He had the talent to rise from the depth, but, when he had reached the surface of the mighty ocean, he drifted with the tide. He could not ride the whirlwind or direct the storm ; and in troublous times was simply the trident of Neptune when a Neptune himself was required.

The Bishop of London, before he took possession of the see, resigned the office of the Master of the Rolls. He was beginning to feel weary of a statesman's life. But when a man has obtained a high position, a greater tax is frequently made upon his time and mind than he had calculated upon paying. He ceases to be his own master, and duties will by circumstances be forced upon him, from the discharge of which he would willingly be excused.

Bishop Warham had resigned the Mastership of the Rolls on the 1st of February, 1502 ; but he was called from the discharge of the episcopal duties, to which he had intended to confine his attention, by the illness of the Lord Keeper. Archbishop Dean, who held the Great Seal, was, comparatively speaking, a young man, and it was supposed that ere long he might resume his duties ; Warham was therefore appointed Lord Keeper on the 11th of August. It was not for any public officer, more especially for a person of Warham's character, to refuse compliance to the proposal of a Tudor ; and Warham only regarded himself as the *locum tenens.* But the unexpected death of Dean,

* Fœdera, x. iii. 21.

within half a year of Warham's appointment as Lord Keeper, caused the great and final change in Warham's life. Warham received from the king the offer of the primacy of All England; and three days before his translation was effected, the title of Lord Keeper was changed to that of Lord Chancellor.

Whatever forms were adopted, the appointments of bishoprics were at that time vested in the king. The *congé d'élire* was then, as now, accompanied by a missive addressed to the electors, requiring, in effect, the convent of Christ Church in Canterbury to regard the election as a mere form, and to elect without hesitation the king's nominee. Its verbosity is very remarkable. The petition to elect a successor to Archbishop Dean having been granted, Henry adds: "We, considering well the see to be one of much honour and pre-eminence, by reason of the primacy thereof, within this our realm, and being fully minded therefore, and for other causes us moving, to provide such a substantial and discreet man, endued with virtue *and cunning and worldly wisdom,* as shall be meet thereunto, and be able not only to execute the charge and cure thereof, both spiritually and temporally, to God's pleasure and to the weal and honour of the said Church, but also, besides that, to do unto us and our realm good and acceptable service, have oft revolved this matter in our mind and ripe remembrance, and by good leisure and deliberation, beholding inwardly, amongst all other, the profound cunning, virtuous conversation, and approved great wisdom of the Right Reverend Father in God, our right trusty and well-beloved counsellor, the Bishop of London, experimentally is known to be of, have therefore, and for his manifold virtuousness and merits, named him as a person meet in our opinion to the aforesaid dignity; willing you therefore to proceed in your election of the said reverend father, according to this our nomination, whereunto we license you by these presents; not doubting but that ye shall have in him such a spiritual pastor and governor as by his demeanour God shall be singularly well pleased, we and our realm well served, and your said Church honoured and advanced."*

The usual forms and ceremonies which were adopted, as we have seen on former occasions, to reserve the rights asserted by the various authorities, who claimed jurisdiction in the election of a prelate, were duly observed. To obtain the confirmation at Rome, oaths were taken by the archbishop-elect to maintain the rights of the papal see in England; and to obtain the restoration of the temporalities, oaths were taken to the king on the 24th of January, 1504, which nullified the preceding oaths by declaring, that the primate elect would assert the liberties of the Church, and, if need should be, maintain the rights of the crown against the pope.

The cross of Canterbury was delivered to Warham by one of the monks of Christ Church, with the usual address: "Reverend Father, I am the messenger of the Great King, who doth require and command you to take upon you the government of His Church, and to love and defend the same, in token whereof I give you this His insignia." He placed the crosier in his hand.† The pall was delivered to him at Lambeth,

---

* This letter was "given under our signet, at our castle at Nottingham, on the 15th day of August." It may have been the *congé d'élire*; and as such I first regarded it; but it is, more probably, the letter missive which accompanied or followed the formal document, and, as a letter from the king, it found its way among the State Papers, from whence I take it.

† Weever, 234. Weever states that in his various buildings Warham's motto appears: *Auxilium meum a Domino.* His arms were: Gules, a fess; in chief, a goat's head erased; in base, three escallops, two and one.—Bedford's Blazon.

on the 2d of February, 1504, by the Bishops of Bath and Lincoln.

The chroniclers have exhausted their powers of description in their minute detail of the splendours of the enthronization feast, which took place on the 9th of March, 1504. We have read of the magnificence displayed on other enthronization feasts, but none surpassed in its grandeur the present ceremonial. When we compare this enthronization and the feast by which it was succeeded, with the frugal entertainment given by Warham's successor, Dr. Cranmer, we read in the comparison the splendid conclusion of one era, and the humble commencement of another, an epoch of new ideas.

The frequent occurrence of festivities during the season of Lent, in the Middle Ages, is opposed to some modern notions with respect to mediæval sentiment; but, when the choice of all the Sundays in the year was open to Warham, it is difficult to surmise why he should select Passion Sunday for his feast day. The courts of law were closed, and business of state suspended; and as every Sunday was a festival, he may have chosen a Sunday in Lent, as being a time when without inconvenience many would attend who would otherwise have been obliged to stay away. When we say, however, that every Sunday was a festival, we must observe that upon the festivities of a Sunday in Lent certain restrictions were nevertheless imposed. Although men ate and drank to repletion, and some of the feasters were obliged, in retirement, to rehabilitate their constitutions by submitting to a course of physic and blood-letting, still the dietary consisted exclusively of fish. The taste of the piscivorous multitude may not have been discriminating. When regaling on well-concocted conger and ling and halibut, dis-

guised under various condiments and sauces, they may
have thought the difference slight between fish and
flesh ; but still the genius of the artist, who presided
over the culinary department, must have been called
into full play, while his taste was displayed in the
various subtleties he devised. The bill of fare, and a
description of the feast, occupy seven folio pages in
Somner. All the honours of the archbishop, and the
offices he had filled, were delineated upon the banquet-
ing dishes in gilded marchpaine and farinaceous
device. The archbishop appeared as Sir William; the
Chancellor of Oxford presented him to the king as the
worthiest son of the University ; the king, surrounded
by his lords, was seen receiving him as such, while, by
labels issuing from their mouths, the praises of the
archbishop were recounted in hexameters and penta-
meters, reminding him of the *vulgus* and verse task of
his school days at Winchester.

On the day appointed, the archbishop entered the
hall in solemn procession, and, taking his seat in the
centre of the table, had for his servitor no less a
personage than Edward, duke of Buckingham. The
descendant of Edward III, not distantly related to
the reigning sovereign, the Lord High Constable of
England, held certain lands, on condition of his acting as the archbishop's high steward ; and he thought
it no degradation to discharge in person the duties
of his office. Attended by the heralds of arms, he
rode into the hall bareheaded, and made obeisance
to the primate. As each dish was brought in by the
appointed officers of the archbishop's household, the
Duke of Buckingham indicated by his staff of office
its position on the table. Backing his horse, he, with
his attendants, left the hall of the archbishop and
repaired to his own. At the expense of the arch-

bishop, the duke was there received with similar ceremony, and his suite were regaled.*

It was an age of pomp and ceremony—the age of the Field of the Cloth of Gold.   The retainers of the lord primate and the officers of the Court of Chancery, the tenants of the archiepiscopal estates, the convent and the city of Canterbury, would all of them have felt themselves aggrieved, if in the splendours of their chief they had not been permitted to have had their share.   It is a mistake to suppose that, in pomp and ceremony, even those who act only as spectators do not take an interest.   A man who prefers the simplicity of a republic, feels that, if he incurs the expense of maintaining a monarchy, the splendours of what he pays for should be brought before his eyes. The philosopher is aware that the obsolete fashions of a feudal ceremonial have a tendency to connect the present with the past, and so to shape the future.   The affectation of simplicity on similar occasions, at present the fashion, is a grand mistake.   He is no philosopher who attends not to little things.

Warham had always been a favourite at Oxford, and the University kept high festival on this occasion. The confectioner of Canterbury was equalled if not surpassed, in the brilliancy of his imagination, by the

---

* Batteley's Somner, Append. 21; Weever, 233; Wood, Annals, i. 661.   In the earlier periods of our history I have frequently given a minute description of feasts, and presented the reader with the bills of fare, as they are preserved in the pages of the chroniclers or State Papers.   I have quoted from books not easily accessible, under the notion that the reader would find instruction and amusement in comparing for himself the resemblances and the differences of ancient and modern customs, more deeply impressed upon the mind when the entertainment is described in the original style.   When we approach modern times, such quotations would answer no purpose; except, therefore, when it is necessary in order to establish a disputed fact to present the reader with the *ipsissima verba* of an author, references will suffice.

pastrycook of Oxford. The Oxford feast was held on the same Sunday in Lent, and the archbishop again appeared in pastry as Sir William. He was seen standing in a bed of flowers, in the midst of eight embattled towers, representing New College, Magdalen, Merton, Osney, Rewley, Black Friars, Austin, and Grey. On each tower was a bedel in his habit and with his staff of office. The king was seen seated with his lords around him, all in their robes. On the right hand of the king sat Sir William, or William Warham. Then the chancellor was seen in his doctor's habit, attended by six bedels, a vergerer, and a crucifer, and he presented " the said Lord William" to the king in some very bad Latin verses; and from the mouth of the king proceeded a label with verses equally bad.

Warham was, like his royal master, under ordinary circumstances frugal, but both were munificent on great occasions.

It was in great state that the archbishop made his appearance at Windsor in the year 1506. The Archduke Philip claimed, in right of his wife, to be King of Castile, and assumed the title of King-Archduke. On his voyage to Spain he was compelled, by stress of weather, to put into Weymouth. By the existing law of nations, a prince landing in a foreign country without a safe-conduct was regarded as the prisoner of the king whose territory he had invaded, and who, on that ground, claimed the right to demand a ransom. The stringency of the law had been relaxed since the days of Richard Cœur de Lion; but the law itself was still in force. The counsellors of the king-archduke would have put again to sea; it was less hazardous to brave the uncertainties of a stormy voyage, than to trust to the tender mercies of the unscrupulous Tudor. But the hospitality with which the royal party was received, reconciled them at length to the difficulty or impossibility of again setting sail. For any advantage to be derived from this windfall Henry VII. would depend upon diplomacy rather than force. The king-archduke and his party were invited to Windsor, where the court was at that time residing, and where a splendid reception awaited the foreigners.*

In those days the primate of all England was treated with the honour due to the first subject in the realm; and the archbishop was invited to Windsor. He arrived too late to officiate at the morning service; and when he entered the state apartments, the hangings of which were of crimson velvet and cloth of gold, he found the two kings standing by the fire-place in close conversation, which he did not disturb. After their private conversation the royal personages joined the ladies. On this day, because it was a holyday, the gentlemen could not hunt; but this did not prevent the ladies from dancing; and among the dancers the young Princess Mary attracted peculiar attention from her elegance and beauty. At the proper time the folding-doors

---

* Of the proceedings of the English court on this occasion a minute description was drawn up by some contemporary herald-at-arms, a transcript of which of later date is preserved in the British Museum. It has been published in the Rolls Series by Mr. Gairdner. In this document it is asserted, in opposition to a statement made by Polydore Vergil, that Philip volunteered the surrender to Henry of the Earl of Suffolk, William de la Pole. The two statements, that of the surrender "unaxed," as is here stated, and that of Polydore Vergil, may be reconciled by supposing—and this, after reading the narrative, we are disposed to do—that Philip had discerned in conversation with Henry, that reasons would incessantly occur to prevent his departure from England until the concession had been made. Philip made a virtue of necessity, and offered as a favour what he knew would be demanded as a stipulation.

were thrown open, and the archbishop and the Dean of Windsor appeared, each clad in his amice, and bringing up the procession which was approaching the chapel. In the chapel the two kings took their seats beneath a canopy of a cloth of gold, the King of England offering, and the King of Castile declining, the seat of honour.[*] The service was now performed by the archbishop, who took his seat in the dean's stall.

On Candlemas Day, the 2d of February, the archbishop was again at Windsor. It was a high festival, and observed with great ceremony. In the procession to the chapel, the sword of state was carried by the Earl of Derby; the kings remained under the canopy until the candles were consecrated. The archbishop sang mass in *pontificalibus*, the Bishop of Rochester carrying the cross of Canterbury. The King of England's taper was borne by the Earl of Kent, and that of the King of Castile by the Lord Ville, Knight of the Order of Toison. The King's taper had a close crown, the King of Castile's an open crown. The magnificence displayed excited the admiration of a contemporary. In the procession he says it was a goodly sight to see so many men of noble birth all well appointed in cloth of gold, velvet, and silk, with massy chains of pure gold and great weight.

Again, on the 9th of February, the archbishop was at court, assisting at an investiture of the Order of the Garter. To add to the dignity of the ceremonial, the archbishop himself, instead of the Bishop of Winchester, administered the oath of the order to the King

---

[*] The essence of good breeding was the same in the sixteenth as it was in the seventeenth century. The story of Lord Stair and Louis XIV. has been often repeated. The action was now anticipated. On one occasion the King of England offered precedence to the King of Castile. The latter paused for a moment, and then obeyed, saying: "I see right well I must needs do your commandment and obey as reason will."

of Castile. When the religious portion of the service
was concluded, Warham appeared in his character
of Lord High Chancellor of England. He was
attended by the Lord Privy Seal, the celebrated
statesman Dr. Fox, bishop of Winchester, and other
members of the Privy Council.

King Henry was seated in his stall as Sovereign
of the Order of the Garter. The Lord Chancellor and
the Lord Privy Seal presented to him the treaty of
peace and amity, which had been agreed upon by the
two kings, duly sealed with the great seal and privy
seal. The counterpart, duly sealed, was presented to
the king-archduke by the Lord St. Py, the president
of Flanders, attended by other members of his council.
Each king, seated in his stall, signed the document
with his own hand. The secretary of the King of
England, the Rev. Dr. Routhall, standing on the steps
of the choir, read distinctly each article of the treaty
in the ears of the people, by whom the nave of the
chapel was densely thronged. A new procession was
formed. The kings, leaving their stalls, approached
the high altar. Kneeling before it, they solemnly
made oath that they would keep the treaty; each
detail of which, point by point, was read. The *Te
Deum* was sung; the trumpets again sounded. At
the chapter-house, the young Prince Henry was in
waiting, and he was invested by the King of Castile
with the Order of Toison d'Or.

Throughout his career, the hospitality of Warham
was conducted on a scale of almost royal magnificence.
Two hundred bishops, dukes, earls, and gentlemen of
lower degree were occasionally feasted in his hall.
His entertainments were always sumptuous, such as
became his dignity; and he was courteous in inviting
his guests to partake of delicacies from which he himself
abstained. His own tastes were simple, and his habits

abstemious.   Wine he seldom tasted ; and it was only
in his old age that he could be persuaded to taste mild
ale, which, according to Erasmus, the English call beer.
Of supper he never partook when he was alone ; and
so he gained time for study, meditation, and prayer.
When guests were present, he sat down with them at
table; and made himself extremely agreeable as a companion, encouraging the jests of his friends, and uttering pleasantries himself ; but of the viands he seldom
partook.   He was a great economist of time.   We
sometimes read with astonishment, of the rapidity with
which the luxurious feasts, provided for the traveller in
an American hotel, are consumed ; but the repasts
in Warham's hall, except on state occasions, only
occupied an hour.

It is mentioned, to Warham's praise, that he never
played at dice, nor did he, as many other prelates,
indulge in field sports.

The income of the Archbishop of Canterbury was at
this time very large.   The incumbent of any great
benefice had too much liberty granted him with respect
to the disposal of it.   He might easily alienate the
estates of the see, and Henry VIII. availing himself of
these facilities, compelled or cajoled Cranmer to make
over to him some of the best manors of the archbishopric.   By similar arrangements, or by long
leases, Queen Elizabeth enriched her courtiers as well
as herself.   Before this time, the attachment to the
Church being more strong in an unmarried clergyman
than his attachment to his family, we have seen the
primates making their successors their heirs.   They purchased manors and erected mansions, and left them to
their see.   Warham is said to have enriched his family
by alienating some of the estates of the see.*   Dis-

* For this insight into the private life of Warham we are
indebted to Erasmus.   See his Ecclesiastes.

regarding the charge brought against him, of nepotism, he sought very properly to benefit his family. His nephew was Archdeacon of Canterbury, the most lucrative preferment, beneath a bishopric, in the country. I find a person of the name of Warham holding a subordinate situation in one of the lodges of his park; so that to his poor relations his family affection descended. But I have not discovered any instance of his alienating any portion of the episcopal property; nor, judging from his character in general, do I think this probable. Indeed, great as his income was, there would be ample demands upon it, when, to a great extent, he had to support the expenses of the chancellorship out of the episcopal revenues. When Warham first became chancellor, the annual salary was only one hundred marks; it was afterwards raised to two hundred pounds. The perquisites of the office, however, were considerable, and Warham looked minutely to every item of expenditure, the consideration of which is not without interest. For commons for himself and his clerks he received one hundred marks. For the repose of the great seal he purchased a new bag of crimson velvet, to supply the place of the leathern bag of which we have so frequently read, and for this he charged the Government fifteen shillings. He received for sixty-two days' attendance, from September 29 till November 30, in his hostel, near Charing Cross, Westminster, at the rate of twenty-three shillings a day, 71*l*. 6*s*. 0*d*. For his attendance in the Star Chamber, in Michaelmas term, 50*l*.; for the month of December, 35*l*. 15*s*. 0*d*. For his winter robes, when so attending, 26*l*. 13*s*. 4*d*. For his service robes twenty marks. He had, in addition, certain tuns of Gascon wines. A variety of other charges might be produced by reference to the Transfer

and other Rolls ; but what is here advanced will suffice
for a specimen.* Such fragments of information, important to the archæologist who has time to pursue the
subject, are valuable to all readers from the light they
throw upon persons as well as upon times. We may
gather from what has been advanced, some further
insight into Warham's character ; and that character
was so similar to the character of Henry VII. and so dis-
similar from that of Henry VIII. that we are at no loss
to understand why Warham should have enjoyed that
favour with the father which was not accorded to him
by the son. He could be magnificent, but magnificence
was the exception, and not the rule. He was generous
in donations to needy friends, or to the reward of personal services or flattery ; but at the same time, none
of his retinue could defraud him out of the smallest
coin, and for the most trifling expenditure he kept and
required an account. He was great on great occasions ;
but under ordinary circumstances he was economical.
In religion he was a reformer, but it was only on a
small scale. His desire was, that the Bible should be
more generally read than it was, but he would confine
the study to only a few who would use it piously
for devotional purposes, and not for a test by which to
sit in judgment on the teachings of the Church. He
admitted the royal supremacy, but he was like a child,
who, having fired a gun, is alarmed by the report. As
a chancellor, Warham has won the praise of modern
lawyers. In writing the history of the Primates of All
England, we have, to a certain extent, been writing the
history of the Lord High Chancellors of the realm.
Although it is incorrect to say, that Henry VIII. was the
first of our kings who appointed a layman to the office of

* Letters and Papers, Henry VIII. c. viii. and the various
Letters among which the information is dispersed.

High Chancellor, yet down to this period the office was so often filled by ecclesiastics, and these very frequently, then or afterwards, lord primates, that we have had frequently to mention the proceedings of the Court of Chancery. At first we have seen the Chancellor ὁ μέγας λογοθέτης, but before the time of Warham he had become a judge.

Full of wise saws and modern instances, if at any time, *summum jus* became *summa injuria*, the common sense of the Lord Chancellor might overrule the letter to enforce the spirit of the law or to give effect to the intention of the legislature ; but already the judge was, to a very considerable extent, bound down by precedents, or by antecedent judgments of the court over which he presided. Warham's chief fault was the fault of his position; the judge was sometimes merged in the ecclesiastic. He would interpret the law of the land by a reference to the Old Testament; and he would warn an executor wasting the goods of a testator, that if he did not make what restitution he could, he would be damned for ever in hell. *

As a statesman Warham retained his popularity while minister of an unpopular monarch, and we presume that he was the adviser of moderate measures. Henry VII. and his ministers were generally unpopular because, towards the close of his reign, he attacked the purses of his people; and this sometimes by proceedings unjustifiable, if not iniquitous. The wise and prudent measures of his government, and the justice with which, in other respects, it was administered, have been too often overlooked. By the regulation of the guilds, and by subjecting their ordinances to the revision of the Lord Chancellor, a burden was removed from the

* See the case given in the Y. B. Henry VII. 46, quoted by Campbell.

working classes.   The statutes against beggars and
vagabonds had been insufferably harsh; they were
mitigated by Henry VII, but were afterwards made
perfectly draconic by his popular son.   The commercial world was gratified by a confirmation of the privileges enjoyed by the merchants of the Hanse.   For
"the ease of his subjects" the king obtained parliamentary authority, to reverse at his pleasure, *the various
acts of attainder*, which had been so frequently
passed in the party-spirit of the late troublous times.

That Warham did not approve, if he countenanced,
the illegal exactions which brought disgrace and ruin
upon Empson and Dudley, I think we may infer from
circumstances which will presently be brought under
the notice of the reader; but from his general character we must presume, that he sympathised with his
master in the opinion that a king could only be
powerful who was, by his wealth, rendered independent
of his people; and we must not forget, that it was
by Warham, that Dudley was recommended to the
Speakership of the House of Commons.   The fact is,
that Dudley and Empson only applied to court affairs
the principle adopted by certain pettifogging clergymen in regard to the ecclesiastical courts.   They
searched out for obsolete laws, and either prosecuted
offenders for the non-observance of them, or enacted
a heavy payment from those who preferred a fine to
amercement.

A king was in those days, his own prime minister;
but Henry was too wise a prince not to consult his
council; and his chancellor must have viewed with
satisfaction the success with which, after a long and
painful struggle, the foreign policy of Henry VII.
was crowned.   Justice has never been done to this
unpopular king; but when we peruse his correspond-

ence with foreign courts which has lately been brought
to light, and see the enormous difficulties of Henry's
position, we shall be inclined to regard him, though
not a brilliant, yet as a very sagacious and far-seeing
statesman.   He raised 'the character of the nation
abroad, and compelled unwilling potentates to respect
his power.   Through his moderation, the struggle
between the kings of France and Spain, for the throne
of Naples, had been set at rest.   Such was the high
estimation in which he was held in Europe, that he
was offered the command of a crusade against the
infidels.   Pope Julius II, in accordance with his name
and character, sent him a consecrated sword.   The
peaceful monarch sheathed the sword, and added
it to the muniments of the crown.   Among the
presents, by which the king and his chancellor
were to be propitiated, came a leg of St. George—a
present from Cardinal d'Amboise, the minister of
Louis XII, on St. George's Day, 1505.   The leg was
enclosed in silver; it was exhibited, by the archbishop's command, in St. Paul's Cathedral.   Warham
was not without superstition; but the friend of Erasmus attached more value to the silver, than the leg;
to the casket, than to the relic.   By those, who, in the
present age, seek notoriety by affecting singularities,
the leg would be worshipped: in the time of Warham,
notoriety was to be obtained by those, who looked upon
the whole proceeding with a scorn they dared not
to express.   Many devout people, however, believed
without examining, and, though mistaken, their
devotion was at least sincere.

   Towards the close of Henry's reign, and after the
death of his amiable queen, the conduct of the king
was such as to cause considerable annoyance and
trouble to his counsellors, and especially to the keeper

of his conscience. His matrimonial speculations were marvellous. The prevalent notion that he had treated Queen Elizabeth with harshness, or even with indifference, so far from being corroborated, is positively contradicted, by such facts of history as have come within our notice. The marriage was not a love-match; but, so far as his impassive nature permitted, Henry became attached to his wife, and the queen was devoted to her husband; in their children they found a tie, which bound them closer to each other. We still possess a letter, which describes the misery of the bereaved parents on the decease of Prince Arthur; and the description of the manner in which both king and queen tendered their mutual consolation is affecting.

The notions prevalent in the Middle Ages, with respect to the marriage state, were lax; such as might be expected when it was represented by the clergy as a mere concession to human weakness or passion. Kings were taught to regard marriage simply as a political arrangement; but even Henry, a wary statesman, could not make up his mind to share his throne with a lady utterly devoid of personal attractions. Among the most ludicrous of the state papers which have been lately discovered, there is none more amusing than that, which contains the directions given to the ambassadors of Henry, who were authorized to propose a matrimonial alliance on the part of the King of England, with the young Queen of Naples. Each feature was to be described, every expression of her countenance was to be observed, and notice was to be taken of her whole demeanour.*

The idea which the king entertained, of obtaining a

* See the Introduction and Report of Francis Marsin and others, with respect to the Queen of Naples, among the Memorials of Henry VII. in the Rolls Series, 223.

dispensation from the pope to enable him to marry the widow of the late Prince of Wales, his son, is revolting to every well-regulated mind. It is a circumstance, however, of some historical importance; for if the marriage had been consummated, the very thought of obtaining such a dispensation could not have entered his mind, and in the divorce controversy of the next reign, this circumstance tends to corroborate the case in favour of Queen Katherine's statement.

It does not fall within our scope to proceed further into the consideration of the matrimonial speculations which bewildered the ever-anxious mind of Henry VII. We are only concerned with his proposal, that, if he could not himself be a suitor to Katherine, she might at least be married to Prince Henry. To this subject we shall hereafter recur.

Between Warham and his sovereign a friendship existed as intimate as the cold and cautious nature of Henry VII. would admit. The king often visited the archbishop, and was his guest at the palace of Canterbury about three weeks before his death. Although he was only fifty-two years of age, the anxieties of a life, always insecure, had told upon a constitution never very strong, and he had become prematurely old. There were upon him unmistakeable symptoms of the consumption of which he soon after died, and he desired to converse with Warham on the state of his soul, and of the account he was to render to that King of kings to whom an earthly sovereign is only the vicegerent. Henry brought with him to Canterbury a draft of his will, in order that to it the great seal might be affixed by the chancellor. The complaints of the people had reached the royal ear, and the conscience-stricken king appointed a commission, at the head of which the archbishop was placed, that restitution might be made to any persons, who could prove themselves to have been wronged, under the late arbitrary proceedings of Dudley and Empson.

Among the various bequests for religious purposes, and for "pious uses," the king directs the formation of a great number of pixes of gold, of four pounds' value each, garnished with the royal arms and red roses and portcullises crowned. They were to be delivered on application to every house of the four orders of friars, and to every parish church, by "the treasurer of our chamber and the master of our jewel house." The royal donor was moved to do this from having often seen to his inward regret and displeasure, in divers and many churches of his realm, "the holy sacrament of the altar kept in full simple and inhonest pixes, specially pixes of copper and timber."[*]

The archbishop was made supervisor of this his last will and testament.

With the death of Henry VII. Warham's career as a statesman may be said to have terminated. He retained the great seal until the year 1515, but he petitioned earnestly to be released from the cares of office, and to be permitted to devote himself to more congenial pursuits. The only person qualified, at this time, to succeed him in the office, was Wolsey, and, owing to his various engagements as a foreign minister, Wolsey was unwilling to add to his labours, so long as the duties of a judge were well performed by one who had no ambition to interfere in politics. How completely Warham had retired from public life, may be perceived, by a reference to the state papers which have, of late years, thrown so much light on history. We find documents in the handwriting of Fox, Ruthal, and Wolsey, but not in that of Warham. With the new king everything was changed, and the methodical lawyer of an effete school of politics could not adapt

* Testamenta Vetusta, i. 33.

himself to the gigantic schemes, by which the great minister of Henry VIII. was raising his country to that high position in the republic of nations, which it has ever since sustained. Although Warham was treated by the king and the queen with the respect due to his high station, he was no favourite at court. The young couple, mutually attached, could not forget that the marriage, by which they found themselves happy, had been opposed by Warham.

Upon this subject we have promised to make a few observations. Henry VII. in the first instance proposed that his second son should marry the widow of his eldest. His object, it is assumed by modern historians, was simply to avoid the repayment of the dower of the princess.* Suddenly, however, we find that, regardless of the dower, he had changed his mind, and the prohibition of all intercourse between the young people had a tendency to convert into a love match what was at first a mere act of state policy. Henry VII. was not a man, who for slight causes either entered upon or retreated from a line of policy, and for his proceedings in this affair we are now able, through the deciphering of the Simancas papers, to account. These papers reveal to us a state of affairs, scarcely intelligible, according to the maxims of modern policy. Before her marriage with Henry, the young Princess Katherine was treated by the king, his father, as little better than a state prisoner. To gain her a position probably at the English court, she was provided by King Ferdinand with a court of her own,

---

* That this was a consideration with Henry, is inferred from his general character; but from the Simancas Letters we learn that the person most urgent for the marriage of the Princess Katherine with Henry, prince of Wales, was not the English king, but her father. The conjectures of the historian are too often accepted as his tried facts.

and her court was the rallying place of a considerable Spanish party then in England. To reduce England to the condition of a Spanish province, was for a long time the day-dream of the ambitious Spaniard. He would not retire from England, but constituted the young princess his representative. That so young a lady, the widow or the *fiancée* of the heir-apparent of the English throne, should be placed in such a situation, would be sufficiently remarkable; but it is still more remarkable, that she did not accept the office as merely one of honour. The advocates, domestic and foreign, of the Spanish interest in England, had been split into factions. The young princess took her side in the controversies; and as she had, and maintained, a will of her own, her father found it difficult to control her.*

Towards the close of Henry VII.'s reign, the relations between him and King Ferdinand of Spain were anything but friendly. Into the causes of their disagreement, it is not our business to enter; we are contented to remark, that there were faults, as in most disputes, on both sides. The quarrel became at length so acrimonious that a war seemed to be inevitable.† Without taking the dower into account, it is not

---

* So little did she account of her dower that she is said to have behaved uncourteously to the bankers Grimaldi, by whom the dower was paid. For the statements here made the reader may be referred generally to the Calendar of Letters, Despatches, and State Papers, placed in the Archives of Simancas and elsewhere, printed in the Rolls Series. The learned Editor, Mr. Bergenroth, speaks of himself as a "calendarer," a new profession; but his right to the title of an historian is so fully established by his introductory chapter that he can claim it when he will. Among calendarers he is equalled by very few, and surpassed by none.

† It was in truth only averted by the serious illness of King Henry. The King of France preached patience to the King of Spain, foreseeing that, without recourse to arms, the controversy might soon be ended by Henry's death.

surprising that Henry should prohibit his son from all intercourse with a court, which, in the king's own country, was plotting against his kingdom. He may not have been able to prove what was actually the case; but he must have entertained more than a mere suspicion, that the King of Spain was actually endeavouring to provoke hostile feelings against his father, in the breast of the Prince of Wales. A letter is in existence, in which Ferdinand commissions his ambassadors to deliver his credentials to the young prince, and to tell him that he, King Ferdinand, "places his person and his kingdom at the prince's disposal." We may, by comparing the Spanish papers with what really took place, presume that the case stood as follows. Henry VII. from political motives would not permit the Lady Katherine to leave his kingdom; so long as she was in England she was a kind of hostage, and her father would act with caution, before he proceeded to extremities. Aware of the hostile designs of Ferdinand, Henry VII, who had at first encouraged the attentions of the Prince of Wales to the Spanish princess, forbade the marriage between the young couple. Ferdinand, when he could not procure the return of the princess to her home, gave her a position in England, beyond that of Princess dowager of Wales, by making her the representative of the Spanish court. Prince Henry, having been already charmed by a lady, whom he had a short time before approached as his intended bride, was known to resent the arbitrary conduct of his father. The King of Spain desired his ambassador to treat Prince Henry as if he were his son-in-law, and offered to assist him, if his father should drive him to desperation.

Among the counsellors of Henry VII. there was a difference of opinion as to the expediency of breaking off the engagement between Henry and Katherine. Warham urged strongly the point of view taken by the king. Whatever he may have secretly thought of the extraordinary conduct of his master, he knew that it would tax his political resources to the utmost, to prevent a war with the King of Spain. He could not advise a marriage between the king's son and the daughter of Ferdinand, so long as Ferdinand was intriguing against England, and forming alliances hostile to her king. Henry VII. dies. A change immediately takes place over the whole aspect of affairs. The King of Spain was the friend, the ally, and sought to be the counsellor of the young King of England.[*] We may say that all consents were obtained to the marriage which were necessary—that of the King of Spain, that of the young King of England, and that also of his father. Henry VII. had desired the marriage so long as there was a good understanding between England and Spain; and now that a good understanding was re-established, he would, if living, have rejoiced to meet the wishes of his son, and to retain the dower of his bride. Henry VII. died on the 31st of April, 1509, and on the 3d of the following June, Archbishop Warham officiated at the marriage of the young king and the Lady Katherine—a marriage productive of many years of happiness, succeeded by a sad, cruel, and tragical termination. I have been

* It would appear from the Simancas documents that Ferdinand expected the succession of Henry to the crown would be disputed. He declared himself ready under such circumstances to send a powerful army to support the young prince, "consisting of men-at-arms, infantry, and artillery, ships and engines of war," and to place himself at their head. Throughout the correspondence with Henry VII. Ferdinand appears to have regarded the position of the Tudor dynasty as precarious. It was long before he could be prevailed upon to address Henry VII. as his brother.

led to investigate this subject, because, until the investigation, the conduct of Warham, in regard to the marriage, appeared inconsistent and unaccountable. The revelation of state secrets made in the Simancas Papers, enables us to account, without recourse to conjecture, for the conduct both of Warham and of his royal master.

It is proper to remark, that a question was started by a Spaniard, the confessor of Queen Katherine, as to the legality of the marriage; and the scruple of the confessor was duly submitted to the consideration of King Ferdinand the Catholic, by his ambassador in England, Gutier Gomez de Fuensalida, knight commander of Membrilla. The king affirmed the lawfulness of the marriage, a dispensation having been duly obtained from the pope; he went on to say, that a sin would be committed by the King of England, if he receded from the engagement, for he had been already betrothed to the Princess Katherine. The King of England might take example from the King of Portugal, who had married successively two sisters and was living happily and cheerfully with the survivor, surrounded by a numerous offspring.* No scruple passed over the mind of Archbishop Warham. From his standing point the case would be thus regarded: the pope could not dispense with a divine law; marriage with a deceased brother's wife was contrary to the divine law; there was, therefore, in such a case, no room for a dispensation: but, on the other hand, a papal

* Simancas Calendars, 8. For the sake of brevity I shall refer to the Spanish State Papers under this title, and to the Calendar of Domestic State Papers as Henry VIII. Calendar. The State Papers published by Mr. Lemon will be referred to as State Papers. The numerous progeny of the King of Portugal might have furnished an excuse to Henry VIII. when his conscience, as he said, was alarmed by the sad fate which attended all his own children save one, and she a female.

dispensation was valid against an infraction of a law of the Church. If, therefore, the marriage had been consummated, then a dispensation was invalid, and no divorce could in any way be obtained ; but if the marriage had not been consummated, then, in point of fact, no marriage had taken place,—there had been a pre-contract only, and here a dispensation was admissible. All that had existed between Prince Arthur and the Lady Katherine was a marriage contract. Such a contract, solemnly made in the presence of the Church, was so far a marriage that if either of the parties had repudiated the contract, and married some one else, he or she would be accounted guilty of adultery, and the children would have been illegitimate ; but to annul such a marriage as this, an incomplete marriage, a papal dispensation would hold good. Upon this point the controversy, into which we shall have to enter more at large hereafter, mainly rested. With a view to that future controversy, it is important that the reader should bear in mind, that when Warham opposed the marriage of Henry with Katherine, the *cathedra*, from which he gave forth his judgment, was not the throne in his cathedral, but the marble chair of the Lord High Chancellor of England. As a statesman, he offered no objection to a marriage against which nothing could be urged when the peace between England and Spain was once restored. Katherine's union with Prince Arthur was regarded by Warham as an act of espousal, investing the Infanta with all the rights of the Princess of Wales. To the public, the announcement of this fact was made, when the bull of Julius II. was exhibited, and more especially when at her marriage with Henry the Lady Katherine did not appear as a widow entering upon her second nuptials ; but was seen in the dress and the colours which betokened a virgin bride. She was apparelled in white satin, embroidered; her hair, "long, beautiful, and goodly to behold," streamed down her neck; a diadem was on her head radiant with gems. She sat in her covered litter borne by two white palfreys. Six noble personages followed on white palfreys. The ladies of the royal household followed in cloth of silver tinsel and velvet, in chariots drawn by horses whose harness was powdered with ermine. The streets were railed and barred from Gracechurch to Bread Street in Cheapside. Every trade stood in its liveries, from the meanest to the most worshipful crafts; at the head were the lord mayor and the aldermen, representing the commercial aristocracy. At the end of the Old Change appeared, at the goldsmiths' stalls, virgins in *white* with branches of *white* wax; priests and clerks attending with crosses and censers of *silver*, to waft a blessing to the royal couple as they passed.

The reader who is interested in ceremonials may find, in the chronicle of Hall, a minute description of the marriage and the coronation which followed its celebration. The coronation services, almost identical with those of the Holy Roman Empire, have been substantially the same in England, from the days of Canute to those of Queen Victoria. Nothing unusual occurred at the coronation of King Henry and Queen Katherine. Although, therefore, Archbishop Warham officiated, as a matter of course, we need not here repeat what has been described on other occasions. To the bridal procession attention has been directed, because it bears upon an historical fact with which both Warham and Cranmer were nearly concerned. After the doubt expressed on the subject of the marriage by the confessor of the princess, the greatest care was taken to impress the public mind with the fact, that the royal bride had

been only nominally the widow of the late Prince
Arthur. What had occurred to the mind of one man
might have suggested itself as an objection to others.
From a letter, of which we have an abstract in the
Venetian Calendar, we may infer that doubts were
from time to time entertained on the validity of the
marriage, though only by a few ; and these few were
persons who were prepared to dispute the papal right,
under any circumstances, to grant a dispensation.
This, however, can scarcely be said to palliate the subsequent conduct of Henry VIII. Because he was in
love with Katherine at the time, and because he was
flattered by the proffered friendship of her father, he
overruled every objection ; and both he and his wife
relied implicitly on the dictum of the wise old King of
Spain, the action of the pope, the acquiescence to the
whole proceeding on the part of the Archbishop of
Canterbury representing the clergy, and the advice of
the Privy Council. When he was weary of his wife,
the doubts were permitted to rise into certainties ;
and a slumbering conscience was excited, if not
awakened, by an illicit attachment.

Of Henry's devotion to his wife, during the first
years of their married life, we have ample evidence in
the State Papers ; in one of these he asserts, some time
after his marriage, that if he were still free to choose,
his choice would fall on the Lady Katherine. Fickle
as he proved himself to be, it was not till the year 1519
that his natural son, the Duke of Richmond, was born.
His attachment was returned by the enthusiastic devotion of his wife. There was not, in her estimation, such
a paragon in the world as Henry ; he was her hero,
her paladin. In his absence, to receive intelligence of
the king's health and news of his proceedings, she tells
Wolsey, is her greatest comfort.

From the delight she felt in sharing the pleasures of
the king, she entered heartily into the gaieties of the
court which she adorned. She danced well; she was
a good musician; she spoke English more correctly
than half the ladies of her court; she was so good a
Latin scholar that she could read with her husband the
works of Erasmus. To her Erasmus dedicated his
treatise " De Matrimonio." In this work he alludes to
the presents he frequently received from the king, and
adds, that in generosity the best of women vies with
her husband. To a dull commonplace artist she would
not have appeared as a beauty, for her features were
not regular, and, when she was not animated, they
were heavy. The artist, however, of genius, would
have seen beauty in the bright intelligence of her
countenance; and the ladies of her court remarked
upon the splendour of her complexion. She was lively
in conversation, while her deportment was elegant and
her manners gracious.*

The archbishop, in the year 1510, was appointed by
the pope to present the king with the golden rose. Of
this royal present we have had occasion to speak more
than once. The rose was dipped in chrism, perfumed
with musk, and consecrated. It was a token of amity
on the part of the Roman pontiff; and its presentation
corresponded with the investiture of a royal personage

---

* This description of Queen Katherine is gathered from various
letters of contemporaries, among the State Papers of Henry's reign.
They are summed up by Brewer in his preface. It is remarkable,
as opposed to the general statement that the queen's religious
feelings and ascetic practices cast a gloom over the court, that when
Campegio had his interview with Katherine, to endeavour to
persuade her to return to a monastery, he accused her of having
encouraged "dancing and court diversions" to a greater extent
than before the commission was granted to the legate.—Collier,
iv. 90.

with an order of national knighthood by a friendly sovereign. It was presented to the king with great ceremony, after the celebration of high mass at St. Paul's.

It was customary to request the primate to act as sponsor to the royal child, when the Queen of England presented to her king and country an heir-apparent to the throne; and to Katherine's first-born, Warham appears as one of the godfathers.

On the 21st of January, 1510, a parliament was held at Westminster. It met in the great chamber of the palace, near the royal chapel, or oratory.* The king assumed his place on the throne, and then directed the Lord Chancellor to address the Lords and Commons in the royal name. Warham's speech was after the usual form, and was listened to rather as a duty than from the hope of ascertaining, from the chancellor's statements, what was likely to be the policy of the Government. The fault of such speeches is the fault which may often be found with sermons. The speaker laboured to prove what required no proof, to establish by argument what had been previously accepted by intuition. Taking for his text 1 Pet. ii. 17, *Deum timete, regem honorificate*, he reminded the king and the magnates of the land of the indisputable fact that, unless they had before their eyes the fear of God, to hope for national prosperity would be vain. The people were to honour the king; but the king was to honour God. The king was honoured when the laws were obeyed by the people; and it was by keeping the commandments that the king was to serve his God. He pointed to the example of our ancestors, who not only made good laws, but also observed and enforced them. He then became figurative and poetical.

* Journals of the House of Lords, i. 3.

Parliament, he compared to the stomach of the nation; the judges acted as the eyes of the commonwealth; counsel, learned of the law, are the tongue; the magistrates in town and country were declared to be the messengers of the king, and those who neglected their duty he compared to Noah's raven. Trial by jury was upheld, and the jurors were to be regarded as the pillars of government; while the collectors of taxes and customs were the spurs of the commonwealth,—and very few of them, he sarcastically remarked, were worth much. These observations elicited much applause, and, we may presume, some laughter. The chancellor, thus encouraged, invoked each separate member of the body politic, and called upon all and each among the lords spiritual and temporal, and the whole commonalty of the realm, to come forward in support of the Crown, in order that Justice, the queen of virtues, might be auspicious in the land. He adverted to a necessity of reform in Church and State, to be effected by the abolition of iniquitous laws, and by the enactment of useful statutes. If the new parliament would act on these principles, God would be feared, the king would be honoured, and the commonwealth would be well administered.

The speech, thus made up of platitudes, was received with great applause, and was much admired. The inference which may be adduced from this fact is, that Warham excelled in voice and manner, and in the externals of eloquence. He was not a man of genius; but among clever men he was in the first rank. Whatever he undertook he cleverly performed, but he only undertook what the circumstances of his position forced upon him. The allusion to a reformation was what might have been expected. We have seen, that for many years, the demand for Church reform, originating in the fourteenth century, had been increasing in its intensity. Among the Simancas papers we find letters from Ferdinand the Catholic, in which this subject is strongly enforced; and until the convention of the Council of Trent, the question among serious men was, not whether a reformation was necessary, but what measures should be adopted to effect the object, and by whom it was to be enforced.

We may lay before the reader in this place the few incidents of Warham's parliamentary life; and we have only to repeat what has just been asserted. He did respectably what he was obliged to undertake; but his speeches were, as must be a man's doings and sayings, when, in what he performs in action or maintains in argument, he feels little interest and takes no pleasure.

On the 4th of February, 1512, parliament again met at Westminster, and Warham thought it necessary to prove what few of his auditors would be inclined to deny or doubt, that it is conducive to the welfare of the country to summon the estates of the realm to assemble in council. He establishes his point by quoting the authority of Valerius Maximus, and King Solomon. The object of a parliament ought to be the preservation of peace; but as peace could not always be maintained, he proved the lawfulness of war by a reference to the wars of Joshua against the Amalekites, and David against the Philistines.*

The prevalent rumours of a rupture between this kingdom and France received confirmation, by this allusion to the lawfulness of war; and the expected demand for a subsidy was made on the sixteenth day of the session. The opening speech was a kind of sermon addressed to the public. But now the lords

* Journals of the House of Lords, i. 10.

spiritual and temporal being summoned, the doors were closed, and the chancellor addressed them in a business-like speech, unadorned by the flowers of rhetoric. It was explained to them, that the King of the Scots had commenced a border war; that the king's officers had been insulted in the execution of their duty, and that the property of his lieges had been wantonly destroyed. In the next place, the lords were informed that the king's ally, the Duke of Guelderland, had been insulted by the King of Castile. Attention was lastly called to the insults offered by the King of the French to the Pope of Rome; an account of which, in a papal brief, the chancellor directed the Master of the Rolls to read to the house.

The House of Lords received with due respect the communication made to it by the crown, through its chief minister. A procession was formed, at the head of which appeared the Lord Treasurer and the Lord Chancellor: they repaired to the House of Commons, and before that house the same statements were laid.*

The subsidies were immediately granted, and various measures were adopted, to enable the king to conduct the war with vigour. The young monarch, full of military ardour, was enthusiastically supported by his people.

No parliament was again summoned until a peace was concluded with the King of France, Louis XII, who was married to Mary, the King of England's sister. On the 5th of February, 1514-15, Archbishop Warham, still Lord Chancellor, was once more called upon to open parliament with a speech. The parliament met at Westminster, in the Painted Chamber; and the king, though he did not speak, was

* Journals of the House of Lords, i. 13.

present. Warham's speech on this occasion gave very great satisfaction.*

He contrasted the selfishness of the existing age with the public spirit on all occasions displayed by the ancients. He complains of the neglect of the common-wealth by those who thought only of their private ends. The republic had, therefore, sickened; physi-cians must be consulted to restore the sick man to health; such medical men were to be found in the king's council, the king being himself the chief doctor. He then changed his figure of speech, and compared his royal master to a schoolmaster armed with a rod: it is necessary that he should exercise proper discipline, and that, in consequence, he should be rightly advised. He admonished the counsellors of the king, that the advice they were to give should be honest, honourable to the king, useful to the commonwealth. He then dwelt upon the duty of the judges, and of all who were concerned in the administration of justice; reminding them of Solomon's injunction to all such: "Love ye justice." In his peroration he called upon them collectively and individually to carry out the work of reformation and amend-ment, concluding with fervour: "So shall ye please God, give honour to the king, and preserve abundant peace and prosperity for the whole realm. *Quod Deus concedat. Amen.*"

We may repeat the remark, that when such an oration as this, was by all parties enthusiastically received, it only proves that Warham was endued with sweetness of voice and a natural eloquence, such as we ourselves occasionally witness in preachers

---

* In the Journals of the House of Lords it is also called, *elegantem quandam et luculentam orationem.*

who, inferior in point of ability, are surrounded by attentive, applauding, and enthusiastic auditors.

Not that Warham was a man of inferior ability; he was, on the contrary, as compared with the generality of men, a remarkably clever person, who had pursued his studies with diligence; but he lacked that genius which is more concerned with the reason than with the understanding, which decides through its intuitions on the course to be pursued, and has acted already, while inferior minds are debating whether action should be taken or not. The ability of Warham is underrated because his whole character is dwarfed by the over-shadowing of the master-mind of Cardinal Wolsey.

Not to interrupt the history of Warham's parliamentary life, I have assumed that the reader has retained in his recollection the history of the splendid events which rendered memorable the early career of Henry VIII. The son had reaped what the father had sown, and Henry VIII. had easily become, what Henry VII. had aspired to be, the dictator of Europe. With the Emperor Maximilian, Pope Leo X. and the King of Spain, the league against France had been formed. On the 30th of June, 1513, Henry had landed on the French territory. On the 16th of August, amidst the applause and astonishment of Europe, the Battle of the Spurs was fought. On the 22d of the same month Terouenne was captured. On the 9th of September the Battle of Flodden was won. On the 29th of September, Tournay was reduced. The glories of Henry the Fifth's reign seemed to be renewed. Nothing could exceed the enthusiasm with which the king was received by his loyal and loving subjects, when on the 24th of November he returned to England. When peace was declared between the kings of

England and of France, the French king had to cede
Tournay and to pay a large sum of money towards
discharging the expenses of the war.   In the field and
in the cabinet all was success and triumph.   All that
was required of the King of England was, that he
should cause his sister Mary to share the splendours of
the crown of France.   Mary had her brother's spirit,
and a woman's heart ; her heart she had already given
to another, and her hand she gave most unwillingly
to a foreigner, prematurely old, debilitated by his
vices ; but she was made to yield.

The French monarch overwhelmed her with presents,
and restored her to her liberty by his death on the 1st
of January, 1515.

For these brilliant successes England was indebted
to the genius of one of the greatest of the ministers to
whose direction the destinies of the country have at
any time been confided.   Thomas Wolsey, not yet a
cardinal, was the adviser, the friend, the boon companion of the king.   He bent to his own purposes the
iron will of Henry.   Sometimes he could hardly refrain
from showing that the king who impetuously issued his
commands was in truth the servant of the minister, who
received from the mouth of his sovereign the orders
which he had himself previously suggested to the royal
mind.   The eleven years of Wolsey's ministry were
years of glory to Henry VIII.   The great cardinal
rendered the proud motto assumed by Henry at the
Field of the Cloth of Gold a reality,—*cui adhæreo ille
præest*.   At the close of the brilliant campaign of
1525, Paris was virtually at the mercy of the English
army.

With the history of Wolsey we are only so far
concerned, as it comes into contact with that of
Warham.

Here we must correct a wrong impression which has prevailed with regard to their relations with each other. In the absence of materials for history, many writers of this period, and the biographers of Wolsey in particular, have had recourse to conjecture. Warham was chancellor; it has been conjectured that Wolsey desired to supplant him, and that he resorted to various artifices with the view of forcing him into a resignation. On the other hand, it is taken for granted that Warham desired to retain the chancellorship, and that when, by the manœuvres of his rival, he was displaced, he became a prey to those little feelings of mortification and jealousy, which predominate in little minds, and from which great minds are not always or entirely exempt.

That these suppositions are without the slightest foundation is clearly proved by the revelations made to us through the documents in the Rolls House, which contain the public and private correspondence of those eminent personages; and through various letters from other quarters selected by the industry, and illustrated by the learning, of Sir Henry Ellis.

For several years before he resigned the great seal, we know for certain that Warham desired to retire, but was not permitted. The permission was withheld because Wolsey, in the multiplicity of his affairs, was unwilling to add to his many avocations the duties which devolved on the chancellor. He could not trust so responsible a post to any of the statesmen who watched his course with envy, hatred, and malice; and the duties of the office were discharged by Warham, whose respect for Wolsey, notwithstanding an occasional difference of opinion, amounted almost to friendship.

In a letter to Erasmus, in 1515, Sir Thomas More

says : "The archbishop has succeeded at last in getting quit of the chancellorship, which he has been labouring to do for some years."*   Andrew Ammonius, referring to this subject as one in which the friends of Warham took an interest, says in a letter to Erasmus, "Your archbishop, with the king's good leave, has laid down his post, which that of York, after much importunity, has accepted."

If we have a fault to find with Warham, on a review of this part of his conduct, we should accuse him of carrying a Christian virtue to an extreme, and of confounding Christian meekness with pusillanimity. He addresses Wolsey with what we may regard as terms of affection, the more remarkable when we bear in mind the stiffness of the age, and the style of letter-writing.   On one occasion, when the archbishop took part with the practitioners in the Court of Arches, who complained of certain infringements upon their privileges by the judges and practitioners in the Lega-tine Court of the cardinal, Warham takes God to witness that he writes under feelings of strong personal attachment to his correspondent.   He concludes, " for I find your grace so loving to me and mine, that I do hide nothing from your grace."

I cannot withhold the following letter from the reader ; it throws light upon the different characters of the two men.   We find in it the gentleness,

---

* Letters and Papers, Henry VIII. 1552.   For the letter of Ammonius, see Singer's Cavendish, i. 31.   Singer makes Ammonius, instead of Erasmus, the correspondent of More.   It must be to the same letter that he refers, though the expressions that he quotes are rather stronger than what I have given above.   He says : "The archbishop hath at length resigned the office of chancellor, which burden, as you know, he had *strenuously* endeavoured to lay down for some years."

amounting to weakness, of Warham's character, and the assumption of superiority on the part of Wolsey, who admonished the Primate of All England as if he had been an inferior. It is a letter from the archbishop to Cardinal Wolsey :—

"Please it your good grace to understand that I have received your most honorable and loving letters, dated at your grace's place beside Westminster, the second day of this month of March, by which I perceive how graciously you take in good part my free and plain writing to the same, whereof in my most hearty wise I thank your grace, assuring you that unless I had had in your grace's undoubted favors and benignity towards me very singular trust and confidence to write without displeasure, not only the plainness of my mind but also such reports as were brought unto me, I would in no wise have attempted to disclose my said mind and report so openly.

"And whereas your grace adviseth me from henceforth to give less credence to all those that have made such untrue reports as be contained in my said letters, studying more to make division than to nourish good amity and accord betwixt your grace and me; surely, albeit I rehearsed in my said letters such reports as were written and spoken unto me, and none otherwise, as I shall answer before God, yet I trust it cannot be gathered of my said letters that I gave any firm credence to those reports. For unfeignedly, whatsoever surmises, sinister reports, or insinuations have been made or shall be made unto me, by whatsoever means they come, they have not, and shall not raise, kindle, or engender in me any part of grudge of mind towards your grace, or else any mistrust in your singular goodness, favors, and benevolence towards me, which evidently towards me and mine by substantial experiment appeareth daily more and more, which your grace's manifold good deeds be more deeply fastened in my heart and remembrance, than can be removed by any words or reports, which your grace's goodness I am not able to recompense with any other thing than with my faithful heart, true love and daily prayer for your grace, whereof your grace, being thus so good lord unto me, shall be so well assured as far as my little power shall be able to extend as of anything in this world, or else I were far unkind and unthankful."*

There is extant a well-written letter in Latin, in which Warham mentions his having sent to the cardinal some small present, *munusculum quod certe perexiguum, neque tanto patre satis dignum extiterat.* The present was only small by comparison. Wolsey was magnificent in everything, and in return he sent through the archbishop, for the shrine of St. Thomas, a costly jewel. The splendid jewel—*jocale illud preciosissimum*—was sent by Dr. Samson, the cardinal's chaplain. It served several purposes: it was a compliment to the archbishop, it gratified the prior and convent—*confratres mei prior et commonachi ecclesiæ meæ,*—it was an offering to a saint whom the servant of a self-willed king desired to conciliate. On another occasion we find Warham so zealous in the cause of the cardinal as to suspend "one Sir Henry, the parson of Seven Oaks, which, as is surmised, hath used unfitting language of your grace, otherwise than seemed him to do." A prime minister of that age shared the protection which pertained to royalty. The letter which Warham wrote does credit to his heart. It was his duty to send the offender to the cardinal, but he states, that the poor man was willing to acknowledge his offence and to sue for pardon. For this reason, it was hoped that the cardinal would be "good, gracious, and piteous towards him." The archbishop added, that he was a poor priest; and that it would be a pity for him to be dealt with severely or put into prison. It was significantly added that he could not bear "any great charge or cost; but if the

---

* The letters quoted are in the British Museum; they have been printed by Ellis, and in the Arch. Cant.

cardinal would be gracious lord unto him, now he would be, at all times, readier to owe unto his grace his service."

In another letter, written like the former from his manor at Otford, and probably in 1522, he complains to Wolsey of some negligence on the part of his subordinates. He begins thus : "*Please it your good grace* to understand that this 22d day of April, in the evening, sitting at my supper, I received the king's grace most honorable letters, dated at Richmond, the 9th day of the said month, by the which I am commanded to send to Greenwich fifty ' habile persons,' sufficiently harnessed, to do the king's grace service in his wars, by the last day of the month of April." He then goes on to say that it was impossible for him to meet the royal demand, unless the time were extended for supplying the complement of men. He had received no letters when the demand was made upon others in his neighbourhood, and such "habile persons" as were in his immediate neighbourhood had been already taken up by other men. He had permitted this under the supposition that no demand would be made upon himself. To send "unhabile persons and other men's leavings, I think should not stand with my poor honesty." If he were to send to further places, to Canterbury, for example, or to Charing, it would be impossible to raise the men by the day appointed. He prays, therefore, for an extension of time. From this letter we see how the army was at this time recruited : in the following we are admitted into the domestic arrangements of the archbishop. There seems to have been very little consideration shown for the convenience of persons whose services were at any time required by the king or his minister. On another occasion, the archbishop was summoned to London;

the king and the cardinal desired to consult him upon
the state of public affairs.   The archbishop says,
writing to Wolsey : "My singular good lord, there is no
subject of the king's grace that would be so glad to accomplish his highness's commandment and your grace's
pleasure as I to my little power would be.   Howbeit,
considering that my horses be at livery at Charing, and
that I have certain provision made as well at Canterbury
as at Charing, and also that I have no provision for
me at Lambeth, against my coming thither, I see not
how it is convenient or possible for me to be at Lambeth in so hasty speed, and namely my age considered
and distance of place."   He concludes with promising
to be at Lambeth on the Friday or Saturday, and then
to give attendance on the king and on his grace.   He
trusted through the cardinal's loving information that
the king's highness would take no displeasure with
him.

In 1522, Warham had the pleasure of consecrating
Dr. Tunstall* to the see of London.   Then, as now,

* Cuthbert Tonstal, LL.D. of Padua, consecrated Oct. 19. He
was the son of Sir Thomas Tonstal and Alice (Neville), born at
Hatchford, York, 1476; educated at Balliol College, Oxford, and
King's Hall, Cambridge; Rector of Chelsea, Dec. 16, 1503 ;
Barneston, March 26, 1507 ; Stanhope, 1511 ; Harrow-on-the-
Hill, Dec. 16, 1511 ; East Peckham ; Prebendary of Lincoln,
April 15, 1514 ; York, Oct. 18, 1519 ; Salisbury, May 26, 1521 ;
Chancellor of Canterbury, 1514 ; Archdeacon of Chester, Nov. 17,
1515 ; Dean of Salisbury, May, 1521 ; Vicar-General to Archbishop
Warham, 1508 ; Master of the Rolls, May 12, 1516 ; Keeper of
the Privy Seal, July 12, 1523 ; Ambassador to Archduke Charles,
Oct. 1515, to solicit the release of Francis I. after the battle of
Pavia ; to Charles V., 1516 ; Worms, 1519 ; France, to visit
Francis I. with Wolsey, 1527, and 1529, to conclude the treaty of
Cambray ; Lord President of the North. He christened and was
godfather to Queen Elizabeth, 1533, at Greenwich ; and stood on
Queen Mary's right hand at her coronation. In 1519, at Brussels,
he

the nomination to a bishopric rested virtually with the king, and Warham, knowing who was the king's adviser, addressed the following letter to Wolsey :—

"Whereas I am informed that it hath pleased the king's most noble grace to name to the bishopric of London Master Cuthbert Tunstall, Master of the Rolls, *at your grace's special commendation, furtherance, and promotion,* I thank your good grace, therefore, as heartily as I can; and, in my poor opinion, your grace could not have owed your favor in that behalf more honorably and laudably than to the said Master Tunstall, being a man of so good learning, virtue, and sadness, which shall be right meet and convenient to entertain ambassadors and other noble strangers at that notable and honorable city, in the absence of the king's most noble grace, if it shall then fortune your good grace to be also absent. And in promoting such a man to that dignity, your grace hath done that thing that I doubt not shall be to the king's grace's great pleasure continually, whereby your grace shall purchase manifold thanks of his noble grace, and I, which am many ways bound unto your grace already, am now much more bound unto your grace, for your said favor shewn to Master Tunstall, in recompensing of the which, if there be anything

---

he was the guest of Erasmus while settling a commercial treaty with the emperor; when his chancellor urged him to punish a heretic he said : "Hitherto we have had a good report among our neighbours, prithee bring not this man's blood upon our head." In 1526, with Sir Thomas More, he bought up the whole of Wiclif's translation of the New Testament, and burned them at Paul's Cross. In 1541, with Bishop Heath, he revised the new edition of the Holy Bible. He was translated to Durham, March 18, 1530, but was deprived Aug. 14, and restored Sept. 13, 1552; again deprived, Sept. 29, 1559. He was the uncle of Bernard Gilpin. He died under the Primate's charge at Lambeth, Nov. 18, 1559; and was buried in the parish church. See Fuller's Worthies, ii. 572; Rymer, vi; Surtees, Durham, i. p. lxvi; Lansd. MS. 980, f. 291-4; Ang. Sac. ii. 228; Foss, Judges, v. 237; Cunningham, ii. 180.; Brit. Biog. ii.

in my power wherein I might or could do your grace pleasure, surely I will be most glad to do it."

Warham was a kind and zealous friend; and
throughout his correspondence with Wolsey the kindness of his heart was displayed. If we decide by
his words and actions, he was singularly free from
those little passions and jealousies frequently attributed to him by those who are conscious that, in
the circumstances under which they have imagined
him to have been placed, would have been experienced by themselves. We find the archbishop, in
another letter, entreating the cardinal to be "good
lord" to Owen Tomson, who was master of the archbishop's mint, and was prosecuted, as the archbishop
thought unjustly, in the Court of Chancery.

This Owen Tomson had been previously sent to
London on the archbishop's own business. Certain
ordinances had been issued for the regulation of the
royal mint in the Tower of London; the archbishop,
in writing to Wolsey, says: "Forasmuch as I doubt
not but that your grace well knoweth that, by the
grants of divers kings, the king's grace's most noble
progenitors, I and my predecessors, Archbishops of
Canterbury, have always had in the palace of Canterbury a mint for coinage, to the great commodity and
ease of the king's grace's subjects within this county
of Kent, and otherwise to the intent that I would
gladly that my mint should in like manner and form
be ordered according to the said new ordinances, I
beseech your good grace to show and declare your
grace's further pleasure and mind in this behalf to my
servant Owen Tomson, this bearer and keeper of my
said mint. Upon knowledge of which I have commanded him to follow the same in everything accordingly." He concludes with saying, "In good faith,

my lord, I desire not this for any great profit or advantage that I shall have by this coinage; but only for the ease of the king's grace's subjects, who more commodiously resort to Canterbury than the Tower."

Thus readily did the archbishop conform to the new regulations of Wolsey's government. Wolsey perceived, though Warham did not, that the regulation of the issue of money must devolve upon the imperial government before this important department in the affairs of state could be satisfactorily arranged. The convenience to which Warham alludes in having a mint at Canterbury was certainly, at this time, not overrated. If a man, being in want of money, was in possession of plate, he sent his plate to a mint, and received it back in the shape of coin. A journey to London with this object solely in view would be troublesome, expensive, and hazardous. The mint at Canterbury was, indeed, at this time, in some danger, and perhaps was only saved because its suppression would have led to the suppression of the mints at York and at Durham, and, in consequence, to the inconvenience of the cardinal. Wolsey's mind was so occupied with foreign politics, that he had no time to carry out his plans for the home government; but, as in this instance, he probably only deferred what his political sagacity perceived to be a necessary reform. Wolsey was cut off in the midst of his career.

We have a letter from Warham thanking Wolsey for the advice he gave the king in this matter. He had been advised by a lawyer whom he had consulted, on Wolsey's suggestion, to obtain a bill for the continuance of his mint, but he would do nothing without the consent and concurrence of Cardinal Wolsey.

We have an account in Cavendish of the splendid arrangements for the celebration of divine worship in Cardinal Wolsey's chapel; and we know the great attention paid by Henry VIII. to the music of the sanctuary; an anthem of his composition is still sung in our cathedrals. Henry VIII. attending service, on a certain occasion, in Wolsey's chapel, was charmed with the singing of one of the children, and the child was immediately transferred from the cardinal's chapel to the Chapel Royal. Wolsey took pleasure in imitating his master and in showing his power even in little things; and having on one occasion attended service in the archbishop's chapel, he served the primate as he had been served himself, and application was made for the transfer of a bass singer from the chapel of the archbishop to that of Wolsey. The letter in which Warham courteously accedes to Wolsey's request is valuable, not only because it shows the friendly terms on which the two prelates lived, and the courtesy of Warham, but also because we learn from it the great care with which Warham attended to the moral training of his household :—

"Please it your grace to know that by my fellow-master, Doctor Benet, your chaplain, I have understood that your grace is desirous to have one Clement of my chapel, which singeth a bass part. For the singular great kindness that I find in your grace, not only the said Clement, but also any other servant of mine which can or may do your grace any service or pleasure, shall be alway at your grace's commandment. Wherefore, according to your grace's mind, I now send the said Clement to your grace, with these my letters, humbly beseeching the same to be good and gracious Lord to him, if it be your pleasure to have him to continue still in your grace's service, assuring your grace that he is of very sad, virtuous, and honest behaviour, and so hath continually used himself for all the time that he-hath been with me in service.

There is not in my house a better ordered, or yet a better conditioned, person. If there be any other service or pleasure that I can do for your grace, upon knowledge of your grace's pleasure therein I shall be glad the same to accomplish to the best of my little power."[*]

CHAP.
II.

William
Warham.
1503–32.

There is another letter, of uncertain date, which shows the archbishop in the character of a friend to the cardinal. Had there been in him the jealousy so often attributed to him, he would have made political capital out of the circumstances to which the letter refers. I can offer no comment upon the letter beyond that which will occur at once to the reader's mind :—

"Please it your grace to understand that at my last coming to Canterbury I was informed of a certain White monk of the monastery of Sutton, in Suffolk, which reported at Canterbury and in other places, that your grace had suppressed the said monastery, and expulsed the religious men of the same, taking from them their lands, jewels, goods, and chattels, by reason whereof reported he that he was compelled (like as other his brethren) to beg, or else to use some craft for his living, and offered himself to serve in a tailor's shop in Canterbury, sometimes to other occupations, by which his report and remiss behaviour I assure your grace there was an evil rumour and bruit in these parts. And when I called him before me secretly to be examined, he denied not but that he did so report, but said it was not true. Forasmuch as this matter toucheth your grace, I have sent him unto your grace further to be ordered as your grace shall think good. Master Hales, Baron of the Exchequer, can inform your grace of this matter more at large.

"At Oxford, the 14th day of May.
"At your Grace's
"WILLM. CANTUAR.

" *To the most* REVEREND FATHER *in* GOD *and my very*
singular good LORD, *my* LORD CARDINAL *of* YORK,
and legate de latere, his good GRACE."[†]

---

[*] Ellis, Third Series, ii. 54.   [†] Ellis, Third Series, ii. 85.

In the year 1519, Charles V. visited England. Warham was at Otford, but having information that the
royal party was to meet at Canterbury, he prepared
to entertain them with his usual hospitality. Wolsey
was so accustomed to dictate his will to others, or to
control them by his influence, that he intended, on
this occasion, to direct the proceedings at Canterbury,
although the expense was to devolve upon Warham.
He wrote to Otford, begging the archbishop to meet
him at Canterbury to assist in making preparations for
the reception of the royalties. Warham despatched to
him the following letter, in which illness was perhaps
the pretext, rather than the real reason for not obeying the summons. Its friendly tone, however, will be
remarked.

" After most humble commendations, I thank your good
grace as heartily as I can, that it hath pleased the same to
advertise me of the established and certain determination of
the emperor's majesty for his repair to the king's most noble
grace, and of the king's grace gifts for the meeting of the
emperor at Canterbury, and for the deducting of his majesty
to Winchester. My lord, I am very much bound to your
good grace for the manifold tokens of great favors and
kindness, which I find daily more and more increase in your
grace towards me, for which if I were able to do your grace
pleasure again, I were far unkind if I would not be very
diligent, ready, and glad to do it. And sorry I am that I can
not be at Canterbury to give your grace attendance, and do
my duty accordingly at your grace's coming thither, which I
assure your grace I would not have failed to have done, if I
had not been diseased now of late, whereof I am not yet
wholly delivered.* Notwithstanding, I trust in God, that by

---

* From his disorder, whatever it was, the archbishop recovered
in time to give a splendid entertainment to his royal guests at
Canterbury. Henry VIII. was accompanied by Queen Katherine,
who had come to meet their imperial nephew. Between the king
and the emperor some state affairs were first adjusted ; and then

that time that I have done my duty to the king's grace at my poor house at Otford, I shall be able forthwith to journey to Canterbury speedily, there to receive the king's grace and the emperor in my cathedral church. If there be anything in those partes appertaining to me which may be to your grace's pleasure, I desire your grace to use it as you would your own."

On another occasion, when the cardinal had invited the archbishop to a private conference on public affairs, the latter was obliged to excuse himself. He could only obey the summons by acting contrary "to the counsel of his physician and by putting himself in jeopardy." He would, nevertheless, give attendance upon the cardinal, about the feast of the Purification of our Lady, if God should send him any amendment of health. He would then supply the information which he was obliged to pretermit in his letters. He adds :—

"I thank your grace as heartily as I can for your grace's *manifold favors*, shewn unto me, many ways heretofore, and now specially that it hath pleased the same, not only to advise me to make mine abode in high and dry grounds at Knowle, and some other; but also to offer to me, of your singular benignity and goodness, a pleasant lodging in your most wholesome manor of Hampton Court, where I should not decease, neither be diseased; there to continue for the attainment of my health as long as I shall think it expedient, by which excellent benevolence and gratitude, expressing evidently your grace's very tender love towards me and my servants, I repute myself so much bounden to your grace as I think myself far unable to deserve or requite your grace's said favors and great humanity. Albeit, at all times I will be ready and glad, with good heart and mind (and so your grace shall find me sure), to do your grace any service or pleasure that may lie in my little power. Which my benevolence I beseech your grace to accept, and take instead and place of mutual beneficence, where my power is insufficient.

CHAP.
II.

William
Warham.
1503-32,

---

the royal personages and their attendants were entertained at the incredible expense of Archbishop Warham.—*Arch. Cant.* i. 13.

"And I entirely thank your grace that it hath pleased the same to write unto me in your last letters that your grace would give order to your officers that as large and ample favor shall be shewed to my nephew, Archdeacon of Canterbury, as to other archdeacons, touching their compositions with your grace for their jurisdictions. And for a conclusion to be taken for my said nephew his jurisdiction, I have now sent this bearer one of his procurators to your grace's officers, to give attendance on them in that behalf.

"As touching my officer, the Dean of my Court of the Arches, I trust I have given him such admonition as he will remember during his life ; and be well ware to busy himself in any matters which may sound to your grace's discontentation and displeasure. And that your grace hath not dealt extremely with him ; but only trained him, with continual attendance for his learning, to be more circumspect in time to come, and that for my sake your grace hath also discharged him of the said attendance, I heartily thank your grace, affirming, without colour or simulation, that neither he, nor any other officer, kinsman, or servant of mine, shall continue in my service or favor which will hereafter willingly fall into your grace's displeasure or indignation. And so I have declared unto them myself, shewing how good and gracious I find you towards me, and how that it hath pleased your grace to write unto me that you will be as good unto them as they can reasonably and justly desire, so that they use themselves accordingly towards your grace and yours, and as they owe to do. In which good and favorable mind I beseech your grace ever to continue, as you shall have me ever your perpetual orator.

"I have now lately set up writings both at Knoll, Otford, and Shoreham, against such as misentreated a certain apparitor of your grace in these parts, that the said misdoers appear before me within xv days, under the pain of cursing. And I trust by that means, or else by other espials, to try them out if it be possible, and then further to order them so that all other shall be ware by them of such wilfulness and contemptuous temerity."*

---

* Ellis, Third Series, ii. 39. The date of the year is seldom given

So far from there being any antagonism between Warham and the great cardinal, the archbishop, on more than one occasion, befriended Wolsey, under circumstances which would have afforded political capital to a rival statesman, or an unfriendly ecclesiastic.

Under the unpopular government of Henry VII. Warham did not incur the odium which brought other members of that king's council into trouble. He was a man of kind and conciliatory manners; and, when he became resident in Kent, his influence, especially in that county, was considerable. The people regarded him as a friend, when the measures of the government were oppressive, and to his intercession they looked when they were threatened by the anger of the king.

Several letters passed between Warham and Wolsey with reference to a tax which the cardinal had unconstitutionally imposed, and which Warham was obliged by his duty to the king to enforce; a duty which he performed with reluctance. Wolsey had always a dislike of meeting parliament; he sought, in consequence, to raise money by other means than through a parliamentary grant. Benevolences had been abolished, and in their abolition Warham had taken part; but, though not in name, they were, in reality, re-established, under what Wolsey in sarcasm, or in policy, was pleased to denominate an amicable and loving grant. Commissioners were appointed, according to Hall, in the year 1525. They sent assistant commissioners into every shire, "to raise money against the time the king should cross the sea." The tenor was this, "that the

in these letters; although the exact date of the letter just quoted is not discernible, Sir Henry Ellis remarks that it must have been rather earlier than 1526, for in that year Hampton Court was no longer Wolsey's "most wholesome manor:" he had given it to the king.

sixth part of every man's substance should, without delay, be paid in money or plate to the king, for the prosecution of his war."[*]

The cardinal, as chief commissioner for London, undertook to carry on the negotiation for this "amicable and loving grant," with the mayor and corporation of London. The dukes of Norfolk and Suffolk and other great men were to act in their several counties; the Archbishop of Canterbury was the chief commissioner for Kent.

The commissioners were to remind the people that now was the time for the king to regain the French crown, and to effect a complete conquest of France; the French army had been annihilated, it was said, by the battle of Pavia. It was calculated that the old enthusiasm in favour of a war with France would be revived; but it was a miscalculation.

On the 30th of March, the archbishop convened a meeting of the noblemen and landed proprietors at Otford, where he, at this time, chiefly resided; almost all the commissioners attended. A few showed some readiness to make contribution to the king's grace for his voyage into France; but he found a great "untowardness and difficulty" on the part of the majority. They did not, however, venture upon a formal opposition, and when they were requested to sign a document to signify their submission, they did not refuse to do so. The archbishop expressed his conviction, however,

---

[*] Sir Henry Ellis observes that, when Wolsey wanted to raise money by unconstitutional measures, he found some pleasant name appropriate to the demand. Previously to the "amicable and loving grant," he had in the fifteenth year of Henry VIII. issued a commission to compel every man with 40l. a year to pay the whole of a subsidy granted by parliament long before it was due. This he called an anticipation. Wolsey's policy was to avoid Parliament; Crumwell's to corrupt or control it.

that there would be a great difficulty in levying the
grant, which, though assented to, was not accepted in
a very amicable or loving spirit. The difficulty of
collecting the money was increased, and the hardship
to which the people were subjected was the greater,
since officers were, at that very time, collecting the last
instalment of a parliamentary subsidy. Many affirmed
that they had not means to meet even the last-mentioned
demand, although for that they had been husbanding
their resources. The archbishop acted as a true friend
to the cardinal. He had secret information, though
he declined to name his authority, of the discontent of
the people, and of their murmurings against the cardinal himself. " It hath been shewn me in secret that
the people sore grudgeth and murmureth, and speaketh
cursedly among themselves as far as they dare; saying
that they shall never have rest of payment as long as
some one liveth, and that they had better die than be
thus continually handled ; reckoning themselves, their
children, and their wives as desperate, and not greatly
caring what they do, or what will become of them."

The other commissioners would only pledge themselves to lay before the people the demand, without
any intention to persuade them to pay it. They would
refer the people to the archbishop as chief commissioner; he expected disturbances, and besought the
cardinal to advise him how to act. It had been signified to the archbishop, that if he meddled in this affair
he would forfeit the popularity he now enjoyed; but
to this sacrifice he would submit for the king's service.

After disclosing still further the murmurs of the
people, the archbishop goes on to show that the attempt
to create an enthusiasm in favour of a French war was
a failure. The public mind had received some principles of political economy. The nobles and gentry in

CHAP.
II.

William
Warham.
1503-32.

attendance upon the king, by spending their fortunes abroad, would enrich the French; while, through the expenses of the war, the English would be thus doubly impoverished. It had now been perceived, that the conquest of France would be actually injurious to England; for it would cause the seat of government itself to be transferred to France. This was the argument employed by the Lancastrian party in the reign of Henry VI.; and it was intended to be significant to the reigning monarch.

In this conference, there was frequent allusion to a forced loan, which had never been repaid. Some of the commissioners, despairing of repayment, contended that it would be only equitable to set off the debt of the king to the people as part payment of the "amicable and loving grant."*

The loan had been a source of much suffering and annoyance; it was an iniquitous manner of raising money without the intervention of parliament. Warham, as has been said, was a popular man in Kent; and it was determined among the people to call upon him to interpose between them and the king, and to entreat him to repay what they had been constrained to lend. There were large assemblages of the people; and the archbishop received information that a mob was on its march to his residence at Knowle. His influence was sufficient to prevail upon the people to commission a deputation of the more substantial yeomen to confer with him, and then peaceably to

---

* This letter is perhaps the most friendly, because it was outspoken, of all the letters of Warham to the Cardinal. It ought of itself to have established the fact that their disagreements, which were unfrequent, were only on public grounds. If Warham had regarded himself as a rival politician to Wolsey, he had only to bring the circumstances mentioned in the letter under the notice of the king, and Wolsey would have been brought into trouble.

disperse. " For commonly," observed the primate, " in a
multitude, the more part lack both wit and discretion;
and yet the same more part will take it upon them to
rule the wiser." He pointed out to the deputation, that
they had fixed upon an inconvenient time to demand
repayment of the loan ; the king having been involved
in extraordinary expenses. He questioned them with
a view to. ascertain whether they had been instigated
by any political adventurers ; he received for reply,
and they were ready to confirm their assertion by oath,
that to their present course of conduct they were urged
by poverty only. Of those who had assembled it
might be truly said, and of their neighbours who remained at home it might be most strongly affirmed,
that they "lacked both meat and money." When
asked why they came to the archbishop, they answered
that he had been at the head of the commission, through
whom the loan had been pressed upon those, who, at
this time, waited upon him ; and they entreated him
to intercede on their behalf with the king, that he
would represent to him their poverty, and implore him
to pay his debt. The archbishop desired them, to prepare a petition, which he would present ; their reply
was that they could not draw up a petition themselves,
and no one had courage to undertake to " write for
them, seeing it concerneth the king's highness."

If Warham had been a great man, he would have
dared the worst ; and, as many of his predecessors
would have done, he would have defended the cause
of the weak. But Warham declined to assist them, or
to permit any of his servants to do so. The people
were, many of them, justly indignant. It was reported
to the archbishop, that they used strong language when
adverting to his conduct. The archbishop immediately
sent a report of what had occurred to the king's

council; and evidently was under an apprehension, that he would be censured for not having had recourse to stronger measures for putting down these insurrectionary movements. He so far served the people, that he warned the council, that some steps ought to be taken to pacify them; and he concludes his despatch with saying: "I have thus, by fair words, answered and partly contented two assemblies which have come to me on this matter; thinking verily by fair words and gentle entertaining they would be better ordered than by rigorous means."

Warham, though not a great, was a good man: if he had not the large heart to place himself at the head of an injured people, and to demand what in justice the government could not withhold; he could, nevertheless, pity and sympathise with the people, and deprecate those strong persecuting measures, which were more in accordance with the spirit of the age, than soft words.

It was seldom, that the Archbishop of Canterbury was on friendly terms with his chapter; and a misunderstanding arose between the prior and monks of Christ Church on the one side, and Warham on the other so serious, that the archbishop ceased to make his palace at Canterbury his chief place of residence. Nevertheless, to him they applied for protection in their difficulties; and the following letter, addressed by Warham to Wolsey, reveals to us the kind of difficulty to which an incorporated society might be at that time exposed:—

"Please it your most honorable grace to understand that I hear say a report, that a servant of the king's grace has come to Canterbury, at the commandment of the king's counsel (as he saith) to have stabling for the king's horses, to be kept at livery within the monastery of my church of Canterbury, showing no letters of the king's grace, or other writings, declaring

the said commandment.   Sure I am that the king's highness
and your grace, well informed of the great charges that the
said monastery hath been and must daily be put into, will be
well contented to spare the same from any such manner of
extraordinary charges.   For the said monastery hath been so
burdened with receiving and entertaining both of the king's
grace's most noble ambassadors and other princes, and of other
honorable personages passing by that way, beside the king's
grace and the emperor's late being there, beside also finding
of men to war, above great subsidies and great loans, that if
such charges or other like should continue, the same might
after be utterly decayed, which I would be very loath to see
in my time.   And I trust verily that your grace, for the
great devotion that your grace oweth to Christ's Church, and
to the blessed martyr, St. Thomas, will be contented of your
goodness to put some remedy that no such new charges be
induced ; but will be so gracious to your religious bedemen
there, as to discharge them thereof, specially where the said
monastery standeth far off from the king's grace continual
abode, to keep any livery of horse commodiously for the
king's grace use."

The amicable relations which existed between the
primate and the cardinal have been traced, as an historical fact, in their mutual correspondence.   We must
not alter facts because we cannot account for them ;
but we may bring other facts in juxtaposition, in
order that we may explain the reason why between
these two great men misunderstandings were inevitable ; and why also these inevitable disagreements
in some public transactions did not lead to any permanent violation of their friendship.   The fact last
mentioned is, no doubt, to be attributed in part to the
yielding disposition of Warham, his indolence, and his
generous determination, on public grounds, not to be
led into a quarrel which might frustrate an important
measure ; to effect which he had made concessions
which may by some persons be regarded as unjusti-

fiable. That Warham was, on some occasions, severely
tried, we shall have to show ; and such trials we should
have expected to find, when the person with whom he
was prepared to act was Cardinal Wolsey. Wolsey
had many of the faults as well as most of the merits
of a powerful, self-reliant, energetic mind. He was
overbearing, dictatorial, impatient of contradiction ;
and, as is the case very frequently with self-raised
men, he was extremely sensitive of any supposed
omission of respect to his station, or deference to his
opinion. When he had a point to carry, he was
regardless of the feelings of others. When they suggested objections, or offered the slightest opposition,
he was equally regardless of their rights. Hence his
enemies were venomous and bitter. Although he was
a man of kindly feelings, he ruled and sought to rule
by fear rather than by love. Upon a mind capable of
kind affections the gentleness of Warham had an effect,
similar to that of the soft answer that turneth away
wrath.

But we must look beneath the surface of things, if
we would do justice to both Wolsey and Warham ; to
the one for yielding, and to the other for grasping,
inordinate power. They had a common public object.
The times required a dictator, before whom the consul
was content for a season to bow his fasces ; the archiepiscopal mitre was to yield precedence to the cardinal's
red hat, and the pillars of the latter were to supersede
the crosier of the primate. To understand what has
just been advanced, we must revert to a subject which
has been fully treated in a preceding volume. In
the introductory chapter to the third book, we have
traced to the miserable condition of the ecclesiastical
courts the increasing unpopularity of the clergy.
Many who did not agree in their opinions in regard to

a reformation of the Church, were unanimous and clamorous in their unanimity for ecclesiastical and clerical reform.

I have stated, that considerable allowance must be made for the one-sided exaggerations of party men in the declamations of Gerson and his contemporaries, in their denunciation of the immoralities of mediævalism; but the facts which come to light in the correspondence of Erasmus and his contemporaries we cannot pass over. Erasmus sometimes employed hyperbolical expressions, and we are not to understand a witty letter-writer too literally; we should not, for example, be justified in believing Germany to be little better than the infernal regions; neither may we flatter ourselves that England was an exception to general corruption—"the least corrupt portion of the world,"—because, as Erasmus says, from its insular position, it is out of it. But Erasmus, though witty as a satirist, was, by no means, severe as a moralist; and society, as represented by him, required a revulsion, such as nothing less than the Reformation could have effected.[*]

Ungrateful princes disbanded their soldiers, when, at the sudden conclusion of a peace, their services were no longer required. The soldiers, becoming ruffians, made a prey of the people who had been previously ruined by taxation to support them in turbulence and crime. Nobles, as selfish as their princes, surrounded their habitations by dependents ever ready for depredation; and these, turned suddenly adrift, when the aristocrat was summoned from the provinces to the court, swelled the bands of robbers. These bands were still further increased by the poor, who were ousted from their farms, now turned into sheep-

---

[*] Erasm. Epist. Append. ccxxxix. cccv.

walks, and were robbed of their commons, through the
inclosure of which the wealthy sought to become more
wealthy.   For the most trivial offences criminals were
condemned to death, and the thief became a murderer
from fear of the halter.   Tradesmen and even pilgrims
found it unsafe to travel by land or by water.   Where
property was secure a sottish selfishness prevailed,
which, thus encouraged by friars, polluted the monasteries themselves.   It was not to be supposed that either
mansions or monasteries would be exempt from scandals, when of all scandalous places the most corrupt was
the Court of Rome.   The age which could tolerate an
Alexander VI, a Cæsar Borgia, and a Julius II, must
have been an age of deep corruption; and the age of
Henry VIII, of Francis I, and Charles V, who sacrificed
millions of lives to amuse themselves on the battle-
field or to usurp dominion, was not an age when life
or property was likely to be much regarded.   The
multitude, who tolerated such popes and applauded
these princes consisted of men, who felt that in such
situations their conduct would have been the same.
Machiavelli would not have written, unless he had
been persuaded in his own mind that he was addressing himself to readers who, while sympathising with
him in his lax and selfish morality, would applaud the
courage which induced him to throw aside the mask
hitherto worn by cowards.   Unless Italy under the
Renaissance had been paganized, Leo X. would not
have presided over a court in which Jupiter and the
deities of Olympus were regarded as highly as the
one and only God Whom Christians are taught to
worship.   That for such a lax state of morality the
clergy was, to a great extent, responsible is a fact which
it is impossible to deny.   To uphold the cause of
morality by word and deed was their first and bounden

duty.   But there is in these cases action and reaction ; the world might have been worse except for their interference ; while they, mingling with the world, too frequently shared in the corruptions, and by sharing, countenanced them.   They were open to strong temptations through the celibacy, which both Rome and the world combined to enforce upon them.

We are, however, happy to know that, if the world was bad, as a fallen world will ever be, there were instances innumerable of men leading sober, righteous, and godly lives.   We can mention, as representative men, contemporaries of Warham, who, in every class of life, proved that the leaven of Christianity was still working in society.   We may appeal to the wonderful sale of the works of Erasmus himself, to show, that moral teaching as well as literature had its many advocates in all parts of Europe ; and, as Erasmus declares, especially in England.   When Erasmus and Luther spoke, theirs was only the voice of genius giving utterance to the pent-up feelings of Christendom.   To the call of Erasmus, preceding that of Luther, the Archbishop of Canterbury and the leading characters in England gave a cordial response.

What is said of the laity is true of the clergy.   Bad as many of the clergy certainly were, we have high testimony to the fact that, as a body, no general charge of immorality could be brought against them.   When the Parliament of 1529 was convened, the House of Commons had been packed, and, to gratify the king's malice against the clergy on account of their being, as a body, opposed to him on the Divorce question, the Commons were required to make themselves acceptable to the king by bringing against the clergy all manner of accusations.   They legislated severely, but wisely ; they attacked them in detail, but no sweeping charge of immorality against the whole body of the clergy did they venture to bring. It is not probable, that men whose very existence, as a body, depends upon their upholding the laws they have vowed to enforce, would be pre-eminent in vice, as Puritan writers affirm. Their temptation would be rather to hypocrisy. There was, we may feel sure, at all times, many a parish priest remote from public view, such as he who is described by Chaucer. We must admit that charges of immorality could be substantiated against several of the clergy who held high positions in society; but they paid the compliment to virtue by concealing their faults from public gaze, and this proves that the public mind was not entirely perverted. Even here modern writers have frequently represented the case as worse than it really was, by giving to the terminology of the sixteenth century the meaning attached to words in the nineteenth. For example, we know from public documents that many of the clergy were married men. The monks made a vow of chastity, as it was called, that is, they bound themselves to celibacy. No vow was exacted from the clergy. They violated a canon, and were obliged to submit to the penalty if it were enforced, but they contrived to escape prosecution. Their marriage was voidable, not void. Cranmer was a married man long before he became, in any sense of the word, a Protestant, and while he was condemning to the stake those who held the Protestant doctrine with reference to the Eucharist. Now these clergy were regarded by rigid disciplinarians as unchaste persons, and were accused of living in a state of concubinage.*

---

* In the year 1521, Henry VIII. issued a proclamation against the married clergy. The document is, on more grounds than one, important. It shows how the royal supremacy existed as a fact,

We may adduce another case. An intrigue between a monk and a nun was regarded as incestuous. The offence was a great one, no doubt, but it hardly substantiates the declaration of some party writers, when they speak of incest as being a common crime of the age, understanding the word in its modern sense.

But when, in a desire to deal fairly to all parties, we have made every allowance that justice can demand, we have still to account for the extreme unpopularity of the clergy at this time.

The bishops during the middle age were frequently, we should speak more correctly if we should say generally, employed in the civil service ; or perhaps we should be still more correct, if we were to say that statesmen, lawyers, and diplomatists received, very frequently, bishoprics as the reward of their services to

before Henry openly claimed it. Though the married clergy are described as few, we may regard this as a mask. If they had been really few in number, they would have been dealt with individually. It runs thus : "The king's majesty, understanding that a few in number of this his realm, being priests, as well religious as other, have taken wives and married themselves, &c., his highness, in no wise minding that the generality of the clergy of this his realm should, with the example of such a few number of light persons, proceed to marriage, without a common consent of his highness and his realm, doth therefore strictly charge and command as well all and singular the said priests as have attempted marriages that be openly known, as all such as will presumptuously proceed to the same, that they nor any of them shall minister any sacrament, or other ministry mystical ; nor have any office, dignity, cure, privilege, profit, or commodity heretofore accustomed and belonging to the clergy of this realm ; but shall be utterly, after such marriages, expelled and deprived from the same. And that such as shall, after this proclamation, contrary to this commandment, of their presumptuous mind take wives and be married, shall run into his grace's indignation, and suffer further punishment and imprisonment at his grace's will and pleasure. Given this 16th day of November, in the thirteenth year of our reign."—Wilkins, iii. 696.

CHAP. II.

William Warham. 1503-32.

the crown. The consequence was, that a resident diocesan, in process of time, became not the rule but the exception. When a diocesan resided, he brought his court with him, and, making his cathedral city a place of importance, he was popular. Of this we have an instance in the case of Wolsey himself. When, on his fall, he intimated his intention of retiring from the world, and of residing in his diocese, Yorkshire rose, as one man, to bid him welcome ; and the jealousy of his enemies in the king's house was excited.

The closed palaces of non-resident diocesans, though doles were issued from the gates to the poor, neither offered hospitality to the gentry, nor afforded employment to the tradesman. Within the sanctuary, the episcopal functions were not neglected. They were, however, discharged by bishops *in partibus*, who chanced to be residing in the country, or by suffragans employed permanently or for the occasion. For the purposes of piety these sufficed ; but, by the worldly, the suffragan was despised, who could not hold a feast in his halls, or take his place among the nobles of the land. The tenants grudgingly paid an income, which was to be spent in London or in foreign lands. This abuse had become a popular grievance, and was made a ground of complaint when it became Henry's policy to attack the clergy. Hence the unpopularity of the hierarchy.

But this, it will be recollected, was not the greatest calamity which devolved upon the Church through the non-residence, in so many instances, of the diocesan. In every diocese, subsequent to the conquest, a spiritual court was established, over which the bishop nominally presided. When the diocesan was employed on state affairs or foreign missions, as he

employed a suffragan or an ἐπίσκοπος σχολαῖος to
perform his spiritual duties, so he delegated his authority as a judge to his chancellor or archdeacons.
These, again, in some dioceses, allowed their officials
to become ordinaries. The courts of these function-
aries gradually and imperceptibly assumed ordinary
jurisdiction, until in the majority of dioceses by the
common law of the Church, archdeacons ceased to act
with delegated authority, and became ordinaries.*
They held their courts nominally in subordination
to the bishop of the diocese, who had right of visitation and appeal, that is, of extraordinary jurisdiction;
but the archdeacons had a seal of their own, and, in
their own name, opened their courts. They held
annual visitations, subject to the triennial visitation
of the bishop; but their obnoxious courts met once
a month, or at stated times.† Although these offices

---

* An ordinary is a judge, who has a certain independent jurisdiction, with which no superior can interfere, except under certain
specified conditions, or on special occasions. The superior officer is
generally regarded as a judge of appeal or a visitor. The visitor of
a corporation aggregate is generally prohibited from visiting except
once in a specified number of years, or to make inquiry under an
alleged grievance. His is not the ordinary, but the extraordinary,
jurisdiction. It is necessary to make the observation for the following reason. In the year 1532, a supplication was addressed by the
House of Commons to Henry VIII, complaining of the conduct of
ordinaries, and Foxe and his followers, either not seeing or purposely overlooking the distinction, speak of this as a supplication
against the bishops. Bishops were the chief ordinaries, the *ordinarii
ordinariorum*, and were therefore included in the censure; but not
exclusively. The terms ordinary and bishop are not convertible
terms; for a bishop may exist without ordinary or any other jurisdiction. An archdeacon or chancellor may be an ordinary; a
suffragan bishop may have no jurisdiction whatever, acting only as
the delegate of the diocesan, *pro tempore*. By confounding the
titles in this instance the real grievance is overlooked.

† Harrison, Pref. to Holinshed.

were, for a short time, held as stepping-stones to higher preferment by great men, yet the archdeacons, as a rule, were men of inferior education, selected as judges from the practitioners of the ecclesiastical courts. Of these courts some exist to the present hour; and the chancellor or judge, though an ordinary, is not unfrequently a layman. In a few dioceses, the archdeacons are merely the delegates of the bishop; but, in the more ancient dioceses, they still have courts of their own.

In the middle ages, the judges and officers in these courts were remunerated, not by fixed salaries, but by the payment of fees; and, in the shape of fees, the demands were sometimes exorbitant. Suitors were compelled to pay, not according to a fixed scale, but according to their supposed capabilities; hence there was incessant wrangling on the subject. It was the interest of the judges and practitioners to absorb all kinds of suits in the ecclesiastical courts. They dealt with matrimonial causes, with probate of wills, with all that related to social contracts. As we have shown before, for every supposed moral offence any one, at any time, might be summoned before an ecclesiastical judge, and, even if acquitted, the case was not dismissed until the fees were paid. So that often it was a saving of time, of trouble, and of annoyance, if not of money, to bribe into silence the clerical accuser of the brethren. These accusers of the brethren were clergymen who, acting as chantry priests, brought down upon the chantries their own unpopularity, and were little better than pettifogging attornies in search of prey. When any of them settled in a neighbourhood, the whole parish was fretted, and reduced to a state of normal irritation. No one knew whether he was safe. For any chance action, word or look, any one might unexpectedly be called to account. The judges, too often selected from this class of the clergy, co-operated with them. With judges and advocates there was but one object, *rem quocunque modo*. If the money could not be extorted by a fine, it might be abstracted as hush-money, though there was really nothing to be hushed. While the high-spirited defied the enemy, the humble and meek paid their money to purchase a quiet life.*

Against these courts, and against the non-residence of the diocesans, the popular feeling was increasing in violence every year. The hostility to the clergy who practised in these consistorial courts extended to the whole order. For the welfare of the clerical body, for the cause of the Church or of Christianity itself, the guilty clergy, unfortunately, cared nothing. No lucre was, in their eyes, filthy, and they went on grinding down the poor and irritating the rich. In the provincial courts, as distinguished from the diocesan, and which sat chiefly in London, there was a superior class of practitioners, and to these vulgar malpractices there was less temptation to resort ; other abuses, however, existed, tending to exasperate the public mind, when the public were looking out for grievances in this direction, and demanding reform.

The Church had, in former times, been the protector of the poor against the rich ; but in this age, when the depression of the poor in every quarter was becoming almost intolerable, the Church was able to do little, and attempted next to nothing. That this was not owing to any want of will on the part of the higher ecclesiastics we have an instance in what occurred soon after Warham's appointment to the primacy. In

* See vol. iii. of this work, p. 35, where the case is fully stated.

the ecclesiastical courts, as in all other courts, a very evil practice prevailed. The judges were dependent for their remuneration partly, as has been just recounted, upon fees, and upon emoluments of office. It was an established custom for a judge to receive money from suitors in their courts. The money was not advanced to purchase a judgment in favour of the suitor, for the money was often proffered and accepted by both parties in the same suit; the object was to induce the judge to appoint the cause for hearing at an early period in the term. The consequence was, that a poor man's case might be delayed for years, owing to his inability to provide this honorarium. Term after term would come to an end before his case could be heard. He saw the rich, one after another, descending into the Bethesda, and, if the water had been troubled by an angel, it would have been troubled in vain, so far as he was concerned. Archbishop Warham determined at once to rectify this abuse. Having matured his plans, early in February 1507, he issued from Lambeth his regulations and statutes for the Court of Audience. They may be found in Wilkins, and consist of nine articles. The second is the one of real practical importance, framed to meet the evil just brought under the reader's notice. It assigned advocates and proctors for poor people without fee, and gratis. All ministers of the court were to waive their fees, in the case of the poor, and to receive nothing. The judge was required to expedite the causes with all possible dispatch, and to take nothing from the parties through the whole course of the process. In the event of any advocate or proctor, so appointed by the judge, appearing unusually negligent or remiss in the management of a poor man's case, or of his refusing to proceed with the cause

without money payment, he was to be for ever dis-
qualified from practising in the court.*

With these facts before them, the biographers of
Warham may well complain of the unfairness of
those historical writers who, following Foxe both in
his imaginations and in his prejudices, represent the
archbishop as having neglected his duty for thirty
years, and of attempting an effete reform in his courts,
only when he was threatened with the interference of
parliament. At that time Wolsey had fallen into
disgrace, and the archbishop merely resumed the
reforms which he had himself commenced at an
early period of his episcopate, and which he had
wisely, perhaps, though unconstitutionally, delegated
to Wolsey.

Warham, a reformer, perceived the weak point
in the ecclesiastical system. He recognised the
iniquitous proceedings of the ecclesiastical courts;
he saw how, for filthy lucre's sake, a large body of
the clergy were not only bringing disgrace upon
themselves, but were also doing injury to the souls
of men, by alienating their affections from religion
and exasperating them against the Church. He acknowledged, that what was intended to promote the
cause of morality was now perverted by the worship-
pers of mammon, and that God was blasphemed in
order that ecclesiastical lawyers might fill their purses
with gold. He attempted a reform : but the guilty
persons had obtained high appointments, and how
they could abuse their powers was to be seen in the
case of Hun, whatever opinion may be formed of
the merits or the demerits of that particular case. A
whole profession, for such these lower practitioners

---

* Wilkins, iii. 65. Godolphin, Repertorium Canonicum, 103,
asserts that the same rule was enforced in the Court of Arches.

had become, were ready to resist the archbishop, not openly but firmly. The *vis inertiæ* of a heavy mass of unscrupulous men, who, in themselves, offered

"A cloudy barrier dense,"

was not to be dispersed, or, by the ordinary course of proceedings, overcome.

The time had arrived when the commonwealth was in danger. It became the duty of the consul to make way for a dictator. We may, with our modern experience, censure the proceeding; but the course of Warham and Wolsey was intelligible and upright. The two primates, Warham and Wolsey, came to an understanding. The ecclesiastical courts could not be extinguished or reformed by any ordinary jurisdiction, or by proceedings under the usual forms of the national Church. The diocesans had permitted a power to rise in their respective dioceses which they could not control. How vast that power was is proved by the fact that these ecclesiastical courts were neither suppressed nor entirely reformed until the reign of Queen Victoria. Even partially to effect the object which Warham had in view, a despotism was required. The only course which presented itself to Wolsey's mind was that, of asserting despotic rights on the part of the pope, of bringing the national Church in subjection to the Bishop of Rome, and of then calling on the pope to exercise those rights through the agency of a legate *à latere*. Wolsey would, as a temporary measure, meaning by that during his own lifetime, supersede all national jurisdictions, including that of the primacy itself. Such a thing had never before been heard of in England. Such powers the pope had never attempted to exercise in any national council, prior to the defeat of the councils in the preceding century. Two centuries ago, such an attempt would have subjected an English ecclesiastic to the punishment of a traitor; and, if made by the pope, would have antedated the extinction of all papal pretensions in England. But Henry VIII. was, at this time, in spite of the remonstrances of Sir Thomas More, a Papist; and to every advice, cautiously offered by Wolsey, the king was prepared to listen.

The case then stood thus: a complete reformation of the ecclesiastical courts in England and of other matters in the Church, was necessary; the Archbishop of Canterbury was not strong enough to overcome the obstruction to reform, which it was the interest of many persons to throw in his way; Warham was willing, therefore, for a time to recede from his high position, and to place all things under the direction of a papal plenipotentiary, a legate *à latere*. This was not to be a permanent surrender of his powers as Archbishop of Canterbury and Primate of All England. Although Wolsey subsequently obtained a grant of the legatine power for his life, it was originally agreed that he should exercise it only for seven years. If Warham had been an ambitious man, he might have sought the legatine power for himself; but his position would then have been more anomalous, and he must have been quite aware, that what the king would concede to his favourite he would not have granted to one who, under these circumstances, would have found in the favourite an antagonist. At all events, Warham acquiesced, without reluctance, in Wolsey's appointment; though he did not realize beforehand the amount of concession which Wolsey demanded. A great work was to be done by a great man, and to accomplish it, the great man was to be invested with all requisite authority, temporal and spiritual.

This point being conceded, however, various details required arrangement; and we are surprised that, in making them, the misunderstandings which took place between the two primates should be so few. Had Warham been of a captious disposition, they would have been multiplied. Wolsey was to exercise extraordinary visitatorial powers; but the common law of the Church of England and her courts, though virtually suspended, was not to be finally superseded. Having effected his object of reform, the legate *à latere* was to withdraw; and on his withdrawal all things were to resume their original position, the corruptions only removed. Thus was the case conceded *à priori*. Wolsey's disposition was to push to an extreme whatever powers he possessed. It was Warham's duty to guard against any such exercise of the legatine authority as might act injuriously upon the permanent authority of existing institutions. We are sometimes surprised to see how easily Warham withdrew an opposition which he offered to some exercise of authority on the part of Wolsey: why did he object, we are inclined to ask, or if he objected why did he not persevere in his objection? Bearing in mind the agreement between the two prelates, we can understand, why Warham may have demurred to a particular line of conduct, when first a case was brought under his notice, and yet be persuaded to acquiesce in the proceeding, when it was proved to him that it did not really interfere with a conceded principle of action. On the one hand, this arrangement was facilitated by the ambition of Wolsey, anxious by grasping at power to further his own designs; on the other, Warham's natural indolence, his infirm health, and his desire of literary leisure, made him sufficiently compliant to the will of the master mind with which he was called to act. Difficulties and objections seldom suggested themselves to Warham's mind, and he was urged to make a complaint when a complaint was made by others. I see no reason for doubting, that both were influenced by high public principle, though temper and self-interest sometimes interfered.   Wolsey felt, that reform was necessary, and, knowing his powers, believed, that he was the only man to effect it, though one year succeeded another without his finding leisure to address his powerful mind to domestic policy or ecclesiastical affairs.   Warham believed that a great end would be accomplished by his submitting, at some self-sacrifice, to the degradation of his high office.   He was occasionally taken by surprise, when Wolsey assumed more than Warham had intended to grant; and when the tenaciousness of Wolsey descended to little points, which we should have supposed to be beneath the consideration of his great mind.   Warham was willing to permit the appointment to the cardinalate, to settle differences.   When Wolsey was translated to York, one of the weak points of his character made itself apparent, by his insisting on his right to carry his cross erect in the province of Canterbury.   Warham was indifferent on the point; but at the persuasion of others offered a feeble resistance.   This point of etiquette—for, though at one time it involved a principle, such it had now become—was settled when Wolsey received the red hat; in accordance with the concession made by Archbishop Chicheley, with which the reader is already acquainted.

When the two primates had come to an understanding, Wolsey was to interest the king in the cause. With the king he found no difficulty; the difficulty

was on the side of the pope, who as a politician had
no inclination to invest the powerful minister of the
King of England with additional authority. This,
however, had the effect of making King Henry the
more determined to carry the point of his favourite.
Times indeed were changed from what they had been
in the reign of Henry V. Henry V. had declared
himself, it will be remembered, ready to sacrifice his
crown rather than permit a Roman cardinal to reside
in England, or the servant of a foreign potentate to
have a voice in the English councils. Henry Beaufort
dared not show his red hat in England, until he had
first obtained a royal pardon from the king for having
been accepted in the cardinalate ; and, when he was invested with the insignia of office, it was done privately
and at Calais. Instead of sharing in the patriotic
sentiment, Henry VIII. became actually a suppliant
to the pope on behalf of his favourite ; and it is not
too much to say that, except for the urgency of Henry
to the unwilling pontiff, Wolsey would never have
been a cardinal. This statement fills the honest mind
with disgust, when it is made in anticipation of
Henry's subsequent conduct to Wolsey and the English
clergy, hereafter to be mentioned. Let it be impressed
upon the mind. We have before us the correspondence on the occasion. We find the pope pleading
as an excuse for his not acceding to the king's
wishes, that it would involve him in difficulties. By
the King of the Romans and by the King of France
similar applications in favour of their ministers would
certainly be made.

When at length, the pope through weakness yielded,
he still demurred to the appointment of Wolsey as a
legate *à latere*. Unless he were, however, appointed
a legate *à latere*, with permission to visit the exempt

monasteries, Wolsey knew that he could not become a reformer. It may be that, aware of the object, and distrusting Wolsey's discretion as a reformer at a time when his attachment to the papal see had not been tested, the pope was averse to the appointment which Wolsey sought, with his usual determination not to be frustrated. In the course of the correspondence, still extant, Wolsey hints that it was only by yielding to the royal demand on this point that the pope could be secure of the friendship of the King of England. Even this hint, significant as it was, was not sufficient. There was to be a bribe delicately administered. On the 7th day of September, the pope expresses his gratification at hearing, that the King of England had granted to him half a tenth from his clergy in aid of the Roman Church. That the object of the grant was understood and duly appreciated is proved by the declaration by the pope of his determination to insist on Wolsey's immediate promotion in spite of all the cardinals. On the 15th of September, Julius, cardinal de Medici, writes to Henry VIII, affirming that Wolsey's promotion was a proof of the pope's anxiety to please the king. On the 20th of September, Sebastian Giustiniani writes to the Doge of Venice, that a courier had arrived from Rome with a statement, that " Wolsey had been created a cardinal *at the desire of the King of England*, who was bent on aggrandizing him with might and main." On the 30th of September, Henry sends an autograph letter from Windsor, to Pope Leo X, affirming, that nothing had given the king so much pleasure, in all his life, as the breve announcing the election of Wolsey to the College of Cardinals, and the additional honour conferred by the pope's oration on the occasion. The *pope had outdone all* the king's expectations, and Henry

esteemed the distinction thus bestowed upon a subject
for whom he has the greatest affection both for his
unusual gifts and most excellent services, as a favour
done to himself.*

This, let it be repeated, is the man who, a few years
after, impeached Wolsey, and not Wolsey only, but
Archbishop Warham and all the clergy of England, for
acceding to a measure of which he was himself the
author. The clergy had violated the laws, in their
ignorance of the stringent enactments, unrepealed
and in full force, against the papacy. They ought,
no doubt, to have brought the law to bear upon
Wolsey, to have denounced and to have prosecuted
him; they ought to have demolished his legatine
courts, when he dared to set them up, in the pope's
name against the spiritual courts of the Church of
England, over which the primate and his suffragans,
now defied, had been appointed by the constitution to
preside. What their fate would have been if to such
a course they had resorted in 1515, it is not difficult
to surmise. The only resistance, faint though it was,
that was offered to the exercise of Wolsey's legatine
power, was offered by the clergy; and against the
clergy, a few years after, Henry VIII, the chief, the
most inexcusable offender, appeared as the accuser,
the judge, the diabolus, and the executioner. We may
withhold our pity from them, and they had only their
ignorance, shared with the king, to urge in their defence. But, be that as it may, if Henry had conducted
himself in a manner so unprincipled and tyrannical
against men or women who had not been admitted to

* See the Letters and Papers, Foreign and Domestic, of the
reign of Henry VIII, Nos. 91, 374, 780, 887, 910, 929, 960.
Others may have escaped my search; but these are abundantly
sufficient.

holy orders, our indignation could have known no
bounds. There are times when the clergy are justly
unpopular for a neglect of their duty; but they are
pledged to seek the favour not of man but of God, and
by the profane and careless, they are most hated when
they best perform this duty.

When the red hat was granted, its arrival in England was anxiously looked for by Wolsey. The
cardinal had promised that the bringer of the hat
should be handsomely rewarded. On the 7th of
October, a letter was despatched by the Bishop of
Worcester,* stating that he had entrusted the precious
treasure to the safe keeping of his friend Bonifacio. A
greater honour was in store for the royal favourite. It
was usual to send the hat (*pileus*) without a ring. On

---

* The see of Worcester appears to have been assigned in this and
the preceding reign as a kind of retaining-fee for foreign prelates,
who were severally employed to act as the King of England's
minister at Rome. Silvester de Gigliis was the nephew, or, as
some said, the son, of John de Gigliis, who had previously held the
see of Worcester. Silvester was arch-presbyter of Lucca. Previously to his consecration he had stalls in Wilts, in Lincoln, in
York, and in Salisbury. He was consecrated at Rome in 1498.
(Stubbs, 73.) He sat in the Council of Lateran, 1512. He was
King's orator at Rome in 1505, and was the Papal collector in
England. He died on the 10th of April, 1521, and was buried at
Rome. (Stubbs, Le Neve, Duffus Hardy.) His predecessor,
John de Gigliis, was a doctor of laws, at Lucca. He was Rector
of Swaffham, Saxeham, St. Michael's, Crooked Lane. He held
stalls in Wilts, in St. Paul's, Lincoln, and York. In 1487, he was
Archdeacon of Gloucester. In 1482, he was Dean of Wells. He
was king's proctor at Rome, and papal collector in England, where
he obtained large sums by the sale of indulgences and pardons.
He held the see of Worcester only one year. He was consecrated
at Rome on the 10th of September, 1497, and died on the 25th of
August, 1498. For the convenience of the reader, I have from
time to time given a sketch of the history of bishops whose history
has been connected with that of a primate. But while in the life

CHAP.
II.

William
Warham.
1503–32.

this occasion, the grateful pope added a ring of more than usual value ; he added also a plenary indulgence to all, who should be present at the ceremony of its reception. Bonifacio would also bring with him the bull of the cardinalate.* The minister who had advised a royal grant to the papal treasury was a man to be held high in honour. On the 7th of November, a letter was despatched by Sir Richard Wingfield to Wolsey, informing him that the hat had arrived at Calais, attended by Bonifacio.

Of the secret negotiations between the English and papal governments, with which we have only lately become acquainted, and of which I have made use, the contemporary public were not, of course, aware. The appointment of a cardinal in England, which, at one time, would have caused a public disturbance, was even now unpopular ; and it was thought improbable that the king would do more than give a silent sanction to the proceedings ; a sanction to be wrung from him by

of a primate, I have written entirely from original authorities, I have not had the means or the time to test the veracity of the statements made with reference to prelates who are only noticed in the notes. I have done so where it has been practicable. Between the episcopate of Silvester de Gigliis and that of Hugh Latimer, two foreigners held the see ; Julius de Medici, in 1521, and Jerome Ghinucci, who is conspicuous in English history, having been employed to collect the opinions of the universities in Italy and Spain in the divorce case of Henry VIII. He was chaplain to the pope, and auditor-general of the Apostolical churches. Professor Stubbs does not give the date of his consecration, which took place abroad. He was consecrated Bishop of Ascoli. He was translated to Worcester, and removed, by order of Parliament, in 1535, as an alien and non-resident. Collier, iv. 196. But I believe he was never resident in England, and that he is rather to be regarded as holding these sees *in commendam*, than in pure and holy matrimony.

* See the Letters and Papers, Foreign and Domestic, of the reign of Henry VIII. No. 994.

Wolsey himself. It was rumoured that the hat had
been already smuggled into the country; that it had
been conveyed hither in a "varlet's budget," or as
others said, "a ruffian had brought it to Westminster
concealed under his cloke."*

Wolsey was determined at once to give the lie to
these malicious reports, and to dismiss the calumnies
by ocular demonstration of the fact, that what had
been done was done with more than the concurrence,
with the hearty approbation, of the king. He was not
the man to despise the importance of little things. He
felt the importance of taking possession of his new
office in a style which might equal if it did not surpass
the magnificence of Warham's enthronization. The
king was popular; Wolsey himself was at this time
popular; and to invite all London, at Wolsey's
expense, to a festival which would give fresh life to
trade, and provide the poor with a feast, was sure
to be a popular act. He also desired to make an
impression upon the authorities of Rome. The unwilling pope had not conceded the legatine authority.
Wolsey determined that he should see how all parties, from the king and the primate to the populace,
regarded his character.

Wolsey himself delighted in ceremony, and never
did he spare expense, whether he was attending his

* Singer's Cavendish, i. 29. I think that we must trace the
existence of the reports, preserved in Cavendish, to the existence
of those absurd reasons by which even in our time almost every
public transaction is preceded; but, if we compare the statements
with the dates of the letters and the other documents we now
possess, we may be confident that they did not influence the conduct
of Wolsey. Everything had been carefully arranged for the reception of the hat, and Sir Richard Wingfield was directed to notify
its arrival in Calais, that everything might be ready for its reception
in England.

master to the Field of the Cloth of Gold, or arranging the details of an entertainment in his own house.

All things were so arranged, that Bonifacio the prothonotary should reach London on the 15th November. At Blackheath he was met by Henry Bourchier, earl of Essex, the Bishop of Lincoln, and a large assembly of persons. The procession was formed. At the gates of the city of London, the mayor and aldermen were ready to bid the hat welcome. A reaction had taken place in public opinion, or the attempt to raise a prejudice against Wolsey had failed. Under the direction of the city magistrates, the streets were lined by the various crafts. The hat was carried by the prothonotary, the Earl of Essex riding on the one side, the Bishop of Lincoln riding on the other.

They quitted the city, and the procession, passing through the Strand and the village of Charing, came in sight of the abbey. The Lord Abbot of Westminster, attended by eight other mitred abbots in splendid copes, appeared at the west door of the abbey; they received the hat from Bonifacio, and conveyed it to the high altar, where, after its long and fatiguing journey from Italy, it reposed.

All the arrangements appear, from the correspondence, to have met with the concurrence of the Archbishop of Canterbury. He did not indeed appear when the hat was received; for the honour of receiving it devolved on the Abbot of Westminster. But on Tuesday, the 18th, he crossed the river and repaired to the abbey. The Archbishops of Armagh and Dublin were already there to receive the Primate of All England; with them were many of the suffragans of Canterbury, together with the mitred abbots of the chief monasteries in the land. The primate was preceded by his cross-bearer, the Lord Bishop of

Rochester.   The sound of trumpets summoned them to
the west door of the abbey, where the ecclesiastics
received the king, the queen, and the queen of France,
Mary, the king's sister.   The nobles, the barons of
the Exchequer, the judges, and the serjeants of the
law were in attendance.   It was soon announced, that
the cardinal with the nobles and gentlemen of his
household had arrived in procession from his palace.
The procession walked up the nave of the abbey, and
when the Lord Cardinal of York had reached the platform, the Archbishop of Canterbury sang the mass, the
Bishop of Rochester bearing his crosier.

The sermon was preached by Dean Colet, of whom
more will be said hereafter.   Colet was one of the
most celebrated preachers of the day; he was also a
personal friend of the archbishop; and his appointment on this occasion was significative.   Colet was
known to be a strong advocate of reform.   In 1512,
he had been appointed by the archbishop to preach
at the opening of the Convocation.   We shall have
occasion hereafter to notice the sermon he then delivered; we shall only say here, that the preacher,
appointed by Warham on that occasion, had denounced
in plain language the wrong-doings of the clergy, and
had especially condemned the scandals and vices of
the ecclesiastical courts, and the newly-invented arts
of ecclesiastical lawyers for getting money.   The
very fact, therefore, of his being the preacher on the
present occasion, indicated the intention of the new
cardinal to act with the archbishop as a reformer.*
It confirms all that has just been advanced in regard

* When we speak of reformers in this chapter, the reader will
remember that we are not, of necessity, speaking of the Protestant
Reformation.   The Theses of Luther were not yet published, and
his name was scarcely known in England.

to the understanding between the primate and Wolsey.

Colet was fanciful at the commencement of his discourse, a thing unusual with him : he affirmed that the cardinals represent the order of seraphim, continually beaming with love to God the Blessed Trinity; for which reason they were arrayed in red, the colour that denoted nobleness. He enlarged on the merits of Wolsey, and exhorted him to be humble in his deportment, and just in the administration of his office. It was an age when great men encouraged plain speaking. Henry VIII, to resist whose will was death, was tolerant of contradiction in argument, and favoured those who, with a certain amount of tact, told him the truth. The courtiers, as usual, imitated the conduct of their masters ; though, in fact, there was nothing in Colet's sermon calculated to give offence.

There was one truth which no one was brave enough to announce—perhaps none were learned enough to be aware of the fact—namely, that when, at the conclusion of the sermon, Dr. Vesey, dean of Exeter and of the Chapel Royal, rose to read the papal bull by which Wolsey was created a cardinal, he, and all present, including the king himself, were *ipso facto* involved in the penalties of a præmunire.

The cardinal meanwhile was lying before the high altar, " grovelling," as the chronicler calls it, before the archbishop, awaiting his benediction. The red hat was solemnly removed from its resting-place on the altar. The cardinal was crowned. When he rose with the red hat on his head, the choir burst forth in a *Te Deum*.

The service ended, the " butcher's son," as plebeians loved to call him, walked proudly down the nave, having achieved the greatness which others had inherited and knew not how to keep. He was supported on the one side by the Duke of Norfolk, on the other by the Duke of Suffolk, proud nobles, who regarded the distinction with mingled feelings. The lord cardinal, a prince of the Roman court, preceded the Archbishop of Canterbury ; one almost revolts from writing the fact, that Warham, though with a good object in view, submitted to the temporary degradation. At the cardinal's palace at Charing Cross, a splendid entertainment was given. The hall and the chamber were " sumptuously garnished by rich arras." The multitude looked on ; and when the nobles had feasted, common people scrambled for the fragments, and the fragments formed another feast. All hostility to cardinals was forgotten. Wolsey was right ; the people love the splendour which they are permitted to participate. A stranger, judging from outward appearances, when witnessing these proceedings, affirmed, that the whole kingdom evinced joy incredible at Wolsey's well-deserved promotion.

A great man he was, for greater is he who achieves greatness, than he who inherits it. Wolsey is treated, therefore, as ungrateful England is used to treat her great men. His faults are engraven as with an iron pen upon a rock, his merits are written in sand ; scarcely legible except by those who search for a man's virtues under the conviction, that the faults in a great man's character are pointed to contemporaries by the finger of envy, and to posterity by the malignity innate in little minds.

It is perfectly consistent to believe that, while Warham and Wolsey acted cordially together in what related to domestic policy and ecclesiastical affairs, there was considerable divergence of opinion

in regard to the foreign policy of the country between the peace-loving minister of Henry VII. and
the energetic adviser of a young king eager to seek
"the bubble reputation at the cannon's mouth."

It was certainly no conjecture of later historians;
it was the opinion of their contemporaries, that the
two great statesmen, Fox, bishop of Winchester, and
Warham, archbishop of Canterbury, were opposed
to Wolsey's policy in giving succour to the emperor
against the French.   Sebastian Giustiniani asserts this
as the court gossip in the year 1516, and, as a proof
that it was not without foundation, he mentions the
circumstance, that those statesmen had withdrawn
themselves from the council for many days and months
past.*

On reference to the state papers we find, that Warham had withdrawn himself from the political world,
not especially on this occasion, but from the commencement of the reign.   He had confined himself
to the legal duties of the chancellor, and, on that
very account, had retained the friendship of Wolsey.
It has been said, that Wolsey, owing much in early
life to Fox, and even to Warham, had driven them
from the helm of government when he had obtained
influence over the young king's mind.   In the case
of Fox, as well as in that of Warham, the injustice
of this charge has been proved.   As regarded Warham, he was not opposed to Wolsey in what related
to the domestic policy of the country, and in ecclesiastical affairs Warham and Wolsey co-operated.
The divergence of their opinions in regard to foreign
politics may have made Wolsey more ready to accede
to the often-repeated solicitation of Warham to be

* Giustiniani, i. 129.

relieved from the burden of the great seal; but we have evidence to show, that no personal feelings of rivalry or of hostility were mixed up with the resignation. Public rumours are not to be overlooked by an historian, but they are not to be accepted as well founded unless they are supported by documentary evidence.

Giustiniani was writing rather loosely, if the correct date is given to his letter—the 17th of July, 1516, for the resignation of the Great Seal had occurred some time before, as may be seen from the following document :—

"1. Memorandum: that on Saturday, 22 December, 1515, in a small and lofty chamber, near the chamber of parliament, William, archbishop of Canterbury, then being Chancellor of England, delivered into the hands of the king the Great Seal, inclosed in a bag of white leather five times sealed by the archbishop's signet, in the presence of Wolsey, Charles, duke of Suffolk, and William Throgmorton, prothonotary, which bag the king had opened and the seal produced, then replaced in the same bag, sealed with the cardinal's signet, and delivered to the cardinal.

"2. Memorandum : that on Christmas eve, Dec. 24, the said cardinal in his chapel at Eltham, after vespers and in the presence of the king, took the oath of office in the form given in English."[*]

Warham soon found himself in a false position, and felt the inconvenience of it; he had retired, as it were, from all but the external rights and dignities of the primacy; and, to effect a reformation of the clergy and of the ecclesiastical courts, he had permitted a temporary dictatorship to be established. It was not his fault, so he thought, if Wolsey had not the time, before his fall, to accomplish what the two

---

[*] Letters and Papers, Henry VIII. 135.

primates had designed.   But if Warham himself was
ready to retire, and to submit to Wolsey's dictation,
it did not follow that such submission would be
conceded without a murmur by those ecclesiastical
lawyers whose opinions had not been asked in regard
to a measure which involved many of them in ruin.

The appointment of a legate *à latere* implied the
appointment of a legatine court.   A legatine court,
though at first only a court of appeal, would, if well
managed, absorb the business of all other courts.   It
is due to Warham, to say that he had the sagacity
to foresee this, and the wisdom to guard against the
possible abuses of the new court.   We learn, from
one of the letters which passed between them, that
Warham and Wolsey had duly considered this subject.   They foresaw the possible collision between the
legatine or foreign court and the national courts of
the Church of England ; and they drew up certain
terms of agreement.   The terms of the agreement are
not stated ; but no terms of agreement could prevent
the practitioners of the different courts from being
involved in controversies ; and in the controversies
of their subordinates the principals were sometimes
compromised.   I shall not weary the reader by laying
before him the extensive correspondence to which
these disputes gave rise.   The impression it leaves
upon my mind is, that the whole subject was treated
by the primate and the cardinal as one of very little
importance.   At the same time, the letters bring out
in strong relief the very different characters of the
two men.   Complaints were made to Warham, and
the practitioners in his courts were really aggrieved ;
but Warham himself had made a great sacrifice for
what he believed to be an important public benefit,
and others ought to do the same.   ·Nevertheless, the

legatine court was generally in the wrong: the national courts only asked to be supported in their constitutional rights, while the legatine court was claiming to try cases, not on appeal, but in the first instance. This was, in effect, to supersede the courts below, to the ruin of the lawyers who practised therein. Warham felt the justice of the plea, and urged Wolsey, though very mildly, to judge each case on its own merits. The overburdened cardinal was irritated by these proceedings. He would remind Warham that they had come to an agreement as to the jurisdictions of their respective courts, and he might silence the complainants by referring them to its terms. He hinted that, in reopening the question, Warham was guilty of a weakness which, as it consumed valuable time, was regarded by Wolsey as culpable. Warham generally submitted. He would sacrifice much for a quiet life. He could say to the complainants that he had pleaded their cause with the representative of the pope, and, if he had not succeeded, it was no fault of his.*

According to Polydore Vergil, the dispute between the primate and cardinal, on one occasion, ran so high, that Warham brought a case before the king. The king, it is said, sent a curt message to Wolsey, requiring him to redress the grievance complained of. It is not probable that, without Wolsey's own consent, Warham would have appealed to the king, at a time when Wolsey had so completely the king's ear. It is possible, on the other hand, that, a misunderstanding

---

* The critic who wishes to contradict the statements given above has only to reprint the letters which passed between Warham and Wolsey in the disputes arising in their respective law courts. A case may be made out on either side. It is by comparing the statements that we come to the truth.

having arisen as to the interpretation of one of the terms of agreement, both Warham and Wolsey requested the king to act as arbiter, and that Henry settled the business in his usual off hand way. He delivered a wise and peremptory judgment, finding pleasure in deciding against the favourite in a matter of no importance. It may be expected that I should notice another statement of Polydore Vergil, and I do so, not because I attach importance to it, but because a passing comment may be demanded on a story which is frequently repeated as a proof of the haughtiness of Wolsey. He is said to have taken great offence when, upon a certain occasion not mentioned, the Primate of All England, in an official letter addressed to Cardinal Wolsey, had signed himself "Your brother, Willelmus Cantuar." The letter of the primate has not been produced. I do not venture to say that it is unproducible, as there are two hundred letters of Warham inedited in the Vatican; but we may be confident that, if such a letter makes its appearance, it will bear a date antecedent to the appointment of Wolsey as a legate *à latere*. When Warham conceded precedence to Wolsey, the etiquette of the age required him to recede from a form of address which was never adopted when an inferior was in communication with one whose superiority he admitted. It was customary, in the middle age, for the chief in every department of Church or State to address his subordinates in terms of condescension or equality. The subordinates were expected, when addressing their superiors, to use their higher title. An archbishop signs himself " brother " when writing to his suffragan, the suffragan replies to " my lord." The presbyter is called " brother" by his bishop ; but the bishop again is " my lord " to the presbyter. The courts of justice were, in this country, for so long a period administered by ecclesiastics, that the same etiquette continues in the legal profession. The puisne judge is, by the chief of his court, addressed as " brother ; " but the chief justice or chief baron receives the lordly title from the other judges occupying the same bench with himself. The puisne judge in addressing the bar distinguishes a serjeant-at-law from the other practitioners by calling him " brother," but when the serjeant pleads before the bench the puisne judge is approached by him as " my lord." In an age when these trifles were regarded as important, it is possible that the mode of address had been discussed between Warham and Wolsey, and the form decided upon which could be objectionable to neither. The usual form adopted by Warham in his letters to Wolsey is, " At your grace's commandment, W. Cantuar."

The whole story is probably a fabrication on a foundation of the slightest possible character. At the same time, the greatest admirers of the ill-used cardinal must admit that in Wolsey there is traceable much of the littleness which sometimes attaches to self-raised men. Suspicious and sensitive, they offend the dignity of others by their frequent self-assertion ; they treat as a personal insult every mark of disrespect, or what they regard as such. Wolsey's self-reliance resented, as an impeachment of his judgment, any proffer of advice. His unconcealed contempt for most of those with whom he was brought into contact acted as a whetstone to the malignity of his enemies, when an ungrateful master, whom he had served too well, left him open to their attacks. This haughty tetchy disposition appears occasionally in his correspondence with Warham. He certainly pushed the powers conceded to him far beyond what Warham expected, and one is inclined to feel indignant at his conduct in regard to the University of Oxford. This is so closely connected with Warham's life that it must be noticed. It is possible that the university reform, which both prelates desired, could have been in no other way carried into effect, and this may account for Warham's quietly submitting to what appears to us very like an insult. We may think that in this affair Wolsey acted wisely; but we may, at the same time, complain of the manner in which even a good work is performed. If, in his general conduct, Wolsey became great by discerning his end from the very beginning and keeping his eye fixed steadily upon it; he created enemies, not because men differed from him in opinion, but because in the furtherance of their common object he was regardless of their feelings; he would make others work, and then he took all the credit of success to himself.

If there was one office in which Warham took more delight than in any other, it was that of the Chancellorship of Oxford. He had, with a very brief exception, remained from early youth attached to his *alma mater*. He had done his duty as reader or professor in the university, if not also as a tutor in his college. He retained his situation as the head of a house, even when his avocations in the law courts of the metropolis, made London his chief place of abode. Although he resigned this office on his nomination to the see of London, yet, as we have seen, he was only for a short time Bishop of London, and soon after his translation to Canterbury, the university evinced its respect by electing him its chancellor.*

* An attempt was evidently made at this time to introduce at Oxford a system which still prevails in some of the Continental universities, where distinct colleges are open to the different faculties. There is a Law College, a Divinity College, a Medical

He is thus connected with the university reforms which took place after he had ceased to reside. They were conducted by the personal friends of the chancellor : with his entire sanction, if not with any very active co-operation. Activity indeed in any of the pursuits of life was not to be numbered among the virtues of Warham ; but, if he was slow to resist evil, he encouraged what was right, and was a learned man.

The reformation of the universities in England, through the influence of the Renaissance in Italy, preceded the reformation of the Church, though the fact is overlooked too generally by the historians of the period.

Even before the chancellorship of Warham the attempt was made to supersede the scholastic and to establish the classical system of education ; to supplant education by philosophy, and to introduce education by language.

In the last century and at the commencement of this, all that related to scholasticism and the works of the schoolmen was subjected to the cheap and paltry criticism of a sneer. Men thought to show their wit when, to a more inquiring age, they simply betrayed their ignorance. Whatever may be the faults of the present time—and they are many,—we do not mention as one, a neglect to do justice to former ages, or to the giants of other days.

College. That this system failed may be a subject of congratulation. The object of a university ought to be to educate a Christian gentleman ; to provide a good education—a liberal education—before removing the mind to the professional point. The great Civil Law School was situated in St. Edward's parish, near St. Edward's Hall. It belonged to St. Frideswide's Priory, and yielded to them, by the name of the Civil Law Schools, three and forty shillings and fourpence, as appears by an inquisition concerning the revenues, taken in 1524.—Wood, Annals, ii. 768.

When Europe was in deep intellectual slumber, scholasticism was admirably adapted to awaken its dormant energies.*

It ought not to be forgotten that, during the two centuries of the predominance of scholasticism, the progress of society, if slow and gradual, was persistent and decided. Results were produced of which the benefits remain to the present hour. It was during that period that the great nationalities were formed, that representative government was made to pass from the Church to the State, that a vernacular literature was created, and a middle class called into existence. It was the schoolmen who by the creation of universities summoned the noble from his castle, where might

---

* In the inaugural lecture of Dr. Shirley, we have presented to us an historical and philosophical view of scholasticism, which, though a sketch, is a sketch so masterly, as to make us sure that his early death was a public loss.

"Ostendent terris hunc tantum fata, nec ultra
Esse sinent."

To him and to Neander's History of Christian Dogmas the modern student of history is under deep obligation. As early as the time of Semler, says Hagenbach, complaints were made of the unjust treatment which the scholastic divines had to suffer. Semler himself observes, "The poor scholastici have been too much despised, and that frequently by people who would not have been good enough to be their transcribers." Luther himself wrote to Staupnitz : "*Ego scholasticos non judico, non clausos oculos ligo— non rejicio omnia eorum, sed nec omnia probo.*" See De Witte, i. 229, Hagenbach, i. 401. In Calvin, the schoolmen still lay down the law to men who in their ignorance revile them. The attack upon such a man as Aquinas by Dean Colet is not creditable to Colet. He betrayed the weakness of ordinary minds, where they are unable to do justice to one party without deteriorating from the merits of another. This is what is meant when men are spoken of as party men. A man may belong to a party, and defend it, but he has no right, when acting as an historian, to conceal the merits of the opposite side.

was triumphing over right, and the student from the monasteries, where theology had exclusive dominion. The universities were the cradle and nurse of scholasticism. To the universities flocked the great middle class, in incredible numbers; and there prince and noble were made to experience, if they did not understand, that knowledge is power.

It does not follow that, because at the commencement of the sixteenth century, scholasticism had done its work, it never had a work to do. Scholasticism had from the end of the fourteenth century, or the begining of the fifteenth, ceased to be a living system of philosophy, prepared to anticipate, to meet, and to control the spiritual requirements of the age; and the students at the university diminished in number when it was found .that the instruction offered was adapted rather for the amusement of pedants than for the business of life.

As applied directly to education, the system of the schoolmen was not designed so much to supply food for thought, as to create the power of digesting it when it had been elsewhere supplied. The object was not to sow the seed, but to plough the intellectual soil. The attempt was to fabricate the steam-engine, and, when this was done, men were too often prepared to gaze at the fabric with wonder, instead of lighting the fire to set it in motion. Men continued to be busy in doctoring the soul, when the inner man was pining for food; they were occupied in improving the plough when it was necessary for the sower to go forth and to sow the seed; when men were preparing to rush they knew not where for the discovery of new worlds, the heads of universities were still questioning the power of their locomotives. The schools, we are told by one who would not have admitted the charge if a love of truth had not impelled him to proclaim it, "were full of quirks and sophistry: all things, whether taught or written, seemed trite and inane. No pleasant streams of humanity or mythology were gliding from among us. Scholars were inconstant and wavering, and could not apply themselves to an ordinary search of anything. They rather made choice of than embraced those things which their reason was capable of."* In short, the leading principles of scholasticism had been petrified into a mere formula. Words were used to which no definite meaning was attached. The schools were occupied in questioning and answering; in laying down theses and counter-theses; in arguments and counter-arguments; in splitting the matter of doctrines according to a stereotyped system. To this the young mind was not willing to submit when fresh sources of information had opened to the European intellect, through the circulation of Greek literature and through the application of the art of printing to the fabrication of books of a more enlarged and general literature.

It was known in England that Italy was awakened to the new learning,—that there was an enthusiasm for Greek, and for all that pertained to classical literature.

The movement in favour of reform commences with an energetic minority; and they who are eloquent upon the ignorance displayed in the English universities, because instances may be adduced of pedantic folly, ought to bear in mind that, when it was found, that the Greek and Latin as pronounced at Oxford and Cambridge was regarded as barbarous by the rising scholars of Italy, an importation of learned Italians was effected, for the better instruction of Oxford. So early as the year 1488, or earlier, Cornelius

* Wood, i. 665.

Vitellius was appointed Greek Professor ; and we are proud of the fact, that it was at Oxford that Erasmus learned Greek ; that an Englishman, an Oxonian, Grocyn, was his instructor ; and that to the talent and real substantial learning which he found in the English universities he bore grateful testimony throughout his life, and on all suitable occasions.

It was soon after Warham's promotion to the councils of Henry VII, when his influence at the court was great, that several of the most distinguished scholars of the day set out on their travels, and proceeded to Italy to make themselves masters of "the new learning."

They went with the full sanction of the English Government ; and, as Warham was of that Government a distinguished member, we may presume that to him they were indebted for their introduction not only to the schools and universities of Italy, but also to the courts of Italian princes.

Of these persons all continued to live on terms of friendship with Warham throughout his life ; he evinced towards them the generosity of a patron without the air of patronage, and they contributed to his enjoyment of a retired life, when he ceased to act as a statesman, a judge or a courtier.

These persons raised the character of England intellectually, as its character was elevated politically by Wolsey. We have the authority of Erasmus himself for saying that next to those of Italy, and scarcely inferior to them, the schools of England were to be ranked ; and that a visit to England was to a man of learning a sufficient compensation, if circumstances prevented his making a pilgrimage to Italy. Although Wolsey was too great a man not to be a patron of literature, his time was so completely occupied by political business that he was the Mecænas rather than the companion of learned men. Henry VIII. was a man of varied accomplishments, interested in literary pursuits, and himself a literary man ; he was affable and accessible ; yet, between love of business and love of pleasure, he had no time to spare, and the court of a great king differed from the courts of the princes of Italy. Men of learning were the occasional visitors rather than the *habitués* of his palace. It was in the manor houses of Archbishop Warham, that learned men found a scholar, imparting and receiving information, using his high station to confer benefits, and forgetting them before gratitude could express its thanks.

Among the foremost of the great men who introduced "the new learning" from Italy, and enjoyed the friendship of the archbishop, Thomas Linacre deserves to be mentioned. Having studied at both of the English universities, he established in each a professorship of Greek. He is present, in his good works, with our own generation, for he was the founder and first president of the College of Physicians. As a physician, a philologist, and a divine, Linacre was celebrated ; he is described by Erasmus as " vir non exacti tantum, sed severi judicii." He studied in Italy, and contracted a friendship with the leading scholars of the age. To Warham he was indebted for the Church preferment which rescued him from the mere drudgery of the medical profession, and enabled him to direct his attention to the higher branches of physical science.*

William Grocyn was a Wykehamist, a schoolfellow of Warham. When, in 1497, Erasmus studied at Oxford, Grocyn had the honour of being his instructor. Grocyn

* Wood, Biog. Brit. ; Fuller, Frein, History of Physic Jortin's Erasmus, Erasmi Epist.

was received as a welcome guest in houses of the highest distinction in Italy, and was intimate with the Medicean family. He had a stall in Lincoln cathedral, but depended chiefly upon the income derived from the mastership of All Hallows College, Maidstone, a piece of preferment conferred upon him by our archbishop.*

Warham extended his friendship to William Latimer, who, having been at one time the tutor of Reginald Pole, assisted Erasmus, in after life, in preparing the second edition of his New Testament for the press. Of William Latimer, it was said by Erasmus that he was " vere theologus, integritate vitæ conspicuus." †

Of Sir Thomas More it is unnecessary to speak. I write not for those who cannot appreciate and admire his calm wisdom, his ever-ready wit, his almost prophetic sagacity in union with a guileless simplicity of character, his inflexible integrity, his sense of justice, his tenacity of purpose. His royal murderer admitted him into a friendship, the hollowness of which was foreseen by More ; and was evinced when More preferred obedience to the dictates of conscience to a compliance with the mandate of a capricious despot.

Whether William Lilly laboured much at the university after his return from foreign travel, is not clear, but it is certain that, having acquired a mastery of the Greek language, he taught it in London ; and to our own generation he has spoken, though now no longer, in the " Propria quæ maribus " and the " As in præsenti." Lilly's Greek Grammar was in use at Winchester School at the commencement of this century. All is now swept away, but St. Paul's School

* Leland, Wood, Bale, Tanner, Jortin's Erasmus, Knight's Erasmus, Knight's Colet.

† Wood, Jortin, Knight, Erasmi Ep.

has a right to boast of its first master, as it has of its founder John Colet; to whom we shall have occasion more particularly to refer.[*]

Lilly studied at Rhodes, and the less learned Colet in Italy, but there is no proof that either of them had visited Florence. Linacre, Grocyn, and William Latimer had, on the contrary, shared the patronage of Lorenzo de Medici, when he had rendered Florence attractive to the student in art, in science, and in letters. They had studied also at Padua and at Rome. Doubtless they had been associated, when at Florence, with the friends and disciples of Savonarola. They had become influenced, if not directly, yet through the instrumentality of others, by the doctrines propounded by that pure-minded man. They returned to England, reformers—not after the model of Protestantism, which did not yet exist,—but still resolved to effect a reformation in the conduct of the clergy, in the management of the monasteries, and in the teaching of the universities. Their inclination was to depreciate scholasticism and mysticism, which they found chiefly in the convents, and they acted under the full conviction that all reformation must commence with the study of the Bible in its original languages.

Such were the contemporaries of Warham, and such their principles; they were Erasmians, although to Erasmus some had acted as teachers.

Erasmus does not appear to have made any great impression or to have won many friendships during his first visit to England. So far from being at that time an accomplished Greek scholar, to Oxford and to Grocyn he was, as we have said, indebted for his first acquaintance with that language.

---

[*] Pits, Bale, Tanner, Wood, Fuller, Knight's Colet.

To Erasmus, to his intimacy with Warham, and to the influence which that intimacy had on the mind of the archbishop we shall have occasion hereafter to revert. We have only to repeat that these university reforms took place antecedently to the reformation of the Church. The opinions of those by whom the university reform was conducted were opposed to Lutheranism, when, about the year 1518, the name of Martin Luther was held up to execration to his subjects of England by the royal polemic, King Henry VIII.

That these and similar proceedings, amounting to a revolution in the university system of education, should meet with opposition, is only what we should have expected. The advocates of change and reform are often as narrow-minded as their opponents, and the most illiberal in their temper are often men who are loudest in the advocacy of liberal principles.

It is happily ordered for the steady advancement of society, that two classes of mind should be in continual action and counteraction; the one class taking for their watchword " *Festina*," the other adding " *lente*." Between the two classes of mind the wise man is to legislate; he sounds the alarum bell to awaken the supine, and he places the drag-chain on the chariot-wheels if a Jehu shall be acting as the charioteer. In the historian, the vice to be avoided is intolerance on either side, a vice from which few historians can extricate themselves, especially when politics or religion are concerned. One cannot but feel sometimes, that the historian who denounces persecution with vehement eloquence would himself have considered the stake as more convincing than the press, if he had lived when fire and fagot were the order of the day.

Party feeling ran high at both the universities when Warham was Chancellor of Oxford, and Fisher

Chancellor of Cambridge. Both at Cambridge and at Oxford a party of Trojans were formed who feared the Greeks " et dona ferentes," and ridiculed the purists who made the style of Cicero the model of Latin composition. The party originated in the wit of the young ; it was afterwards increased by some who ought to have been wiser ; and those who remember how, half a century ago, they could hardly restrain their laughter when the head of a house, from the university pulpit, declared against the system of examinations, then newly introduced, warning his audience that it would end in the world giving them " the bye-go," will not be surprised to hear that, even from the university pulpit, the study of Greek was denounced, when that study was forced upon every student. But, even when they are blinded by party rage, men are not altogether fools ; and we must remember that, although they had little to say in vindication of their conduct, still something was adduced which commended itself to the mind of dullards. What they objected to was not the study of Greek on the part of the learned few, but the forcing its study on all members of the university. It was said to be useless to encourage the study, since in the Vulgate the student of theology had a version of Scripture of which the authority was equal to that of the original. As to Ciceronian Latin, it was represented as absurd, when Latin was used to express modern ideas, to bind oneself down to a model which was not with those ideas even remotely connected. In this opinion Erasmus himself to a certain extent coincided. The war waxed strong ; there were on the one side a Hector and a Paris, supported occasionally by a Priam, but they fought against the novelties in vain. By those who regard as fools and persecutors all who are in authority, reference is sometimes made to this party, as a proof of the blindness of the universities to the requirements of the times. But when we remember, that the Greeks were soon able, in recording their literary exploits, to say "Troja fuit," we may be excused if we arrive at an opposite conclusion. It is granted that there was opposition; but when we mention the names of Grocyn, Linacre, Tunstal, More, Colet, and the two chancellors Warham and Fisher, and when we add to this the testimony of Erasmus, who places the English universities in the van of the educational institutions in Europe, we regard the opposition as insignificant though it was troublesome; and we may see, in the antecedent reform of the universities, the foundation laid of those principles which led, in due course, to the reformation of the Church.

Such controversies as these must be of continual occurrence so long as human nature, in its virtues and in its faults, remains such as it is. There were difficulties, however, in the way of Warham which were peculiar to the age in which he lived. The controversies between Greek and Trojan were put down, with the usual weapons of controversy, by those great men whose names have just been given. Antecedently to this controversy, there had been a dispute between Northerners and the Southerners, such as we have seen prevailing in former years, though never before with so much temerity and fierceness. In the High Street, in the front of St. Mary's Church, a battle had been fought, in which three scholars had been wounded, and some had lost their lives. Among the wounded or slain were some of high standing in the university, under which head we may perhaps class some of the young scions of the aristocracy. It is only thus we can account for the extreme violence with which the nobility, as a class, are said

to have urged the king, Henry VII, to cancel the
university charter. The feeling against the university
was so strong, that nothing but Warham's influence
with the king could have saved it. While acting as a
buttress without, Archbishop Warham was also a pillar
giving support to the university by his benefactions.
His contributions were munificent towards the completion of St. Mary's Church and the erection of the
divinity school.

The charter of the university was again in jeopardy
at the commencement of the new reign; but Warham obtained from Henry VIII. a renewal of the
charter of King Edward IV, and he also secured for
Oxford the honour of a royal visit in 1510. Upon
several of the nobles, as if to conciliate them, degrees
were at this time conferred.

The attention of the chancellor was directed to the
very unsatisfactory state of the university statutes.
All things were in a state of transition. Some of
the statutes had become obsolete, others required to
be adapted to the altered state of society. As in the
courts of law, so in the university, there were informers, who were constantly exacting money, under the
threat of prosecution for the non-obedience of statutes
which had long fallen into desuetude. Young men
found themselves sometimes accused of perjury. They
went, in their alarm, to the commissioners. By the
commissioners licence was given to the students to
select advocates from the regents, and to the regent
masters licence was given to absolve the students
from the penalties attached to the disregard of the
statutes. This was a state of things so unsatisfactory,
that Warham appointed another commission to reduce
the statutes and ordinances into some intelligible
method. The commissioners found the difficulties so

many, or their caution was so great, that their progress did not keep up with the impatience of the university reformers.   There were, at the same time, frequent misunderstandings between the university and
the civic authorities to be settled : and new regulations
had to be made with reference to the election of proctors.   In short, Warham encountered the difficulties
to which every one is exposed who, in attempting to
reform, desires to act according to precedent, and to
pay a due regard to all vested interests.   There was
much talk of university reform, and little progress
was made in it.   In 1518, the subject was brought
before Wolsey.   The king and Queen Katherine
being in progress, arrived with a splendid retinue at
Abingdon, and took up their abode in the abbey.
The queen unexpectedly signified her intention of
visiting Oxford, and a loyal reception she met with
from the masters and the students.   The visit had not
been previously planned, and, when the royal pleasure
was signified to the authorities, the chancellor was
unable to reach Oxford soon enough to take his place
at the head of his university.   He was at Otford,
whither a despatch was forwarded to him containing
an account of the proceedings.   The scholars had
welcomed the queen with every demonstration of
love and joy.   After visiting the several places of
interest, she paid her devotions at St. Frideswide's
Priory, to the sacred relics of that virgin saint ;
and that done, says Anthony à Wood, " she vouchsafed
to condescend so low as to dine with the Mertonians,
for the sake of the late warden (Rawlins), at this
time almoner to the king, notwithstanding she was
expected by other colleges."*   On her departure, Cardinal Wolsey honoured the Convocation House with

* Wood, II. i. 14.

his presence. He was surrounded by the nobles and others who held office in his household; and "he spake an oration," in which he declared his *readiness at all times to serve* the university to the best of his ability. His words were not idle words. He was always grand in his conceptions, and thoroughly practical. He signified his immediate intention of founding new professorships to meet the requirements of the age; and, alluding to the difficulties which had arisen from the unsatisfactory state of the statutes, he offered his services to correct and reform them, to remove the discrepancies which had lately given rise to many complaints, and to render them conformable to the altered circumstances of the times.

The proposal was accepted with enthusiasm by those who had become impatient through the dilatoriness of Warham. The grievances were great and practical; any day any person might be subjected to annoyance from an obnoxious neighbour threatening prosecution for a breach of the statutes; scrupulous consciences were only half satisfied by confession, and an alternation of repenting and sinning and sinning and repenting. The system of prosecuting for the non-observance of obsolete statutes, which had excited the public feeling against the Ecclesiastical Courts, was adopted by reformers in the university. The dilatoriness, it was urged, of Warham argued either incapacity, or inattention to the business; and here was the first man of the age offering to bring down his mind from high affairs of state to this comparatively small matter. Wolsey was at the height of his popularity. His talents, great as they were, were magnified in men's minds. They whispered of his low origin, they saw him an ἀναξ ἀνδρῶν. He was avaricious of work. Up to this time, in whatever he had attempted he had succeeded. He was a man of progress. Although not a man of technical learning himself, yet he was the patron of learned men. The character of the lectures he proposed to institute indicated the direction his reform would take—he proposed to endow professorships in medicine, philosophy, mathematics, Greek, rhetoric, and humanity; and, at the same time, he established new chairs in theology and civil law. His ideas with respect to his new college, if vague, were sufficient to convince the heads of the university, that they had to deal with one of the master spirits of the age.

Anthony à Wood believed that the intention of Wolsey was to do all that in him lay to further the interests of the university, and in this opinion the impartial reader will concur. His natural disposition, self-reliant and haughty, loved power; but his object in obtaining power was to be a benefactor, not of himself only, but of his Church and country. His was an enlarged selfishness, which made his Church and country only part of himself. One grand mark of superiority he possessed: he left a sense of his power impressed on the minds of all who approached him. Offensive by his self-assertion to those who were proud like himself, he inspired confidence in all who, conscious of their own weakness, desired to find the arm on which they reclined equal to the weight they put upon it.

To the members of the university it appeared, that they had, at length, secured the services of the very man, who could, if he were willing, effect through his influence with the king and pope, the object they had in view.

It appears extraordinary, that the university should have taken for granted, that Warham should at once

T 2

have acceded to these proposals; and we have, in
his conduct on this occasion, an instance of that disregard to the feelings and privileges of others which
involved Wolsey in much unpopularity. He thought
not of the chancellor of the university, but assumed
at once, that he who had not objected to the exercise
of legatine authority, would acquiesce, without remonstrance, in a measure of reform which the chancellor
had failed to effect, but which the legate, armed with
the exceptional powers of a dictator, would be able to
accomplish. Warham perceived the state of the case.
He had undoubtedly given his consent to the appointment of a legate *à latere*, but he was not prepared to
acquiesce in Wolsey's assumption, that the powers with
which he was invested extended to the university.
But if the all-powerful favourite chose to interfere,
opposition would be useless. He protested, but did
not offer opposition; he contented himself with warning the university, that the measure proposed was
exceptional and revolutionary.

In a well-written Latin letter, he reminded the
university that to make and to reform the statutes
was a duty which devolved upon and was attached to
" the venerable society of regent and non-regent
masters " acting as a council to the chancellor. He
observes that " all the statutes of the university do in
general, and severally, tend to the advancement of
learning and scholastic discipline; if the whole
authority respecting such statutes should devolve upon
any person besides those who are at this time vested
with it, the university, considered as a society, would
be dissolved. A mere empty name, a shadow of power
would only remain to it, and the authority which it
formerly exercised wholly terminate in the person to
whom you desire it to be transferred. But if the

cardinal should be pleased to declare his sentiments concerning a regulation of the statutes, or in what respects he would have them altered, restored, or methodized,.and should lay his scheme to that end before the university for their confirmation, if it should appear so salutary and well concerted as might justly be expected from him, there would then be no question but all persons would readily come into it."

The letter had no effect. Wolsey, who revolted from the control of parliament, was not likely to permit himself to act as the mere servant of the Convocation of Oxford. Besides, there was an inconsistency in Warham's argument. It was proposed for the occasion to supersede the authority of the chancellor, simply on the ground that the evil was so great, that exceptional legislation had become necessary. The constitutional authority to which Warham referred, had been found insufficient to supply a remedy. An enthusiasm was excited in favour of Wolsey. The university expressed its pride at the high position in Church and State which had been achieved, through his transcendent abilities, by one of the alumni of Oxford. A decree was proposed, and unanimously passed on the 1st of June, investing the cardinal with full power, on his own authority, to revise the statutes, and make such regulations for the better government of the university as might be suggested to his wisdom.*

* The resemblance between Oxford and Otford has misled Fiddes, who supposes that Warham was at Oxford during these transactions. The letters may be found in Fiddes' Collections, Nos. 16, 17, 18, 19, 20, 21. On this and one or two other occasions, Wolsey and Warham are addressed as "Your majesty." The words to Warham are "*et dum felicissime vivat Majestas tua.*" It was not appropriated *exclusively* to crowned heads till a later period. Modern biographers of Wolsey are sometimes guilty of an anachronism, by calling him "his eminence." The title *eminentissimi* was conceded to the cardinals by Pope Urban VIII. in the year 1631.

Although the name of the chancellor is not attached to the decree, yet the conduct of the cardinal, or rather of the university, made no alteration in the friendly relations between Warham and Wolsey. Warham, a theorist, contended, lukewarmly, for a principle; Wolsey, as a practical man, sought only for power. Of the letters already presented to the reader, several were written, in the most friendly terms, subsequently to the events just narrated.

We find the two prelates acting in concurrence under circumstances far more offensive to our feelings. About the year 1521, the works of Luther had obtained circulation in the university of Oxford. It had not been long before, that the name of this celebrated man had been first heard beyond the schools of Wittenberg. It was on 31st of October, 1517, that Europe was electrified by the publication of his Theses. The events of his history then proceeded in rapid succession. His interview with Cajetan took place at Augsburg, in the following year, and in 1519, his interview with Miltitz, his controversy with Eck, and his dispute at Leipsic. In 1520 he had been excommunicated by the pope, and in the December of that year he burnt the bull and the papal decrees. Every one was now interested in watching his conduct, and surmising what that conduct would be at the Diet of Worms.

That he should have sympathisers in England as elsewhere was only to be expected; but they were comparatively few in number. It did not follow that, because Warham was an advocate of reform, he must also be a follower of Luther. The king was still popular; and the king was an enemy of Luther. What would happen if it should come to the king's ears that there were many in either university who received with approbation the writings of the king's opponent, it was difficult to say. It is pardonable if those who were at the head of affairs took alarm. Warham, always timid, was much excited when he received a letter making inquiry upon the subject from the cardinal. Warham's reply we possess. The alarm was great.

"It is," he said, "a sorrowful thing to see how greedily inconstant men, and specially inexpert youth, falleth to new doctrines, be they never so pestilent, and how prone they be to attempt that thing that they be forbidden of their superiors for their own wealth. I would I had suffered great pain on condition this had not fortuned there, where I was brought up in learning and now am chancellor, albeit unworthy. And I doubt not but it is to your good grace right powerful hearing, seeing your grace is the most honourable member that ever was of that university.

"And where the said university hath instantly desired me by their letters to be a mean and suitor unto your grace for them, that it might please the same to decree such order to be taken, touching the examination of the said persons suspected of heresy, that the said university run in as little infamy thereby through your grace's favour and justice as may be after the quality of the offence.

"If this matter concerned not the cause of God and His Church, I would entirely beseech your Grace to tender the infamy of the university as it might please your incomparable wisdom and goodness to think best. For pity it were that, through the lewdness of one or two cankered members, which as I understand have induced no small number of young and uncircumspect fools to give ear unto them, the whole university should run in the infamy of so heinous a crime, the hearing whereof should be right delectable and pleasant to the open Lutherans beyond the sea, and secrete behyther, whereof they would take heart and confidence that their pestilent doctrines should increase and multiply, seeing both the universities of England infected therewith, whereof the one hath many years been void of heresies, and the other hath before now taken upon her the praise that she was never defiled; and nevertheless now she is thought to be the original occasion and case of the fall in Oxford." *

We can easily understand how the intolerant urged the king to make inquiries, and how both Wolsey and Warham feared lest an outbreak in favour of Lutheranism would be visited upon them.†

Both Warham and Wolsey admitted that a reformation was necessary : they were both of them prepared to conduct a reform, they were in consequence the more annoyed when, by their excesses, wrong-headed persons offered a real impediment to the reform which they would fain effect. But we may affirm both of Warham and of Wolsey, that they were neither of them persons of a cruel disposition. Many a lordly persecutor assumes to be, and has a character for being a philanthropist.

In the early part of his career we find Warham sitting in judgment upon heretics, and at the close of his career, under the command of Henry, he was obliged to do the same. In 1511, six men, most of them

---

* Ellis, Third Series, i. 239.

† Fuller speaks of Warham as a persecutor, "especially towards his latter end." He says "he was a still and silent persecutor of poor Christians." He gives no authority for the statement, and Fuller is no authority himself. We know that by poor Christians were meant those whose principles were the same as Fuller's ; but it is difficult to know what is meant by stillness and silence. How were the stillness and silence penetrated by the worthy historian? It is more remarkable that Foxe, who has a keen eye for a persecutor, while holding up to reprobation Fitzjames, bishop of London, and Nix, bishop of Norwich, does not, so far as I can find, conjoin with theirs the name of Warham. The age was cruel, men were doomed to death for the most trifling offences; and I doubt not that Warham would have pronounced sentence upon a heretic, if it had pertained to his office to do so. But I do not think that he was a man more cruel than some zealots of a later period, who might be named.

natives of Tenterden, were summoned before the archbishop's court, then sitting at Knowle. They had declared that, in the sacrament of the altar, the consecrated elements were not the body and blood of Christ, but material bread and wine. They rejected the sacrament of baptism, and held confirmation and confession to be unnecessary. Marriage also they considered as unprofitable to the soul; they denied extreme unction, pilgrimages, and saint-worship.

With the exception of their opinion with respect to matrimony and baptism, what they asserted would now be generally received; but, regarded from Warham's standing point, they would appear to him as revolutionary. Heresy was prevalent at Tenterden, for the court resumed in the afternoon to receive the abjuration of two other men from the same place. The court sat again on the 5th of May, when the archbishop pronounced judgment. A penance was enjoined. The abjurors were to wear the badge of a fagot in flames on their clothes during their lives, or until they received a dispensation. They were required, in the cathedral church of Canterbury, and each in his own parish church, to go in procession carrying a fagot on his shoulders, a sign that, though pardoned, they had incurred the highest penalty of the law.

The court sat at Lambeth on the 15th of May. Many abjurations were received; a few persons were handed over to the secular power as relapsed heretics; but, though they were condemned, there is no record of their execution, and we may feel so sure that if execution had taken place the fact would have been discovered and proclaimed with exultation by Foxe, that we may charitably conclude that they were permitted to escape. The policy of Warham and Wolsey was to keep things quiet by enforcing the rigour of the law; but we

CHAP.
II.
～～～
William
Warham.
1503–32.

must remember that the vindictive feelings had not as yet been excited on either side. Warham and Wolsey were human beings like ourselves; they no more delighted in deeds of blood than any modern philanthropists; what philanthropists can do when their passions have been excited enthusiastically in favour of a cause, we may read in the history of the French Revolution. The idea of murdering men for their opinions is horrible enough; but many horrible acts have been done by well-designing men. We must, at the same time, remember that there was a large body of men, vehement, as men in every age have been vehement, for the suppression of those who deviated from the constituted order of things. By these persons the primate and the bishops generally were severely censured as being lukewarm in their prevention of heresy. Royalty itself was enlisted on the side of intolerance. The king had written against Luther, and were the bishops to be less zealous against the pestilent heresy of Germany than their royal master?* The feelings of the common people were excited on the same side. There was a violent feeling against the foreign merchants and mechanics who were settled in London. The foreigners were watched with a jealous eye. The Germans were suspected of heresy. We are surprised to read of four merchants

---

* Of King Henry's book against Luther I have not occasion to speak. Henry must have foreseen that Luther would attribute any merit which the book possessed to those who assisted the king in its composition. He would represent the king as merely nominally its author. The king, anticipating this, was careful not to consult divines. He did consult Sir Thomas More, a layman; but, from a letter from Pace to Wolsey, it would appear that the king did not consult even Wolsey. There is no more ground for doubting the authenticity of Henry's book than there is for doubting the authenticity of the Life of Julius Cæsar by Louis Napoleon.

of the Steelyard doing penance at St. Paul's Cross, for having, without a dispensation, eaten meat on a Friday. The party feeling must have been violent which pushed matters to such an extreme, in an age of much practical laxity, when Cardinal Wolsey himself was accustomed—under a dispensation to meet the cravings of his appetite for the support of his overtaxed frame,—to regale on flesh on days of abstinence. The penance was performed under circumstances of more than ordinary solemnity. It occurred in 1521. The well-fed cardinal attended, under an escort of eleven bishops. At the west door of St. Paul's he was censed, and "under a canopy of gold," held by four doctors. He went in procession up the nave to the high altar, where he made his oblation. The procession then returned to St. Paul's Cross. There on an elevated platform a throne was erected to receive him, "under a cloth of estate." On his right hand, but upon seats on a level with his feet, sat the pope's ambassador and the humiliated Primate of All England; on his left the imperial ambassador and the Lord Bishop of Durham: the other bishops sat on two forms, "outer right forth."* The sermon was preached by Bishop Fisher, and was pointed against Lutheranism. The same subject was treated by the Bishop of Rochester in the sermon he preached at the penance of Dr. Barnes. Dr. Barnes had been tried for heresy, and, sentence being given against him, he was compelled to bear a fagot.

* Letters and Papers of Henry VIII. 481. Wolsey was, during the year 1521, particularly active in his endeavours to suppress Lutheranism. There is a letter of his to Booth, bishop of Hereford, in which the bishop is required to cause search to be made for all books and pamphlets composed or edited by Martin Luther, and within fourteen days to give account of them to the cardinal.— Ibid. 487.

That Warham was not a persecutor, and that he desired to allow to every one the latitude granted by the Church, is revealed to us by his conduct towards Dean Colet, whose case I have reserved for special consideration. The subject is in this connexion the more important, because, by knowing the principles of Colet, we may infer those of the archbishop.

John Colet was a man of fortune, the son of Sir Henry, sometime Lord Mayor of London. He was in after life vehement in denouncing the abuses of the Church; but at its commencement, he himself exhibited an example of the maladministration of the Church's preferment. He was only nineteen when he was preferred to the great living of Denington,* in Suffolk, a piece of preferment which he held afterwards with the deanery of St. Paul's, and kept to his dying day. He had a prebend in the cathedral of York. His father also presented him to the church of Thoyning, in the diocese of Lincoln.† He had stalls in the church of St. Mary-le-Grand, and in the cathedral of Salisbury. These preferments he obtained before he was even in deacon's orders; it was doubtful whether he were even a sub-deacon or more than an acolyte.‡

Thus splendidly endowed, John Colet studied at

---

* The income of this living of Denington amounts at the present time to 850l. a year. The population is considerable.

† I do not find this living in the Clergy List, unless it be Thurning. We have the presentation to the living, which was probably purchased by Sir Henry as a good investment. "*Henricus Colet, miles—Præsentamus dilectum nobis Johannem Colet, Rectorem eccles. paroch. B. Mariæ de Denyngton Norvic. dioc.; ad ecclesiam de Thoyning dioc. vestræ modo vacantem per mortem Ricardi ultimi rectoris. Dat. ult. die mensis Sept. 1490. Reg. Russel ad Lincoln.*"

‡ Knight, 20. He remarks that Calet was the usual mode of pronouncing Colet, and that this title gave name to Colet's family.

Oxford, and probably at Cambridge.* On the conclusion of his studies at the English universities, he
went first to Paris and then to Italy. Whether he
went in company with his distinguished countrymen,
of whom mention has been made before, is more than
doubtful; but that he formed in Italy an intimacy with
Grocyn, Linacre, William Lilly, and William Latimer
is certain. We know of Grocyn and of Linacre that
they were admitted into the highest literary circles of
Florence, and shared the studies of the Medicean
princes. If Colet had also been at Florence, such an important fact in his history would not have been omitted.
He was at Rome, and there he probably met with
Grocyn and Linacre, with William Lilly, who had
lately arrived from Rhodes, and they all went to Padua,
where William Latimer was perfecting himself in
Greek. These were all friends of Warham, and all
found in him a protector or a patron. The study of
Greek was an European enthusiasm, and to introduce
those studies, or rather to render them a part of the
curriculum at Oxford, was their object, and in this
object they succeeded. On their return home they
were each of them engaged in raising the literary
character of their country; finding a home, whenever they required one, in the mansions of the
archbishop, who, soon after their return, retired from
public life.

Colet repaired to Oxford. He declined applying for
priest's orders, from the tender regard, as Knight supposes, which he had to the dignity of the sacred office
and function, though this regard did not prevent him
from enjoying the emoluments of a pluralist. He did
not hold any office under government, and, therefore,
on his ordination, he would have been compelled to dis-

* Polydore Vergil, 6. vi.

charge the duties of a parish priest for which he was not prepared. He thought, no doubt, that with his foreign experience he might be more usefully employed as a lecturer at Oxford;* and, as a Master of Arts, he was not only authorized to lecture, but, strictly speaking, he was required to do so.

The young man's lecture-room was filled, not merely by undergraduates, but by doctors in divinity and law, by abbots, and dignitaries of the Church, proving what has been stated before, that, although there were opponents to the new learning, there was no attempt on the part of the authorities at the university to put it down. He only met with that opposition which was sure to be raised against him by those who, in their interpretation of Scripture had committed themselves to a system of interpretation adverse to that which Colet maintained. It would appear that the other young men who had visited Italy had agreed, when they returned to England, to commence their work by expounding the Epistles of St. Paul; for a similar course was pursued at Cambridge.† At Oxford, Colet became acquainted with Erasmus, and he received from Erasmus some of those well-turned compliments with which that great scholar repaid his benefactors. We gather from the letters of Erasmus, that Colet was a man of great ability; not a good Greek scholar, but a plain-spoken, honest man, who had great command over language, so as to make himself thoroughly intelligible when handling a difficult subject. He was, however, a man of hasty temper, who, when assailed, so spoke as to convert an opponent into an enemy.

* As M.A. he might lecture at Oxford; but could not lecture elsewhere until he was a doctor, except by special licence.
† Knight, 26, 28.

The labours not of Colet only or chiefly, but of that learned band of brothers who had gone from the English universities to Italy, thence to bring forth the new learning, were successful, and the success was rapid as well as great. It must have been after their time that Erasmus uttered the memorable sentence, that he found so much learning and polish in England —not mere shallow learning, but profound and exact, both in Latin and Greek—that, except for his being able to say that he had been there, he should have ceased to entertain a wish to visit Italy.

While Colet was lecturing at Oxford, Warham was Lord High Chancellor of England; and to his influence with King Henry VII. we are to attribute Colet's appointment to the deanery of St. Paul's. There it was open for Colet to pursue his career as a lecturer, and he had a more extended sphere of action. The learning of the university was now brought to bear on the metropolis. In London as at Oxford his persuasive and lucid eloquence gathered around him large congregations from the court as well as from the city. The rich and the noble sat with the merchant and his apprentices. Jesus Christ and Him crucified was the one subject of his discourse. He did not split hairs with the schoolmen, but he adhered to the New Testament and the Apostles' Creed. This was to him an exhaustless subject.

But, with all his merits—and the merits of the founder of St. Paul's School were many and great— Colet had faults which made him unpopular. He was narrow-minded; he could not take one side without becoming a vehement assailant of those who walked not with him; he could not uphold the new learning without attacking Thomas Aquinas, and his language was often violent and incautious. He had

devoted admirers and friends; but the enemies of such
a man were likely to be bitter. He made himself a
party man in London when to form a party was inex-
pedient, and by a strong party he was, of course,
opposed. He was, moreover, ascetic in his habits, and
not given to hospitality, when hospitality was a de-
canal virtue, not to be dispensed with.

The word "hospitality" in the middle age had a
more extensive signification than it has at the present
time. The dean and each member of the chapter had
to provide, at his own expense, a common table for
the members of the establishment of every degree.
This was indeed the remuneration of the subordinate
members of the corporation. At first, a common fund
was established; but this fund was in process of time
broken up,—the members of the chapter received divi-
dends, and the inferior officers stipends. Still the
custom of keeping hospitality lingered in many
cathedrals, and in a modified state remained to our
own times. Each dean and prebendary during his
residence kept a certain number of public days; this
was especially the case in Durham. In Colet's time,
hospitality was in a transition state. The various
officers of St. Paul's cathedral received their salaries,
and they expected the dean to keep a table for them,
if not, as in times past, every day, yet probably on
every festival of the Church, at a time when festivals
were numerous. We can easily understand how these
entertainments in London, among the lower class of
the clergy and their dependents, degenerated into
riotous living, and brought discredit on religion. The
austere dean determined to effect a reform. The
munificence of the founder of St. Paul's school was
such as to secure him from the suspicion of penuriousness, and Colet acted probably with the full

approbation of Warham and the higher ranks of the clergy. It is not precisely what you do that gives offence, but an unhappy manner of doing it. Colet so conducted his reform as to excite against himself the animosity of all the underlings of his church. The dean found it more difficult to contend with the Cretan bellies of his petty canons, than to struggle against the Bœotian intellects of his opponents at Oxford.

The Bishop of London was Richard Fitzjames.[*] He was a violent party man, and his party was directly

[*] Richard Fitzjames, descended from an ancient and knightly family, was born at Redlinch, in Somersetshire. Dallaway gives his pedigree. Educated at Merton College, Oxford, he became a fellow in 1465. He served the office of proctor in 1473, and on the 12th of March, 1483, he was elected warden. In the same year he became vice-chancellor. He was a student, and became a Scotist. Like a Calvinist in those days, he confounded his scholastic opinions with Christianity, and, as they do, regarded as undeserving the name of Christian any whose opinion did not accord with his own. He does not appear to have been more intolerant than some modern prelates of strong party feelings, though he was invested with more terrible powers to enforce his doctrines. He held a prebend in the Cathedral of Wells, in the year 1475, and of that church became a residentiary. On September 18th, 1483, he was appointed treasurer of St. Paul's. He was chaplain to Edward IV. and master of St. Leonard's Hospital, in Bedford. In June, 1495, he was Lord High Almoner to Henry VII. On the 21st of May, 1497, he was consecrated at Lambeth to the see of Rochester, and on the 29th of November, 1503, he was translated to Chichester. On the 2d of August, 1506, he was removed to the see of London. On the 11th of February, 1503, he preached the funeral sermon of Queen Elizabeth. He expended large sums of money in building, and encouraged magnificent works of architecture, particularly by completing the fabric of St. Mary's Church, at Oxford. His brother was Sir John Fitzjames, Lord Chief Justice, and in conjunction with him the bishop founded Burton School. He was mixed up with the sad story of Richard Hun, of which I shall have occasion hereafter to speak. He died Jan. 15, 1521, and was buried at St. Paul's.—Dallaway's Sussex, i. 67; Wood, Athenæ, ii. 720; Ang. Sac. i. 381; Fuller.

opposed to that which regarded the dean as one of its leaders. Colet dwelt upon the facts of Christianity, and thought scorn of the speculations of the school-men, while the party to which Fitzjames belonged reasoned *à priori*, and assumed the facts to be such as would substantiate their intuitions or their logical conclusions.

The underlings of St. Paul's were aware, that the bishop would be happy to support them in any charge of heresy they could bring against their dean. While they were opening their mouths in vain for a supply from the fleshpots, the dean was providing the mental pabulum which they were unable to digest, and determined if possible to represent as poison.

Colet was incautious, or rather went out of his way to express his contempt for the theology of which the Bishop of London was the advocate. The dean declared he had searched Scripture in vain for any confirmation of the peculiar teaching of "the subtle doctor," who was an apostle to Fitzjames. It was not Fitzjames only that he offended : the theology of the Bishop of London was the theology of other divines, and in his proceedings against Colet he was supported by other prelates. The Bishop of London was himself a narrow-minded man, but we can hardly sympathize with those writers who represent the opponents of Colet as necessarily fools; nor can we excuse Colet from a charge of narrow-mindedness, though his narrowness lay in an opposite direction.

It was now that the patronage of Warham was needed to protect the weak against the strong. Charges were brought against the dean by the inferior clergy of St. Paul's, to which the bishop lent a ready ear.

The bishop could not, however, proceed summarily against the dean, or cite him, as he might have done a parochial clergyman, into his court. It is said "to pertain to the dignity of any member of a cathedral chapter, that it is only in chapter that the bishop can speak to him." The bishop, with reference to the chapter in a cathedral of secular clergy, neither had nor has, ordinary jurisdiction; his power is simply that of a visitor, and he can only interpose his authority at a visitation. To protect the dean and chapter from vexatious proceedings on the part of their visitor, the bishop cannot hold a visitation more frequently than once in seven years; unless he be requested by the dean and chapter to visit for the purpose of making new statutes; or unless a representation be made to him of the existence of abuses which require extraordinary powers to investigate. In the latter case, however, an appeal will lie against the visitor to the metropolitan. If it be alleged, that the pretext for a visitation is vexatious, the archbishop is to decide whether the visitation shall be held or not.

The Bishop of London signified to the dean and chapter of St. Paul's his intention to hold a visitation, that he might inquire into the doctrines advanced from the pulpit by the dean. The dean and chapter appealed. It was necessary on the appeal to state the specific charges which were to be brought against the dean, in order that the archbishop might judge whether they were of sufficient importance to render the visitation necessary. The charges in the present case were so trivial as to render the action of the bishop almost ridiculous. Colet was a disputatious man, and fond of argument; the archbishop therefore may have been afraid of his friend, lest he should in some way have committed himself. But it was found that in preaching he had confined himself to a simple exposition of Scripture. His vehemence, which was considerable, exhausted itself in condemning the inconsistent conduct and lives of ecclesiastics; he had not accused the Church of holding any unscriptural doctrine. He was not, indeed, prepared to do so. He desired to ascertain for himself, and to induce others to ascertain, what the Scriptures teach. What he could not find in Scripture he abstained from noticing. All that his accusers could do was to infer his heresy from his silence, and their inferences were sufficiently strange. It was said, that he had instructed the people that images ought not to be worshipped. If Colet was the companion of Erasmus, when Erasmus visited the shrine of St. Thomas of Canterbury, we can imagine that the preacher gave offence by his contemptuous manner of treating the subject. The *ipsissima verba* would have been produced if his language had been as provoking as his manner. But, be that as it may, this was the strong point with his opponents, who were hard pressed to substantiate their charges against him. The dean was lecturing on the twenty-first of St. John. The hungry subordinates of the cathedral were all attention. The cathedral was filled with an attentive audience. The preacher remarked on the repetition three times of the word " Pasce." He pointed out the forced construction placed upon Scripture not unfrequently by the schoolmen. They agreed, and the preacher agreed with them, that the word " Pasce, Pasce," twice repeated, were to be understood in a metaphorical sense; and that the reference was to spiritual food. But, when the word " Pasce " was repeated the third time, the petty canons had hitherto instructed the people to believe that our divine Master alluded to that virtue of hospitality in relation to things carnal in which the dean was deficient. It was considered monstrous, that the dean in his preaching should understand the injunction in a metaphorical sense. It was contrary to the doctrine of the schools, therefore it was heresy. We shall, in the progress of our history, find men accused of heresy because they have understood Scripture in a sense different from that adopted by Calvin ; it was the same evil principle which was now at work, resulting from an oblivion of our Lord's command that we should call no man master. They indeed, whose god was their belly, gloried in their shame, when on this ground they brought an accusation of heresy against the ascetic dean.

Bishop Fitzjames was not only a violent party man, a leader among the Scotists whom Colet attacked : he was also old, sensitive, and tetchy. It was the custom, as we are informed by Erasmus, for the clergy of the Church of England, at this period, to read their sermons ; the practice was censured by the "men of the new learning," and Colet had more than once complained that these written sermons were read in a cold, unaffecting manner. Now the Bishop of London was an offender in this respect, and the dean was accused of using the pulpit to bring the bishop of the diocese into discredit.

The archbishop, when the case was brought before him, saw that, at best, the proceeding originated in mere party feeling, the Scotists being anxious to silence an opponent, and that the flame of party spirit had been fanned by malice. He decided that the dean had not exceeded the limits which the Church permitted to freedom of thought and speech ; he gave judgment, accordingly, for the reformer against the prosecutor. The bishop appealed from the metropolitan to the king—another instance of the practical supremacy of the crown ; the king refused to interfere. The dean of St. Paul's remained unmolested, not the most discreet of men, but venerated for his learning, his sincerity and his piety.

If we are inclined to accuse Warham of indolence we must admit that his indolence did not imply lack of courage. His determination, as a reformer, is evinced in his choice of one so bold, so uncompromising, and plain-spoken as Colet to address the clergy when the convocation assembled in 1513. This took place before the appointment of Wolsey to the office of legate *à latere,* and confirms what has been said before of the reasons which induced Warham to submit to an arrangement which was a temporary degradation of himself. Warham had not the sagacity to see how necessary it was to commence with the reformation of the *Church.* His object was to reform the *clergy;* and, as the first step, he desired to expose their malpractices to public view. His opinions on this head concurred with those of Colet, and he compelled Colet, in opposition to his own inclinations, to the performance of an invidious and ungrateful office. The sermon delivered by Colet on this occasion is the more important, as it may be regarded as indicating the opinion of Warham.*

The preacher began by adverting to the fact, that he should have shrunk from the office, if the duty had not been imposed upon him " by the most reverend father and lord, the president of this Council." Following the example of the fathers of the Council of Constance, he was vehement in his denunciation of the

---

* The sermon, in Latin, is found in the Appendix to Knight. The date given by Knight is 1511. Burnet provides us with an abbreviated translation, and gives the date 1513. As Parliament did not sit in 1511, and did sit in 1513, we may presume that a convocation was not summoned for 1511, and I therefore take 1513 as the correct date.

pride and ambition of churchmen, their feastings, banquetings, vain babblings, sports, plays, hunting, hawking, lust, and concupiscence. All this is too rhetorical to be of much real value. He is more practical when he complains of the burdens of episcopal visitations; of the grand grievance of all, the corruption of the ecclesiastical courts; of various new inventions resorted to for the mere purpose of extorting money from the poor and needy; of the avarice of officials in the exaction of their dues; of the great abuses in the probate of wills and the sequestration of first-fruits; on the vigorous enforcement of laws which, through the fines imposed, brought profit to the court, and of the shameful neglect of all others that tend only to the reformation of manners. The crying evil of the ecclesiastical courts, for the reform of which Warham was prepared to make great sacrifices, is so strongly urged as to induce the supposition that before the sermon was delivered it was submitted to the inspection of the primate. Colet then again became rhetorical, and taking up the popular topics, warned the superior clergy, the "holy fathers," against simony and nepotism, whereby it happened that boys and blockheads and sots had obtained preferments in the Church.* He again became practical, and exhorted the bishops to put in force the canons which forbade any man in holy orders to be a merchant, a usurer, a hunter, a gamester, or a soldier; especially those canons which restrain the clergy from haunting taverns and from keeping company with suspected women. He boldly rebuked the bishops, who were, too many of them, anything but spiritual, earthly rather than

---

* The reference to boys holding preferments comes with a bad grace from Colet, but of this kind of inconsistency men are often guilty when they indulge in rhetorical phraseology.

heavenly, savouring of the things of this world more than of the spirit of Christ. He urges this the rather because he held high the priestly dignity, which is greater than royal or imperial dignity, and equal even to that of angels. He concludes with a peroration, eloquent from its earnestness and powerful from the evident sincerity of the speaker.

To what extent the advice of the preacher was followed is not recorded. We only know, as has been before narrated, that Warham gave up the cause of reformation in despair ; or rather that he permitted it to be attempted by Wolsey, armed with the extraordinary powers of a legate *à latere.*

Although Wolsey had no time, during the few years of his being at the head of the government, to carry any great measures into effect, he was thoroughly in earnest when he commenced his career as legate, and was jealous of Warham's interference.* He knew

* No one is more inclined to do justice to Wolsey than Mr. Brewer, and there is no one whose opinion is so worthy of attention in whatever relates to the reign of Henry VIII. He observes of Wolsey, " Throughout the whole period of his long administration, and through all his correspondence, it is remarkable how small a portion of his thoughts is occupied with domestic affairs, and with religious matters still less. Looking back upon the reign, and judging it, as we now do, by one great event and one only, it appears inconceivable that a man of so much penetration and experience should have taken so little interest in the religious movement of the day, and regarded Luther and the progress of the Reformation with so little concern." To this we must add that he would not permit others to act, when he was unable to act himself ; a fact from which we infer that he fully intended to direct his powerful mind to domestic and ecclesiastical affairs, when foreign politics would permit him to find the time. It is to be remembered that the title of Protestant had only been partially assumed in 1529, and that the Articles of Torgau were not drawn up till 1530. We may say that Wolsey's struggle, not merely for power but for existence, began in 1527.

that, if he had been himself the Primate of All England, he would not have permitted the Metropolitan
of York to be invested with powers which virtually,
though only for a time, superseded the authority of
the Archbishop of Canterbury, and he suspected that
Warham, though he had conceded the authority,
would be jealous of its exercise. We have seen how
Wolsey assumed, in what related to ecclesiastical
courts, certain powers beyond what Warham thought
necessary and expedient; and we have also seen how
the timid and indolent nature of Warham cowered
before the master mind of Wolsey, and how Wolsey's
haughty spirit was melted into friendship towards the
yielding primate.

When we pass from the courts of law and the university to the legislative transactions of the two
prelates, we have nearly the same story to tell. There
was, at the commencement of their joint career, the
same misunderstanding, the same proud assumption
of authority on the one side, and the same mild resistance and subsequent surrender on the other The
reader will only understand the real state of the case
if he bears in mind, that what is now to be narrated
occurred soon after the appointment of Wolsey
as cardinal and legate, before he understood the
character of Warham, and before the amiable disposition of Warham had conciliated the friendship of
Wolsey.

Warham and Wolsey, even at this time, to a certain
extent, had come to an understanding. They both
agreed in the opinion that a reformation of the Church,
or at all events of the clergy, was a subject of the
greatest importance. They both agreed that to effect
this by the ordinary constitutional authority of the
Archbishop of Canterbury was a thing impossible.

Both agreed that it was desirable that a legate *à
latere* should be appointed, and the unambitious
Warham was quite aware that, if a legate was to be
appointed, the appointment would rest upon Wolsey.
But Warham expected that the legate would co-
operate with the primate; whereas Wolsey determined that Warham should only act as the first
minister of the legate. Warham, from his point of
view, thought it important that, as the two were to
act together, their respective jurisdictions should be
clearly defined. Wolsey could hardly object to such
an arrangement, but he never intended to adhere to
it. An agreement had been made with reference
to the limits of jurisdiction to be observed in the
legatine court; on the first misunderstanding on the
subject, we have seen how quietly Wolsey remarked
to his correspondent that he had entirely miscom-
prehended the nature of their agreement. When in
a dispute one party assumes the exclusive right to
place his own interpretation on the law, it only remains for the other party to yield with what grace
he may, or gird himself for the battle.

In what related to the conduct of convocations
and synods, the two prelates had come, as Warham
supposed, to a clear understanding in the presence of
the king. The king did not lay down the law, or
give much thought to the subject, but he gave his
sanction to what the two prelates proposed. Wolsey
was convinced that, although when the king was determined upon a subject there was no alternative,
and that obedience must be rendered to the royal command; yet, having the king's ear, he was also confident
that, when the king was not personally interested or
committed to a subject, he would support his minister
in any construction it might be expedient to place

upon an expression of the royal mind. Wolsey offered no objections to the proposals of Warham.

Everything being, as Warham supposed, arranged and settled, the archbishop was prepared to act.

In the Convocation of 1513, the archbishop had employed the eloquence of Dean Colet to signify to his suffragans and the clergy of his province, the nature of the reforms he intended to introduce into the Church. Nothing however was done till the year 1518. He was now prepared to propose certain measures of reform. It never occurred to him that those measures were to be initiated by the legate; the legate was, he supposed, only to be called in when extraordinary power was requisite to enforce the measures. Leaving it to Wolsey, as Archbishop of York, to convene the clergy of the northern province, the Archbishop of Canterbury summoned his suffragans and his clergy to meet him at Lambeth, there to hold a synod for the adoption of immediate measure of reform.

To his astonishment he received the following letter from Cardinal Wolsey :—

" MY LORD, after hearty commendations. This day, to my no little marvel, I have seen the copy of such monitions as you have directed to your suffragans, commanding them by the same to repair to Lambeth, where you intend to keep a great counsel with them, for the reformation of divers great enormities, expressed in your said monitions and committed through your province; alleging that the rather ye be moved so to do, forasmuch as it hath pleased the king's grace, like a noble and virtuous prince to move you thereunto. My lord, albeit such and many other things, as be specially expressed in your said monitions, be to be reformed generally through the Church of England, as well in my province as in yours, and being legate à *latere*, to me chiefly it appertaineth to see the reformation of the premises, though hitherto, not in time coming, I have ne will execute any jurisdiction as legate *à latere ;* but only as I shall stand *with the king's pleasure ;* yet assured I am that his grace will not I should be so little esteemed, that you should enterprise the said reformation to the express derogation of the said dignity of the see apostolic, and otherwise than the law will suffer you, without my advice, consent, and knowledge ; nor you had no such commandment of his grace, but expressly the contrary. And that well appeared when his grace and highness willed you to repair to me at Greenwich, sitting in administration of divines in the choir, at which time I appointed to have special communication with you apart, afore any monitions should be sent forth. Wherefore, my lord, since you have done otherwise than was agreed at that time and the king commanded you, necessary it shall be that forthwith you repair to me, as well to be learned of the considerations, which moved you thus to do besides my knowledge, as also to have communication with you for divers things concerning your person, and declaration of the same of the king's pleasure further, as at this time it shall not be much incommodious unto you thus to come to me, forasmuch as I intend to be at Richmond eight or ten days, from whence your place of Mortlake is not far distant, where you may for the time right easily and pleasantly be lodged, and we both with little pain often repair together, as the case shall require. And thus heartily fare you well. From my house of York," &c. *

Upon this extraordinary document it is necessary to make some remarks. We must first renew our observations on the carelessness or the malignity of Foxe, and of the historians who take him for their authority, when they assume that, until the clergy were attacked in the parliament of 1529, Warham and the superior clergy had taken no steps to remove the acknowledged grievances of which the laity complained. The first thing Warham did after his appointment to the primacy was, as we have seen, to effect a salutary reform in the ecclesiastical courts. He then brought the subject of reform before the convocation.

* Wilkins, iii. 660.

When he found it impossible for the Primate of All England, by the exercise of his ordinary functions to effect this object, he sought extraordinary powers through the Church of Rome, and accepted a legate, *à latere*. Upon the appointment of the legate he commenced operations, by convening the synod to which we have just referred.

An Englishman may feel just indignation at the unprecedented measure to which he had recourse, when he permitted a legate *à latere* to assume office in England; but we can hardly accuse him of not attempting a reform, and we are not justified in saying that all was a failure, because, through circumstances, Wolsey never found time to discharge the extraordinary functions conceded to him. It is one thing to condemn the proposed measures, and it is another thing to affirm that they were never taken.

The next thing to be remarked is the deference which Wolsey paid to the king,—the supremacy which he acknowledged in fact, if not in words. To this we add, that he did not perform a single legislative act without the king's entire permission,—a circumstance which renders Henry's subsequent treatment of the cardinal as extraordinary as it was cruel and iniquitous.

The tone of Wolsey's letter is perfectly savage. At the same time, we must admit that there were circumstances which might give him provocation, if not justly, yet not to our surprise. We must bear in mind, that this letter was written in 1518, that is, before friendly relations were established between the primate and the cardinal. Wolsey was not acquainted, at the time, with Warham's character. It appeared to him that Warham was the aggressor. The archbishop was here assuming the right of initiation; it appeared that,

CHAP.
II.

William
Warham.
1503-32.

although he had invoked the assumption of legatine powers by the cardinal, he intended him only to
play a secondary part,—to be called in when, by the
ordinary processes of the canon law of the Church,
the archbishop was unable to carry his point. To
play a second part, however, was a thing intolerable
to Wolsey, who must be first or nothing. It appeared
to him that Warham was playing a deep and unfair
game. Warham was not likely to do this ; but we may
presume that the cardinal was so far right that when
conceding legatine power to Wolsey, Warham originally designed to be assisted, not to be superseded.

We will further remark on the grotesque rudeness,
the uncontrollable violence, of Wolsey's letter. We
see, in one of the most accomplished men of the age,
how a high state of civilization in what pertains to
the externals of society was not inconsistent with a
character almost like that of a barbarian in the individual. In the correspondence of ambassadors, the fact
is sometimes mentioned that they met with rudeness in
their conversations with Wolsey, and that in his expressions he placed himself under no restraint. This
is mentioned rather as an incident, not as anything
unusual in the intercourse of public men. Men were
not educated to restrain their passions ; everything was
violent and cruel. The cruelty of the age must be
taken into account when we speak of persecutors. Men
were impatient of contradiction ; and, in their impatience, they hesitated not, if it were not inconsistent
with the policy of the state, to bring an opponent to
the scaffold. If we pass from England to France, from
Henry VIII. of England to Francis I. and Henry IV.
of France, it would seem as if no bounds could be set
to the passions of anger and lust, when the ability to
indulge those passions was conceded.

No man seems to have had less power to restrain his passions than Wolsey : though urgent for the reform of the clergy, he was an unmarried father of children ;* though a man of really kind feelings, he desired to make men fear rather than love him.

Warham, as usual, succumbed.† The interview between the primates took place ; the result was, that a synod for the purpose of effecting a reformation of the Church was called ; but not in the name of the Archbishop of Canterbury. It was summoned in the name of the legate, and was to meet on the first Monday of the ensuing Lent. When the appointed time arrived nothing was done; for the plague was raging in London.‡ When at length, in the Lent of the following year, the synod did meet, although certain articles were adopted, yet nothing of importance was transacted. Wolsey had not possessed the leisure to lay down the laws which the synod were to enact. But he carried one point of importance to himself. The suffragans of Canterbury submitted to his domination, and published the articles, not under a mandate from their metropolitan, but by order of the legate.

There might be a question, when the authority of a legate was, by the royal permission, exercised in England, whether Warham had authority to summon *a synod* in his own name as distinguished from a convocation. The proceeding was irregular, and, without consulting the king, the archbishop did not venture to act. But, when a convocation was to be called,

---

* See the letter of John Chesy to Master Crumwell. (Ellis, 1st Series, vol. ii. p. 92). The thirty-eighth of the articles exhibited in Parliament against Wolsey, speaks of two natural children.

† Regist. Car. Booth, Hereford, fol. xxxvii.

‡ The reader is referred generally to Wake and to Wilkins, iii. 660, 661, 681, 682.

there was no doubt in any one's mind that it ought
to be called without reference to the legate. As a
matter of course, the writs for the convocation were
issued in the name of the Archbishop of Canterbury,
as those of York in the name of Wolsey, in his
capacity of Archbishop of York. In the year 1523
the Convocation of Canterbury, not summoned for
any special purpose, but with the single view of
granting a subsidy to the Crown, assembled, as was
usual, in St. Paul's cathedral. Wolsey, as Archbishop
of York, summoned his suffragans and clergy to meet
him at Westminster. The Northern clergy might well
complain of having been compelled to take a long,
hazardous, and expensive journey for the convenience
of their metropolitan ; but this was not an affair of
the Southern convocation.

The clergy of the province of Canterbury met.
They proceeded to the transaction of business, in the
chapter-house of St. Paul's. Suddenly, to their surprise, a messenger arrived from Westminster. The
Convocation of Canterbury, the Primate of All England,
his suffragans, his clergy, were required to appear
immediately before the lord legate at Westminster.
However surprising the call may have been, no one
seems to have hesitated for a moment to obey the
mandate of the royal favourite. But it is not to be
doubted that, in the interval between the meeting of
convocation and their being summoned to appear before
the legate at Westminster, something had occurred,
of which no record has been preserved, which had
excited feelings of indignation in the irascible cardinal.
He had permitted the Convocation of Canterbury to
assemble ; he had co-operated with the Archbishop of
Canterbury, by calling at the same time the Convocation of York ; they had actually assembled. This was

not, therefore, a case parallel with the former one. It is possible, that the legate had received information, that, besides being called upon to vote a subsidy, certain questions were to be brought under discussion, which Wolsey determined to have discussed only when the legate was present.

Warham was not the man to raise an objection. The clergy again were prepared to admit, as they had admitted before, that if there were a legate *à latere*, he might convene a synod. But Wolsey was not, on this occasion, to have it all his own way. The Convocation of Canterbury was united with the Convocation of York, and met as a synod at Westminster. Wolsey was lord paramount. The business, however, most pressing,—that for which the two convocations had been summoned,—related to the granting of a subsidy; yet when to the amalgamated convocation the cardinal proposed a grant of money to the king, it was humbly represented to him, that it was by convocation only that a subsidy could be voted; that in obedience to a mandate from the cardinal they had assembled in synod; but that they could only vote money in their character of proctors for the clergy, and that for this purpose the clergy of Canterbury must return to St. Paul's, and act independently of the Convocation of York. Wolsey at once perceived, that he had taken a wrong step,—that in every diocese there would be persons ready to plead the illegality of the vote in order to excuse themselves from paying an unpopular tax, and that payment, in many instances, would, under such circumstances, have to be enforced by the strong arm. Resort to extreme measures would involve the government in unpopularity, and the love of popularity was in Henry an amiable weakness, inducing him sometimes to abstain from an evil

action, and, at others, to vindicate his conduct as
we see it vindicated in the preambles of his Acts of
Parliament.

Into the merits or demerits of the case, how far the
conduct of Wolsey was a wilful act of aggression or
how far a mere act of self-defence, we cannot, with the
materials we possess, venture to affirm. The popularity of the cardinal was waning, and the people supported the primate and his clergy. Hall, the chronicler,
always hostile to Wolsey, alludes to the transaction
as something unprecedented and unjustifiable. "The
cardinal, by his legatine power," he says, "dissolved
the Convocation of St. Paul's, cited by the archbishop,
and he summoned the archbishop and all the clergy to
Westminster, which was *never seen before in England*,
whereof Master Skelton, a merry poet, wrote—

> "'Gentle Paule, laie down thy sweard,
>   For Peter at Westminster hath shaven thy beard.'"*

Throughout these transactions we are inclined to
complain of the apathy of the primate, and yet, after
his concession of the legatine power to Wolsey, it is
difficult to say how, as a good man, who desired the
well-being of his Church and country through the
instrumentality of another, he could have done otherwise than he did.

Warham had, as far as it was possible for him,
retired from the world; and, in perverting a high and
important office into a station in which he might enjoy
his *otium cum dignitate*, he yielded to the influence
of the age in which he lived. We have only to refer
to the biographers of great men, the contemporaries of
Warham, to see that this was the object at which the

* Yorkshiremen entertain much respect for the name of Skelton,
but in these lines the malice is more apparent than the wit.

leading characters of the day were aiming. They laboured to acquire high station, fortune, and fame; and, these acquired, they hoped to devote the rest of their days to the enjoyment of those literary pursuits which, ever since the fall of Constantinople, had been not merely a fashion, but a rage. When from defect of primary education a man could not himself take a position among learned men, still by the scholars of the day, he might surround himself, and to their Mecænas an immortality of fame was accorded by the men of erudition who were fed by his bounty or encouraged by his patronage. There was, no doubt, some self-deception on the part of great men who were conscious that their genius tended not so much to a mastery of the intricacies of literature and science, as to the government of their fellow-creatures; but still, in their self-deception, we see, that the idea of human happiness related to the possession of a princely income, to the cultivation of the intellect, and to the enjoyment of a literary society. We can hardly believe, that the time would ever have arrived when Wolsey would have voluntarily relieved himself from the labours of a statesman; but we have his own authority for saying, that what he desired was to retire from public life. What he talked of was actually accomplished by Charles V. It was with the object of enjoying in an aristocratic retreat the fruits of his labours, that Crumwell hoarded his money and erected his palaces. It was thus that we account for his obtaining his earldom just before his execution: his ministry had failed to accomplish what he had proposed to the king, and he asked the king to permit him to retire upon an earldom, the honours of which his wealth, *hard* earned, if not *well* earned, would enable him to sustain. Henry acceded to the proposal, though he afterwards deter-

mined upon his ruin. If Erasmus did not retire
to some remote abode, and would not have tied himself to any particular locality, his life was a life of
literary enjoyment. Colet, at one time, thought of
seeking a retreat in the Charterhouse.

That there should be this anxiety on the part of the
great men of the world, to realize in retirement the
fruit of their labours, will appear natural, if we
observe the difficulties by which the great men were
surrounded, and the dangers they had to encounter.
How great these were may be inferred from the effect
which the labours of public men produced upon their
natural constitutions. Of the public characters of the
day we scarcely find one who was not prematurely
old. We are accustomed to regard Henry VII. as an
old man : and, as a man well stricken in years his
portraits exist to represent him ; and yet when he died
Henry VII. was only fifty-two years of age. The
marriage of Louis XII. with the Lady Mary of
England was regarded as a misalliance on account of
the age of the bridegroom ; yet when, shortly after the
marriage, the bridegroom died, he was only fifty-four
years old. Maximilian was only sixty when he paid
the debt of nature, and Charles died at fifty-nine.
Francis I. was fifty-three, and Henry VIII. only fifty-
six. Wolsey was bowed down to the grave by his
cares, his sorrows, and his fears, an old man at fifty-
five. Statesmen felt that their lives, as well as their
fortunes, were held at the will of their monarchs, and
monarchs courted war until they experienced the
miseries it entailed. They were in constant dread of
the rivalry of surrounding sovereigns, or the machi-
nations of rebellious subjects ; of pretenders to their
thrones, and of the dagger of the assassin. To these
fears we may attribute some of their most iniquitous,

despotic, and tyrannical actions; in self-defence, as they supposed, they became legal murderers.

William Warham, when, in high station, and with the command of great wealth, he resigned, contrary to Wolsey's wish, the great seal, was an object of admiration, respect, and envy to his contemporaries. He had effected, at a comparatively early period of life, what they still hoped to accomplish. The mere functions of his office of archbishop he had a pleasure in performing; and no man finds pleasure in complete idleness. We desire to be free from work which we are compelled to perform; but self-imposed labour is acceptable He was sometimes forced by circumstances to come down from his shelf; but, until quite the close of life, he was ever anxious, after engaging in a controversy, which he contrived to make as short-lived as possible, to retire from public life, and to resume his not inglorious ease.

Although Warham was ready to protect the interests of the prior and convent of Christ Church whenever they were attacked, yet, like many of his predecessors, he did not regard their vicinity as adding to the pleasures of a residence at Canterbury; and consequently the palace of the metropolitan city never became his chief place of abode. From the date of his signature to the various documents which we still possess, we find, that his favourite residence was at Otford. On this manor he spent no less a sum than thirty thousand pounds. He had here a spacious park, well stocked with deer, and, although the delicate state of his health prevented him from indulging in field sports, yet he found pleasure in rural pursuits. As he refreshed himself at the well of sweet waters, which owed its origin to the discernment or the merits of St. Thomas of Canterbury, and gazed upon the lovely prospect over the park to the chalk hills beyond, on which the eye of Becket had often rested, he may have contrasted the fiery temper of the saint contending against the crown for every vestige of right pertaining to the see, with the meek submissive temper of the then possessor of the domain. In the transition state of the Church neither St. Thomas on the one side, nor ourselves on the other, may be able to understand what could have been the sentiments of a primate of the sixteenth century. Although they were contending against evil from opposite quarters, we may believe both to have been acting conscientiously; and we may pray that, in all ages of the Church, the successors of those good men will contend, as the exigencies of the Church may require, that the things of God may be rendered to God, and the things of Cæsar to Cæsar.

At the manor, of late years called the palace, of Lambeth, the archbishop resided when duty required his attendance at the court. It was at that time a lovely residence—a *rus in urbe*, although, in point of fact, the city had not made much encroachment on the southern side of the river. The green fields, in the midst of which the manor-house stood, extended over unbroken pastures, or pastures broken only by hedgerows, to the Surrey hills. From the windows of the hall the eye rested on a continuous line of palaces from Westminster to the Tower. The river was the great street of London. With the gilded barges of the nobility and the painted boats of the middle classes, a gayer scene would be presented to the eye by none of the great cities of Europe. As the archbishop went out "at the even tide" to meditate like Isaac in the fields or on his terraces redolent with flowers, there came up, we are told, from the various boats as they passed, those sweet strains of music which, resounding in our busiest thoroughfare, induced the foreigner, when he returned to his native land, to speak of " merry England." The cares, the labours, the filth, the wretchedness, the disease which abounded at that time even more than now, were to be found in the filthy, plague-stricken streets, which were visited by those only who were compelled to traverse them on account of business. The aristocratic and the gay were on the river, the streets were to them what the city is to us.

It was, however, so easy for the aristocrat or the courtier to cause his boat to stop at the quay at Lambeth, or for the citizen to cross the river on business; it was so easy for the king to send over to Lambeth and command the archbishop's attendance at Westminster, even when there was no great pressure of business; that Warham was not a constant resident at this manor; but, even when he had to attend to public business in London, he would often have his establishment at Croydon, and come to Lambeth for a few hours in the day.

His habits, as we have seen from the testimony of Erasmus, were unostentatious, and in his ordinary dress and in the arrangements of his household he affected simplicity. Erasmus, indeed, somewhere remarks, that the archbishop differed herein from the other great men of the age, by giving to his friends, however humble in life, a cordial shake of the hand.

But although he avoided all ostentation and parade when he was entertaining the literary friends of whom we have given a description, yet on great occasions he exercised the rites of hospitality on a scale of great magnitude. His tastes lay so much in that direction, that we suspect it was the infirm state of his health which induced him to relegate, without a remonstrance, the entertainment of princes to the cardinal, whose love of splendour was almost puerile.

Wolsey was not unwilling to entertain royalty at Warham's expense. Sometimes he incurred the remonstrances, but never the disapprobation of the archbishop,—not his disapprobation, for what he did he had a right to do. Even to the end of Elizabeth's reign, the sovereign did honour to a royal visitor, and saved the public exchequer, by billeting him, so to say, on one of the nobles of the land. It was one of the taxes to which the aristocracy were liable.

It was thus that the archbishop was called upon to entertain the Emperor Charles V. on one of his visits to England. With what splendour Warham could on great occasions make his appearance we gather from the record, which has been preserved, of his reception of Cardinal Campeggio in the year 1518.

This mission of Campeggio was long antecedent to his well-known attendance about what was called " the king's business," or the divorce question. The object of this his first embassy was to obtain from the king a grant of money for the pope. Wolsey, aware that the embassy would fail in its immediate object, was extremely anxious to obtain for the legate an honourable reception, in order that he might, nevertheless, secure his friendship at Rome. The king was quite prepared to do what the cardinal desired, provided he was not required to make the grant ; and he sent Lord Abergavenny and other lords to wait upon the legate on his landing in Dover. The Bishop of Chichester represented the archbishop on this occasion ; the archbishop himself, with his crossbearer, the Bishop of Rochester, remaining at Canterbury ; at which place the legate arrived next day, July 24th. The archbishop exhibited to the legate the splendid shrine of St. Thomas, before which the legate knelt, and made an offering. The prior and monks, after presenting to him the other relics to be kissed, gave him a splendid entertainment in the hall of the convent. There was no religious ceremonial. Campeggio had come to England not as the representative of the Bishop of Rome, but as the ambassador of the Sovereign of the Papal States. The archbishop met him not with mitre, pall, and cope, but as the first among the gentlemen of Kent, and a privy counsellor of the king. The morning after Campeggio's arrival, Warham appeared at the head of a splendid cavalcade; a thousand horsemen, his tenants or retainers, in full armour, and with gold chains around their necks. They passed, banners raised, trumpets sounding, through Sittingbourne, Bexley, and Rochester, to Otford, where the hospitality of the primate was such as to cause the admiration of his grateful guests. The splendour exhibited by Warham on this occasion was, however, as nothing when compared with that which was displayed by Wolsey. Wolsey knew, that a visit from a Roman cardinal was unpopular with the clergy as well as with the people, that the archbishop only did what the proprieties of his office required, and that the king merely yielded to the wishes of his favourite, and condescended to enjoy the entertainments which Cardinal Wolsey provided at his own expense. Wolsey was not to be thwarted; the splendour of his entertainments conciliated the king and the multitude who participated in them, and astonished the foreigners; for this reception of Campeggio was, in point of magnificence, never surpassed. Although the embassy failed in

obtaining a grant of money, it would have to report of
the hearty goodwill of Cardinal Wolsey, of his boundless wealth, of his favour with the king, and of his
general popularity.

When the archbishop had recovered from the fatigues
of entertaining the legate, he went privately to Lambeth, that he might be in attendance upon the king
on the 3d of August. On that day, the king was
publicly to receive the legate. It was a civil transaction, a political arrangement, and Warham was there
not as the Primate of All England, but as the first
personage in the House of Lords. He passed over to
the palace at Westminster, and there in the royal
dining chamber, with the lords spiritual and temporal,
together with all the great officers of state, he awaited
the arrival of the king. On the king's arrival, his
majesty took his place in the centre of the hall, the
archbishop and the other lords spiritual on his right
hand, the dukes and temporal peers on his left. The
anomaly was, that one of the representatives of a
foreign potentate was, on this occasion, the minister of
the King of England. Wolsey appeared with Campeggio applying to the king and realm of England for
aid against the enemies of God. He asked in the
name of Leo X. what it had been agreed in the council
of Henry VIII. should not be granted. The legates
saluted the king, and the king graciously raised his
hat. He proceeded to the top of the hall, Cardinal
Wolsey on his right hand and Cardinal Campeggio on
his left, their pillars, crosses, and hats being carried
before them. The sword of state was borne before
the king by the Earl of Surrey. The king ascended
the throne. On the right, the primate and the lords
spiritual retained their places, and the lords temporal
stood on the left. Fronting the throne were seen two

chairs of state covered with cloth of gold.   The larger
of these chairs was designed to bear the great personal
weight of Cardinal Wolsey, who took the lead in this
foreign mission to the court of England.   Cap in hand,
he made a Latin oration to the king. The king received
it most graciously.   Henry was always pleased with
an opportunity of displaying his personal advantages,
and his acquirements as a scholar.   The king, standing
in front of the throne, returned an answer in the same
language, "most eloquently and with great gravity."

Campeggio's brother followed, and he stated more
in detail the objects of the mission—the desire of the
pope for the peace and unity of Christendom, and the
importance of a crusade against the common enemy,
the Turk.*   An answer was made by a member of the
government, dictated, we may presume, by the king
himself. The King of England needed not to be reminded of his duty as a Christian man.

The king and the legates then withdrew into the privy
chamber, and there they were closeted together for an
hour.   There were not a few who felt indignation on
these occasions, when Wolsey, by the exclusion of
other counsellors, made it apparent to all that he
only had the ear of the king.   A splendid banquet followed.

The whole object was to proclaim to the foreigner
the power of Wolsey in the English court.   We are

---

* Hall adds that they declared, as one of the causes of the legation,
a desire to effect a reformation of the clergy. It is possible that
such a subject might be mentioned *ad captandum ;* but it would
have so changed the character of the proceedings to have introduced
Church matters, that it is improbable.   But the case seems settled
by the fact, that in the original documents there is no reference to
the subject.   It was probably discussed in private, as we know it
had been an object with both Wolsey and Warham.

expressly told that no business was transacted, and that no respect was shown to the court of Rome.*

Towards the close of his life, Warham became a valetudinarian. So early as the year 1525, he was advised by his physicians to abstain as much as possible from public business, and to take up his abode at Knowle, as being a situation high and dry.

To this circumstance we have had occasion already to allude. We will only remark here that the illness continued till 1529, and was evidently the breaking-up of his constitution. He made it an excuse for not receiving Campeggio, when that legate again visited England on "the king's business." * He wrote to Wolsey :

"Please it your good grace to understand that this, St. Matthew's day, I received your grace's most honourable letters, dated at Oking, the xviiith day of September, by which I perceive it is the king's grace's pleasure and yours that I should determine myself to receive the most reverend Cardinal Campegius, legate *de latere*, at my church now shortly, and the same to entertain in the best manner and accompany to Rochester, &c.

"So it is, if it like your good grace, I was at Canterbury lately, intending then to have continued thereabout the most part of this winter, but I could not have my health iii days together at the time of my abode there, whereby I was forced for the safeguard of my health and life to return from thence. And if I should now journey thither and hither again, especially in the ending of this month of September or in the beginning of October (in which times I am most troubled with my old painful disease of my head), I assure your grace I think verily I should not escape without extreme danger of my life. For albeit I keep myself now as precisely as I can, yet I daily feel grief and betokening of the coming of my sickness which I fear more than ever I did, and which

---

* Papers and Letters, Henry VIII. 4362, 4366, 4371.

was not wont fail me about this season. And I think that after the shaking of my head in my horse-litter I should not be able to do that thing that I should come for. And albeit I would be right glad specially for the king's grace's pleasure and commandment; and for my duty to the See Apostolic, and also for my own observance that I owe to the said most reverend legate, to await on the same by the way from Canterbury, yet in my opinion it were not most meet for me to accompany the said most reverend legate, he riding on horseback and I in my litter, for I am not able to ride iii miles together on horseback. In consideration whereof I beseech your grace that, as I have ever found you good and favourable lord unto me, so it may please your grace to be mediator for me to the king's highness, to hold me excused of the said journey to Canterbury, my age, impotency, and danger of life graciously considered. Assuring your grace that if I thought I should be able to endure the said journey, and be able to do the king's highness any acceptable service by the same, I would ask no pardon thereof; but do it with as good will as ever I did thing, and as I have at all times been ready when I have been commanded, and will be during my life, as far as I shall be able, and I send unto your grace at this time the steward of my house, who can inform your grace of the truth concerning the premises, to whom I beseech your grace to give your credence. At Otford, this present St. Matthew's day."

We will now attend Warham in his retirement; and we will group some occurrences, without reference to their chronological order, in order that we may not interrupt the narrative when we have to bring under the reader's notice those first decisive steps towards the Reformation, which render the last years of Warham's primacy memorable and deeply interesting.

And here a question arises, which may take the reader by surprise: Was Warham a married man?

In a private letter, written in 1518, by Erasmus to Archbishop Warham, he entreats the primate to intercede in his behalf with Henry VIII, in order that he might obtain from the king a small subsidy, of which he greatly stood in need. He addressed the archbishop as his Mecœnas. In this letter he alludes to the archbishop's " sweet wife and his most dear children."[*]

Jortin cannot omit a reference to this letter, but he makes the remark, " here must be some error, for in the same letter mention is made of the archbishop's wife and children. · Perhaps the letter should be inscribed to Lord Mountjoy."

We may be inclined to think there is some mistake, since we find no allusion by any other writer to the wife and children of Warham, and no other allusion by Erasmus himself. We may decide against his marriage, but still it is possible, that Archbishop Warham may have had a wife and children. His successor, Archbishop Cranmer, was certainly a married man. A puritan writer would reply, that Cranmer was a Protestant ; but antecedently to the reign of Edward VI. a Protestant Cranmer certainly was not. No one was more zealous than he in putting in force, with unmitigated severity, the cruel laws against the Protestants, as well as all other reputed heretics.[†] His wife, throughout Henry's reign, was kept in the background. Henry, at one time, knew that he had what he called a "bed-fellow," but he merely regarded Cranmer as he regarded Wolsey, as a concubinary priest.

Only persons of very strict religious principles

---

[*] " *Bene vale cum dulcissima conjugali liberisque dulcissimis.*" —Erasmi Opera, iii. 1695.

[†] I shall have occasion hereafter, in my life of Cranmer, to remark on the extreme injustice done to that eminent man by those who represent him as a Protestant in disguise during the reign of Henry.

objected to the residence of a concubine in the house of a clergyman ; and when nephews were spoken of, it was in a sarcastic tone implying the existence of a nearer relation. In either case, the lady was treated with equal respect or disrespect ; she was generally selected from the humbler classes of society ; her questionable position in society rendered the connexion objectionable in the higher ranks of society. Nevertheless it was important, though it was a secret transaction, for the female admitted into a clergyman's family to prove that the marriage ceremony had been performed, for upon that circumstance depended the legitimacy of the children. The marriage was voidable, but void, and if the marriage were proved, the legitimacy of the children was not disputed. At the same time, a clergyman, though not bound, like a monk, by an oath of celibacy, was regarded, on his marriage, as one who had violated the canons of the Church or the statutes of the land ; hence the marriage was generally clandestine, and rather admitted, in the presence of friends, than openly avowed.

Allusion has been made to Skelton, the poet ; he declared on his deathbed that his concubine was really his wife, but that from prudential considerations he had not owned her as such. Many there were who were cravens in this respect like himself, but who, to save their children from the brand of bastardy, made their confession at last.

Under these considerations, as I have said, we abstain from a hasty conclusion with respect to Warham, and cannot assume, as Jortin does, that the letter published in the works of Erasmus, as addressed to Archbishop Warham, was, beyond all doubt, intended for some other person. On the contrary, we have internal evidence to produce which, though not such as completely to establish the authenticity of the letter, will have some weight with some classes of mind.

Erasmus takes occasion to inform his correspondent that he was in want of a horse,—an acquisition of great importance when journeys were for the most part made on horseback. He says, " *Equo commodo est mihi opus, sed tu soles in re equestri parum esse felix, adjuta, tamen, si quid potes.*" There is a little sarcastic pleasantry here, which is just in the style of Erasmus. He would not have written thus to everybody, but he alludes to a transaction, which had already taken place between his correspondent and himself. We are reminded of one of the most amusing letters of Erasmus, in which he says to the archbishop: " I have received a horse from you, not handsome, but a good creature, for he is free from all the mortal sins except gluttony and incorrigible laziness. He has all the virtues of a holy father confessor, being pious, prudent, humble, modest, sober, chaste, and quiet; he neither bites nor kicks. I suspect that by the knavery or mistake of some of your domestics, another horse has been sent me in the stead of what you intended. I have given no directions to my groom, only if by chance any one will give a handsomer horse and a good one he may change the saddle and bridle." *

We would not force the expressions of a well-bred man like Erasmus to an extreme. But it would seem that, when writing to the archbishop, he mentioned a lady who, on his visits to his grace, had received him with courtesy, and who had done the honours of the house, without knowing or caring whether the religious ceremony had been performed, he spoke of her in the terms which he regarded as likely to be most acceptable to her.

---

* Erasmi Opera, ii. 814 ; Ep. 697.

Wolsey was himself a concubinary priest, and to the appearance of a lady presiding over the household in one of Warham's manors, he would have nothing to object ; but if Wolsey had discovered, that in an hour of weakness Warham had yielded to the wishes of the lady and his children, and had become clandestinely a married man, we discover another ground for the despotic influence which Wolsey certainly exercised over the mind of Warham. We have alluded before to a proclamation by the king against the marriage of the clergy, and we have observed the very moderate terms in which the proclamation was worded. This proclamation was issued when Wolsey ruled without a rival in the court and over the mind of Henry VIII. The proclamation may have been intended as a hint to Warham, that he was in the power of the minister ; and when what was done terminated only in, what we can hardly call a threat, but only a hint, we can assign a reason for the expressions of gratitude which appear sometimes in the letters of the primate, and for which we are unable otherwise to account. What would have happened, had Henry been told that his primate was a married man, it is impossible to surmise ; for the actions of Henry depended frequently upon the caprice of the moment. Until quite the close of Warham's career, Henry was devoted to the pope, and felt himself called, as Defender of the Faith, to uphold the discipline of the Church. He would have treated as a good joke the discovery, that the primate had a concubine dwelling in his house ; but he would have resented an infraction of the laws both of Church and State such as his marriage would have implied.

To the majority of my readers the arguments in favour of Warham's marriage will appear insufficient. It was proper, however, that I should notice the case ; and I repeat that, if there existed a secret which placed Warham in the power of Wolsey, we can then understand the unresisting submission of Warham to the insults of Wolsey, for which we have found it so difficult to account. But, whether a lady presided over the establishment or not, Warham's house was the resort of the learned, and especially of the reforming divines ; his guests were placed at their ease, and among Warham's guests none was ever more welcome than Erasmus.

It was not, however, till his third visit to England, that the intimacy commenced, which lasted through life, between Archbishop Warham and Erasmus. Of their first interview Erasmus has himself left an amusing description.

The archbishop had signified to Grocyn his readiness to receive, at Lambeth, the distinguished scholar who made his boast that the foundation of his Greek studies had been laid at the university of which Warham was the chancellor.

There still lingers among us a custom prevalent in the sixteenth century. When a physician calls upon us, and we have received his advice, we present him at parting with an honorarium. A similar treatment was expected by a scholar when calling on a Mecænas in the sixteenth century. The scholar would present his patron with some work, and attach to it a suitable dedication, and on his departure he expected his fee. This system of patronage continued, with some modifications, to the middle of the eighteenth century. An author was paid for a dedication.

On the occasion before us, Archbishop Warham received Erasmus with his usual affability and kindness. They conversed together. Erasmus was invited to

dinner, and after dinner the conversation was renewed.
Nothing could be more agreeable than the meeting.
Erasmus, at parting, placed in the hands of the archbishop a copy of his version of the "Hecuba" with
a dedication. At the same time, Warham was evidently determined to give a salutary hint to his friend.
He was aware, that this version of the "Hecuba" had
already done similar service when Erasmus paid his
respects, in the course of his travels, at other courts.

The translation was merely an exercise which
Erasmus had performed when, studying Greek in
the University of Louvain. This he had transcribed ;
and, carrying copies with him, when he called upon
a great man, he presented a copy to him, with a suitable dedication, and received his fee. A very small
fee, however, the archbishop placed in his hand on
this occasion.

When the two friends left the manor-house of
Lambeth and took boat, Grocyn, delighted with the
reception his companion had met with, asked, in a
whisper, what the fee was which the archbishop had
given, expecting a large sum to be named. The fee
was so ridiculously small, that the two friends, when
Erasmus named it, burst into a roar of laughter. Presently the great scholar asked whether the archbishop
regarded the book as worthless, or whether the small-
ness of the fee was to be traced to the penuriousness of
Warham. Grocyn was provoked at the latter insinuation, and mentioned to Erasmus the comments which
had been made on the easy manner in which he
was accustomed to abstract money from the pockets
of his patrons. There was always something of the
spirit of Grub Street mixed up with the genius of
Erasmus. He was, however, a perfect gentleman. Soon
after he let the archbishop understand that the rebuke,

justly incurred, had been well received, by adding to a translation of the " Iphigenia," that of " Hecuba," and by sending both, with a new dedication, to the archbishop.

Never again had Erasmus to complain of want of generosity on the part of Warham. Although he thought it right to show, that he was not to be imposed upon, Warham continued, through life, to heap favours on the grateful Erasmus. He gave him not less than 550 nobles, and, by offering him a living, endeavoured to secure his residence in England. He collated Erasmus to Aldington, near Ashford, on the 22d of March, 1511. Erasmus, when he found that he was expected to reside, resigned the living on the plea that he could not speak English. This was a sentiment in advance of the age; and Warham could not see the force of his friend's reasoning. We have so frequently adverted to the prevalent feeling, that so long as the parish was well served, it was no concern of the parishioners whether the money was paid to the absentee rector, a portion of it being deducted for the support of his deputy, or whether the rector were to discharge the duties in person, and possibly not so well. The feeling of the age was against non-residence and pluralities; but the reason was, that the people desired that the money drawn from the locality should be spent among themselves; and, so far as Erasmus was concerned, on the present occasion, we cannot attribute to him the higher motive for his conduct. His clear intellect saw the force of the argument against non-residence, and adduced it as the pretext for his refusing the living when he found that the archbishop offered it to him with the express object of providing him with a comfortable home in this country, where, if it was not a distinct stipulation, he would be expected to reside.

A roving life was more to the taste of Erasmus, and to a certain extent, it was, in his case, a necessity. A scholar was obliged to change his residence frequently; now for the purpose of consulting libraries; at another time to be in the vicinity of one of the few printing presses then in existence. Erasmus offered no objection, when the archbishop resorted to a measure equally objectionable in point of principle to that which he had previously proposed, and against which the parliament soon after petitioned. When the new incumbent was nominated to Aldington, the living was saddled with a pension to Erasmus, who, though he declined the responsibilities, accepted the income.

It is impossible to read the works of Erasmus without being attached to the man, though, in money matters, he was not very particular. But he was not entirely without a sense of moderation and modesty for, on one occasion, he said that he had received so much from Archbishop Warham that it were scandalous to take more of him, even if he should offer it.*

Warham argued that pastors ought to contribute to the support of one who was the instructor of pastors. By a scholar providing food of thought for scholars, the expenses incurred were many and great: he had to consult manuscripts, to employ transcribers, to keep his horses for travelling; and of the profit arising from the sale of his works it was considered beneath his dignity to share. It would be a degradation for the scholar to sink into

CHAP.
II.

William
Warham.
1503-32.

---

* Ep. 150. But this sentence is qualified by what ensues; he says : "Even our friend Linacre thinks me too bold, and though he knows my state of health, and that I am going to London with hardly six angels in my pocket, exhorted me most pressingly to spare the archbishop and Lord Mountjoy, and advised me to retrench, and learn to bear poverty with patience."

the tradesman. The printer undertook the expenses of publication, and, although the sale of the works of Erasmus was large and rapid, the expenses of printing were at this time so great, that the profits were not likely to be considerable.

Archbishop Warham did not himself shrink from sharing the burden by which an income was to be provided for Erasmus. He saddled the living of Aldington with an annual payment of 20*l.* and to this sum he added 20*l.* from his own purse. Erasmus was thus endowed from England alone with an income equivalent, at the present calculation, to 400*l.* a year. When we find him continually asking for help, we must suppose that there was mismanagement somewhere, and that, while the expenses were great, the scholar was not economical.

Attached though he was to England, yet Erasmus openly declared, that he would not sacrifice his liberty for any amount of income: and in this declaration we discover the real grounds of his refusal.

The praise of England was frequently in the mouth of Erasmus. In his third visit, when he was between thirty and forty years of age, we find him on one occasion laughing at himself, for, like other humourists, he found amusement occasionally in making himself his own butt, though he would have resented the liberty had it been taken by any one else. Writing to one who knew the unaccountable habits of the scholar, he represents himself as having become a perfect horseman, though from other portions of his works we may discover that he had no little difficulty in keeping his seat on horseback; he had almost become a hunter, he was a tolerable courtier, and could actually make his bow in a courtier-like style; he hinted that he was almost inclined to marry, and the ladies in

England, he said, had a delightful custom of greeting even strangers with an innocent but pleasant salute.* He praises everything, even the climate, which he found most agreeable and most healthful. " I have found," he says, " so much civility (*humanitas*) so much learning, and that not trite and trivial, but profound and accurate, so much familiarity with the ancient writers, Latin and Greek, that, except for the sake of seeing it, I hardly desire to visit Italy."

His happiness it was to visit the archbishop, who, he says, "treats me as if he were my father, or my brother." He speaks of the archbishop's learning, his piety, his earnest desire to discharge the high functions of his office, and to sustain the cause of literature. "Of those who are kind to me," he exclaims in a letter to the Abbot of St. Bertin—

" I place in the first place Warham, archbishop of Canterbury. What genius ! what copiousness ! what vivacity ! what facility in the most complicated discussions ! what erudition ! what politeness ! From Warham, none ever parted in sorrow. This conduct would do honour to a monarch ! With all these qualities, how great is Warham's humility ! how edifying his modesty ! He alone is ignorant of his eminence ; no one is more faithful or more constant in friendship."†

After the archbishop's death, Erasmus thus wrote of him to one of his correspondents :

" How fully soever Warham might be occupied with the

' * This passage, as Dean Milman, in the Quarterly Review, observes, has given rise to much solemn nonsense. The whole passage is composed in that easy Latin, which could only have been accomplished by one who was accustomed to think in that language.

† Perhaps the eulogy of Erasmus, if exaggerated by friendship and gratitude, will be still more in favour of Warham than the sneers at his weakness in which some modern writers, from party motives, indulge.

concerns of the kingdom, they never trespassed upon his archiepiscopal duties. He might even be thought to be engrossed by these: he found time almost every day to say mass; to give audiences; to receive ambassadors; to attend the royal councils; to visit some parts of his diocese, and even to read. Conversation with the learned and literary occupations were his only recreations. Sometimes two hundred persons dined at his table; it was frequented by bishops, dukes, and lords; it never took more than an hour of his time; he drank no wine, he was very cheerful; he never supped; but if some of his intimate friends (and he admitted me among them) remained with him till that hour, he sat down to table with them, eating nothing or scarcely anything himself. He was fond of wit, and occasionally witty, but his wit had no bitterness. He left behind him no more money than was necessary to pay his debts."

We have already alluded to the inclinations of Warham to the cause of reform. He was a deeply religious man, more inclined to mysticism than to scholasticism. His religion was more tinctured with superstition than that of Erasmus; but still we may gather from Erasmus what the sentiments of the archbishop generally were. Erasmus dedicated to Warham his edition of St. Jerome; and in the dedicatory epistle, Erasmus was too much of a courtier to commit the archbishop to opinions and sentiments which he was not careful to avow. He complained of the little care which had been taken to preserve the patristic manuscripts; and he compares this with the lavish expense which had been sometimes incurred on works worse than useless.* He did not despise the simple and well-meant piety of the vulgar; but his

* Jortin, i. 78. The dedication to Warham and the Life of St. Jerome are not inserted among the works of Erasmus; but they are given by Jortin. Jortin and Knight, in their text or in the Appendices, have gathered together all that pertains to English history from the deeply interesting and important letters of Erasmus.

surprise was great at the perverse judgment of a
multitude who ought to have known better. " We
kiss," he says,

" The old shoes and dirty handkerchiefs of the saints ;
and we neglect their books, we abandon to mouldiness and
vermin the works which of all their relics are most holy
and valuable, on which they bestowed much pains, and
which still exist for our benefit. It is not difficult," he continues, " to discover the causes of this conduct. As soon as the
manners of princes degenerated into brutish tyranny, and the
bishops were intent upon acquiring profane dominion and
wealth, instead of teaching the people their duty, the whole
pastoral care fell to the share of those who are called friars,
or brethren, and religious men ; as if brotherly love, Christian
charity, and true religion belonged only to them ! Then polite
literature began to be neglected, the knowledge of the Greek
tongue was much despised, the knowledge of Hebrew still
more. The study of eloquence was thrown aside. The Latin
tongue, by a new accession of barbarisms, was so corrupted
that it could hardly be called a language. History and
antiquities were disregarded. Learning consisted in certain
sophistical quibbles and subtleties, and all science was to be
fetched from the collectors of sums, that is, of commonplaces
of philosophy and divinity. These compilers were always
dogmatical and impudent in proportion to their ignorance ;
they were glad to have ancient authors disregarded, or, which
is very probable, they gave a helping hand to destroy those
books, which if they had ever read it was to no purpose,
because they were not capable of understanding them."*

Warham agreed with Erasmus in thinking, that a
reformation could only be effected by rendering the
leading men of the day good Biblical scholars ; and,
as the lower class of mind is influenced by the higher,
the people would soon be eager to receive that Scrip-

* See Erasmus, Roberto Piscatori, Ep. xiv. and the various
excerpts from Erasmus in the Appendix to Jortin. To the
panegyrics on Warham additions might be easily made.

tural instruction by which alone the existing abuses in practice and doctrine could be rectified. To Erasmus, therefore, Warham extended both his assistance and his patronage, when the former prepared first his Greek Testament and then his Latin translation for the press.

It is observed by Professor Brewer that, although the New Testament was printed at Basle, where only a sufficient supply of type used by the band of men of learning there congregated, could be found; yet in the preparation of this great work English scholars were employed. They assisted in collating the MSS. while English prelates, let it be observed, supplied them with the funds for carrying on the work. He took up his abode at Cambridge, for there Bishop Fisher appointed him Lady Margaret's Professor of Divinity. Gratefully, enthusiastically, as we have seen, does Erasmus acknowledge his obligations to Warham. Having descanted on the modesty, the labours, the genius of the archbishop, and having dwelt on the generous patronage he extended to learned men, Erasmus continues:

"Had it been my good fortune to have fallen in with such a Mecænas, as the archbishop, in my earlier years, I might have done something for literature. Now born as I was in an unhappy age, when barbarism reigned supreme, especially among my own people, by whom the least inclination for literature was then looked upon as little better than a crime, what could I do with my small modicum of talent? Death carried off Henry de Berghes, bishop of Cambray, my first patron; my second, William, Lord Mountjoy, an English peer, was separated from me by his employments at court and the tumults of war. By his means it was my good fortune, then advanced in life, and close upon my fortieth year, to be introduced to Archbishop Warham. Encouraged and cheered by his bounty I revived, I gained new youth and strength in the cause of literature. What nature and my country denied me, his bounty supplied."

It is the more important to notice this, because it is customary to misrepresent the state of learning in this country at the period just preceding the Reformation. The way was prepared for the reformers by the struggles after improvement made by men whom it is customary only to revile. If we say that among the bishops there was only a minority of learned men we shall only say what may be said of them in almost every age. Learned men are not always practical men; and men engaged in their studies, especially if they are plain-spoken, honest men, are not likely to make friends among courtiers; but Erasmus expressly states to Dorpius that he laid his Annotations on the Vulgate before divines and bishops of integrity and learning. We draw too large an inference from the angry, sarcastic, and witty remarks made by Erasmus on the divines of the age, if we presume that all were dishonest or fools who went not the full length of the Protestant Reformation. Erasmus mentions with gratitude not only those large sums of money with which in addition to his salary Warham from time to time relieved his wants, he alludes also to grants made to him by other prelates.

It is sometimes assumed that a mediæval archbishop must have been a man void of wit and humour. We read in modern histories, that if such a person ventures on a joke it is what is called "a grim joke." Erasmus, however, particularly dwells on the facetiousness of Warham, through which he was wont to place himself on a footing with his guests, while by his manner he showed that no one was to take a liberty with him or with any of his companions. The jokes of the age were coarse, and we may give the following letter as a specimen :—

"To Erasmus.—If it be the usual form to commence a letter

by wishing health to the healthy, much more fitting is it that
I should do so when writing to the sick. Although I augur
that, since the Feast of the Purgation of Mary is now past,
you have been purged of your stones, let me ask what right
have those stones to a place in your body? Upon this rock
what would you build? I cannot suppose that you think of
erecting a noble house or anything of that kind. And so,
since you cannot have any possible occasion for stones, get rid
of them as soon as you can, and pay any money to carry
them off. I indeed will purchase them, and, to save you
trouble and expense, I have sent you by the son of my London
goldsmith thirty nobles, which I require you to charge with
ten legions. Gold is a medicine of considerable efficacy.
Apply it to the recovery of your health, which I should be
glad to purchase at a greater rate. For I know you have
many excellent works to publish which cannot be done without health and strength. Take care, therefore, to get well;
and do not any longer defraud us, by your longer sickness, of
the hopes and fruits of your labours. From London, 5th of
February."[*]

The conduct of Warham with respect to the translation of Scripture into the vernacular, notwithstanding
the explanations already given, is perplexing. He
cordially supported Erasmus in his new edition of the
New Testament in his Latin version, and in all that
related to the circulation of the New Testament. Yet
he is known to have taken measures to suppress
Tyndal's noble·translation of the Bible into the vernacular; that translation which was itself a revision,
and which, still further revised, is the basis of the
authorized version.

We must briefly revert to the subject with a view
of seeing how it presented itself to his mind. The
ground on which he supported Erasmus's translation
was that the Vulgate was itself a translation, and that

---

[*] Erasm. Ep. cxxxiv.

Erasmus's work was an appeal from a version to the original. Tyndal's translation was only a "doing into English" of the Septuagint and the Vulgate. The argument, if it had been true, is weak ; but it would suffice to a man looking out for a pretext for withholding his sanction from what would appear to be a legitimate inference from premisses supplied by himself.

But why did he object to the free circulation of the translated Bible ? This is the question, the answer of which must be continually kept before the mind, if we would do justice to all parties.

A demand for a version of the Bible in the vulgar tongue was a party cry,—the cry not merely of the religious reformers, such as Cranmer and others of his school ; but still more loudly of the political reformers, the men of Crumwell's school. The cry for a reformation resounded from one end of Europe to the other, from Italy especially, for in Italy the corruptions were most glaring. What steps were to be taken ? Western Europe gave the answer. There is one book which all agree to be the work of men under the guidance of the Holy Spirit, and the enunciations of which we all agree to be infallible. "To the law and the testimony :" when the Church speaks not according to this it must be in error. This was admitted by reformers of the Erasmian school. But the reformation, they contended, must be carried on gradually by persons in authority. "We will give to them an improved edition of the Bible, in the Latin language, the language of all literary men, and we must abide by their decision." "Let Colet," said Warham, "denounce the corruptions of the clergy; let Erasmus translate the New Testament into Latin, and supply us with paraphrases, and by degrees we shall discover and acknowledge your faults and supply a remedy."

The political reformers raised what may be called the radical cry of the age, a demand for an English Bible. Place the Bible in every man's hand, and every man will be competent to reform the Church. Warham and men of that class knew how violently opposed were many to authorized or least tolerated practices of the age, especially those which bore upon their purses. Such persons were only asking for a pretext to justify their insubordination, and Warham knew that if their passions were inflamed, the lives and the property of the clergy would be at the disposal of the demagogues of the day. This at least was the fear of the great conservative party of the time, and they were soon able, by pointing to the excesses committed in Germany, to show that their timidity was not to be despised. When men's lives and properties are in danger, they are not particular about their logic.

A large number of the religious reformers, of whom I take Cranmer, Ridley, and Latimer as types long before they assented to the leading dogma of Protestantism, were found abetting the political reformers, not from sympathy with them in their insubordination, but from the conviction that the fears of the Erasmians were not worthy of consideration. They were men of faith, and said, "Do what is right, leave events to God; maintain the truth, and though the consequences may be at first unpleasant, yet the truth will have the Almighty for its defender. The Church is corrupt: we do not deny it. How far it is corrupt let the people see. When people see how unscriptural the Church has become, they will secure at once the reformation which it is folly to postpone." The feeling on both sides is intelligible, if we consider it impartially. On both sides there was much that was right, and something which was wrong. Our estimate of the right and the wrong will depend to a certain extent on our own temperaments, or the principles in which we have been trained. The politician, looking only to worldly results, was naturally vacillating. It was the interest of Henry VIII. sometimes to court the one party and sometimes the other. He knew that the party of the religious reformers were always ready to abet him when his patronage was extended to an English Bible ; but that their tempers were sufficiently Erastian to induce them to remain quiescent when the Government decided on a particular course of action. We shall hereafter see him effecting that kind of compromise in which he delighted, by persuading the one party to accept the Bible, and the other to permit it to be read under certain restrictions.

Whenever Henry desired to intimidate the clergy, he threatened them with an authorized version of Scripture. Conscious as they were of the inconsistency of much which was done and preached with the teaching of the Bible, they were ready to submit to the dictates of their master. Whenever he would win their favour, he proscribed the English Scriptures. The course he pursued towards the close of Warham's career is to be attributed rather to the vacillations of the archbishop, who was then approaching his end, than to a variety in the policy of the king, in which however a change soon after, under the influence of Crumwell and Cranmer, took place.

When the question of the divorce comes under consideration we shall find the king exasperated at the unwillingness of the clergy to support him in the matter. He felt, however, that he had gone unwarrantably far in placing them under the penalties of præmunire for conduct of which he himself was guilty ; he felt some remorse for his treatment of Wolsey ;

he was aroused to the impolicy of exasperating the clergy beyond endurance ; he was aware, that it was whispered that the opponent of Luther was himself beginning to Lutheranize ; and he determined to deprive the clergy of the power with which such a notion, if it became prevalent, would invest them.

These observations are offered to enable us to account for an extraordinary document * which we find in Warham's Register, under the date of the 24th of May, 1530. It is a very able document, whether drawn up by Warham himself, or by some one employed under his direction. Judging by what we know to have been a common practice with Henry VIII, we may presume, that it was corrected by the royal hand ; it was certainly drawn up by the king's command. To do justice to the author, whoever he was, we must not forget, that the real object with those who drew it up and caused it to be published was, a justification, in spite of all that had occurred,—the assertion of the royal authority and the rejection of the Pope of Rome by the convocations of the Church of England,—of those who refused to meet the rising clamour for an authorized version of the Scriptures.

Convocation had asserted the royal supremacy ; parliament had not yet followed its example. The country was divided, perplexed, alarmed. The laity were prepared to attack the clergy, but not to touch the Church.

A royal commission was appointed. The Archbishop of Canterbury was chairman. The commission was to report on certain books which, to the horror of some of the laity eminent for their bigotry, were said to be replete with heresy, and were, it was affirmed,

---

* It has been printed by Wilkins, iii. 728.

surreptitiously though widely circulated. The commission assembled at Lambeth, at the close of the year 1529, and they were required to make their report before the following May.

This report contained a long list of errors and heresies which abounded in the books complained of. It is, and was probably intended to be, a mere party document. A catena of errors is presented to us; this course is frequently uncharitable and unfair, since from the statements made, inferences are deduced as indisputable, which they to whom the heresy is imputed would have been among the first to dispute. There can be no doubt that Luther's great doctrine of justification by faith only did alarm some of his contemporaries, and might be used to alarm others who saw not his object in asserting it. He asserted the doctrine to show that man, to the last hour of his life, was a sinner pardoned through the merits of the Saviour imputed to him in his acceptance of the Lord Jesus as his sole Redeemer. This overthrew at once the dogma of supererogatory merits, saint-worship, indulgences, purgatory, almost the whole fabric of the papacy. But we can easily understand how the commissioners may have been really alarmed, when books were circulated in which men were warned " to beware of good works, because they were not of God." It is to be remarked, that it was against good works, not bad works, that Luther was supposed to preach, since a reference to their good works induced men to rely for justification, not on the sole merits of our Lord, but upon what was done by themselves, or by others for them. Men of learning were roused to indignation when they were told, not merely that the university system required an alteration, but that " whosoever he was who ordained an university, he was a star that fell from heaven, for he taught moral virtues for faith, and opinions for truth," whence it was said "universities are the infernal cloud, and open the gate to hell."

In the nineteenth century, there are many who would condemn our ancestors for their commissions and reports, but still we must admit that they had ground for some alarm, though it may have been carried too far. Certainly too far they went, when, because opinions, apparently hostile to good works, were held by that good man, William Tyndal, it was assumed, that his sole object in translating the Scriptures was to gain circulation for these tenets, and to further the cause of insubordination in the Church and of rebellion against the Government. It had been said, in justification of Tyndal, that the king had himself promised to authorize a translation of the Bible. This promise was one of those convenient falsehoods by which public men sometimes meet a public clamour. Wiclif's Bible was prohibited, because it was said to be filled with errors ; the king had promised a version to be made by learned men, which should be a correct representation of the original. The principle on which Tyndal acted had therefore been conceded, and it was demanded either that Tyndal's version should be authorized or the king's promise redeemed. The only answer to this reasonable demand was, that when such dreadful heresies, as that, for instance, which made good works damnable, were deduced from Scripture by wilful men, resorting to Scripture for political purposes, the time had not come when the king could be advised to publish a translation of the Bible, such as the Church might approve. In short, the king did not withdraw his promise, but followed the advice formerly given by Wolsey : he delayed.

When the report was to be presented, the king made the procceding his own, by receiving it under circumstances of peculiar solemnity. On the 24th of May, 1530, the commissioners met at Lambeth. With the archbishop at their head, they proceeded to Westminster. Here they were ushered into the old chapel, or the chapel of St. Edward, on the west side of the parliament chamber. They found the king on his throne, or chair of estate. The report was read, and, from a report to the king, it was issued under an alteration of form, as a royal proclamation. In the royal proclamation, now first read, the titles are given of the several books concerned. The proclamation concludes thus : "The king, our sovereign lord, of his most virtuous and gracious disposition, considering that this noble realm of England hath of long time continued in the true catholic faith of Christ's religion, and that his noble progenitors, kings of this his said realm, have before this time made and enacted many devout laws, statutes, and ordinances for the maintenance and defence of the same faith against malicious sects of heretics and Lollards, who, by perversion of Scripture, do induce erroneous opinion, sow sedition among Christian people, and fondly disturb the peace and tranquillity of Christian realms, as lately happened in some parts of Germany ; his highness, like a most gracious prince, of his blessed and virtuous disposition, willeth now to put in execution all good laws, statutes, and ordinances ordained by his most noble progenitors, kings of England, for the protection of religion." He proceeds to call upon all his lords spiritual and temporal, and upon all who hold office civil or ecclesiastical, as they would avoid his high indignation and displeasure, that they assist him in suppressing publications and in silencing preachers who teach anything contrary to the determination of the Catholic faith and the definitions of Holy Church. He requires them to assist the ordinaries in measures to be adopted for carrying the laws into effect, and for preventing the importation of foreign books.

This proclamation, an act of the royal supremacy, was published a year before the king's assertion of that title, which took the country by surprise. We are often offended by a name, when the name is only an expression of an admitted fact.

The report, or whatever we may call the instrument which was executed before the king at Westminster, and witnessed by the notaries public, was also published. It is a confused paper, in which Warham comes forward, as Primate of All England, to commend it to the attention and observance of all members of the Church. He resumes his proper position as the head of the English Church. The authority of Wolsey was no longer recognised; the primate speaks without reference to the cardinal, and we trace in the document something of the garrulity of old age.

It was probably on account of this proclamation, and a mandate to the same purpose addressed not long before to his suffragans, that Fuller complains of Warham's exhibiting a persecuting spirit towards the close of his life.

There was no enthusiasm or zeal in Warham's constitution, and he simply did what by circumstances he was required to do. We may refer his acceptance of the office of papal collector, in the matter of indulgences, to a similar desire on his part of leading a quiet life. We must not, however, judge of his conduct by the feelings excited in our own minds, when mention is made of the papal system of indulgences. It was well known that recourse was had to the sale of indulgences merely because the papal treasury was exhausted, and this was regarded as a legitimate means of raising money. Application had been made, as we have before mentioned, to the convocation of England to grant a subsidy to Leo X. for the prosecution of a war with the Turks. Considerable pressure had been made upon Warham to induce him to constrain the clergy to make the grant, and to use his influence with the king, to consent to the proceeding. The archbishop did not refuse to submit the papal requisition to his clergy, and the brief was laid before convocation.* But without comment he communicated the refusal of his clergy. He reminded the papal authorities of the generosity of the English clergy to Julius II, and exposed the insincerity of the pope by reminding him that the victories of Henry VIII. over the French had removed all dangers from the Holy See.

The demand for this subsidy had been opposed by a very large minority in the college of cardinals. But the proposal for a sale of indulgences, on a larger scale than heretofore, was well received.

Leo X. was in want of money. He might call upon all Europe to contribute towards the rebuilding of St. Peter's Church. As regards the pious, an appeal was made to the religious sentiment : was it becoming that the bones of those martyrs whose relics were revered by all Christendom, should, as was the case in the present ruined edifice, be exposed to the elements ? An appeal was also made to the charitable.

* Papers and Letters of Henry VIII. No. 1312. In No. 3160, we find the oath taken by Silvester Darius, as papal collector ; but in No. 3688 he is spoken of as sub-collector.

A belief in purgatory prevailed, and was at the root
of almost all the worst superstitions of the age.   To
be relieved from the pains of purgatory, the rich would
bequeath large sums of money, that masses might be
said for their souls, and payment would be made to
obtain, for the departed members of a family, an
early release from the penalties they had incurred by
sins which, though venial, had been many and great.
This was the origin of chantries. But now, for a
comparatively small sum of money, the poorest might
be placed upon a spiritual equality with the rich.* The
statesman was exonerated by this from the necessity
of imposing a tax, when the money he might otherwise have to raise was voluntarily proffered.   These
sophistries were but as the spider's web, when the
hand of the noble Luther was raised against them.
But Henry VIII. was the opponent of Luther, and he
would have been a bold man who should in England
have given weight to Luther's arguments.   Against the
chance of opposition, in England, to the sale of indulgences, Leo X. had taken due precaution.   A fourth
of the money, if not a third, arising from the sale of
indulgences, represented as an act of mercy as well
as of piety, was granted to Henry VIII.† We are
expressly told that to this iniquitous delusion, not
now invented for the first time, but for the first time
conducted on this gigantic scale, the universities were
opposed, and, among the opponents, were the parochial

* In France, a contemporary writer states that whoever shall put
ten sous Tournois into the money-box would go to Paradise, for ten
sous a-piece all sins were forgiven, and souls would escape from
purgatory.—Brewer, Pref. ii. ccv.

† The kings of France and Spain were equally enriched, so was
the Elector of Mentz, Reformer though he was.—See Ranke's
Reformation, 831, where the whole history is given.

clergy.   Erasmus denounced the iniquitous system;
and we must conclude that against this system Warham could argue in private, but he had nothing of the
martyr in his composition; and, when Henry VIII.
commanded him to encourage the profitable sale of
indulgences, Warham offered no resistance or remonstrance.   Believing in purgatory, and accepting the
opus operatum to its full extent, he would argue that
it could do no harm, that it might do good in a
spiritual as well as in a temporal sense.

Between Warham and Fisher there seems to have
continued a friendship throughout their career.   They
were neither of them enthusiasts, but they were men
of similar dispositions.   Between Warham and another
great contemporary, Fox, bishop of Winchester, no
cordiality appears to have existed.   Even when they
acted together as members of the Privy Council of
Henry VII, we find them differing in opinion in regard to the marriage of Prince Henry with Katherine.
At a later period, a dispute arose between them upon
a question having reference to the prerogatives of the
metropolitan, as bearing upon the rights of his suffragans.*

CHAP.
II.
William
Warham.
1503–32.

* The question related, I have little doubt, to the right claimed
by Warham to hold a provincial or metropolitical visitation. I have
searched in vain for information on the subject. I believe that no
documents or records touching the alleged dispute exist in the
episcopal or capitular archives of Winchester. I am informed
by Mr. Baigent, whose diligence as an antiquary is well known,
that he can find no reference to it in his notes. There is no reference
to the subject in Warham's Register in the Lambeth library, which,
as I have observed before, is the least important of all the archiepiscopal registers. Richardson, in his addition to Godwin, merely
mentions the fact, that Fox contended with other bishops, concerning the prerogative of Canterbury, against Archbishop Warham, to
the prejudice of the See. But he gives no authority. I find the
statement, however, relating to such a controversy, confirmed by two

It is interesting to find questions arising even at this period, relating to rubrical difficulties before the Reformation.

The festival of Corpus Christi was instituted in the year 1264. It was to be celebrated on the Thursday after Trinity Sunday. In the year 1529, the vigil of the Nativity of St. John the Baptist fell on that festival, and application was made to the primate to know on what day the fast was to be kept. The primate, perplexed, wrote to the pope. It was not a point on which Leo X. would feel much interest; but he assured the primate that, having taken counsel with his brethren, he had come to the conclusion that, when the vigil of St. John Baptist should fall on the feast of Corpus Christi, the fast should be kept on the Wednesday preceding.*

Warham was engaged in another controversy, to which we have had occasion in a preceding volume to refer. In a letter dated " At Lambeth, 4 June, in the year of our pontificate 5," the archbishop addressed a letter to the Abbot of Glastonbury, in which he mentions that it had lately come to his ears, that a certain tomb of the holy Dunstan had been openly erected by the abbot, by which he would have it inferred that the sacred body was buried in their chapel. The archbishop produces evidence to show that the aforesaid saint, who had preceded him in

letters, Nos. 3066 and 4552, among the State Papers. These show that the King and Queen Katherine took an interest in the proceedings, and nothing more. The controversy was continued under Cranmer and Gardyner. Perhaps some critic may be more fortunate if he will inquire further into this matter. For the dispute between Cranmer and Gardyner, see Cranmer's Letters (Parker Soc.), 304, and Strype's Cram. i. viii.

* " Declaratio jejunii vigiliæ Sancti Johannis Baptistæ contingentis in die Corporis Christi."—Ex. Reg. Warham, fol. 26.

the archiepiscopal dignity of Canterbury, had been duly buried in Canterbury Cathedral, where his body had lately been discovered. By his blindness, rashness, or boldness in asserting that the saint was buried at Glastonbury, the abbot was bringing scandal to the Church of God, and leading the people of the realm into no small error, *superstition*, and confusion; for can it possibly be believed, without mistake, that the body of one saint should be in different places, or that one body, instead of the other, should be considered sacred and adored? That so great a disgrace and abuse might not gradually proceed to still worse evil, and that the truth of the matter might become more evident, he earnestly exhorted, as well as begged and required, his fraternity to appear before him, in his own person, if possible, but, at all events, by deputy, at the next occurrence of the Feast of the Translation of the holy Thomas the Martyr. The abbot was directed to bring with him such writings and records as favoured their pretended title; and, as an act of prudence in the meantime, the archbishop advised the abbot not to suffer the pretended body of St. Dunstan to be disclosed and venerated by the people in any way.

To this, Richard Beere, the abbot of Glastonbury, made reply. He admits that, with the full concurrence of the bishop of the diocese, he and his brethren had removed the tomb of St. Dunstan, their patron and saint, from one place to another, because the shrine being easily touched, the hands of persons who approached it were often found to pilfer the pieces of gold and silver with which it was adorned. It was removed to a higher position, beyond the reach of pilferers. They did not allege that his body had been buried at Glastonbury; but what they asserted was that, after the destruction of Canterbury by the Danes, his sacred bones were conveyed to that place. He suggests that, while the greater portion of his remains had been conveyed to Glastonbury, some particles might have been retained by the monks of Canterbury, and these were what had been lately discovered: he will be glad to have it found that, while the monks of Glastonbury possessed the posterior and upper portion of the skull, the monks of Canterbury had the forehead or anterior portion, and then, without scandal or tumult of the populace, Dunstan, like some other saints, might be honoured in different places. He could not prevent the remains of God's saint from being disclosed or venerated by the people, lest haply he should be fighting against God. The people in the neighbourhood having been accustomed from time immemorial to pay their devotions at the shrine of St. Dunstan, at Glastonbury, a tumult would be occasioned if they were to discontinue a custom which very generally prevailed; it would be more reasonable for the monks of Canterbury to conceal their newly-discovered relics until the proposed inquiry as to their authenticity could be made. He pleads the infirm state of his health as an excuse for not waiting upon his grace; but assures him that he is always ready to obey his commands, so far as they might be done without detriment to the rights of his church and monastery.*

This correspondence taking place immediately before the Reformation is worthy of notice. Within a few years, the shrines of St. Dunstan, whether at Glastonbury or at Canterbury, were demolished; and the money, misappropriated to the purposes of super-

* Ang. Sac. ii. 229—231. The originals may be found in Vol. I. of this work, p. 422 *et seq.*

stition, was devoted to the purposes of a profligacy which, though equally opposed to the practices of true religion, is regarded with feelings of greater toleration.

When we remember the celebrated pilgrimage of Erasmus and Colet, if Colet is personified by Gratianus Pullus,* to the shrine of St. Thomas of Canterbury; we may presume, that the archbishop, who, privately, agreed with them in opinion, acted on this occasion less from any impulses of his own, than from instigation of the monks of Canterbury, whose rights he was sworn to maintain, and whose perquisites were likely to be diminished. Credulity had been the fault of the past ages, about to be superseded by a general tendency to scepticism. We are not surprised at the occasional inconsistencies of Warham, Fisher, and More, and, to a certain extent, of Erasmus, when the prevalent feeling in their minds was, that superstition should be denounced on the one hand, while, on the other, care was to be taken lest the spirit of inquiry should develop itself into a latitudinarianism nearly allied to irreligion.

These observations are intended to introduce to the notice of the reader an extraordinary imposture, which obtained more importance than it would otherwise have deserved, through the attempts of both parties, when parties were formed on the subject of the divorce, to make out of it, to use a modern expression, political capital.

The age, the high station, and the infirmities of Archbishop Warham were probably his protection when he committed himself to the ridiculous but tragical affair, which conduced, among other things,

---

* This may be considered as a fact established by Erasmus himself in his *Modus orandi Deum.*

to the legal murder of his friends, Bishop Fisher
and Sir Thomas More. It is not indeed improbable,
as Sir Henry Ellis remarks, that, if Warham's life
had been prolonged two years, he would himself have
been subjected to a charge of misprision of treason.

So far as we are justified by our documents in
arriving at a conclusion, we have no reason to suppose
that Warham was influenced, in any part of the transaction, by any political feeling. From politics, indeed,
he carefully abstained, except when political subjects
were forced upon his notice. He was probably led
on by the easy indolence of a man who, in retirement, requires some amount of excitement, and seeks
it in the passing occurrences of the moment, sometimes very trifling.

Elizabeth Barton was residing, in a menial capacity,
at Aldington, in Kent, the living which had been
offered by the archbishop to Erasmus. Being affected
by some hysterical disorders, she was visited by the
pastor of her parish, a man of the name of Maister,
who was surprised to hear her, when lying apparently
in a kind of trance, uttering frantic and incoherent
sentences, which, probably in ignorance, he regarded
as inspirations, and of a prophetical character. Maister
made a communication upon the subject to his diocesan, the archbishop. The treatment of such a case
in the sixteenth century differed widely from that
which it would have received in the nineteenth, and
was contemplated with different feelings. The first
inclination would now be to regard the case in the
light of a mere disease, to be submitted to the physician ; or else it would be denounced as an imposture.
In the sixteenth century the inclination would be to
look at it with awe as a Divine or a diabolical visitation. It might be found, on investigation, to be an

imposture ; but the *onus probandi* would be with the sceptic. The remarkable impostures, such as those relating to spirit-rapping, which are now believed by noble lords and literary gentlemen, whose incredulity and infidel propensities are only visible when the Bible is concerned, are sufficient to moderate our censure of Warham, Fisher, and More, when they were inclined to give credit to the ravings of Elizabeth Barton. The archbishop, having heard the exaggerated statement of Maister, directed him to watch the case, and to note what, under her fits of inspiration, the young woman might say. It does not appear that either Maister or his patient had any intention, in the first instance, to deceive. By herself and by her pastor, Elizabeth Barton was thought to be inspired. He was amazed at what he had witnessed, and, finding the archbishop equally astonished, he then became anxious, for his own credit's sake, to increase the marvel, or, at all events, to show that he had not been deceived. His credulity increased the disorder of the young person : and, under the notion that she was inspired, the contortions of her body became more violent, and her hysterical utterances more frequent. She was told that to conceal the workings of the Holy Spirit within her would be a sin, and there soon became method in her madness. Maister was a man himself of inferior capacity, and was, like the girl, a dupe before he became an impostor. He consulted one Bocking, a monk of Christ Church, whom he met when he went to Canterbury. Bocking appears to have been altogether an intriguing, avaricious, and designing man. He saw clearly how they might make a gain of godliness. The young woman heard the priests affirm that she would be restored to health if she prayed before an image of the Virgin Mary, in the chapel of Courtop Street.* She soon had a vision of the Virgin, and the suggestions of the priests became a mandate of Our Lady. She was carried to the chapel. She lay long prostrate before the image. Her prayer was heard. A miracle was wrought; she was apparently restored to health.

The consequence was that wealth flowed in upon Maister and Bocking from the numerous pilgrimages which were made to the image of the Virgin.

It is to be remembered, that this imposture, cleverly managed, covered the space of eight years; it was no sudden evanescent transaction: it was gradually developed. Elizabeth Barton declared that the malady had left her, and the servant-girl was sinking into insignificance. She had been the subject of a miracle: others in their own cases imagined the same; and nervous diseases of various kinds were healed by a pilgrimage to the image in the chapel of Courtop Street.

Another step must be taken, or the occupation of Maister and of Bocking would have been gone. The disease was cured; this was the fact that brought grist to the mill of Aldington. But what had been at one time a disease was now a Divine visitation. There were contortions of the body, and she was frequently to be seen in a trance; at such times, she saw visions and received revelations from the Virgin. It was hardly fitting that such a person should continue nothing more than a servant-girl.

It was arranged, that there should be a great gathering in the chapel of those who had received benefit through the intercessions of Our Lady, before whose image, the work of men's hands, multitudes had fallen

---

* Otherwise Courte of Street. See Cranmer's Remains.

down in the chapel of Courtop Street. Elizabeth
Barton was there, and all eyes were fixed on one
through whose instrumentality so many diseased persons had received the blessing of health. Suddenly
her whole frame was convulsed ; the contortions of her
face were frightful. She spoke, for a revelation had
been made to her, of Our Lady's will : that will was
that Elizabeth Barton should receive the veil. There
were but few monasteries that would receive the profession of a penniless girl ; but here was a Divine
command and a case of miracle ; and where were the
religious that would refuse obedience, or forego the
fame which attached to a wonder-worker? Elizabeth
Barton was removed to a nunnery, St. Sepulchre's, at
Canterbury. She was now under the immediate care
of Dr. Bocking, who became her spiritual adviser or
ghostly father.

All had succeeded so far. Her patrons were enriched by the pilgrimages to Aldington. Elizabeth
Barton herself, now called the Holy Maid of Kent,
was in a place of comfort and respectability, receiving
visits from the great and the good. Among her visitors was the Archbishop of Canterbury, who wrote
thus to Cardinal Wolsey :—

" Please it your grace, so it is that Elizabeth Barton, being
a religious woman, professed in Saint Sepulchre's, in Canterbury, which had all the visions as Our Lady of Courtop Street,
a very well disposed and virtuous woman (as I am informed
by her sisters), is very desirous to speak with your grace
personally. What she hath to say, or whether it be good or
ill, I do not know ; but she hath desired me to write unto
your grace, and to desire the same (as I do) that she may come
into your grace's presence. Whom, when your grace have
heard, ye may order as shall please the same. For I assure
your grace she hath made very importune suit to me to be a

mean to your grace, that she may speak with you. At Canterbury, the first day of October." *

Wolsey was not likely to be hurried away by enthusiasm, and evidently treated the whole proceeding with contempt; hence he incurred the enmity of the nun and her accomplices. But Warham thought the case to be of sufficient importance to bring it before the king, to whom he presented a roll on which was written many of the nun's rhapsodies. The king submitted the document to Sir Thomas More, who was astonished to find the inspired utterances unworthy of notice. " I find nothing," he said, ."in it, that I can esteem or regard : a simple woman, in my mind, might have spoken it all."

These statements, however, show that a sensation had been caused through the proceedings of the Holy Maid of Kent, long before an idea was entertained of making political capital out of the case. It would appear that, however it may have been with respect to others, Warham viewed it in its religious and not in its political aspect. It can hardly be said to have assumed a political character before Warham had passed to that place where " the wicked cease from troubling, and the weary be at rest." He only knew that in her trances she was heard to rebuke sin, and

---

* Ellis, Third Series, ii. 137. It is interesting to compare this letter with one on the same subject, written by Cranmer, and to be given in his Life. The change of feeling which had already taken place, is worthy of remark. Warham was afraid of shocking the religious feeling by not believing the miracles of the Nun of Kent; Cranmer was afraid of shocking the same feeling by appearing to believe in it. Warham was, perhaps, less of a believer than he supposed himself to be ; Cranmer, perhaps, believed rather more than he professed. In the filthy spirit which loves to imagine impurity, it has been asserted in after times, without the shadow of a proof, that Bocking had an intrigue with the Nun of Kent.

that she, an unlettered girl, gave utterance to the most orthodox dogmas, and denounced the new learning. Had her patrons been contented with this state of things, all might have been well. But when persons have once lived on excitement, it is to them as to the man who indulges in spirituous liquors: there must be fresh causes of excitement, or a depression ensues, which it is too painful to bear.

They passed into the world of politics. The country was divided into two great factions, the party of the king and the party of the queen. The men of the new learning, the Reformers in general, were on the king's side, as his mistress, Ann Boleyn, had signified her inclination, so far as was safe, to extend to them her patronage. They were intellectually powerful; but at present numerically weak. The great bulk of the nation, the people, the women especially, and the clergy, were vehement in their feelings of indignation at the insults offered to a lady whose conduct as a wife and as a mother had been exemplary, who had maintained the dignity and decorum of the English court, who had become a thorough English woman, and now was to be treated as a foreigner.

The Holy Maid of Kent became political. By whom she was prompted it does not appear; but the divorce was condemned, and she was directed to warn Queen Katherine and her daughter not to acquiesce in any arrangement which might have this object in view.

Into the details of her conduct after she had become simply and consciously an impostor it is not necessary for me to enter. The history is well known. It is known how cruelly her case was brought to bear upon the fate of some of the greatest persons this country has produced. How Henry and Crumwell wished to represent the case so far as it concerned Warham, may be seen from the act of attainder against Elizabeth Barton, Edward Bocking, and their accomplices. It says :—

"And for ratification of her false, feigned revelations, the said Edward by conspiracy, between him and the said Elizabeth, revealed the same to the most reverend father, William, late archbishop of Canterbury, who by false and untrue surmises, tales, and lies, of the said Edward and Elizabeth, was allured, brought, and induced to credit them, and made no diligent searches for the trial of their said falsehoods and considerations, but suffered and admitted the same, to the blasphemy of Almighty God, and to the great deceit of the prince and people of this realm."[*]

We now pass on to observe that, however anxious Warham may have been to convert a high and holy office into a splendid retirement, where he might enjoy his *otium cum dignitate*, he was compelled to learn, that man looks in vain for a Sabbath in this sublunary world ; the Sabbath of the Christian, though predestined to be eternal, will not commence until this world and the fashion of it shall have passed away.

In 1527, the subject of the divorce, which was destined to occupy an important place in the history of England, was first mooted ; and then only among a chosen few to whom the king's "secret matier" was confided.

---

[*] Mr. Amos shows, that in two of his works Lord Coke lays it down that the affairs of the Nun of Kent and her confederates were not treason. The parties attainted were not heard in their own defence before either house of parliament. That they were impostors is clear, but of the extent of their imposture we cannot speak. We know not how far they might have disproved the charges brought against them if they had been heard. It is fortunate in these days that men are not doomed to die for their impostures.

There is some difficulty in ascertaining how and under what circumstances the question of the divorce first arose. The difficulty will diminish, however, if we admit, that the idea of the divorce did not *originate* in the king's passion for Ann Boleyn. This intervened after the subject had been mooted; and it complicated the whole affair.

It is expressly stated by Pole, that the idea of the divorce was suggested by Cardinal Wolsey. Pole, though a slow man, was not likely to misstate a fact wilfully, and he only repeated what was the prevalent opinion, and confirmed it by his own authority. It is said that this was denied in the legatine court, and in the presence of the king, by Wolsey himself.[*] But this is not precisely accurate. We gather what Wolsey asserted from Henry's reply. What the king stated was, that the religious scruples by which he was influenced had not been suggested by Wolsey or by any one else, but had originated in the piety of his own royal mind and tender conscience. When the foreign ambassadors, in reference to certain matrimonial alliances relating to the Princess Mary, objected that a question might be raised on the ground of her legitimacy, then the passing notions which had disturbed the king's mind received confirmation. Now we know that, among his political speculations, Wolsey entertained the notion of a marriage between Henry VIII. and Renée, the daughter of Louis XII. of France.[†] Wolsey, with that disregard to private feelings which is characteristic of statesmen when the interests of the public are concerned, suggested that there was just enough of doubt about the legality of

---

[*] Poli Apol. ad Cæs. The emperor, in his answer to Henry, made the same assertion; but his authority was Pole.

[†] Le Grand, iii. 166, 168.

Henry's marriage with Katherine to enable the marriage to be set aside by some one or other of those countless subterfuges by which popes were accustomed to override the law, and to accede to the will of princes, when princes were prepared to defer to the decisions of a pope. The king, weary of his wife, listened graciously to the proposal of his minister, and called to mind the misery he had endured for years, under the impression that, instead of being a married man, he had been living in a state of concubinage. Would the queen, from motives of patriotism towards her adopted country, consent to a separation from the man to whom she had given her heart? This was the question which it was easy to ask, and to which it was not difficult to divine what the answer would be. The queen, when she suspected the object of the minister, who from that time became her aversion, acted like a fond woman and a devoted wife. She thought to win back her husband's heart by redoubling the splendours of her court, which she did to such an extent that Campeggio deemed it his duty to remonstrate with her on the countenance which she gave to dissipation. A further proof she gave of her determination to maintain her position as the king's wife in her toleration of his infidelities. The infamy was great when Ann Boleyn kept up a court in rivalry to that of the queen, under the same roof; but we may complain of the weakness of Katherine in submitting to the insult. It is difficult to say what she could have done, when she was so entirely under the dominion of a despot. She probably hoped that, through her forbearance, the time would come when she should regain her husband's heart; but the fact is to be noticed, since it has been the custom with Protestant writers to represent the gloom of her character, and the consequent dulness of her court, as a palliation of the king's conduct.

When the king and his minister had determined to apply for a divorce in the king's behalf, the next question was to ascertain the general feeling of the country upon the subject, and especially the feeling of those statesmen who had concurred in procuring the dispensation from Julius II. From the part Warham had taken in that transaction—having first opposed the marriage of Henry with Katherine, and having then officiated at its celebration—to secure the co-operation, or, at all events, the silent sanction of the primate, was now important.

Warham was on a visit, in the year 1527, at Dartmouth, the guest of Sir John Wiltshire, when he was waited upon unexpectedly by the cardinal. It must be remarked that Wolsey's object was simply to discuss the policy of a divorce, without any reference to Ann Boleyn. Ann Boleyn had not come on the *tapis*. The cardinal enlarged on the king's scruples. He admitted that they were not shared by the queen. Katherine was a pious woman, but her conscience was less sensitive than that of her husband; and as for the king himself wishing to be separated from his wife, the cardinal was commissioned to assure the primate that Henry's sole desire was the "searching and trying out of the truth."

On the political aspect of the affair, there was much to be said, though less than is sometimes supposed. That some fears were entertained of the consequences likely to arise out of a disputed succession we may infer from the fact, that on this subject the king's friends dwelt much. But these fears were really entertained only by a few. Sir Thomas More, opposed as he was to the divorce of Katherine, openly declared that he was ready to acknowledge the right of parliament to regulate the succession to the throne. He held to the old English principle, the hereditary right of the family, to be regulated by the decision of the nation. The various acts of parliament regulating the succession passed in Henry's reign, and the quiet manner in which the Ladies Mary and Elizabeth severally succeeded to the throne, all suffice to show that the succession was subject to parliamentary arrangements; and the contempt with which the attempts of Mary queen of Scots were met, in her endeavours to act in defiance of the law of parliament, only corroborates the fact.

At the same time, the fact that she had a party to support her, and that, throughout the reigns of Mary and Elizabeth, pretenders to the crown from time to time appeared, and that, from jealousy of their pretensions, blood was cruelly spilled on the scaffold and in the field, must be adduced to show that a party also existed which upheld the doctrine of uncontrolled hereditary right to the crown. It was not yet ascertained, nor was it ascertainable, whether this notion, for the maintenance of which Jacobites afterwards fought and died, was a doctrine only of a minority in the land.

The heir-presumptive was a girl; and a female had never yet succeeded to the English throne. The claim of a female in the case of the Empress Maud and the late Elizabeth of York, had, with their own consent, been set aside.

The question started by foreign diplomatists as to the legitimacy of the Lady Mary, had been especially brought forward and strongly urged by the Bishop of Tarbes; at least such was the statement made to Warham, who had originally regarded the match, not from the religious, but from the political point of view.* How much importance was attached to this interview with the primate may be inferred from the fact of the cardinal himself waiting upon Warham; and also from the notification, that he watched the archbishop's countenance as he made his communication to him, to see what impression his arguments would make. Wolsey "carefully watched the fashion and manner of my Lord of Canterbury;" and Warham evidently received the royal communication better than was expected. There was never any enthusiasm or chivalry about the man, and now, instead of throwing his ægis over a poor, persecuted, unbefriended queen, he consented to take the hard, dry legal view of the subject. He determined that, without regard to the queen's wishes, " the truth and judgment of the law" must be followed,—law without justice, and judgment without mercy. It had been supposed that he would take up the queen's cause; but, when he declared himself on the king's side, Wolsey supplied him with directions how to proceed if the queen sent for him.†

Thus stood the case with the archbishop; and, when the royal intention was divulged, the people in general approved of a measure which would give the king a

---

* I think Dr. Lingard, in the Appendix P to vol. iv. has established the point that the objection, said to be urged by the Bishop of Tarbes to the legitimacy of the Princess Mary, was a mere fiction agreed upon by Henry and the cardinal to cajole the primate.

† State Papers, i. 195, 196. When we read this letter we easily understand why, on Wolsey's fall, the great seal was offered to Warham. Henry feared that the queen might be supported by the primate; he was, therefore, to be made keeper of the king's conscience.

young wife, and secure a male heir to the throne. They thought not much of the subject; and as for kings and queens, it was so usual for them to marry and to be unmarried for the good of their subjects, or for political objects, that the people did not contemplate any great opposition on the part of the queen. Wolsey had made up his mind as to the person who was to occupy the second seat on the throne when it should become vacant. The people in general fixed on Margaret, duchess of Alençon. All were well pleased with a king who yielded to the dictates of conscience, and for the sole welfare of his people was ready to receive or repudiate a wife, according to the requirements of his council and the exigences of his country.

But a change soon took place in the opinion of the public. All persons were astonished and many were shocked when the news spread, which was at first incredible, that the king of whose scrupulous and tender conscience so much had been said, whose single aim had been the good of his subjects, had determined to elevate his mistress to the seat from which he had resolved to dethrone the royal lady who for seventeen years had rendered respectable as well as brilliant her husband's court, and concealed his evil doings from the public eye.

The matronage of England was insulted; the clergy united with them in an expression of indignation. The expression was deep though not loud, because a despotic power was exerted to suppress it; party writers, at a later period, have ignored its existence. But we have the strong assertion of Wakefield, made to no less a person than to King Henry himself, that, if the people were aware of Wakefield's having changed his side and of his advocating a divorce, which he had previously opposed, they would stone him to death.* Wolsey, to quiet a disturbance, was obliged on one occasion to proclaim that, happen what might, the husband of the Lady Mary would be the heir to King Henry's throne.† The women were so enraged that, on another occasion, they threatened the very life of Ann Boleyn. So impossible was it found to prevent the clergy from attacking her from their pulpits, that, by an unheard-of exercise of despotic power, when Cranmer succeded to the primacy, he was obliged to close all the pulpits in his province, except to those who received a special licence to preach. The sagacity of Wolsey foresaw the result of this act of infatuation on the part of Henry ; and when the king first signified his intention to him of marrying his mistress, the cardinal remained for hours, on his knees, imploring him not to be guilty of an act so deplorably rash ; an act, in truth, which in any one except Henry himself would have cost him not only his crown but his life.‡

It was fortunate for the king, that he now found two counsellors who have left each of them a name, equally distinguished in history with that of Wolsey himself ;—Thomas Cranmer, wise to suggest great measures, and Thomas Crumwell, unscrupulous in carrying them into effect. Cranmer urged the king to transfer the question of the divorce, through an exertion of the royal supremacy, from the papal to the national

* Knight's Erasmus, Append. ix. p. 28.

† Le Grand, iii. 204.

‡ Cavendish, 139. The arguments said to have been employed by Wolsey on the occasion are to be found in Le Grand ; they are all of a political character. Not long after, another faithful minister, Sully, sued in vain to Henry IV. of France, when that monarch, under an infatuation similar to that of Henry of England, determined to insult the morality of nations by causing his mistress to be crowned.

courts; by Crumwell the king was advised to apply the Supremacy to a visitation of the monasteries with the view perhaps, in the first instance, to mulctuary proceedings rather than to their suppression.

Upon the subject of the Supremacy, something has been said in the introductory chapter of this book, to which the reader is referred, and something will presently be added. It has been shown that in every reign the royal supremacy, as a matter of fact, was asserted. When by their own misconduct, and the political management of the authorities at Rome, the general councils were suppressed, and from the time of Martin V. it had been maintained that the supreme authority in the Church rested not, as was before contended, in the councils, but in the Bishop of Rome: the rights of national churches were virtually suppressed. The century preceding the Reformation was one of extreme laxity in what related to doctrine as well as in what related to conduct. The papal power was no longer resisted, as in times past, by the king, the clergy, and the people of England. The clergy permitted their primate to be, in effect, superseded by a legate *à latere;* the people were universally discontented, but they had confidence in their king; and King Henry VIII. was, in the earlier part of his reign, a violent and unreasoning papist. Instead of upholding the clergy of the Church of England against the pope, he disliked the clergy and abetted the pope, when the pope attempted to exercise that authority over them which the king's predecessors had resisted.

But Henry in action was not consistent. He did not, until the close of Warham's primacy, assert his supremacy theoretically, or as a matter of right; but, if his will was thwarted, then, as a matter of fact, the Supremacy was shown in reality to exist.

In no instance was this more clearly manifested than in the case of Dr. Standish, the consideration of which I have therefore reserved for this place.

Dr. Henry Standish, warden of the Minorities of London, was one of the most popular preachers of the day.* He was a prudent man, and one who, contrary to what we should expect in a friar, maintained, like Cranmer, the rights of the national Church, even when they clashed with papal assumptions. We may account for this tendency in Standish, when we find him to be a courtier, and one of the king's counsel learned in the law. The antagonism between the friars and the secular clergy still existed, and in the towns the friars had the ascendency; they mixed more freely with the people, and were the better, or at all events the more popular, preachers. It was by the secular clergy and the upper classes that the friars were disliked: by the former, because they set at nought every parochial regulation and ridiculed the incumbents; by the latter, on account of their vulgarity, and the petty arts by which they cheated the ignorant.

---

* Erasmus had a quarrel with Standish, and represents him as a man of consummate ignorance and impudence. We must regard these as the words of an angry man. Standish was very probably not a proficient in classical literature. But even here we must qualify the assertion of Erasmus. Unless Standish had some acquaintance with Greek, he could hardly have entered into a controversy with Erasmus on his translation of the first verse of St. John's Gospel, *In principio erat sermo* instead of *verbum*. That he sought to damage Erasmus with the king by accusing him of heresy may be adduced as a proof of his malignity, but not of his ignorance. But Erasmus could retaliate, and we know that Standish resented a charge of ignorance when brought against him, as Erasmus did a charge of heresy. In 1519, Standish was advanced to the see of St. Asaph, commonly called at that time St. Asse. Erasmus thought it witty to speak of him as *Episcopus à Sancto Asino.*

Standish was the more powerful, because his position was exceptional. He was at the head of the friars, and could command their services; he was popular through his preaching; he was hostile to the secular clergy, and the London incumbents in particular; he was learned in the law, and knew that by the law the king was over all causes and persons supreme; he maintained the royal cause against the clergy, and thus, having a common cause with the nobility, with them also he was a favourite. In 1512, an act of parliament was passed, by which murderers, robbers of churches, and housebreakers were deprived of their clergy, unless they were in holy orders. Against this act, Richard Kidderminster, abbot of Winchcombe, declaimed in 1515, from the pulpit at Paul's Cross. He represented it as an act opposed to the liberties of the Church. The act only so far invaded the liberties of the Church as to prevent the Church from extending its protection to persons guilty of these offences, not because they were in holy orders, but because, being able to read, they were *qualified* for ordination. The abbot, however, went still further: he asserted that the lords spiritual and temporal, as well as the commons, by whom the bill was passed, had incurred the censures of the Church. The preacher was impeached, and the king appointed a commission, consisting of a certain number of divines and a certain number of temporal lords, before whom the case was to be argued. The commission met at Blackfriars, and was attended by the judges.* The secular clergy generally

* Letters and Papers, Henry VIII. In No. 1313 we have Keelway's account of this affair. Keelway lived in the reign of Elizabeth, and his statements must be corrected by the account of Dr. Standish and Convocation, No. 1314—a contemporary document.

supported the abbot. Standish was the leading counsel against him. He contended manfully, that what was passed for the good of the realm could not be against the liberty of the Church,—the realm and the Church consisting of the same persons. The commission did not come to an agreement; the bishops were unwilling to accede to the demand of the lords temporal, that the Abbot of Winchcombe should be made to apologize. Party feeling ran high. Among the lower classes, it was taken up as a quarrel between the secular clergy and the friars; in the upper classes, it was a controversy between the lords temporal and the lords spiritual.

As is usual in such cases, party feeling hurried both sides into extreme measures which could not be justified. The clergy, wrong from the beginning, put themselves still further in the wrong, by prosecuting Dr. Standish in convocation, not only for heterodoxy in some of the arguments which, as counsel in this case, he had employed; but for heterodox opinions which were deduced from lectures he had given,—the heterodoxy of which would certainly not have been noticed, except for his conduct in this affair. The lords temporal asserted, that by this proceeding the convocation had incurred the penalties of a præmunire. The accusation is remarkable; it shows that it was considered as already possible that a whole corporation as well as an individual might incur those awful penalties, and this probably first suggested this policy to which we shall have occasion presently to advert.

The affair was patched up. When the king became himself a partisan, and showed symptoms of anger, the bishops only thought of the least undignified manner of escaping from the difficulty. On a comparison of the several statements, I think the facts may be fairly stated as follows :—The king demanded and received an explanation from the convocation, and then took the case into his own hands. He summoned the judges and the members of the Privy Council to meet him at Baynard's Castle. The judges gave judgment that the convocation, by its proceedings, had incurred the guilt of præmunire; appending a threatening clause to the effect, that the spiritual lords had no place in parliament except by virtue of their temporal possessions, and that therefore the king could hold a parliament by himself, the lords temporal, and the commons, without summoning the spirituality. This was a significant hint, and Wolsey, with his usual quickness of decision, kneeled before the king, and solemnly assured him that nothing had been intended prejudicial to the prerogatives of the crown. Assuming that he himself was the head of the clergy, he alluded to the fact, that it was impossible for one like himself, who owed his advancement solely to the royal favour, to assent to anything that would be derogatory to that royal authority on which he was wholly dependent. He prayed the king to permit the matter to be referred to the pope and his council at Rome. This was the form in which he thought it best to let the matter drop, and as the king was at this time (1515) a violent advocate for the rights of the papacy, it was not probable that he would refuse.

Instead of letting the matter rest here, however, the Bishop of Winchester and the Archbishop of Canterbury prolonged the discussion, the former provoking the king by a sarcastic remark on Dr. Standish; and the latter eliciting an opinion from the chief justice stronger than had yet been given, by weakly alluding to the conduct of some of his predecessors in office, whose conduct he praised, but was by no means prepared to imitate. Warham remarked that in former days, many holy fathers had resisted the law of the land on this point, and some suffered martyrdom in the quarrel. Fineux, the chief justice, answered that the correcting of clerks had been practised by many holy kings, and many fathers of the Church had agreed to it. Then, turning to the bishops, he added: "If a clerk be arrested by the secular authority for murder or felony, and the temporal judge commits him to you according to your desire, you have no authority by your law to try him." Hereupon the king said: "We are, by the sufferance of God, king of England, and the kings of England, in times past, never had any superior but God. Know, therefore, that we will maintain the rights of the crown in this matter, like our progenitors; and as for your decrees, we are satisfied that even you of the spirituality act expressly against the word of several of them, as has been well shown you by some of our spiritual counsel. You interpret your decrees at your pleasure; but as for me, I shall never consent to your decrees more than my progenitors have done." *

* The king evidently alluded to an argument *ad hominem* adopted in the course of his pleading by Dr. Standish. The counsel on the other side maintained that there was a decree of the Church expressly opposed to the act of parliament, and that decrees of the Church all Christians were bound to obey. Standish met him by an *ad captandum* argument; all bishops, he reminded his opponent, were by the decrees of the Church required to be resident in their cathedrals at every feast; but yet this decree the majority of the bishops of England disregarded. The reader is to be reminded that the case of Dr. Horsey and the merchant Hun, of which Foxe and Burnet have made so much, occurred at this time, when party feeling ran very high. It seems clear that Dr.

This occurred in 1515, at a time when Henry VIII. was a devoted supporter of papal rights; we may rather say of the pretensions of the see of Rome, unacknowledged by the English constitution.* His feeling was, that he would support the pope, when the pope could establish his pretensions; but, at the same time, he would maintain the prerogatives of the crown, according to which the king was in all things supreme. The two powers having co-ordinate jurisdiction, the supremacy of the pope over the clergy was to be rendered consistent with the supremacy of the king over all, whether of the clergy or of the laity.

But, although the king asserted his supremacy, he did not perceive how it bore upon the question of the divorce, until he admitted Cranmer to his counsels.

Horsey was wrong in the first instance in prosecuting him; but we have the high authority of Sir Thomas More (Works, 297) for regarding the verdict of the coroner's jury bringing in a charge of murder against those who had the custody of Hun when in prison as the dictate, not of justice, but of party rancour. The party feeling which the case still excites is attributable in part to the supposition that Hun was prosecuted in the legatine court. In an attack on the legatine court, the clergy would have gladly joined. Hun was prosecuted in the national court of the Bishop of London, which had existed from the time of William the Conqueror. The legatine court, as we have seen, was introduced by Wolsey, and was intended by him to supersede other ecclesiastical courts.

* Henry went so far in his deference to the see of Rome that when he showed to Sir Thomas More his book against Luther, Sir Thomas says, " I moved the king's highness either to leave out that point,"—what he had said of the primacy of the pope,—"or else to touch it more tenderly; for doubt of such things as might hap to fall in question between his highness and some pope, as between princes and popes divers times have done. Whereunto his highness answered me *that he would in no wise anything mind of that matter;* of which thing his highness showed me a secret cause whereof I never had anything heard before."—More, ed. Cayley, i. 188.

The mind of this illustrious man was a legal mind: he was greater as a lawyer than as a theologian. It was a providential blessing to our Church that Cranmer and his master were so attached even to the technicalities of the law, that this circumstance acted upon them as a restraint in the midst of proceedings which necessarily bore a revolutionary character.

Wolsey, on the other hand, brought the mind not of a lawyer or of a divine, but of a statesman, to bear upon ecclesiastical affairs. He looked to the end, but disregarded the means. In defiance of the constitution and of the law, he had introduced the legatine courts, and this proved to be the cause of his fall, by perplexing the whole subject of the divorce.*

The divorce, according to Wolsey's view, could only be settled by the pope; and the pope would act through his legates. Hence the country was insulted, and the constitution violated, by the opening of a legatine court to try the case, and to sit in judgment on the King and Queen of England. The very notion of the thing stirs up the blood of an Englishman, and this was one of the causes of Wolsey's unpopu-

CHAP.
11.

William
Warham.
1503–32.

* The word "divorce" is used throughout this controversy; but the reader must bear in mind that a divorce in the strict sense of the word could not be pronounced. The question was whether the dispensation obtained to legalize the marriage of Henry and Katherine were a legal document,—whether the pope had power to legalize the marriage. The pope might dispense with a law of the Church, but not with a law of God. If Arthur were really married to Katherine the pope's dispensation was null: if it were merely a contract without consummation it was a marriage, but only in the eye of the Church, and a dispensation would hold. If the marriage were consummated, then it was a marriage in the sight of God, who prohibited marriage with a deceased brother's wife. Therefore, when the pope granted a dispensation for the celebration of the marriage, he was acting *ultra vires*. Hence the importance attached to the consummation.

larity. In his own case he had established the precedent of holding a court, not in the king's name, but in that of the pope, and, in regard to the divorce, he could only suggest the formation of a similar court with enlarged powers. Cranmer's clear and sagacious mind perceived where the difficulty lay, and he suggested the remedy. The Church of England was a national Church, and was not, as Wolsey regarded it, a mere dependency upon Rome. The national Church had, from time immemorial, possessed ecclesiastical courts: the king, as supreme over all causes and persons, ecclesiastical and civil, was bound to see that the decisions of those courts should be carried into effect. The pope had no right to initiate proceedings; he had no right to hold a court within this realm; the divorce must be pronounced in England and in English courts, and then against the decision an appeal to Rome might lie. The English courts having sat in England, and decided, if, contrary to the law of the realm, an appeal were carried to Rome, there judgment would be given, not on the king, but on the proceedings of the English judges. Let the divorce be decided in England, and the ministers of Henry knew how to obtain a verdict, when the king had determined what the verdict should be. Either party might appeal; in the interval between the judgment and the appeal the king might act as he pleased —*that* was no business of Dr. Cranmer. Before his acquaintance with Dr. Cranmer, the king had been advised to obtain the opinion of the canonists and universities. Let an opinion be obtained favourable to the divorce; let the English courts, armed with this authority, decree the divorce; and it was not probable that the courts of Rome would reverse the judgment.

As this subject will come repeatedly before us, it is

as well to be precise, and to point out the difference between the counsels of Cranmer and those of Wolsey, Gardyner, and Bonner, all equally in favour of the divorce, and all willing to go great lengths to compel the pope to grant it. Cranmer asserted that the case was to be tried in the English courts, with the power of appeal to Rome. The others supposed that proceedings must be initiated in a foreign—the papal —court. Their object was to terrify the pope, and to compel him, not only to institute a legatine commission without delay, but to appoint such judges as would decide as the king wished. They admitted the papal claim to act in the first instance; but wished to make the pope, from political considerations, an unjust judge. Cranmer had no intention to deny the papal rights; but he asked, as an English lawyer, what those rights were. He called upon the king to exercise that authority which, as we have seen, he claimed, and, by the exercise of his supremacy, to prevent the pope from originating proceedings. The others were not prepared, as Cranmer was, to deny the pope's right to initiate. Cranmer saw the weak point in his own case from the beginning,—the admission of a right of appeal to Rome from the judgment of the English court. We infer this from the extreme anxiety we shall afterwards find him exhibiting, when he gave what is called the Dunstable judgment, lest an appeal against this judgment should be lodged by the queen. On this account, Henry demurred to act at once upon Cranmer's advice; he persevered, until circumstances rendered his marriage with Ann Boleyn a necessity, in acting on the advice of Gardyner and Bonner; and he hoped to intimidate the pope. He understood Cranmer's advice to be, Obtain a sentence in your favour in the English courts;

marry upon it; then, if there be an appeal, it will have reference, not to the first marriage, but to the second, not to the king, but to the judge.

Although we have brought this subject under one point of view, we must now return to the consideration of the measures adopted by the king antecedently to the acceptance of Dr. Cranmer's counsel, which will come under notice in Cranmer's life. The question was, how to deal with the clergy? When the question related simply to the divorce, they were prepared to acquiesce in whatever the Government might decide upon doing. When it was known, that the king was infatuated by his attachment to his mistress, for whose sake he would sacrifice his country as well as himself; when it was known that his mistress would be satisfied with nothing less than a share of his throne; every manly sentiment was enlisted on the side of the insulted majesty of Katherine. The clergy, and,— until Ann Boleyn allowed it to be supposed, that in her the advocates of reform would find a patron, —to a very great extent the people also, were, as the people generally are, on the side of injured innocence.

Wolsey, deeply depressed, still laboured in his master's service. His supplication to Henry not to disgrace himself in the eyes of Europe, or to forfeit the high character which Wolsey, at his own soul's risk, had won for him, had not only been in vain, it was a petition which led to Wolsey's own ruin. Ann Boleyn was mistress of the king's secrets. She knew that Wolsey had opposed her marriage with the king, and she never forgave. She in her own mind exaggerated Wolsey's power. He could, she thought, obtain for her the crown matrimonial, if he would. He refused to do so; he should die. Whereas, in point of fact, Wolsey lacked the means of doing what could only be ac- complished by a renunciation of those principles, in the fearless maintenance of which his strength had lain. He foresaw the end. He knew the king's weakness and his strength; his weakness inciting him to give pleasure at any cost to those who were near him, and in whose pleasures he could participate,—his strength of will, which was death to all who appeared, even through non-exertion, to resist it. Wolsey soon began to betray his own weakness—a weakness which reduced the foremost man in all the world to a state of abject cowardice. There are some who are irresistible in their might, when they ride upon the wave, and, amidst the plaudits of admiring multitudes, steer through the threatening rocks and quicksands, strewed with shipwrecks, into the haven; but who sink into nothingness when the cheering support is withdrawn. Such were Wolsey at Leicester, and the first Napoleon at St. Helena.

Warham, though feeble in health, apathetic, and lukewarm, remained on the king's side throughout the controversy. In a letter from Henry VIII. to Benet, written the year before Warham died,* Benet is directed to represent to the pope the injustice of citing Henry to Rome; and, acting on Cranmer's suggestion, he is to propose that the case should be adjudged in England by the Archbishop of Can- terbury. In the instructions to Benet, the king observes :—

"Ye may sodenly ex abrupto say: 'And why, syre, should ye not suffer the Archbishop of Canterbury to determyne thys matier in Inglande, who ys metropolitane, and hathe the hole jurisditione established there only for thys purpose, *ne causæ evocentur* yf hyt were done there, and as the Kynges Highness,

* Letters, Foreign and Domestic, Henry VIII.

my master, desyryth? Ye alredy knowe, as I have before shewed you, yt shuld be justly determined, for so all lerned men conclude.' . . . We doubte not but the Archbishope of Canterbury wyl gladly for discharg of his duetie entrepone hymselfe yn the same."

The eulogy which follows, paid by Henry to Warham, the year before his death, may be cited as an honourable testimony to the archbishop's merits :—

" And for the person of Bisshop of Canturbury ye may say ther canne be no person in Christendome more indifferente, more miet, apt, and convenient then the sayd archbisshop, who hath lernyng, excellent high and long experience, a man ever of a singular zele to justice, and *at the fyrst* of the Quene's Counsayl, but also for hys age, beyng above fourscore yeres, &c. . . . He should not fynd a personage, &c."

With the proceedings of the legatine court on the subject of the divorce we are not concerned. The legatine court was held in defiance of the laws of England, and the canons of her Church. The rights of the Church of England were ignored. The people were justly indignant at seeing their king submitting to be tried in his own realm, by a foreign court,—an indignity to which the country had never been subjected, except in the reign of King John. The whole proceeding reflected disgrace upon all parties. The Archbishop of Canterbury was too timid to defend the rights of his province, or rather of the two provinces of England, for of All England he was Primate. A powerful king was putting forth all his strength to crush a noble-minded woman, the jealous feelings of whose loving, broken heart he ostentatiously insulted. The pope prevaricated. The aristocracy of England, converted by Henry and his father into courtiers, had received or were in expectation of, the substantial favours which the crown only could confer. The House of Commons was packed. The universities were intimidated. The clergy were persecuted. The laws of God and man were violated. But while the great men were at fault, the country was sound at heart. The common people were still true to their generous intuitions, they were loud in their exclamations of disgust when Campeggio arrived in England. The women continued to make the queen's cause their own, they openly accused the king of incontinence, and did not hesitate to assert the truth,—that the king's conduct was to be traced, not to principle, but to passion. They honoured the wife who had borne her faculties meekly but royally; and they repudiated the ambitious mistress whose conduct was as disreputable as it was heartless.

The royal criminal, however, was not to be thwarted. The more he was opposed, the higher rose the intellectual power of Henry, directed by an indomitable will. He was equal to the occasion. He soon settled matters among his courtiers, for their hopes, perhaps life itself, depended upon the servility of their votes and the steadiness of their support. Among the commons of England Lollardism prevailed to a considerable extent. There were among the learned not a few, as we have seen, determined upon effecting a reformation of the Church, and at the head of this party the king wisely placed Ann Boleyn. It was given out that she favoured the "new learning," and thus, without compromising the king, all Reformers were permitted to regard her as a patroness. We all know how religious faction can wash even a blackamoor white. It is curious to observe how from the days of Henry VIII. to those of Lewis XIV, and from Lewis XIV. to the time of George IV, royal mistresses have sought to attach popular religious parties to themselves, and how religious parties have accepted them.

The king convened a meeting in his palace at
Richmond, not only of the Privy Council, but of the
mayor and civic authorities of London, who, rather
than the House of Commons, represented the commercial
aristocracy and the moneyed interest of the country.*
With that *bonhomie* and hearty good humour which
rendered him always popular, he laid before them his
whole policy, foreign and domestic, and claimed their
support.   The oration, as it was called, made a favourable impression, as is always the effect of royal addresses and royal condescension.   But still the people,
the women, were against the king.   The clergy might
influence them; but the clergy either openly supported the queen or at best were lukewarm.   Wolsey
saw the danger of exasperating the royal mind, and inconsistently laboured to win them to the king's side.
He persuaded Warham to make a similar attempt; but
all they succeeded in doing was, to prevail on them
to throw the responsibility from themselves by pro-
posing to submit the whole question of the divorce to
the arbitration of a council at Rome; that is, to have
no trial, but a special council called to legislate on the
case.   This was of course a mere evasion.   The king
determined to intimidate the clergy.   Although a
reverence for the sacred office still lingered among the
people, the clergy, as we have seen, had made themselves
sufficiently unpopular.   Of this the archbishop and his
suffragans were well aware.   In the case of Dr. Standish

---

* See Stow, 541.   There is some difficulty in the chronological
arrangement of this period of our history.   I follow Stow when I
refer to the royal oration at this time.   When dates are not given
in ancient documents something must be left to conjecture, and
when we begin to conjecture there must be varieties of opinion.
There is no doubt as to the occurrence of the facts, though their
exact order is not ascertained.

which has been already given we have some insight into the prevalent feelings of the Londoners. This was more apparent in an event which took place about the same time. A merchant of London, named Hun, had been prosecuted for heresy, and, being committed to prison, was found hanged in his chamber. Although, according to Sir Thomas More, who though a determined defender of the Church, was by no means an advocate of the clergy, Hun was *felo de se*, yet the chancellor of the diocese was accused of having caused him to be murdered, and was prosecuted accordingly. Against his indictment in a temporal court his partisans protested; and one of the bishops declared that the London juries were so prejudiced against the clergy that they would find Abel guilty of the murder of Cain.* We are not to construe too literally the *obiter dictum* of a party man; but, after all allowances, the exactions of the clergy, out of which the prosecution of Hun arose, had roused the public feeling against them. The friars, it is to be observed, took an active part against the secular clergy.

The king knew that his support was of more importance to the clergy than the clergy were willing to believe. He had only to side with their opponents and their adversaries would be irresistible. The king did not attack the Church. The Church was not attacked by the parliament when it was assembled. On one occasion, indeed, Bishop Fisher asserted that a feeling hostile to the Church or to Catholicism in general, prevailed in the House of Commons, and he so

CHAP.
II.

William
Warham.
1503-32.

* The story is given in Burnet. It is difficult, perhaps impossible, with the evidence we possess, to give a verdict in this case either one way or the other. If we read the statements with a view to acquit the chancellor, we have a case; and a strong case we have if we take a brief against him.

offended the members, that they addressed an angry remonstrance to the king against the bishop. Even in 1531, we find the House of Commons retaliating on the bishops, and complaining that they did not evince a sufficient zeal against heresy. Many evils existed and required reform, but they originated not in any fault found in the organization of the Church, but in the maladministration of the clergy. Sir Thomas More expressed the feeling himself, when he declared that what was wanted was not new laws, but a strict enforcement of existing laws.

Under these circumstances, it was rumoured, the rumour of course originating with the king himself, that a parliament would be called.

To parliamentary government Wolsey had been practically opposed. With the exception of one session, parliament had not met for fourteen years. We are not to suppose that a parliament at this period, resembled such an assembly as that which has represented the learning and ignorance of the country, its philanthrophy and its malignity, its religion, superstition, and infidelity, during the last thirty years. But under a different form, we may, perhaps, find the virtues and the vices in similar combination, the impotence, folly, and wickedness of man being overruled by a superintending Providence.

The parliament which met in 1529, memorable equally for its merits and its faults, was an assembly in the deliberations of which the king did not hesitate to interfere, and which acted to a considerable extent under his dictation. He took the initiative in the legislation, and several acts are represented as originating in "the goodly and gracious disposition of the king." The House of Lords consisted of the lords spiritual—that is to say, of the two archbishops, sixteen bishops, two guardians of the spiritualities, twenty-six abbots, and two priors—and the lords temporal, in number at the first meeting of a parliament which lasted for seven sessions, of forty-four peers. In the House of Commons there were two hundred and ninety-eight members. From the original correspondence, which is now in the hands of the public, we find that the House of Commons was elected almost always under the influence, and most frequently by the direct interference of the Government. The chronicler, Hall, speaks of the fact, and apparently with approbation, that "most part of the Commons were the king's servants." On one occasion, in a preceding parliament, the Earl of Surrey was informed that a subsidy had been granted of unprecedented amount, "the more part being of the king's council, his servants, or gentlemen."

Such were the three estates of the realm, the lords spiritual, the lords temporal, and the commons; they were summoned to do the bidding of one who would have scorned to have been styled, as is the custom lately introduced, one of the three estates of the realm, and who regarded himself simply as their lord and master, seeking their advice, and requiring them, according to the letter of the law, to give legal validity to the dictates of his will.

At the same time, the king knew that his will they might resist, and although on such resistance they would be dissolved, and not permitted to meet again, he was nevertheless aware that a law-loving people would become discontented, and that to a discontent, founded on reason, any pretender to the crown, and such was sure to appear, might appeal with every possibility of success. The three estates, therefore, were to be intimidated and managed.

To govern the clergy resort was also had to intimidation. The conduct of the lords spiritual in submitting to
the royal dictation in the House of Lords is surprising.
The common supposition, that they were looking to
preferment does not meet the case. They were
generally men who had risen to the highest position in
the Church, and although translations were possible,
they did not offer a sufficient bribe to allure them to
silence when direct attacks were made upon their constitutional privileges. It is very difficult to rouse into
enthusiasm and zeal those who feel that they have a
falling cause to defend ; they are more likely to call
into exercise the virtues of submission, when they feel
the ship sinking beneath them, than to display the
heroism which fires the heart when the standard is, at
peril of life, to be planted in the enemy's battery.
The lords spiritual were guilty of the unpardonable
fault of despairing of the fortunes of the spiritual
republic. They thought, so far as the abbots were
concerned, that their case was hopeless, and they were
prepared to make the best bargain they could for
themselves individually.*

* A similar feeling depresses the clergy of our own generation.
There is no fear of the spiritual well-being of the Church of England. The clergy may be tempted to become republican from seeing
how the Church thrives in republican America. But so far as the
Establishment is concerned the feeling that little can be done is de-
pressing. The state of public feeling may be gathered from public
events. In Queen Anne's reign the queen, as the representative of a
grateful nation, went in state to St. Paul's, amidst the plaudits of
the people, to return thanks for Marlborough's victory. Not once on
any occasion has Queen Victoria evinced a regard for the public services of the Church. The national religion is treated with scorn
before it is denationalised. What makes the treatment of the
Church more marked is this, that when the Sultan visited this country,
the Government gave him, as a national act, a splendid entertainment,
with the avowed object of conciliating the inhabitants of India by
showing respect to the Mahometan religion through its head.

Of the lords temporal, the majority were courtiers grateful for favours received, or more grateful still for promises made of favours to come. An hereditary aristocracy, succeeding to wealth and honours by the chance of birth, are always jealous of an aristocracy which is theoretically the result of professional merit. Between the nobles and the ennobled clergy there has always been a jealousy, which would induce the lords temporal to join in measures calculated to humiliate those who had precedence in their common house.

The commons were almost all of them placemen, or men expectant of place. They were contented with bribes less valuable, though more directly offered, than those which now win supporters to the one side or the other of the House. If they evinced independence when a subsidy was required, "they were spoken with and made to say ' Yea ;'—it may fortune," says a contemporary writer,—" contrary to the heart, will, and conscience."

This is not asserted to depreciate the three estates of the realm in Henry's time, for men will always be corrupt, or corruptible, until they become saints ; but the form and extent of the corruption is noticed, since it is important to understand the fact, that Henry VIII. was a despot under constitutional forms ; and that for what was done, in the name of the king and the three estates, the king himself was, to a great extent, the responsible person.

The parliament met on the 3d of November, 1529. Wolsey was already in disgrace. When Warham had declined the seals, Sir Thomas More was appointed Chancellor. He was the personal friend of Warham, a leading person in the Erasmian school of reformers, to whose memorable saying allusion has before been made—" I could not provide better provision than are in the Church provided already, if they were as well kept as made."

The king had acted with his usual sound judgment in selecting for his advisers two such men as Warham and More. The sentiment uttered by More expressed the principles upon which the king designed to act: Uphold the Church, reform the clergy. The difference consisted in the fact, that Henry acted as an impassioned man, the other two on principle only. Both Warham and More had committed themselves on this subject. Warham had endeavoured to reform the crying evil of the day, the ecclesiastical courts; he had appointed Colet to address to the clergy a sermon which must have sounded to many as a bill of indictment: to effect a reformation of the ecclesiastical courts, he had bowed his cross before that of Wolsey, and, he had permitted the establishment, for a season, of a legatine court within his province. The worst class of the clergy were too deeply interested in the iniquities of those courts to take timely warning, and things had gone on from bad to worse, and were now at their worst. The king, enraged at the clergy for not supporting him in the question of the divorce, had a strong case against them. He knew that, whatever the general feeling of the country was as to his "secret matier," an attack on the ecclesiastical courts would be popular, and it was the first measure of the new parliament.

It has been before remarked that the clergy were not attacked on the ground of immorality. That there were cases of gross immorality to be produced when reference was made to the life and conduct of ten or twelve thousand men is not to be doubted; but these must have been regarded as exceptional cases. At all events, as a body they were not arraigned.

The proceedings of the first session of this parliament, in regard to ecclesiastical affairs, were skilful, moderate, and well-conducted; such as we should expect as emanating from that good man, Sir Thomas More, the friend and counsellor of the king and of the primate.

Three bills were introduced: one to regulate the testamentary jurisdiction of the spiritual or consistory courts; another to regulate mortuaries, a payment which had caused as much disturbance as the demand, in our days, for church-rates; and a third to prevent the clergy from engaging in farming or in trade, or from holding more benefices than one, except under peculiar limitations; it also legislated against non-residence.

The reader of these volumes has read enough, and more than enough, of the abuses requiring correction in the consistory courts; and he will not be led astray by the rhetoric of party or Puritan writers, who would represent the action under this parliament as the first attempt to remedy the evil.

So early as the reign of Edward III. an act was passed in which complaint was made of the outrageous fines for the probate of testaments by the ministers, deputies of bishops, and by other ordinaries of the holy Church. The king charged the Archbishop of Canterbury and other bishops that they cause the same to be amended. If they refused, then by an act of his supremacy, it was accorded that the king should cause to be inquired by his justices of such oppressions and extortions, to hear them and determine them, as well at the king's suit as at the suit of the party, *as in old time hath been used.**

Henry claimed no powers beyond those which had been exercised by his ancestors.· He sought to correct a grievance which was sure to rise, not only in eccle-

---

* Edward III. st. i. c. 4.

siastical courts, but under all other jurisdictions, so long as the officers of the court, and, to some extent, the practitioners, were paid by fees, not limited by law, but demanded according to the supposed exigencies of the case. An exorbitant fee was demanded, and the person upon whom the demand was made would frequently meet the unjust demand rather than encounter the toil, trouble, and extra expense of carrying the case by appeal from one court to another, with the possibility in the end of not receiving justice. The officer of the court, the ordinary or the practitioner, was thus able to make any demand he might think fit, looking, not so much to the case, as to the ability of the client to meet his demand. We have seen how Archbishop Warham endeavoured to correct the grievance on his first coming to the primacy; but we must not forget that in so doing he was only following precedent. By a constitution of Archbishop Mepham, it was enacted that, for the insinuation of the testament of a poor person, the inventory of whose goods should not exceed one hundred shillings, nothing should be demanded.* Archbishop Stratford also, it will be recollected, attempted to meet the evil by fixing the fines. By a constitution of his, *no fee whatever* might be taken by any ordinaries, and among the ordinaries the bishops are included. He permitted the clerks writing the insinuations to receive sixpence for their labour, and no more.† A regular gradation of fees, when large sums were accounted for, was laid down by the primate; but in every instance they were remarkable for their moderation.

What was now done was nothing more than the parliamentary enactment of a constitution already made by a primate of the Church.

* Lyndwood, 170.   † Ibid. 181.

The second bill had reference to mortuaries, an ecclesiastical demand which had been the cause of violent altercations between the clergy and the laity. The payment was, like church-rates in modern times, resisted sometimes from mere factious motives by the Lollards; but the resistance, from whatever motive, was too often justified by the unjust and exorbitant demands made by the clergy.[*]

A mortuary was originally an oblation made at the time of a person's death; in early English times it was called soul-shot. It was due to the parish church of the deceased person; and the payment was enforced so early as by a law of King Canute. This payment was made the subject of subsequent legislation; but there was no regulation as to the amount of the fee: this depended upon the custom of a parish: and the clergy too often asserted, that modern custom should be superseded by ancient custom, when the fees required by ancient custom (they themselves being the historians of the fact) exceeded that which had been latterly tendered. The statute of Henry in this, as in the former instance, was a regulating statute. It did not deny the right of the clergy to the fee; but it affirmed, that question and doubt had arisen upon the order, manner and form of demanding, receiving and claiming mortuaries, otherwise called corse-presents. It was ordered, therefore, that no manner of mortuary should be taken or demanded of any person, who, at the time of his death, was not in possession of moveable goods worth ten marks. From a person possessed of more than ten marks, but under thirty pounds, the parson might not take more than three shillings and fourpence for the whole, and so on, the largest sum allowed to be taken being ten shillings. Parsons and

* 1 Still, 171.

other ecclesiastics were permitted, however, to receive
any sum bequeathed to them or the high altar of the
church, such being regarded, not as a fee to be claimed,
but a free gift to be received.

These two bills passed through the House of Lords
without difficulty. The third was calculated to excite
considerable opposition. It was one of those many
bills which, touching apparently the surface only, was
intended to penetrate more deeply and to make an
incision into the very principle which had hitherto,
and for many years, rendered the Church, in point
of fact, a secular possession; the resource, not of
theologians, but of lawyers, diplomatists, and statesmen. What the bill proposed was simple enough,
and what rendered the task of its opponents more
difficult was, that it was based upon principles the
validity of which it was impossible to deny.

We have frequently shown how different was the
view taken of the objects for which the Church was
endowed in the fourteenth and fifteenth, and the early
part of the sixteenth century, from that with which
we are familiar in the nineteenth. An ecclesiastic was
bound to promote the glory of God and the welfare of
his fellow-creatures, in things temporal as well as in
things spiritual, as God should provide the means.
When kings could summon the whole nobility of the
land to fight their battles, they often found it next to
an impossibility to supply the civil offices of the state
from the ranks of the aristocracy. The clergy became
statesmen, diplomatists, and lawyers, and they were
supported and remunerated by the preferments of the
Church. They performed their ecclesiastical duties by
deputy, and the endowments of the Church were regarded as designed, not for the benefit of any particular place, but for the maintenance of those who, in

fighting the battles of the Church militant, required a large income, and the means of supporting many retainers. As the aristocracy became less warlike and more learned, they desired to see the bishops confining themselves to their peculiar and pastoral duties, without intruding any longer into offices, the duty of which the laity could discharge as well as they, and for which there were many aspirants.

The secular spirit exhibited by their superiors pervaded, as we have seen, the lower ranks of the clergy, and they became lawyers, farmers, tradesmen, ready to do anything for money. It is impossible to omit our special duties and undertake others, not immediately devolving upon us, though in themselves equally important, without deterioration of character. To this secularity on the part of the clergy we have traced that degradation of the clerical character of which the country complained; and now, when the arts of peace were cultivated, we are not surprised that to the laity, the conduct of the clergy in engaging in the different objects of worldly pursuit, with peculiar advantages, should be deeply offensive. It was under the impression of feelings such as these, that a bill was introduced into parliament which had for its object the prevention of clerical farming or trading, for abolishing pluralities, and for enforcing residence.

But we must, in fairness, look on the other side. What was proposed, though it met with the approbation, doubtless, of those quiet unobtrusive parish priests who, unknown to the world, were administering the Gospel in remote and retired districts, was regarded by a large body of the clergy as nothing less than ruin. It was, and it was designed to be, a revolutionary measure. The farming and trading had

reference chiefly to the regulars, and what were the
monks to do if they were no longer to cultivate their
estates and bring the produce to market? At the
same time, the reference to pluralities and non-residence would render it impossible for the higher ranks
of the clergy to engage any longer in state affairs.
There could be no future Wolsey; the chancellorship
must henceforth be in lay hands; and the eloquence
of the clergy would be no longer heard in the courts
of law. We have, in our time, been accustomed to see
the bishops and clergy abstaining from politics almost
to a fault; but, though we cannot sympathise in the
alarm felt when this measure was first brought forward, we may try to understand it. If the legislation
of the country, it was said, should pass exclusively to
the hands of the laity, as it must be, if the bishops
were without exception compelled to reside in their
dioceses sometimes as difficult to reach as the diocese
of a colonial bishop of the present age, what would
become of the property of the Church? Why were a
large body of landed proprietors, because they were
clergymen, to be virtually excluded from the councils
of the nation?

That there was some truth in the objections thus
urged is proved by the fact that, when the measure
was carried, the dispensations for non-residence and
for holding pluralities were so numerous, and so easily
to be obtained, that it became a restriction rather than
an abolition of the practice against which it was
originally directed. The abolition of pluralities and
the enforcement of residence was not finally carried
till the reign of William IV, and even now it is
questionable whether what is correct in theory is
working well for the Church. We are not surprised,
at all events, at hearing that, when the bill was intro-

duced into the House of Lords, it met with considerable opposition from the lords spiritual.

The object of the king, at this time, was to alarm, but not to throw over, the clergy, and he therefore interposed his good offices. There was a conference between the two houses, and the last bill, according to some writers, was at the king's suggestion remodelled. They were finally passed, with the sanction of the lords spiritual.*

---

* In the debates, the venerable, aged, but still energetic Bishop of Rochester, a friend of Erasmus, and encourager of the new learning, argued with so much vehemence and eloquence, as to give offence to certain captious members of the House of Commons. It was said that the bishop had dared to cast suspicion upon the orthodoxy and upon their attachment to Catholicism. The speech is given in Baily's Life of Fisher. The bishop explained that his words were to be understood in a parliamentary sense. Purists in morals, and historians whose inaccuracies in their statements of facts favour their party views, affect to be shocked at the insincerity of the pious bishop's explanation. We will state, therefore, his defence : A complaint having been made to the king, he sent to my lord of Rochester to come before him ; "being come, the king demanded of him why he spake in such sort ; the bishop answered, that being in council he spake his mind in defence of the Church, whom he saw daily injured and oppressed by the common people, whose office it was not to judge of her manners, much less to reform them, and, therefore (he said), he thought himself in conscience bound to defend her in all that lay within his power ; nevertheless, the king wished him to use his words more temperately, and that was all, which gave the commons little satisfaction." The words actually used by Bishop Fisher were as follows : " My lords, beware of yourselves and your country, beware of your holy mother the Catholic Church ; the people are subject unto novelties, and Lutheranism spreads itself amongst us. Remember Germany and Bohemia, what miseries are befallen them already ; and let our neighbours' houses, that are now on fire, teach us to beware our own disasters : wherefore, my lords, I will tell you plainly what I think, that except you resist manfully by your authorities this violent heap of mischiefs offered by the commons, you shall see all obedience first drawn from the

In this the first session of parliament, the clergy had nothing to complain of. In the progress of our history we have had to speak of parliaments much more stringent in their enactments, and displaying more hostility against the clerical body.

A hint had now, however, been given to the clergy of what they might expect if the king's protection were withdrawn, but the hint was not taken. As a body they refused to argue before the people in favour of the divorce, and party feeling soon made them oppose it. When the advocates of reform among the lower orders espoused the cause of Ann Boleyn, the clergy were naturally led to argue more strongly in favour of the injured Katherine. The reforming party sought to win the king, and, though they did not succeed, they had the satisfaction of seeing him come down with irresistible force upon their opponents. The king had at his right hand in Crumwell a bold adviser, who suggested a measure of gigantic iniquity, by which the king and his mistress might avenge themselves of the clergy, while the exchequer, left exhausted by Wolsey, might be replenished without the demand of a subsidy from parliament.*

It was discovered, all of a sudden, that the whole English nation was involved in the penalties of a

clergy; and secondly from yourselves; and if you search into the true causes of all these mischiefs, which reign among them, you shall find that they all arise through want of faith."—Baily's Life of Fisher, 96. Baily is a pseudonym. I only mention this that I may not seem ignorant of the fact. I shall quote the book as I find it.

* We find that the laity were at first alarmed by the desire, expressed by the House of Commons, to include the laity in the bill of indictment for the clergy, introduced into parliament after they had paid their fine. The Government stated that the laity should rely on the king's generosity.

præmunire for having yielded to the legatine authority of Wolsey. The laity were at first alarmed, not knowing what despotic act was about to be performed. They must of course be absolved, for it would have covered the Government with ridicule, if an attempt had been made to outlaw a whole nation, even if a great nation should have yielded to the insult; especially when the grand criminal was their accuser—the king himself. But it was soon surmised that the indemnity of the laity might be purchased at the cost of the clergy ; and the people were well pleased to see the clergy taxed to support the piety of the king or the prodigality of his court. The case, when argued against Wolsey on its abstract merits, was easily decided. The statute of præmunire, passed in the reign of Richard II, asserted that " The crown of England hath been so free at all times, that it hath been in no earthly subjection, but immediately subjected to God in all things touching its regality, and no other, and ought not to be submitted to the pope." By the same statute it is enacted that " They who shall procure or prosecute any popish bulls and excommunications, in certain cases shall incur the forfeiture of their estates, or be banished, or be put out of the king's protection." This, however, was not the only statute that could be hurled against the cardinal. The reader, accustomed to the statements of post-Reformation Romanists, and of historians who stultify themselves by admitting those statements without examination, may probably not be aware of the anti-papal character of the statute law of England anterior to the time of Henry VIII. By a statute of Henry III. the pope's canon law had no place in England, except so far as the king and parliament permitted.* To the king was given the last

* 20 Henry III. c. 9.

appeal of all his subjects, the patronage of bishoprics,
and the investiture of bishops; no subject could be
cited to Rome without the king's licence, no legates
could be admitted without the king's permission and
an act of courtesy; when any legate was admitted he
had to accept an oath, not to do anything derogatory to the king or his crown. To issue a papal excommunication in England without the king's consent,
or to bring over a papal bull, involved the offender in
the forfeiture of all his goods. Bramhall, summing up
the statutes, says, "So the laws of England did not
permit the pope to cite or excommunicate an English
subject, or dispose of an English benefice, or send a
legate *à latere*, or to receive an appeal out of England
without the king's consent."*

The iniquity of the proceeding as against Wolsey
rested with the king. We have already called attention to the fact, abundantly proved by the royal
letters still in existence, that the unwilling pope was
almost compelled by the king to grant the cardinal's
hat to Wolsey; and that, even after he had conceded
the cardinalate, he was reluctant to accede to the
king's resolve that he should also be appointed legate
à latere. That after this the king should visit his
own offence upon the head of his servant, faithful to
him if to no one else, and certainly, in the opinion
of his contemporaries, the foremost man in all the
world,—this is something so monstrous that we are

---

* See the Stat. of Clarend., the Stat. of Carlisle (35 Edward
I. c. 4 § 3), the Artic. Cleri (9 Edward II. c. 14), (the Stat. of
Provisors), 25 Edward III. (Stat. 6, § 5), [2] 7 Edward IIL.
c. [1]; 16 Richard II. c. 5 (Statutes of Præmunire), Placit.
an. 1 Hen. VII. et an., 32 et 34 Edward I. (and the Just. Vindic.
c. iv. vol. i. pp. 141—148). See more of this in the Introductory
Chapter. See also Bramhall, i. 137, ii. 298.

at a loss for words to express our contempt for the
meanness to which, in his vengeance as in his love
affairs, Henry VIII. could stoop. Wolsey was aware
that he was transgressing the law when he accepted
the legatine office ; but he contended that the king
had a dispensing power, and he was careful to obtain
a licence under the great seal before he ventured to
exercise the legatine authority. He showed his
precaution, because, at the same time, it was pleaded
that those old laws relating to the supremacy of the
crown and the independence of the Church of England,
had from the early part of the fifteenth century become
obsolete. Thus fortified he had, as the king's prime
minister, discharged the functions of legate, with the
entire approbation of his royal master, for fifteen
years. In a letter to his judges he mentions the
existence of this licence in his coffers ; but his papers
had been seized, and he consequently had no means
of self-defence.

Soon after Wolsey's death a bill was filed by the
attorney general in the court of King's Bench, at the
suit of the crown, against the whole clergy of England
for having submitted to the legatine authority, which,
in defiance of the statutes of præmunire and of provisors, the late cardinal had exercised. The iniquity
of the proceeding in this case was even more flagrant
than that which was displayed against Wolsey himself.
In the royal councils, the high and haughty tone of
Cardinal Wolsey was now replaced by the subtle
cleverness of the wily Crumwell. The only persons
in the country who had offered any opposition to the
legatine court were the clergy. They had not,
indeed, taken sufficiently high ground : they had not
dared to oppose the royal will by referring to the
acts of præmunire and provisors ; they had not, when

the king supported the pope, resented, like their predecessors, all papal aggressions ; but, from interested
motives it may be, they had been opposed to a jurisdiction which was likely to absorb all ecclesiastical
business, and was ruining the judges and advocates
of the ancient ecclesiastical courts of the Church of
England. We have seen that, throughout his episcopate, Warham's peace was disturbed by the indignation
of the clergy, who forced him, against his will, or in
spite of his indolence, to come into collision with the
cardinal. Warham and some of the higher clergy
were equally guilty with Wolsey, though in yielding
to the legate they made great personal sacrifices ; but
the clergy in general were unjustly accused, although
when the charge was against them, they relapsed
into a supineness difficult to understand. Whether
they had thought the laws obsolete or not, the laws
of the land they had undoubtedly transgressed, and
they had nothing to do but to throw themselves on
the mercy of the king,—a mercy to be bought and
sold. The clergy taxed themselves, and the laity
were interested in permitting the king to extract from
their coffers a large sum, for this would render him
less exorbitant in his demand upon the laity. The
courtiers were amused at the extreme cleverness of
the king or his adviser. There was no one to take
the part of a body of men who, by the misconduct of
some among the most prominent of its members, had
become unpopular. The question now had reference
only to the amount of the fine which the king, in his
mercy, would condescend to accept as a peace-offering
from his clergy. They had followed his example ;
and, for doing unwittingly what he had done with
his eyes open, they must suffer, while the real criminal
would be enriched. The convocation met on the

29th day of March, 1530,* and was continued to the 28th day of March, 1531.† · The representatives of the clergy had not now, as usual, to vote such a subsidy as their constituents might be willing to pay ; they were to await the dictation of the crown. It was understood that a liberal vote would be followed by an order from the crown to stay further proceedings, which in the court of King's Bench had been already begun against the clergy of England. But the question did not come before them in such an undignified form. The king demanded a liberal grant of his clergy, on the high ground that some acknowledgement was due to him for the services he had rendered the Church in writing against Luther, in repressing heresy, and in protecting the clergy against the insults of heretics and their other enemies. The benevolence which the grateful clergy were expected to offer amounted in the province of Canterbury to the sum of 100,844*l*. 8*s*. 8*d*., in that of York to 18,840*l*. 0*s*. 10*d*. —an enormous sum compared with the present value of money.

The attention of the king and of the country having been called to the ancient laws of the realm, and to the canons of the Church of England, it was understood that, according to those laws, and until the fifteenth century, the royal supremacy was a fact of which no doubt had ever been entertained.

It was on this ground that the clergy had been guilty of a præmunire ; they had insulted the crown, by ignoring the supremacy of the king in all causes, and over all persons. Of this fact they were now to be reminded. They were not only to admit that they had done wrong, but, with a view to future legislation, they were to understand the ground on which their

* Wilkins, iii. 724.   † Ibid. 746.

submission to the authority of the pope was an unpardonable offence. Upon this subject the archbishop conferred not only with the judges and privy councillors, among whom were the bishops, but with the prolocutor of the Lower House of Convocation, with the deans and other persons* who took a prominent part in the proceedings of the assembly. The result of this conference was, that the royal supremacy should not be voted as something new, but that, in the formula making the grant to the king of a fine imposed, because his supremacy had been overlooked, the supremacy should be introduced as something not to be disputed. This statement is made on the only authoritative document we possess bearing on the subject; and the statement is important, for it clearly shows that the assertion of the supremacy was made by the highest subordinate authority, the Archbishop of Canterbury, not with a hostile intention or with a sinister intention.

The subsidy was voted on the 24th of January. The conference then took place as to the form in which the grant should be made, and the indemnity expressed. On the 7th of February, the archbishop summoned the Lower House to meet him. When he came to the words "of the English Church and clergy, of which the king alone is the protector and supreme head,"†—there was a demurrer on the part of some of the clergy.

* Wilkins, iii. 725. Of Warham's opinion concerning the supremacy there can be no doubt: he said, according to Foxe, in speaking to the king, "that it was the king's right before the pope's."

† Without the shadow of authority it is conjectured by some writers that the assertion of the supremacy in this form was suggested by Cranmer. It may have been the case; but we are to

They were not so depressed as is sometimes supposed, for they refused to admit the title without further explanation and discussion. There was no disposition on the part of the king to push matters to an extremity, nor was the opposition factious. The subject was under discussion for several days. The objection was not to the fact itself. The clergy were willing to admit what they could not deny, that the King of England had, till of late years, been in all causes, ecclesiastical as well as civil, supreme ; but the objection was to the terms in which it was expressed. The Lower House specified their ground of resistance : "lest peradventure, after a long lapse of time, the terms so generally included in the article might be strained to an obnoxious sense."*

remember that Cranmer was not by any means a Protestant at that time ; that this subsidy was proposed as a reward to the king for his constant zeal against Protestantism and all heresy, in which Cranmer joined. There is no reason to suppose, or rather there is every reason that we should not suppose, that Cranmer would suggest such a measure without consulting the primate, with whom he was on friendly terms. (See Strype's Cranmer, book v. c. iv.) We have before us the fact, that Warham was the person who introduced the clause to convocation, and finally we have the plain assertion of Cranmer himself. Brooks, not long before Cranmer's burning, charged him with first setting up the king's supremacy. To which Cranmer replied, "That it was Warham gave the supremacy to Henry VIII, and that he had said he ought to have it before the Bishop of Rome, and that God's word would bear it. And that upon this the Universities of Cambridge and Oxford were sent to, to know what the word of God would allow touching the supremacy, where it was reasoned and argued upon at length ; and at last both agreed and set to their seals, and sent it to the king, that he ought to be supreme head and not the pope.

* "Ne forte post longævi temporis tractum termini in eodem articulo generaliter positi in sensum improbum traherentur."—Atterbury, Rights, 82. "In the thirty-second session (Feb. 7), the most reverend (the archbishop), having had private communication with

The clergy, in spite of·all that had occurred, retained their independence, and when the king proposed a compromise they at first rejected it. At last, Arch-

certain counsellors and justiciaries of our lord the king, began to treat with the prolocutor, deans, &c., on the matters contained in the articles added at the beginning of the book of the grant of the subsidy, which were of this nature :—1. Of the Church and Anglican clergy, of whom he alone is the protector and supreme head. 2. Of the fear and peril which our most invincible king has banished from us, and provided that in quiet and secure peace we may be able to serve God and give due heed to the cures of souls committed to our charge by his majesty and the people entrusted to him. 3. The privileges and liberties of the same, which do not detract from his regal power and the laws of his realm, by confirming he defends. 4. That he would deign to grant a general forgiveness and pardon for all their transgressions of the penal laws and statutes of this realm, as well as other laws, in such ample form as had been granted in that parliament to all his subjects (the statutes of præmunire being imposed on us in addition). 5. So that all the laity may thence be burdened. The last article, after consultation had with the bishops and Lower House, was easily granted in the thirty-third session (Feb. 8), when the king's justiciaries exhibited a copy of the articles of exceptions to the general pardon of our lord the king, of which mention occurs in the fourth article, concerning which the justiciaries of the king affirmed that they had no authority to conclude it until the bishops and clergy had come to a conclusion with respect to the first article. The notion of the king's supremacy did not well commend itself to the prelates and clergy, and they wished it to be modified. During three sessions, therefore, conferences were entered into with the king's counsellors as to how they might incline the king's mind to express that article in softened terms. The king then, by the Lord Rochford, remitted the motion in this form: " Whose protector and supreme head, after God, he alone is," and refused to have further discussion with the prelates and clergy upon that matter. At length, on the 11th day of February, the archbishop proposed the article of the king's supremacy in the synod in the terms given above. Wilkins, iii. 725.

The subject is one of such great importance that I have thought it expedient to present to the reader the original document upon which the statement rests.

bishop Warham informed the clergy, that the king was willing to accept the form in the following terms: "of the English Church and clergy, of which we recognise his majesty as the singular protector, the only supreme governor, and, so far as the law of Christ permits, even the supreme head." This was carried *nemine contradicente.* When the archbishop put the question the majority were silent. The archbishop remarked that silence gave consent. He received for answer, "Then we are all silent." The debate, however, was resumed in the afternoon, and the formula was in due order agreed to by both houses. It was subscribed by Archbishop Warham and all the bishops in the Upper House, and by a large majority in the Lower House.

We have shown in another place, that the dispute was, as those who were at first opposed to the archbishop admitted, chiefly verbal. There was a fear entertained that the temporal authorities should interfere in functions purely spiritual.

The conduct of the archbishop and of the clergy met with very general approbation from the other public bodies. The expression of satisfaction, at the assertion of national independence, on the part of the universities and other ecclesiastical corporations, became more enthusiastic when, in 1534, the old doctrine was affirmed, that a general council represented the Church, and was above the pope and all bishops, the Bishop of Rome having had no greater jurisdiction given him by God in the Holy Scriptures, within this realm of England, than any other foreign bishop.*

But to return to Warham. The convocation of Canterbury met again on the 16th of October, 1531,

---

* The recognition of the royal supremacy thus took place in convocation long before it was admitted in parliament.

and was continued to the 21st of March, 1532, N.S.
It was chiefly occupied by ecclesiastical business relating to testamentary matters and clergy discipline.
The meeting last mentioned, however, obtains a more
general interest from the fact, that on this day the
celebrated Hugh Latimer made his recantation. There
seems to have been some conversation in preceding
meetings, on heretical notions propounded by Latimer
and his friends, Dr. Crome and Bilney. It is not stated
what the articles were which were exhibited against
him, and it is useless to conjecture on the subject.
Latimer was in advance of his age, and being a
straightforward, outspoken man, he often spoke without discretion, on subjects which he had not sufficiently examined. Noble lords and commoners
not distinguished for a tolerant spirit, declared
that decided steps ought to be taken to put down
these novel practices and this unorthodox teaching. But the clergy dealt tenderly with Latimer,
who was a general favourite. He was called upon to
recant, and, on his refusal to do so, he was committed
for contempt of court, and declared contumacious.
Being declared excommunicated, he was delivered to
the custody of the archbishop. When a prisoner was
committed to the custody of some great man made
responsible for his safe keeping, the captive was permitted to associate with his custodian; and we may
presume that through the conversation of Archbishop
Warham, Latimer was persuaded, by his recantation,
to enable the archbishop to withdraw his excommunication pronounced before as a matter of course. At
all events, on the 21st of March, debate took place in
the two houses of convocation; and it was remarked
that, under certain conditions, Hugh Latimer might be
absolved. The archbishop was not present; the Bishop

of London acted as his commissary, and before his
lordship, on the day following, Hugh Latimer knelt
down and submitted himself. He craved forgiveness ;
he acknowledged that he had been in error. "My
lords," he said,—

"I do confess that I have misordered myself very far, in
that I have so presumptuously and boldly preached, reproving
certain things, by which the people that were infirm hath
taken occasion of ill. Wherefore I ask forgiveness of my mis-
behaviour; I will be glad to make amends; and I have
spoken indiscreetly in vehemence of speaking, and have
erred in some things, and in manner have been in a wrong
way (as thus) lacking discretion in many things."*

He humbly asked to be absolved, but his pardon
was not immediately granted. On the 10th of April
the absolution was at length, pronounced ; but it was
not decided whether he should be subject to penance or
what the penance might be. He was directed to be
forthcoming on the 15th of the same month. His enemies had been, in the meantime, active, and before the
appointed day other grounds of complaint were lodged
against him. Another adjournment took place on the
19th. It would seem that Latimer only admitted that
he had been guilty of indiscretion ; but he denied
his having propounded heresy. He was, on a smaller
scale, undergoing a temptation similar to that under
which Cranmer fell. He now appealed to the king.
The friends who advised him to pursue this course
gave wise advice ; they thought that the king would
seize the opportunity to show that the supremacy was
no idle assumption, and that over one of his own
chaplains he could and would throw his ægis. But
they were mistaken. The king would see that justice

---

* Wilkins, iii. 747.

was done to all his lieges; but he said, that it was for convocation to decide upon a case of heresy; and, consequently, through the Bishop of Winchester, the king referred the case to convocation.

It was a humiliating episode in the life of a good and conscientious man, who afterwards died for his principles. But Latimer himself would have repudiated the defence set up for him by some of his admirers, that, in making his recantation, he was insincere. We may easily understand how certain new opinions had commended themselves to his judgment, and how he propounded them in order that he might provoke discussion; but these notions had not as yet become to him a fixed principle. They were merely opinions, and he would not assert them in opposition to the great majority of his brethren. But, whatever his feelings may have been, or however influenced, Latimer, who had seen what the sufferings of the stake were, for he had assisted at one execution, if not more, shrunk from the flames at the present time. When his appeal to the king had been rejected, he then knelt down before the convocation, and said,—

"That where he had aforetime confessed that he hath heretofore erred, and that he meaned then it was onely error of discretion, he hath since better seen his own acts, and searched them more deeply, and doth knowledge that he hath not erred only in discretion, but also in doctrine; and said that he was not called afore the said lords but upon good and just ground, and hath been by them charitably and favourably intreated. And where he had aforetime misreported of the lords, he knowledgeth, that he hath done ill in it, and desireth them, humbly on his knees, to forgive him; and where he is not of ability to make them recompence, he said he would pray for them."*

* Wilkins, iii. 748.

After making this submission, Hugh Latimer was, at the special request of the king, taken again into favour. Latimer gave his solemn promise that he would obey the laws and observe the decrees of the Church. The Bishop of London, lord *locum tenens*, absolved him, and restored him to the sacraments.

The archbishop made a point of attending the meeting of convocation on the 12th of April. For his convenience the houses were adjourned from St. Paul's to the Jerusalem Chamber, at Westminster.

He had submitted to the two houses a supplication from the House of Commons to the king, containing an attack upon the clergy, to which the king desired a speedy answer.

It was not an attack upon the bishops, but upon ordinaries generally; and, therefore, it was necessary that the subject should be discussed in the Lower House of Convocation; for, in point of fact, there were more ordinaries in the Lower House than in the higher.

Of the discussions we possess no record; but we have the result in an able reply to the commons, which is remarkable for the ability with which it was drawn up; as might be expected, when we are told that the real author of it was no less a person than Bishop Gardyner. Gardyner admits, indeed, that he was no divine, but he was certainly one of the ablest lawyers of the day, and it is to law that the supplication chiefly refers. He said that they, the ordinaries,[*]

---

[*] Wilkins, iii. 751. A transcript of what is entitled the answer of the ordinaries is to be found at the Rolls House. A portion of it, *ex* Registr. Cantuar. is printed in Wilkins, iii. 750. According to Hall, the commons began to complain of those grievances wherewith the spiritualty had oppressed them soon after the meeting of parliament in 1529; but the journals of the House of Lords agree

had perused the supplication in which complàint was made by the commons, zealous against heresy, "that much discord, variance, and debate had arisen among the king's subjects, spiritual and temporal, in his grace's Catholic realm, as well as through new fantastical and erroneous opinions, grown by occasion of seditious and overthwart-framed books compiled, imprinted, and made in the English tongue in parts beyond sea, contrary and against the very true Catholic and Christian faith, as also by the uncharitable dealing and behaviour of divers ordinaries, their commissioners and substitutes in the concern, and often vexation of the king's said subjects in the spiritual courts, and also by other evil examples and misuses of spiritual persons."

To such an assertion as this there could be but one answer, and that a simple contradiction. This contradiction is given in a passage of considerable eloquence, and with a display of moderation and good temper. It is admitted, "that there may be evildoers among the clergy, but the king is entreated not to draw an unfavourable conclusion against the whole body from the circumstance of there being a few delinquents. Although the ordinaries perceived and knew right well that there was as great a number of well-disposed men in the commons as ever they knew in any parliament, yet they were not ignorant of the sinister informations and importune labours and evil

with the registers of convocation, showing that the supplication was not presented till 1532. Of the ability displayed in the reply of the ordinaries, one of the most learned lawyers of the present day has expressed his admiration. The reader will observe that the answer is described as that of the ordinaries, not of the bishops, as Presbyterian writers have given it. The subject is mentioned in a preceding note.

persuasions of evil disposed persons, pretending a zeal for justice and reformation, by whom some right wise sad and constant men were persuaded to receive as true what was not really the case."

The reader of these volumes has before him a sufficient number of facts to enable him to form his own conclusions on the real merits of the case. We have always, in history, to steer our way between the two extremes, by which each case is overstated. If we may judge from the conduct towards an accused person sometimes exhibited on the bench by no less a person than Sir Edward Coke, and the gross temper evinced by Bishop Bonner when he sat in judgment upon heretics, we should not be surprised, as the ordinaries were willing to admit, that instances might be produced in which judges were provoked to indecent behaviour on the bench; yet we may concede that, generally speaking, the ordinaries could be borne out in their contradiction of the specific charges brought against them by the commons. At the same time, we have seen that a low class of clergy existed, whom we can only describe by recource to phraseology from the adoption of which we should shrink, if it were not necessary to adopt the vulgar language to describe the conduct of which the vulgarly vicious alone were guilty. We have spoken of clergy who, in fact, were pettifogging attornies touting for business. They would watch for any expression which might receive an heretical interpretation, and would demand a bribe to abstain from prosecution, or if the prosecution ensued, resort to that bullying process which minds of the same stamp as that of Bonner would mistake for wit. We doubt not, that it was part of that system which made the consistory and other ecclesiastical courts perfectly odious.

It was natural that the commons, in their complaint, should pass from the inferior court to the great
court of convocation. It was complained, that laws were
made in convocation not in harmony with the statute
laws of the realm, touching on temporal affairs, independently of parliamentary or even of royal sanction.
These laws encroached in some instances on the royal
prerogative ; the infringers of them were made not only
to incur the terrible sentence of excommunication, but
also " the detestable crime and sin of heresy ;" they
bore with peculiar hardship on some of the humbler
classes, causing them great trouble and inquietude.

To this charge the reply was, that since the temporal
and the ecclesiastical legislators agreed in holding that
their authority to make laws was grounded upon the
Scripture of God and determination of holy Church,
the ordinaries felt convinced that if the laws were
sincerely interpreted, no contrariety or repugnancy
between them would be found to exist ; but that, with
regard to the laws of the realm and the canons of the
Church, the one would be found aiding, maintaining,
and supporting the other. The ordinaries, speaking
in the name of the convocation, added, " If it shall
otherwise appear, as it is our duty, whereunto we shall
always most diligently apply ourselves, to reform our
ordinaries to God's commission, and to conform our
statutes and laws, and those of our predecessors, to the
determination of Scripture and holy Church, so we hope
in God, and shall daily pray for the same, that your
highness *will* if there appear cause why, with the
consent of your people, temper your grace's laws
accordingly ; whereby shall ensue a most sure and
perfect cognition and agreement, as God being *lapis
angularis*, to agree and enjoin the same." As the constitution then stood, the parliament was to legislate for

the country in things temporal, the convocation in things spiritual. The convocation had been accused of encroaching upon the rights of parliament, and to the charge brought against the clergy they had given their answer. But more than this was now demanded of them ; in that which was acknowledged to be their own sphere of duty, they were required to submit to the king, and not to enact canons without the royal assent. Here, without receding from those rights, which they believed to be inherent in their office, the clergy humbly desired that, " as had been done heretofore, so henceforth the king would show to them his mind and opinion, and what his high wisdom should think convenient, that they would gladly hear and follow, if it should please God to inspire them so to do, with all submission of humility." They besought the king to tread in the steps of his progenitors, and to maintain and defend such laws and ordinances, as they according to their calling and by the authority of God shall for His honour make, to the edification of virtue and maintaining of Christ's faith, whereof they said, " your highness is defender in name, and hath been hitherto in deed a special protector."

As to the charge that convocation had attempted to invade the royal prerogative, they were content to leave their cause in the king's hands, and prayed that he, being so highly learned, would of his own most bounteous goodness " facilly discharge and deliver them from that charge, when it should appear that the laws made by them or their predecessors were conformable and maintainable by the Scripture of God and determination of the Church, against which no laws can stand or take effect.

Here was a king seeking to make himself a despot, who had bribed or intimidated his parliament to regard his will as law, bravely resisted when endeavouring to violate the rights with which the constitution had vested the convocation of the clergy. They who are really the opponents of despotism will admire the spirit with which Henry was opposed in his attempt to place himself above all law whether of God or man; even though the opponents were neither men nor women, but only the clergy. The tendency of the age, however, was to invest a single man with despotic power, and to elevate him who, according to the old custom, had been the foremost and first in a nation, to the position of a Cæsar. In every country in Europe the attempt was made, and in some cases with success; our liberties were regained under the Stuarts, but they were nearly lost under the Tudors. Detesting a spirit of tyranny in every one, from the monarch on his throne to the most despicable member of the Lower House of Parliament, we cannot but sympathise even with a Gardyner, when we find him resisting the aggressions of a monarch on the rights of the subject.

Henry VIII. was extremely indignant at the reply of the ordinaries, and resumed his attack by expressing his displeasure against Gardyner, the supposed author of the offensive document. Gardyner had probably expected, with the Duke of Norfolk, to share the counsels of the king on the fall of Wolsey. But Crumwell, though not ostensibly in office, and treated with either condescension or contempt by the courtiers, had already obtained the ear of the king, and it was part of his policy to bring Gardyner into discredit with his royal master. Gardyner was put upon his defence, and his letter of exculpation is still extant. It is curious to find a bishop palliating his conduct, if he were proved to be in error, on the ground that he was not learned in divinity; but, while expressing his readiness to yield to any proofs which the king, as a divine, might produce, he refers to Henry's zeal against both Luther and Wiclif, and then reiterates the assertions made in the public document.[*]

The king, in placing the answer of the ordinaries in the hands of the Speaker of the House of Commons, said, " We think this answer will scantly please you, for it seemeth to us very slender." He thus encouraged the House of Commons to continue its controversy with the Convocation, and concluded by saying, " You be a great sort of wise men : I doubt not you will look circumspectly in the matter, and that it will be indifferent between you."

The whole subject was brought again for discussion before the convocation, which met on the 29th of April, 1532. The debates continued till the 6th of May. Although on some occasions the Bishop of London acted as the archbishop's commissary, yet on a reference to the acts of convocation I find that the archbishop was able generally to attend.

The difficulty of coming to a conclusion was great, on account of the different opinions prevalent in different sections of the convocation ; they can hardly be called parties, for there were no leaders, neither was there combined action either for or against the Government. There were certainly many persons in convocation who, like Cranmer, were ready to support the king, whatever the royal determination might be ; with these acted generally another party who discussed every measure on its own merits, but who represented the old Anglican and anti-papal feeling ; there was a party alarmed at the progress of Lutheranism, and having little confidence in the king, who were ready to

---

[*] Wilkins, iii. 752 ; Atterbury, Append. vi. a.

throw themselves at the feet of the pope, and to yield to all the papal demands in return for papal protection. Wolsey's party, indeed, had split into two sections: some of his adherents would like to see the legatine power revived; while others, seeing this to be impossible, were prepared, like Crumwell, to abet the Protestants, without becoming Protestants themselves. The king's friends said, "Make everything over to the king;" the other party felt that the king, supported by parliament, was all-powerful, and that, although they would have to yield, they might fight the battle inch by inch, and save what they could. All were agreed, whether in parliament or in convocation, as to the duty of opposing Lutheranism and Lollardism, and of suppressing heresy.

When the 6th of May arrived, and nothing had been done, the Upper House of Convocation desired the Lower House to prepare a new reply to the supplication of the commons, and by a committee a new document was drawn up, which was presented to the lords on Monday, the 8th of May. "It is a paper," says Atterbury, "drawn up with great spirit and firmness;" he attributes it, from internal evidence, to an author not the same as he by whom the former document was penned. It is manfully contended, that the prelates of the Church have authority to legislate freely in what pertains to faith and to good manners, necessary to the soul's health of their flocks. They establish their position by reference to Scripture, to history, and to the king's own book, "most excellently written against Martin Luther for the defence of the Catholic faith and Christ's Church, in which he doth not only knowledge and confess, but also with most vehement and inexpugnable reasons and authorities doth defend the same."

Yet, these considerations notwithstanding, they were content to promise, with reference to new laws, that they would not publish or put forth any constitutions without his highness's consent, except those which concern the maintenance of faith and morals, and the reformation and correction of sin. As regards the old laws made either by them or by their predecessors, as it is pretended, contrary to the laws of the realm or the prerogative of the crown, they would engage to revoke and annul them, so that "your right honourable commons shall now dare execute your laws without fear or dread of our said laws, if any such there be."*

The answer, drawn up by the Lower House of Convocation, was submitted to the Upper House. It received the sanction of their lordships, and a committee was formed consisting of the bishops of London and Lincoln, the abbots of Westminster and Burton, together with Sampson, dean of the chapel, and Fox, the almoner, to carry the answer to the king. They were directed to be instant with the king that he would preserve and protect the liberties and immunities of his clergy as his noble ancestors had done.

Convocation reassembled on the 10th. of May to receive the report of the committee. They had to state that the king was not satisfied with the amended form of reply, and Fox, the almoner, submitted to the Convocation a document, with nothing less than which, he said, his majesty would be content. It was the result of the interview with the king, and ran thus:

"1. That no constitution or ordinance shall be hereafter by the clergy enacted, promulged, or put in execution, unless the king's highness do approve the same by his high

---

* Ex. MS. Cott. Cleop. F. 1. fol. 101, printed in Wilkins, iii. 753.

authority and royal assent; and his advice and favour be also interposed for the execution of every such constitution among his highness's subjects. 2. That whereas divers of the constitutions provincial, which have been heretofore enacted, be thought not only much prejudicial to the king's prerogative royal, but also much onerous to his highness's subjects, it be committed to the examination and judgment of thirty-two persons, whereof sixteen to be of the Upper and Nether House of the temporality, and other sixteen of the clergy, all to be appointed by the king's highness; so that, finally, whichsoever of the said constitutions shall be thought and determined by the most part of the said thirty-two persons worthy to be abrogate and annulled, the same to be afterward taken away, and to be of no force and strength. 3. That all other of the said constitutions, which stand with God's law and the king's, to stand in full strength and power, the king's highness's royal assent given to the same." *

It now became evident, that the king would accept of no compromise or modification of the terms : the convocation must surrender at discretion. He was supported by the House of Commons, and if not by a majority, yet by a considerable number among the members of convocation. Fox was directed to present the articles to convocation, not for discussion, but for acceptance and subscription ; long debates, however, ensued. For the convenience of the archbishop the convocation still sat at Westminster ; but, having no regular place of meeting they were dependent upon the courtesy of the abbot and monks of Westminster. They had to adjourn from St. Catherine's chapel to St. Dunstan's, an adjournment which makes some of the Puritan historians merry, though, from what appears, the members of the convocation were preparing not to invoke a dead bishop, but to consult a living one. A committee was appointed to seek the advice

* Acts of Convocation, Atterbury, 89 ; Wilkins, iii. 749.

of Fisher, bishop of Rochester, who, for some reason or other, was unable to attend convocation personally. What his advice was we do not know. The king was impatient : he began to talk of a divided allegiance, and an *imperium in imperio*. He courted the commons.

The convocation reassembled on Monday, the 13th of May. The archbishop presented the three articles to the Upper House. The house assented to the king's terms on the first article, that without the royal licence they would frame no new canons. In the Lower House an amendment was moved and carried, to the effect that the concession here made should be confined to the term of the king's natural life. With respect to the proposal, that there should be a commission of thirty-two persons for a revision of the ancient canons, to this neither house would agree. They were willing, however, to submit to the judgment of the king himself : they were willing to moderate and annul them at his suggestion, but by their own ecclesiastical authority.

There was now an inclination on both sides to recede from the assertion of extreme principles. The king appointed six noblemen to hold a conference with the Upper House of Convocation ; and they were men who were by no means hostile to the Church, the Duke of Norfolk being at the head. The Upper House of Convocation could not be persuaded to submit to the terms proposed with reference to a revision of the old canons, and the committee of noblemen had to report to the king that, let the consequence be what it might, this was the final resolution of the clergy.

While the conference was going on in the Upper House, there was a debate in the Lower House of Convocation. Here, at length, the clergy agreed by a considerable majority to accept the proposal of the king without modification, or any alteration whatever.

The archbishop and the Upper House were waiting in some anxiety to know how their resolution would be taken by the king, when the prolocutor came up with the resolution of the Lower House, admitting the *whole* terms proposed by the king. Warham desired the lower clergy to retire to their own house, and there wait until they were summoned to hear the king's pleasure.

At noon the answer came. It caused the greatest satisfaction, for it terminated an unpleasant controversy. The king would consent to the submission of the clergy, without the terms which gave such reasonable offence to the prelates. He would be satisfied if they promised not to enact, promulge, or put in use *new* canons without the royal licence.

A new draft of the submission was now engrossed, and on Thursday, the 16th of May, 1532, it was presented by the Archbishop of Canterbury to the king.[*] The form was as follows :—

"We, your most humble subjects, daily orators, and beadsmen, of your clergy of England, having our special trust and confidence in your most excellent wisdom, your princely goodness, and fervent zeal, to the promotion of God's honour and the Christian religion, and also in your learning, far exceeding in our judgment the learning of all other kings and princes that

---

[*] See Wilkins, iii. 739, 746, 748, 749, 755. See also Wake, 476, 477, 545, 546 ; Atterbury, 84, 90, 521, 528, 535—548 ; Append. to Collier, xix. xx. ; Strype's Memoir, 1, i. 198, 209 ; Fiddes, 524. It is to be remembered that two years elapsed before this submission, passed in convocation, was confirmed and enforced by act of parliament. The act bound the clergy to the performance of the promise contained in their submission.

we have read of, and doubting nothing but that the same shall still continue and daily increase in your majesty, first do offer and promise *in verbo sacerdotii* here unto your highnesss, submitting ourselves most humbly to the same, that we will never from henceforth enact, put in use, promulge, or execute any new canons or contitutions provincial, or any other new ordinance, provincial or synodal, in our convocations or synods, in time coming, which convocation is, alway hath been, and must be assembled only by your high commandment of writ, only your highness, by your royal assent, shall license us to assemble our convocation, and to make, promulge, and execute such constitutions, ordinaments, and canons provincial or synodal, which have been heretofore enacted, but thought to be not only much prejudicial to your prerogative royal, but also overmuch onerous to your highness's subjects; your clergy aforesaid are contented, if it may stand so with your highness's pleasure, that it be committed to the examination and judgment of your grace, and of thirty-two persons, whereof sixteen to be of the Upper and Nether House of the temporalty and other sixteen of the clergy, all to be chosen and appointed by your most noble grace. So that finally, whichsoever of the said constitutions, ordinaments, or canons provincial or synodal shall be thought and determined by your grace and by the most part of the said xxxii persons, not to stand with God's laws and the laws of your realm, the same to be abrogated and taken away by your grace and the clergy. And such of them as shall be seen by your grace and by the most part of the said thirty-two persons to stand with God's laws and the laws of your realm, to stand in full strength and power, your grace's most royal assent and authority once impetrate fully given to the same."

We have now brought to a conclusion the public life of William Warham. In his primacy, the Reformation commenced in the reassertion of the royal supremacy, and the submission of the clergy.[*] These two great

---

[*] The submission of the clergy was agreed to on Wednesday, the 15th of May, 1532. The Clergy Submission Act was passed in parliament in the spring of 1534.

objects were effected in convocation, some time antecedently to their adoption by parliament.

It was not till two years later, the 31st of March, 1534, that convocation, again in advance of parliament, decreed that "the Pope of Rome has no greater jurisdiction conferred on him by God, in holy Scripture, in this kingdom of England, than any other foreign bishop."[*]

Whether Warham would have consented to the latter proposition is more than doubtful ; though revulsions of feeling and renunciations of opinions are rapid and unexpected in a revolutionary age. It may be doubted whether Henry VIII. would have rejected the pope in 1532, in the terms used by convocation in 1534.

There exists on Warham's part, a protest to the effect, that he neither intended to consent, nor with a clear conscience could consent, to any statute passed, or hereafter to be passed, in the parliament of 1529, derogatory to the rights of the apostolic see, or to the subversion of the laws, privileges, prerogatives, pre-eminence, or liberties of the metropolitan Church of Canterbury.[†]

The reader who does not come new to this subject, but has, through these volumes, traced the history of religious opinion in the Church of England, will easily understand the position of Warham, and will perceive that there was no inconsistency between his protest and his acts.

The Church of England, as an independent national Church, possessed certain rights, certain laws, privileges, prerogatives, pre-eminence: the King of England

[*] Wilkins, iii. 769 ; Heylin, 7.

[†] The original is to be found in the Longueville MSS. in the possession of Lord Calthorpe. It is printed by Wilkins, iii. 746.

possessed certain rights and authority within this
province, and in regard to both the provinces, the
entire Church of England : the Bishop of Rome,
until the year 1534, possessed certain rights in this
realm of England, undefined and undefinable, and the
cause in consequence of continual disputes.   There
was no inconsistency in saying, "While we assert
the just rights of the Church of Canterbury, we
do not intend to encroach on the royal prerogative ;
while we admit the prerogatives of the king, we do
not deny that the Bishop of Rome,"—the term applied
at that time to the pope,—"has also certain rights ;
but where there is any doubt upon the subject, we seek
an adjustment."

It had been discovered that the kings of England,
almost until the reign of Henry VIII, had claimed and
exercised a supremacy over all persons and causes
within their dominions. Warham was persuaded upon
this point and acted accordingly : " but," he added,
"though I concede to the king the prerogative he claims,
yet I do so with a full understanding, that this is
consistent with my maintaining the privileges of my
Church of Canterbury, and any jurisdiction that the
Bishop of Rome may legally possess." It was said, that
the clergy by their canons and constitutions and the
independent legislation of the two houses of convocation, had encroached on the royal prerogative. Warham was persuaded, that this was the case, and urged
convocation to submit to the principles laid down by
the king for their future government ; but in granting
to the king what he considered his right, he protested
that against king and pope he would maintain, in
consistency with the other rights, the liberties of the
Church of England.

Soon after Warham's death it was discovered that the

Bishop of Rome had no divine right in England, and .
the jurisdiction he sought to exercise, being a usur-
pation, was by this Church and realm rejected.

Whether Warham would have been open to conviction on this point can never be known. But certainly
his was a candid mind, and his tendency was to yield
to persons of stronger will than his own. Perhaps
some readers will be of opinion, that his protest would
not have prevented his acting with the king's government, when the time came for asserting that, while the
prerogatives of the crown were greater than he had
supposed, for the pretensions of the pope there was
no foundation in Scripture.

There is a letter from Warham to the king about
his courts, to which it is difficult to assign the date.
When Warham commenced his primacy, he desired
to reform the ecclesiastical courts : finding the difficulty of cleaning the Augean stable, he permitted the
legatine authority to be established : the Hercules
whose aid he invoked perished without completing
the work which proved to be beyond his strength ;
but confusion had ensued, and the king's courts
were in consequence assuming the jurisdiction which
Warham had yielded, as a temporary arrangement,
to the legatine court. Against this proceeding, it is
said, that he appealed to the king.*

It has been seen that, throughout the controversy
between the king and the convocation, Warham,
though acting as a moderator, was on the king's side.
With the king he grew into favour, and the archbishop
had frequently the honour of receiving his sovereign at
Knowle.

* The letter is given in Collier, iv. 199. Its authenticity may
be questioned.

On the questionable authority of Harpsfield, Warham is said to have predicted that Cranmer would be
his successor in the see of Canterbury. In noticing
this report, I would observe on its extreme improba-
bility. Dr. Cranmer was probably brought under the
notice of the archbishop as a lawyer who had suggested a mode to be pursued for the accomplishment
of the king's wishes in regard to the divorce. But
before Warham's death Cranmer and Crumwell had
scarcely emerged from obscurity. They had obtained
a place at court, but courtiers of the old school hardly
thought them worthy of notice. They had won the
king's ear before their power was known. There was
one man who seemed to be marked out for the
primacy, Bishop Gardyner, who never forgot or forgave the slight which was passed upon him when he
was overlooked and a new man was placed on the
throne which he had regarded as his own.

In August, the archbishop, who had bravely performed the duties of his high office through the stormy
debates of convocation, retired into the country, and
visited his nephew, Archdeacon Warham, at St.
Stephen's, near Canterbury. He went there to give
final directions as to his tomb prepared for the reception of his corpse in a chapel which he had built in the
Martyrdom. Travelling in those days, whether on
horseback or in a litter, was not to be undertaken by
an old man without danger. The archbishop was
much fatigued by his journey. His debility increased ;
he was confined to his bed ; he was preparing for
his great change. He summoned his steward to his
bedside, intending to give directions as to the disposal
of his property. He had been generous and munificent, and when he inquired what money remained
in his coffers, he was told thirty pounds. The good

old man smiled. He, was not likely to see another rent day. He said, "*Satis viatici ad cœlum.*"

The splendours of his enthronization, we may suppose, passed before his mind, and he certainly felt as old men feel, "Vanity of vanities, all is vanity."

Between the hours of two or three, on the 22d day of August, 1532, William Warham expired;* and soon after, the event was announced to the Church by the tolling of the great bell of the cathedral.

The body was conveyed to the church of St. Stephen's. Here it lay in state. In the gloved hand was placed the cross of Canterbury; a magnificent pall was laid upon the corpse; lights were burning at the head and at the feet. The chaplains incessantly chanted the psalms.

The cathedral was, in the meantime, prepared for the obsequies, and everything was ready for the ceremonial by the 9th of September. On that day, at two o'clock in the afternoon, the body was placed in the nave.

On Thursday, the 10th, the cathedral was filled by a multitude attracted by piety, by gratitude, by curiosity. Mass was said; a sermon was preached; the religious rites were duly performed.

An adjournment took place to the palace, where the archbishop's character for hospitality was sustained to the last. A repast was prepared for all invited guests; but a repast in those days was not confined to the invited guests within the hall. The crowd outside asserted their right to appropriate whatever

---

* See the certificate in the Heralds' Office. Professor Stubbs gives the 23d as the date of his death from the Register. He died at St. Stephen's, and his death was not known in Lambeth until the 23d.

they could lay hands on. A general scramble was
the consequence, and, though the noise was at the
time subdued, it was scarcely possible to suppress
the excitement and quarrels which a scramble implies.

This diversion was intended to clear the church of the
mob. When the multitude was dispersed, the body of
the defunct archbishop was raised, and in deep silence
it was carried to the Martyrdom. There was no
religious office performed while the corpse of William
Warham was placed in the sepulchre he had himself
prepared for it. The members of the archbishop's
household, and his officers of state stood around, their
occupation done; one by one each approached the
coffin, and breaking his staff cast it into the grave.
The silence was at length broken by the herald, who
proclaimed the style and title of the deceased.

All things being done decently and in order, every
man, we are told, went to the palace, where again a
sumptuous dinner was prepared.*

Of the archbishop's benefactions to Winchester, New
College, and All Souls', mention has already been
made. His theological books went to All Souls'
College library; his canon law books, with the
prick song books belonging to his chapel, to New
College; his lectionaries, grayles, and antiphonals to
Winchester College.

---

* A certificate in the Heralds' College Office, London, printed in
the Athenæ Oxoniensis.

CHAPTER III.

THOMAS CRANMER.[*]

Preliminary Observations.—Cranmer opposed to Protestantism in early
Life.—Parentage and Birth.—His early Education.—Sent to Cambridge.
—Is elected a Fellow of Jesus.—His first Marriage.—His Life at the
Dolphin.—Appointed Reader of Buckingham College.—Becomes a
Widower, and is restored to his Fellowship.—Whether he was offered
Promotion in Wolsey's College at Oxford doubtful.—Proceeds to the
Degree of D.D.—Does not distinguish himself at the University—Dis-
charges the routine Duties of a Master of Arts and a Doctor.—Becomes
Tutor to Mr. Cressy's Children.—Introduction to Henry VIII.—The
Divorce Case.—Cranmer sent with Embassy to Rome, to plead the
King's Cause.—He is favourably received by the Papal Authorities.—
The Pope confers upon him the Office of Grand Penitentiary of England.
—Opinions of the Universities on the Divorce Case.—Cranmer returns to
England.—His Opinion of Pole's Letter on the Divorce.—He defends
Persecution of Heretics.—Ambassador to the Emperor.—Unsuccessful
Negotiation.—He lingers in Germany.—Has little Intercourse with the
Lutherans.—Falls in love with Osiander's Niece, and contracts a
second Marriage.—Appointed by the King Archbishop of Canterbury.—
Sincere in his Reluctance to accept the Office.—Is consecrated.—His
Enthronization.—Convocation.—The King secretly married to Ann
Boleyn.—Cranmer pronounces the Nullity of the King's Marriage with
Queen Katherine.—Cranmer's description of Queen Ann's Coronation.
—Indignation of the Public against the King and the Archbishop.—
Harsh Measures of Cranmer.—He silences the Pulpits.—Recurrence to
the History of the Nun of Kent.—Cranmer protected by Military Force
at his Visitation.—His provincial Visitation.—Opposed by the Bishops
of Winchester and London.—Legislative Enactments.—Election of
Bishops.—Archbishop invested with power to grant Dispensations
hitherto granted by the Pope.—Suffragan Bishops.—Protestant Persecutors.—Legal Murder of More and Fisher.—Archbishop's Retirement.
—Trial of Ann Boleyn.—Unjustifiable Conduct of Cranmer.

CHAP.
III.

INJUSTICE has been done to the character of Cranmer,
and his conduct has been exposed to the censure of

Thomas
Cranmer.
1533-56.

[*] Authorities.—The life of Cranmer, like the other lives in these
volumes, has been written from original documents, some of which

superficial readers, in consequence of the false position into which he has been forced by his friends, his have only lately been brought to light. I was careful not to read any modern writers until the life was completed about two years ago. In former times, I had been acquainted with the biographies of Cranmer written by Archdeacon Todd and Mr. Le Bas, both of whom I had the honour of numbering among my friends. I only remembered that, when I read their books, they left on my mind the impression that they came forward, not as historians, but as advocates. They each of them held a brief for Cranmer, and, on renewing my acquaintance with their writings, I found them more one-sided than I expected. The student is bound, after reading their books, to have recourse to Dodd and Lingard. The fault, however, is not in the misstatement of facts, but in the inferences which they deduce from them. It is not my business to enter into controversy with any modern writers. I simply state the facts as I find them, and I endeavour to discover the principles on which they rest. Tracing the origin and progress of our Reformation to the overruling Providence of God, and not, as I have shown in the introductory chapter, to any meritorious action on the part of man, I am not under a temptation to extenuate the faults of reformers, or to overlook the virtues of their opponents. The work of God is equally effected by the perverseness of a Pharaoh and the willingness of a Paul. Men, as *persons*, may be rewarded or punished; as *things*, whether willingly or otherwise, they will be compelled to act as God pleased. Most of the important documents relating to Cranmer, as well as his own writings, have been printed. The Remains of Thomas Cranmer have been edited by Dr. Jenkyns. They have been carefully reprinted, collated, and compared with the originals, for the Parker Society, by the Rev. E. J. Cox. Scarcely anything worthy of notice relating to Cranmer has escaped the researches of Dr. Jenkyns, and the gleanings and industry of Mr. Cox, if we except a legal document on the subject of the Divorce, which has been discovered in the British Museum by Mr. Pocock, who has favoured me with the perusal of his transcript. I have, of course, searched the State Papers and the Journals of the House of Lords. The Anecdotes and Character of Archbishop Cranmer, by Ralph Morice, his secretary; and another contemporary Life and Death of the Archbishop, have been published by the Camden Society. I believe that Cranmer's Commonplaces, said to exist in the British Museum, have not been printed.

CHAP.
III.

Thomas
Cranmer.
1533-56.

advocates, and biographers. A general opinion, through their misrepresentation of the facts of the case, prevails to the present hour, that Cranmer was born and bred a Protestant ; and a Protestant too of the modern type. If such had been the case, it were impossible to acquit him, when to our reprobation he is held up as a hypocrite. In consigning to the stake the noble-minded men who,—holding the same principles as he is himself assumed to have held,—added to their faith the manliness—which he did not possess—to avow it, he might well, under such circumstances, be denounced as the vilest of persecutors and the meanest of mankind.

I have no inclination to vindicate the character of Cranmer, and in his conduct there was much which was indefensible ; but it is my duty, as an historian, to guard against the distortion of facts ; while, as Christians, we are bound to make due allowance for a person who, in a position, not sought for but forced upon him, was surrounded with peculiar and unusual difficulties. The reader must be reminded of the fact, that Cranmer was certainly not a Protestant before the commencement of the reign of Edward VI. ; and the question may, indeed, be fairly asked, whether, in the modern acceptation of the term, a Protestant he ever became.

When first Cranmer appeared as a public character, although parliament had not yet acknowledged the royal supremacy, the supremacy had been asserted by the convocation ; and in the sentence of the convocation Cranmer acquiesced. The act of convocation, as Cranmer himself declares, was attributable, not to him, but to Archbishop Warham, and all that Cranmer did was, when the principle was once admitted, to carry it into practice. But the royal supremacy was not at this time regarded as inconsistent with the legitimate claims of the papacy. There were two powers exercising co-ordinate jurisdiction, and, a misunderstanding having arisen, they required adjustment. The royal supremacy was held by Gardyner and Bonner as well as by Cranmer; the question between them was not as to the fact but as to the extent. Cranmer actually went to Rome to argue the case; and, so far from being regarded as an enemy, he was received with honour, and was preferred.

When it was found impossible to adjust the respective jurisdictions, it was declared, first by convocation, and then by parliament, that the pope hath no more authority in England than any other foreign bishop. From this time there was a breach between this country and the see of Rome; but Cranmer and Henry, though antipapists, were not one whit nearer to Lutheranism. They both of them rejected the *sobriquet* of Protestant, and declared it to be their resolution to uphold the Catholic faith. Papists were condemned to the stake, because it was contended, that the assertion of papal supremacy was opposed to Catholicism; and to the same stake, for the same reason, because they were opposed to the Catholic faith, Protestants were consigned. Cranmer and Henry may have been in error as to their view of Catholicism, but it was for this that they contended, and it is only when we bear this in mind, that we can understand what has given rise to much sarcastic rhetoric, when historians have mentioned the fact, that Papists and Protestants were condemned to death by the same Government. Henry and Cranmer were neither Papists nor Protestants, but they professed to be Catholics. Their conduct in condemning those to death who refused to accept their definition of Catholicism may have been iniquitous ; but, though not justifiable, it is at least intelligible.

The real work of the Reformation was the changing of the Mass into a Communion, as will be hereafter shown, and this involved the dogma of transubstantiation. This dogma, in its acceptance or rejection, became the test of the two parties. It is not to be supposed that many could understand the merits of the case, so far as the dogma was itself concerned ; but as men can fight and die for the flag which is carried in front of a regiment, because it tells of the side to which they belong, so, by asserting or denying the dogma, they proclaimed themselves Papists or Protestants. Henry VII. was dead before Cranmer renounced transubstantiation, and, until he did this, it is a mistake to speak of him as a Protestant.

The Cranmers or Cranmars* had been settled in Nottinghamshire from early Norman times. Through the marriage of Edward, the great-grandfather of the future archbishop, with the heiress of Aslacton in the parish of Whatton, they assumed, at the close of the fourteenth century, a respectable position in society. They ranked with the rising class of country gentlemen. The retainer who had become a farmer, grew into a yeoman ; the yeoman bore arms and became a country gentleman, from whose younger sons the professions were replenished.

At Aslacton, on the 2d of July, 1484, was born Thomas Cranmer, predestined to be the sixty-eighth Archbishop of Canterbury. He was the second son of a father bearing the same Christian name as himself. He had two brothers and four sisters.

---

* The surname of Cranmer, written with his own hand, occurs, I believe, only once in the documents bearing upon his history. In his letter to the Earl of Wiltshire, in 1531, he signs himself Cranmar.

Thomas Cranmer was unfortunate in his early education.   When we take into consideration the character of the man, there is something affecting in the statement he gives of the treatment he received when a boy.   The boy was " cowed and crushed," and from this early " cowing," it is long, if ever, before a youth rises to that manliness of character which is ranked, among Christian dispositions, next to faith.   Speaking of Cranmer, Ralph Morice, his secretary, says, " that his father sent him to school with a marvellous severe and cruel schoolmaster, whose tyranny towards youth was such, that, as he thought, the said schoolmaster so appalled, dulled and daunted the tender and fine wits of his scholars that they more commonly hated and abhorred good literature than favoured or embraced the same : whose memories were also thereby so mutilated and wounded that for his part he lost much of that benefit of memory and audacity in his youth that by nature was given him, *which he could never recover, as he divers times reported*." *

The injurious effects of this treatment were partially

---

* Morice, Anecdotes of Archbishop Cranmer, 239. The passage is important as throwing light on Cranmer's character, although I have not seen it noticed by any modern biographer. Some curious instances of the severity of masters are given in Knight's Colet, and in the Letters of Erasmus. Cranmer would not perhaps have fared better at Eton. The verses of Thomas Tusser, on Nicholas Udall, schoolmaster of Eton, have been often quoted:—

> " From Paul's I went to Eton, sent
>   To learn straightways the Latin phrase,
>   Where fifty-three stripes given to me
>   At once I had.

> " For fault but small, or none at all,
>   It came to pass, thus beat I was,
>   See, Udall, see the mercy of thee,
>   To me, poor lad."

counteracted in the case of Cranmer, by the field sports,
—"the civil and gentlemanlike exercises," as Morice
calls them,—in which, encouraged by his father, the
boy excelled. Throughout his life, in the intervals of
business, Thomas would follow hawk and hound, and
although short-sighted he could take a good aim with
the long bow. When he became Archbishop of Canterbury, the game was carefully preserved on his
manors, in order that he might the better enjoy the
sport. He was a bold and skilful horseman, as his
secretary not only tells us with feelings of satisfaction
and pride, but looking back to the days when his
master had become one of the grandees of the nation,
he delighted to remark that, when Primate of All England, Cranmer was ever ready to mount the horse
which no groom in his stables could manage.

At the age of fourteen, Thomas Cranmer was sent
by his widowed mother to Cambridge, and there, as a
member of Jesus College, he resided for many years.

In the Life of Warham we have refuted the statement, that the universities at this time were unequal to
meet the requirements of the age. We have the testimony of Erasmus to the superiority of the English universities, and to the number of learned men by whom
our country was distinguished. Between the extremes
of self-laudation and of self-depreciation by which the
English have been, at all times, distinguished, it is
sometimes difficult to discover the truth; under the
prevalence of party feeling institutions and persons
are too frequently depreciated. One thing, however,
is remarkable : hitherto the reader will have observed
very little has been said of Cambridge ; that university,
as compared with Oxford, had been in comparative
obscurity. From that obscurity it was now to emerge.
During the early period of the Reformation, during

the reigns of Henry, Edward, and Elizabeth, the
greater number of our distinguished men and great
reformers emanated from Cambridge, which has
always maintained a friendly rivalry with her sister
university.   We may attribute this, in part, to certain
controversies inimical to learning which took place,
about this time, at Oxford, to which attention has been
already called.   The Trojans, though they had their
origin in Cambridge, became tyrannically powerful, for
a time, in Oxford, and the peaceful student retired
to Cambridge.   But the pre-eminence of Cambridge is
to be greatly, if not chiefly, attributed to the residence
there of Erasmus, and the munificence of his patron
Bishop Fisher, to whose transcendent virtues and
noble qualities justice, through the party spirit of
Puritans, has never been done.   He it was, who
appointed Erasmus to the chair of the Margaret Professor; and so great was Fisher's zeal in the cause of
Greek literature, that in his old age he desired to
place himself under Erasmus as a student of that
language. With the generous assistance of the Lady
Margaret, he did more than any other man in
England to promote the cause of education; and so
wise and judicious were his measures, that students
in either university are, at the present hour, receiving
food and raiment from funds which his royal mistress
placed at his disposal.   Such is the man whom
Puritans too generally love to defame, because he
would not fall down, with the costly sacrifice of
an upright conscience, before His Majesty King
Henry VIII.

In the university there were then, as there have
always been, the industrious, the dissipated, and certain indolent revellers in literature, distinguishable
from the real and conscientious students.

The question with which we are concerned relates to the studies and position of Cranmer; and of Cranmer we have nothing to record. For a quarter of a century he was resident in Cambridge—twenty-five years of excitement, of reform, and of progress; and yet we can only remark and lament, that among the distinguished men of the university the name of Cranmer does not appear. From the deeply interesting letters of Erasmus we can give the character of many of his contemporaries; but, though Cranmer lived almost in the same street as the great scholar, of Cranmer no mention is made. Erasmus had occasion to thank Cranmer, when Cranmer had become Archbishop of Canterbury, for some favour conferred upon him; but no allusion is made to any former intimacy between them when both had been resident in the same university.

Cranmer, although, by no means, deficient in scholarship, and although he was pre-eminent as a writer of pure English and as a translator, was never ranked among the men of learning. He was, however, acute as a lawyer, and had a thoroughly legal mind. Some legal documents afterwards drawn up by him have excited the admiration of modern lawyers. I think, therefore, that we may conclude that, although he neglected no branch of study, and chose the Scriptures for his subject when he became a professor or doctor, he directed his mind chiefly to legal studies, with a view of making the law his profession. He would scarcely have married, if he had intended to become an ecclesiastic. It is true, that after he had become a priest, Cranmer again fell in love and took unto himself a wife.*

* Dr. Redman, who was strongly opposed to the marriage of the clergy, when he was asked in convocation for a legal opinion on the subject, gave the following as his legal opinion :—

But it was one thing for a priest, under the influence
of a violent passion or strong affection, in spite of the laws condemning the marriage of the clergy, to make
the young woman to whom he was attached what the poor people still call " an honest woman ;" and it was another thing for a young man commencing his career in life to adopt a measure which, if discovered, would have acted as a certain impediment to his preferment. Having become a Fellow of his college, it would have been dishonest to have concealed his marriage, and his marriage young Cranmer did not attempt to conceal.* He had become a Fellow of his College in 1510 or 1511, and by those who were watching for a vacancy among the Fellows, Cranmer's marriage would soon have been discovered, even supposing that a man of his upright mind could have committed a fraud by concealing it.   He might have cohabited with the object of his affection if she would have consented to

"I think that although the word of God do exhort and counsel priests to live in chastity, out of the cumber of the flesh and the world, that thereby they may the more wholly attend to their calling, yet the bond of abstaining from marriage doth only lie upon priests of this realm by reason of canons and constitutions of the Church and not by any precept of God's word ; as in that they should be bound by reason of any vow, which, in as far as my conscience is, priests in this Church of England do not make. I think that it standeth well with God's word, that a man which hath been, or is but once married, being otherwise accordingly qualified, may 'be made a priest.'"—Strype's Memorials, 223.

    * The deep degradation of the clergy through the constrained celibacy of their class, is mentioned by Sir Thomas More.   His words are best given in the Latin :—"Theologus asserebat conclusionem famosam cujusdam limpidissimi doctoris, qui fecit illum singularissimum librum qui intitulatur *Directorium Concubinariorum,* plus eum peccare qui unam domi concubinam quam qui decem foras meretrices haberet ; idque cum ob malum exemplum, tum ob occasionem sæpius peccandi cum ea quæ domi sit."—Tho. Mori, Apologia pro Erasmo.

become his concubine ; but Cranmer's strong sense of moral propriety prevented him from adopting such a course as this.

It is, then, highly probable that Cranmer intended originally to practise as a lawyer ; that he remained long at the university to study law and to make the requisite independence by taking pupils ; that he afterwards changed his mind, and received holy orders, when, having to choose a subject upon which to lecture, he selected the Holy Scriptures ; but that before this time, Erasmus had left Cambridge.

The marriage of Cranmer with an innkeeper's daughter must have been regarded as a misalliance. His wife, "Black Joan," was a near relative of the landlady of the Dolphin Inn. An innkeeper occupied a respectable position in the social scale. As we see in the "Canterbury Tales," he mingled on terms of equality with his guests, and became their companion. In a monastery, the prior presided at the hospitable board of the convent ; and the guest, at parting, left, as a gift to the house, an offering sufficient to meet the expenses to which he had subjected the community. When monasteries were less frequent or less hospitable, inns were opened, where payment was made directly to the innkeeper, and the visitor was at liberty "to take mine ease." Nevertheless, the innkeeper still received the visitor as his guest, and at the social meal "mine host" presided and led the conversation. This custom still lingered in foreign hotels at the early part of the present century, and the landlord presiding at the *table d'hôte* was often an intelligent, well-informed, and agreeable companion. Cranmer's marriage was not regarded as disreputable, for although, as a matter of course, he forfeited his fellowship, he found an income to support his wife by accepting the appointment of reader or lecturer at Buckingham Hall, a hall which afterwards developed into Magdalen College.   Nevertheless, the family of the young squire of Aslacton was not likely to look with a favourable eye on his alliance with an innkeeper's niece ; and, although this connexion brought him into contact with general society, and so was advantageous in the formation of his character, a severe judge might think the taste questionable of a young man who, when he might have sat at the feet of Erasmus, preferred the social comforts provided for him in his home at the Dolphin.

Whatever may have been, however, the comforts of the Dolphin, Cranmer was not destined to enjoy them long.   Before the termination of the first year of their union his wife died in childbirth.   The child also died, and was buried with its mother.

It may be that Cranmer's mind was now first turned to more serious things, and that he found that consolation in the sacred volume of which he desired others to participate by placing a version of it in every one's hand.   His zeal for the promulgation of Scripture, though shared in by Erasmus and Warham and Fisher, became such a marked feature in his character, that he was suspected of being a Protestant long before such he really became.

On the death of his wife, Cranmer claimed to be reinstated in his fellowship ; and the claim was admitted.   His wife had died, before his year of grace was expired ; and, although the statutes excluded the Mariti, yet he could prove, that there was no statutable objection to the Maritati.   Disconsolate for the loss of his wife, he thought that he should never wish to marry again ; and, without prospect of a family to be dependent upon his exertions, he determined upon seeking admission into holy orders. Having been ordained in the year 1523, he soon after proceeded to the degree of Doctor of Divinity. A Doctor of Divinity, or Professor of Theology, was expected, if he remained in the university, to give lectures on some chosen and special subject. Some chose one subject, some another; but, as we have seen, in every age there were many doctors in our universities who made choice of lecturing on Holy Scripture. There was no discouragement, it will be remembered, in the mediæval Church, of the study of the Bible,—but the Bible as *a whole* was to be studied only by the learned few. The mass of the people were to be satisfied with the various selections provided for their edification in the services of the Church and the primers.

About this time Cardinal Wolsey, having suppressed numerous monasteries, determined to found a college at Oxford, which in its magnificence was to surpass any collegiate institution throughout the world. By those who look out for proof of the high estimation in which Cranmer was held in his own university, it is said that, when a selection was made from the most distinguished men in either university to become fellows of the new college, Cranmer was one of those who were chosen, and that he declined, for no assignable reason, the lucrative and honourable post.* The story is problematical, but, if it be true, it is a proof in addition to those which will be hereafter produced, of the unambitious character of Cranmer's mind, and

---

* Strype states this on the authority of Foxe. But it is curious to observe that the first Canon who became Subdean in 1527 was Thomas Canner. Wood, Colleges, 422. Foxe was likely enough, either in carelessness or by design, to mistake the name—to have supposed Canner to be Cranmer, and then to have represented Cranmer as having refused what in point of fact was never offered to him.

of his desire to remain in literary retirement. An ambitious man would not have refused an offer to be placed under the eye of the great man, at whose disposal lay all the best preferments in Church and state, a generous patron, quick to discern merit and always ready to reward the labours of men of learning. Be this as it may, from inclination and from circumstances Cranmer remained in obscurity. He filled in due course certain university offices; and became one of the public examiners in the Divinity School, and, as such, he is said to have been severe and strict.

A quarter of a century passed away since Cranmer's matriculation, and still Dr. Cranmer continued to be what we should now call a private tutor. He had under his care two young men who were, through their mother, related to himself; when, in 1528, the sweating sickness reappeared in the country, and committed havoc among the colleges of Cambridge.* The filthy condition of the towns made each great city little better than a pest-house; and the inhabitants, when they had the means, rushed into the country. Dr. Cranmer accompanied his pupils to the house of their father, in the parish of Waltham. In the neighbourhood of Waltham the king had now fixed his abode. Alarmed at the death of two gentlemen of his privy chamber and others among his courtiers, who, having sickened in the morning, were before the sunset dead men, Henry had wandered from place to place, his temporary and lonely residence being indicated by fires lighted day and night, both to purify the atmosphere and to warn off intruders. But now the fierceness of the pestilence having abated, and his alarm being less exaggerated, he was settled at Tytynhanger, a house belonging to the Abbot of St. Albans.

* For an account of this disease, see Grafton, 412, Hecker, 222.

Although public business had been at first suspended, and even the great subject which had occupied the minds of men—the divorce—had ceased for a time to be discussed, the king now began to direct his attention to state affairs, and summoned his ministers to an occasional interview. They were, so to say, billeted upon the neighbouring monasteries and gentlemen's houses. Persons engaged on the king's business were able to command all services, and to make themselves at home in every house.

At Mr. Cressy's house, Dr. Cranmer met two great men, Dr. Gardyner, the Secretary of State, and Dr. Fox, the Lord High Almoner; the former historically known as Bishop Gardyner from his elevation to the see of Winchester,—the latter becoming, in course of time, Bishop of Hereford.* The divorce question became a subject of conversation, and Dr. Cranmer freely stated his opinion. Such contradictory statements have been made with reference to Dr. Cranmer's opinion upon the divorce question, that it is not easy, at first sight, to understand what his opinion really was.

The view taken by Cranmer appears to me to be perfectly intelligible, and he adhered to it consistently from first to last.

All parties were agreed, at that time, (for Ultramontanism, as it now prevails, did not then exist,) that, although the pope could grant a dispensation to supersede, for a particular occasion and purpose, a law

---

* I have not hesitated to accept the tradition of the interview between Cranmer, Gardyner, and Fox at Waltham, because it appears to be corroborated by circumstantial evidence. Suspicions of its authenticity have been entertained, under the idea that it rests only on the authority of Foxe. But this is not the case; it is mentioned by Parker, and, more important still, I have found it also in Morice, the archbishop's secretary, who says that Gardyner and Fox lodged with Mr. Cressy.

of the Church, no papal dispensation would extend to
a law of God.

The question, therefore, to be first decided was
this,—whether the law of God prohibited a marriage
with a deceased brother's wife.

It is sometimes supposed, that Cranmer suggested
that this point should be submitted to the judgment
of the canonists and the universities, but it is almost,
if not quite, certain that this measure had been resolved
upon, some time, before Cranmer came on the scene.*

The question, therefore, now was, what steps should
be taken in the event of the judgment of the canonists
and universities being in the affirmative.

Gardyner, Bonner, and others of that school would
reply, "Clement must be coerced to give a righteous
judgment." We have seen in former times, how men
who did not deny the papal prerogative were not, in their
own opinion, acting inconsistently, when they resorted
to threats, and even violence, to have the prerogative
exercised in their favour. Strong language had been
used by Bonner and others in the interviews with
Clement; even a rupture between the Church of England and the see of Rome—a temporary rupture—was
threatened. In modern Italy, we have heard men
cursing their patron saint and even trampling upon
his image, who nevertheless the next moment, would
fall down and worship him, and would certainly aim his
stiletto at a Protestant who should speak of the saint's
nonentity. This illustrates the state of feeling towards
the pope as it existed in the minds of Gardyner and
Fox. They held that the pope ought to decide in favour
of the king,—that he should even be compelled to do

* Cavendish ascribes to Wolsey the suggestion of a reference to
the universities, and he is followed by Fiddes. Wordsworth, Ecc.
Biog. i. 539 ; Fiddes, Wolsey, 444.

so; but, until the papal judgment was officially given, the king might not marry again.

To the lucid and legal mind of Cranmer, who had no private ends to answer, and who, at that time, cared neither for king nor pope, the rights of the case were so clear as to seem to him to be self-evident.

It was not, strictly speaking, a question of divorce, it was a question simply as to the nullity of the marriage. If the marriage of Henry with Katherine, was a marriage contrary to the divine law, it was, in point of fact, no marriage at all. The parties had lived together in a state of concubinage. There had been no sacrament. If there were no marriage at all, then the king was a bachelor; if the king was a bachelor he might marry whom and when he pleased, without any reference to Rome,* provided it were not within the forbidden degrees. The fact might be decided by the ordinary ecclesiastical courts of the national Church. Let then the canonists and universities declare that for a man to marry his deceased brother's wife is contrary to the divine law, let the evidence be produced, before the ecclesiastical court, that Katherine had been married to the king's brother—and the king's cause would be gained.†

This was not a sentence pronounced *ex cathedrâ*, it was only a private opinion hazarded in the course of conversation, though it was the opinion of one who

---

* The statements which have been made of Cranmer's opinion are complicated and contradictory; but, after comparing what is reported on the subject with his conduct, I am convinced that I have presented the reader with the real state of the case.

† All the disgusting investigation as to the consummation of marriage bore upon this point. The friends of the queen maintained that, the marriage not having been consummated, it was no marriage at all. If the queen had only been betrothed to the king's brother, then there was ground for a papal dispensation.

had probably amused himself by reflecting upon a subject which at this period was engrossing the public mind.

When the party separated, Dr. Cranmer may have found recreation in following hawk and hound on Mr. Cressy's domains; but, whether this was the case or not, he soon returned to his ordinary pursuits and to the superintendence of the studies of his pupils. Of the conversation he thought no more. Although he may have looked back with satisfaction to the honour he had received in being admitted to the society of men so eminent in station, as were the secretary and almoner of the king, it was with surprise, that, soon after his return home, he received a summons to wait upon his majesty at Greenwich.

It appeared afterwards that, in the course of some discussion with the king on the divorce case, the opinion of Dr. Cranmer was mentioned either by Dr. Gardyner or by Dr. Fox. Of Cranmer the king had never heard even the name, but the acuteness of his judgment was immediately recognised by the quick sagacity of the king, who exclaimed: "Who is this Dr. Cranmer? Where is he? Is he still at Waltham? Marry," said the king, "I will speak to him: let him be sent for out of hand. This man, I trow, has got the right sow by the ear."*

A mandate from Henry VIII. was not to be disobeyed; and, when Henry was desirous of making a

---

* This expression induces me to think that the report of this conversation is substantially correct. No one would invent the vulgarity of "having the right sow by the ear," and put it into the king's mouth. But uttered by the king with his usual *bon-homie*, and in a manner indicating it to be a quotation, it would be remembered as a species of witticism. The vulgarity consists, not in the words used, but in the manner of using them.

favourable impression, no one could more perfectly act the gentleman. A few civil words uttered by royal lips have such a magic influence on a large class of minds, that royalty ought always to be popular, and Cranmer's was the kind of mind to be enslaved by royal condescension and kindness. The king penetrated the character of Cranmer at once. He spoke to him of what he called his conscience; and, forgetting that his queen had a conscience too, he desired to be relieved from the burden by which he imagined himself to be distressed and perplexed.

He had been informed that Dr. Cranmer had devised a plan by which the king might be extricated from his difficulties, and he prayed him as a favour to devote himself to the cause. Cranmer showed some reluctance to withdraw himself from literary pursuits, and to become the leading counsel in the lawsuit —for this in fact was the king's proposal. This is apparent from the tone which the king now assumed. "Master doctor," he said, "I pray you, and nevertheless, because you are a subject, I charge and command you, all other business and affairs set apart, to take some pains to see this my cause to be furthered by your device, so that I may shortly understand whereunto I may trust."

Upon Cranmer, as his first task, was now imposed the duty of placing his argument on paper. He was enjoined to produce a treatise in which his argument was to be supported by the authority of holy Scripture, of the general councils, and of the fathers.

And now might Cranmer truly say,

"A change came o'er the spirit of my dream."

He is no longer writing in a dull cold chamber, looking out on a duller quadrangle, or in a public library, where neither candle nor fire was permitted, but in the splendid library of the Earl of Wiltshire, at Durham Place,* looking down upon the great thoroughfare of London, crowded with boats and barges of every description and size. The student has become a courtier. Henry had reasons of his own for not lodging him at Greenwich, where, though the queen still lived, the Lady Ann was the ruler, and ruled like a despot. He commended the doctor to the hospitality of the lady's father,† the Earl of Wiltshire ; and of that lady's position in Henry's household no one had a right to complain, if the arrangements met with her father's consent, that father not being then known as one of the basest of men.

Here Cranmer was at a sufficient distance from the royal residence, and at the same time near enough to admit of frequent conferences with the king. That such conferences took place is shown by the speech which Henry was reported to have made, to the effect that there were no difficulties which he was not ready to encounter, if he had only Dr. Cranmer at his elbow.

Cranmer, an unknown Cambridge man, was appointed one of the royal chaplains. He is said to have held the emoluments of the Archdeaconry of Taunton, and of some other benefice of which the name is not known ; but the duties he did not perform.

When the treatise was completed, Henry asked Cranmer whether he would venture to maintain his argument at Rome ; and Cranmer expressed an earnest desire to be so employed. He was not a Protestant ; and he had nothing to fear at Rome. He was, as his countrymen had been for centuries, a thorough Angli-

* The Adelphi now occupies the site of Durham Place.

† Ann Boleyn was at court generally called the Lady, till she became the Marchioness of Pembroke.

can, prepared to defend the king's cause against that of the pope; but he had not exceeded, as all admitted, the latitude usually allowed to an advocate, even the devil's advocate, to say all he could on behalf of his client. His argument was that the king's marriage with his deceased brother's wife was not merely void-able, but *ab initio* void.

The treatise, having received the royal *imprimatur*, was laid before the two universities and the House of Commons.* To both Oxford and Cambridge, accompanied by the Secretary of State, Dr. Gardyner, and by Dr. Fox, the Lord High Almoner, together with other great men, Dr. Cranmer now went to discuss the subject of the divorce. Such was the mode of enforcing and eliciting public opinion, before the press had become its organ. Cranmer, so supported, argued with great success; and it is said that at Cambridge he won to the king's side six or seven distinguished men, who were previously opposed to his cause. The result of the mission may be admitted by those who think that there were other modes of effecting the change beyond the eloquence of Dr. Cranmer.

An embassy to the papal court having been resolved upon, Henry attached to it an advocate who had proved himself to be both logical and eloquent. With a refined policy, by which it was proclaimed to the world that Henry's admiration of the Lady Ann had not passed the bounds of propriety, the Earl of Wiltshire, her father, was placed at the head of the commission.† The powers of the commission were large and indefinite, and it appears that the Archbishop-elect of

* The treatise is said to be lost, though I suspect that we possess it, among the manuscripts in the British Museum.

† The pope was at this time at Bologna.

York and the Bishop-elect of London at one time
joined the embassy.   The object was that " the matter
of the divorce should be disputed and ventilated."*
It was known at the papal court that Cranmer was
rising in the favour of Henry, and accordingly he was
received at Rome with every mark of respect.   The
pope accepted a copy of the treatise with courtesy,
but he postponed indefinitely a public discussion.
The question related not to the existence of papal
authority in the abstract, but to the limitations of that
authority in the present instance ; whether proceedings should be initiated at Rome, or whether Rome
should remain passive until an appeal was made from
the decision of the court below.   That the powers
assumed by Rome had, of late years, been much exaggerated, was beyond a doubt, and equally beyond a
doubt was the inexpediency of permitting a discussion
which would, though commencing with a particular
case, involve the abstract question.

Although the pope postponed *sine die* the hearing
of Cranmer's argument, yet for the advocate himself
he took every opportunity of showing his respect.   A
clever lawyer, who had suggested a new view of the
king's case, one who appeared, as the mouthpiece
of an embassy of much importance, and who was
rising in favour at a court where the question was
eagerly asked, " Who is to be the successor of Wolsey "—was a person not to be despised.   The pope
therefore conferred upon Cranmer an office which was
lucrative as well as honourable.   Cranmer was appointed by the pope " Penitentiary of England." †

CHAP.
III.
~~~
Thomas
Cranmer.
1533–56.

</div>

---

* Morice, 242.

† The importance of the office may have been seen in the fact
that Sixtus IV. conferred it upon one of his nephews.—Ranke, i.
38.

Upon him was conferred the power of granting all papal dispensations; and for such dispensations the fees required were by no means small. One of the proposals made for meeting Henry's object was, to grant him a dispensation to contract another marriage during the life-time of Kathcrine; had this point been carried, the dispensation would have passed through the hands of Cranmer; and it is probable that on this account the appointment was made.

If the conduct of the Roman clergy did not create the same amount of indignation and disgust in the mind of Cranmer as it had done in the case of Erasmus and Luther, we must remember, that his visit was later than theirs; and if the reforms introduced by the piety of the good Pope Adrian VI. had produced no other effect, they had caused the clergy to assume a virtue if they had it not, and to comport themselves with decency and decorum. Nevertheless, there can be no doubt that Cranmer's visit to Rome produced on his mind an impression unfavourable to the papacy, and rendered him more ready to hear in Germany, which he visited in furtherance of the king's matter, the various arguments used in favour of the *regale* in opposition to the *pontificale*. He did not, however, as yet dispute the existence of certain papal rights in every country; but he saw more clearly the necessity of placing restrictions upon the exercise of those rights. His ancestors, with this object in view, introduced the statute of præmunire, and those which were directed against provisions and provisors. The new circumstances of another age required the revival of such legislation; or even an attempt to make the laws against the papacy more stringent.

Cranmer remained abroad for some time; but he appears to have been almost exclusively occupied as a lawyer, arguing in favour of what was called the king's cause. He commenced in Italy; he continued his labours in France and Germany. He was engaged in some secret conferences with the Elector of Saxony and other princes, who had joined the Protestant league. Because these conferences were secret, it is, of course, impossible to trace him from one place to another. Towards the close of the year 1530, he probably for a short time returned to England. That he was in England in 1531 we learn from a letter addressed by him from Hampton Court to the Earl of Wiltshire, bearing date the 13th of June of that year.*

The letter is a remarkable one, for he states with candour and conciseness the arguments used by Reginald Pole, in direct opposition to those of Cranmer himself, urging the king to submit his whole cause to the sole judgment of the pope.

The king, though prepared to act upon Cranmer's advice, if the pope could not be brought to terms, hesitated to do what would immediately provoke a rupture with the emperor. He retained confidence also in the sincerity and diplomatic skill of the King of France, who undertook to negotiate with Clement. Everything counselled delay; for, although the courtiers boasted, that the canonists and the universities were everywhere in the king's favour, yet the king himself was aware that, even if literally speaking they were correct, the public opinion was against him. Henry knew full well, that a verdict notoriously obtained by bribery, coercion, or intimidation would carry with it no moral weight. In order to induce the English universities to decide as the king willed, recourse had been had to proceedings the most unjustifiable and iniquitous. The chivalrous spirit of the younger

* Lansdowne MS. 115, fol. i. Holograph.

masters had been roused in the cause of their persecuted and insulted queen; and by an act of despotism* they were deprived of their votes. In Italy and in Spain, the king's cause had found little favour. The Sacramentarians† and Swiss reformers refused to discuss the subject on its own merits. In Germany the Lutherans were reported by Cook, the king's agent, to be " utterly against his highness in the cause ;"‡ and honest old Luther gave utterance to the feeling which lurked in the soul of every true-hearted gentleman not blinded by party zeal : " Whether the marriage were at first legal or illegal," he declared that " separation, after so many years of cohabitation, would be an enormity greater than any marriage could have been, however improper that marriage might have been in the first instance."

How far Cranmer was mixed up in those measures, by which men were bribed, coerced, or cajoled, it is impossible to say. We know, however, that he had now entered into the cause with all the fervour of a partizan, and we fear that he considered no means to be unlawful, which was conducive to the end he had at heart. With the injured queen he was unacquainted, and to his feelings of compassion no appeal was made from that quarter ; at the same time the king was his friend and benefactor, and as Cranmer thought, and as was literally the fact—so far as the question was a dry question of law—the king had right on his side.

The violence with which men can enter into such a

* Equal despotism was manifested towards the University of Paris by Francis.

† Persons so called because they affirmed that the Sacraments were outward visible signs, without inward spiritual grace. *Lucus a non lucendo.*

‡ This was not strictly true, as Osiander and a few others took the opposite side.

cause, as that in which Cranmer was now concerned, can be well understood by those who remember the vehemence with which the cause of Queen Caroline was supported or assailed. Little was thought of the real merits of the case, but one party supported the queen, under the idea that by so doing they were furthering the cause of justice, and another party were zealous for the king under the notion that they were counteracting a tendency to revolution.

Cranmer had to report of the German princes, that they could not be moved to take an interest in the divorce question. They were naturally unwilling to enter on a course of conduct, which, if it obtained the precarious support of Henry, would be personally offensive to the emperor. They could clearly see that Henry had only a personal object in view, and that when his point was carried, he was not prepared to render them any valid support in their controversy with the emperor. To them Luther was an authority; and among the most bitter opponents of Luther, King Henry had been distinguished, and he would not recant. If either Henry or Cranmer had been Protestant, a powerful league might have been formed, and the Reformation might have become more uniform and complete. But though Henry had a quarrel with the pope, and though the anti-papal feeling was, as in most of his countrymen, strong in Cranmer, yet both of them were opposed to Protestantism. In religious matters they sympathised rather with the emperor. He like Henry was, at this time, prepared to set bounds to the papal pretensions; but both Henry and Cranmer were determined to uphold the authority of the Church. Under these circumstances an embassy was appointed to the emperor, and Cranmer was commissioned to act as minister-plenipotentiary of the King of England. His legal abilities, his zeal in the king's cause, his acquaintance with Rome, his intercourse with Protestant princes, his conciliatory manners, all marked him out as peculiarly fitted for the situation. But he certainly did not seek it, and there is no reason to doubt his assertion that he had no wish to become a public character.

Cranmer's commission as "Conciliarius Regius et ad Cæsarem Orator," bears date the 24th of January, 1531-2, when Warham was Archbishop of Canterbury. Some delays took place, and he did not leave England till the end of June or the beginning of July.

The real, though not the ostensible object of Cranmer's mission was the furtherance of the king's cause in the matter of the divorce. The policy of the king was to induce the princes to purchase his support, by aiding him in his cause ; or on the other hand, to make it clear to the emperor that, by withdrawing his opposition to the divorce, and by securing Henry as his ally, he would be able, without trouble, to establish his supremacy in Germany. But the ambassador, Dr. Cranmer, soon found he had to contend against adverse circumstances, which proved to be too powerful for himself and his master. On the side both of the emperor and of the German princes, there was an increasing desire for a suspension of hostilities, if it were only for a season. Cranmer had forwarded to the king a copy of the edict of the 3d of August, 1532, when, at the conclusion of the Treaty of Nuremburg, the emperor announced the general peace of Europe, " until the meeting of a general free and Christian council."

Cranmer's mission to the emperor was at an end; but he lingered in Germany, and had no desire to hasten his return to England. He was not engaged in theological discussions ; and the German divines were politically, as well as on spiritual grounds, opposed to the Grand Penitentiary of England. They were the supporters of Luther; and Cranmer represented the royal opponent of Luther. They regarded as heretics all who refused to subscribe to their dogma of consubstantiation; and for holding, or at all events for propagating, the dogma of consubstantiation, Cranmer was prepared, as it was soon after found, to consign the criminal to the tender mercies of the state, which would silence him by the stake. In their Erastianism they might have found a common sentiment, and in a determination to circulate the Scriptures; but, even in their antagonism to the pope, Cranmer was not at this time prepared to go as far as the Lutherans.

With one man only could he fully sympathise. Osiander was, like himself, an enthusiastic student of Scripture, and was eminent as a critic of the Greek Testament.* They were both of them discontented with the existing state of things; they saw the necessity of reform; but could neither of them, at that time, decide what the reform ought to be. They were not either of them at that time Papists, neither were they Protestants. Osiander disliked though he feared Luther, he tyrannised over Melancthon. His mind was in sympathy with no one; he was a self-opinionated man, who entertained such singular notions on theological subjects that, as Mosheim remarks, it is easier to say what he did not than what he *did* believe.† He was at this time employed on his Dissertations, and this attracted to him the mind of Cranmer. But it was not by the learning of Osiander that Cranmer was

---

* His name was Andrew Hoseman; the name of Osiander was assumed, according to the pedantic custom then prevalent in Germany.

† Mosheim, ii. 576, edit. Stubbs.

detained in Germany; the bright eyes and sweet temper of Osiander's niece had made an impression upon the susceptible heart of Cranmer; who, having recovered from the loss of his Joan, was passionately in love with the fair Margaret.* They married; and this marriage may be adduced to corroborate Cranmer's own statement, that he never sought, desired, nor expected the primacy of the Church of England.

It did not seem probable that the primacy would be offered to Cranmer. He was a new man, just emerging from obscurity; and there was at the king's right hand a faithful minister, perhaps even a kinsman, who ranked high amidst the statesmen of the day, Stephen Gardyner. Gardyner was as zealous as Cranmer in the cause of the divorce, and not less zealous in supporting the Royal Supremacy. If he was less sincere than Cranmer, of his sincerity or insincerity no man could judge, perhaps not even himself.

If Cranmer had been an aspirant to the primacy, he would have foreseen that his marriage would have offered an impediment to the fulfilment of his wishes. If he loved his wife he would have shrunk from placing her in a very delicate position, when she who, in private society, was his wife, would be treated on public occasions as if she were only his concubine.

Cranmer's ambition was the prevalent ambition of the age, that of acquiring a high character in the literary world, with the means of enjoying literary leisure. Erasmus set the example which men were anxious to follow: we have seen in the life of Warham how the *otium cum dignitate* was the end which many great men placed before them as the reward of their exertions. This Cranmer might fairly expect; it seemed to be within his grasp. He had lately been leading the life

* "Puellæ cujusdam amore irritatus."

suited to his disposition and character. He had been
received at court with all the honour which great men
were delighted to evince towards men of learning; and
in his own king he had a patron and friend, in whose
palaces he was sure to be a welcome guest. He might
expect from the king's generosity a sufficient number
of sinecure benefices to enable him to live in comfort,
and to enjoy that independence which Erasmus failed
to realize. To a man so situated, and going only occasionally into public, a wife would be at all times a
comfort, never an inconvenience. She might accompany
him when he visited the courts of the German princes ;
and, if he were summoned to places where she would
not be a welcome guest, he might leave her for a short
time in Nuremberg, or in some happy home in England.
His position as king's chaplain was, in a worldly point
of view, one of high respectability. It gave him a
certain status wherever he might go ; and the learned
were prepared to welcome him in the universities or in
their homes, whenever he sought their society, or
desired amicably to discuss any of the great subjects
which occupied the minds of men. In the most
solemn moments of his life, Cranmer affirmed that he
never sought the primacy, and would have avoided the
honour if with safety he could have done so.

The king, however, did not make the offer of the
archbishopric without having first duly considered the
whole subject ; and what came in the form of a favour
Cranmer knew was in reality a command. The straightforward manly course would have been for Cranmer to
have said, as a mediæval prelate had said before him,
when refusing to obey a summons from the pope, " I
have married a wife, and therefore I cannot come." But
the cowed boy of Aslacton had not this manliness of
character ; and he was aware that the excuse would be

set aside at once, by a command to put away his wife.
Whatever might be the insults to which they might be
subjected, Cranmer and his Margaret determined not to
part. He sent her before him to England, there to provide a home for herself, preparatory to future arrangements which would depend upon circumstances. He
had, meantime, recourse to a measure which usually
commends itself to weak minds. He delayed his
journey to England as long as he could, in the hope
that, on reconsidering the matter, the king might
change his mind.

When, at length, he arrived in England, he found
that the home government had been employed not in
reconsidering the appointment to the see of Canterbury, but in expediting measures for the speedy
consecration of Cranmer, already archbishop-elect.

At the end of January, 1533, the king had notified
to the pope that he had nominated Dr. Cranmer to the
see of Canterbury; that his election by the prior and
convent had taken place; and that his desire was that
all expedition should be used in the issue of the bulls
of confirmation. The king had reasons of his own for
wishing that none of the customary forms should be
omitted; and the pope was desirous to meet the wishes
of a king to whom he was under great obligations, and
whose requests respecting the divorce he was unable at
present to meet. The bulls were issued as a matter of
course; the first eight bearing date the 21st of
February; the ninth being dated the 22d of the same
month, and the tenth and eleventh the 2d of March.

The reader has been frequently reminded that the
nomination to vacant sees was virtually as much in the
power of the crown before the Reformation as after
it; that the election, saving theoretically the right of
chapters, and the grant of bulls, saving theoretically

the papal claims with reference to confirmation and provisions, had become mere forms.*

There was no reluctance on the part of the papal authorities to confirm the election of Cranmer. He was indeed one of the king's counsel in the matter of the divorce, and on some points he raised legal objections to the exercise of the papal power; but such was the case with respect both to Gardyner and to Bonner. Both of these ambassadors had used much stronger language to the pope than had escaped the lips of Cranmer; and, though neither of them had any sympathy with the Protestant movement on the continent, they had threatened the pope, and warned him that England might be compelled, if he did not do justice to the king, to bid defiance to the papal power and act independently.

These observations are offered, and to those who have perused the former volumes of this work will be perfectly intelligible, because it is sometimes made to appear that Cranmer acted with dishonesty towards Rome in order to obtain the papal sanction to his appointment.

An objection was raised, and a difficulty interposed, not by the papal authorities, but by Cranmer himself. His was a legal difficulty, which was solved by the lawyers whom he consulted, and not by casuists or divines.

Among the forms required by the papal authorities was an oath to be taken by the prelate elect to the effect that he would maintain and defend, against all men, the regality of St. Peter; that he would conserve the rights, honours, privileges, and authorities of the Church of Rome, and of the pope and his successors;

---

* The reader has been also reminded, in the history of several centuries, that the opinion is erroneous which would represent the reduction of the *congé d'élire* to a mere form as originating at the Reformation.

and that he would not be in any council, treaty, or any other act in which anything should be imagined against him or the Church of Rome, their rights, seats, honours, or powers. He was sworn to resist and persecute heretics and schismatics, and annually visit the threshold of the apostles.

This oath had been taken ever since the twelfth century without compunction or reluctance, and without any protest on the part of the king or of the national Government. It meant nothing, because this oath was followed by another, in which the archbishop or bishop elect solemnly on oath declared that he utterly renounced and clearly forsook all such clauses, words, sentences, and grants, as he had made or should hereafter make to the pope's holiness in behalf of the bishopric to which the king had nominated him; that he utterly renounced whatever had been hurtful or prejudicial to the king, his heirs, dignity, privilege, or estate royal; that he was ready to live and die for the king against all people. He solemnly with an *oath acknowledged himself to hold his bishopric of the king, and of the king only*; and, on the ground of this oath, he prayed for a restitution of the temporalities of the see, which would otherwise have been withheld.

This latter oath was considered as superseding the former oath, and both oaths had been taken without hesitation by Warham and his predecessors for centuries. The oaths were taken as mere forms. The bishop elect would maintain all papal rights except when they stood opposed to the prerogatives of the crown, or the statutes of the realm, or the canons of the Church of England. He would uphold the prerogatives of the crown and the laws of the land against all papal aggression; leaving it an open question for the lawyers to decide what authority the pope might legally exercise. The pretensions of the pope anterior to the Council of Trent were very different from what they have become since.

It was a bad state of affairs, intended simply to reserve rights, the king to nominate, the chapter to elect, and the pope to confirm ; though it was well known that, except when the Government was more than usually weak, the royal nomination was the only thing practically necessary.

It is under the most solemn circumstances that in the nineteenth century a chapter proceeds to election ; and the forms appear to be useless, because the electors would be, not indeed burned, for burning is now illegal, but outlawed, deprived of their property, and exposed to the assaults of any one who should raise up his hand against them, unless they obeyed the command of the sovereign, who is himself under the influence of his ministers ; but now, as formerly, the form is observed, that under altered circumstances for good or for evil, the Church may be prepared to act independently.

But the cautious mind of Cranmer started a difficulty. Wolsey had accepted the legatine commission ; in accepting a commission from the pope, and exercising it in England, even with the full sanction of the crown, he laid himself open to the penalties of a præmunire ; the Statutes of Præmunire and Provisors having rendered any such appointment by the pope in England, under any circumstances, highly penal. Since the iniquitous proceedings on the part of the king,—the constitutional proceedings on the part of the people,—which put into execution the statutes just mentioned, the convocation had declared and the parliament had ratified the declaration of the royal supremacy. If, then, Cranmer took the usual oaths, against which he entertained no conscientious scruples on religious grounds, what guarantee had he that he should not be subjected to the penalties of a præmunire for taking an oath, which might be represented as inconsistent with the enactments relating to the supremacy?

The treatment of Wolsey had shown that the old antipapal statutes had not become obsolete; the new enactment had made them more stringent.

Cranmer was in a delicate position. He was required by the king to act contrary not only to the Statute of Præmunire but to the Act of Supremacy also. There would have been no difficulty formerly. It was assumed that the king had a dispensing power; and consequently the forms were observed without fear of consequences. The king was willing to exercise his powers with respect to Cranmer. But the royal dispensation had not been sufficient in the case of Wolsey. Yet the king's will and word ought not to be disputed or doubted. Therefore Cranmer was obliged to rest satisfied with a protest, which was to be a document, available if Cranmer was at any time brought into trouble, to free him from all the penalties which might otherwise devolve upon him for violating the law.

Such is the explanation given by Cranmer himself. When he was probing his conscience towards the close of life, his conscience did not reproach him for what he did on this occasion. Called upon to do what his predecessors had done, he started a legal difficulty. To meet the difficulty, by the king's direction, he consulted the lawyers. He acted on their advice; the protest was duly recorded, and he dismissed the subject from his mind, until at his last trial he was called to account for his conduct.

The only individual who was personally interested in the proceedings was the king, and his object was to satisfy Cranmer as speedily as he could, and not to offend the only man who could, under existing circumstances, render him the service he required.

The infatuation of Henry with respect to Ann Boleyn had been little less than monomania. She, by refusing his solicitations, inflamed his passion, and for a season domineered over the king in a manner which probably surprised his courtiers as much as it has surprised posterity. The impartial reader cannot but come to the conclusion that Henry had at length triumphed over her virtue, and that, if a divorce had been much longer delayed, she would have become a mother before her marriage had taken place.*

---

* The passion of Henry VIII. of England for Ann Boleyn has a parallel in that of Henry IV. of France for Gabrielle d'Estrées. It would seem that men at this time, unaccustomed to put a restraint upon their passions in early life, became victims to a predominant vice at a period when we might have expected self-restraint. Gabrielle was so determined to exhibit her power to the world, that to meet her wishes for a coronation, Henry IV. risked his crown. Perhaps more astonishing than the passions of the kings was the quiet manner in which the two nations submitted to what was in fact a national insult. Henry VIII. was not, like Charles II, a coarse sensualist. He required in the object of his attachment sentiment and intellect. He did not rove from one mistress to another. His passions were not easily excited, but when once excited, he was on that point a merciless madman. Ann Boleyn, a woman not of ardent feelings, but of great ambition, domineered over her lover by encouraging without indulging his passion. But every impartial reader of history must be convinced that Henry at length triumphed over her virtue, such as it was. She was created Countess of Pembroke, on the 1st of September, 1532, and was endowed, before the Reformation, with £1,000 a year out of the bishopric of Durham, and another £1,000 out of the court lands. The king married her on the 25th of May, 1533. An earlier date has been assigned, with the obvious purpose of creating an opinion that the child of which at her coronation she was pregnant, was conceived in wedlock.

There is no other way by which to account for the hurried marriage of the king, and the mystification which exists as to the date of the ceremony. While there was no prospect of a family, the king could tolerate the delays of law; but when the birth of a child was expected, he expedited the marriage with Ann before the nullity of his first marriage with Katherine was pronounced, in order that there might be no question as to the child's legitimacy. Everything now depended upon the validity of Cranmer's view of the marriage between Henry and Katherine. Gardyner, as well as Cranmer, held it invalid. But if Gardyner had been archbishop, he would have waited until the nullity of the marriage had been declared in the papal or legatine court. Years might have passed before the divorce could be obtained; months would certainly have intervened, and the expected heir to Henry's throne would have been illegitimate.

Cranmer, on the other hand, contended, it will be recollected, that by the canon law of the Church and the statute law of the realm, the initiative should be taken, not in a papal court, but in the court of the national Church; he maintained that sentence should be given by the Archbishop of Canterbury, as the Primate of All England. When this was first propounded by Cranmer, he would probably have admitted of an appeal to the court at Rome; but since that time, with a view to this very case, it had been declared that the Bishop of Rome had no more authority in the Church and realm of England than any other foreign bishop. Cranmer was therefore prepared to resist an appeal, although he was evidently doubtful as to the mode of action to be adopted if an appeal should be made.

We now see why Cranmer unexpectedly, to the

chagrin of Gardyner and the astonishment of England,
had been nominated to the see of Canterbury; why
everything had been done, even before his return to
England, to expedite his consecration; and why such
care was taken to attend to all the old forms. The king
was anxious that nothing should occur which should
throw doubt on the validity of Cranmer's consecration.
At any other period, instead of providing Cranmer
with a pretext for observing the forms now declared
to be obsolete, he would have applauded the zeal with
which he defended the royal supremacy. Soon after,
there was an enactment to render illegal the importation of bulls from Rome under any and every plea and
sanction; but now, as the divorce was to be pronounced
by Cranmer, everything was to be avoided which
might raise a question as to the regularity of any of
the antecedent proceedings.

Cranmer travelled slowly to England in the hope
that his capricious master might change his intention
with respect to the primacy. But it never entered
into Henry's mind to suppose that his will would be
disputed; and on Cranmer's arrival in this country,
he found that, through the energy of the Government,
all the steps necessary for his consecration had been
already taken.

No time was lost when the legal instruments were
ready. There was to be no great display; no journey
to Canterbury. The prior and his chapter had been
required to grant a dispensation that the consecration
might take place at Westminster; and on the 30th
day of March, 1533, at St. Stephen's chapel, Thomas
Cranmer was consecrated, the Bishops of London,
Exeter, and St. Asaph officiating.

Much was to be done before Cranmer's enthronization could take place, and it was delayed till the 3d

of November. The appointment was far from popular, for Cranmer had done nothing as yet to justify his extraordinary rise; and the people of Canterbury would have preferred an aristocrat : Cranmer therefore acted with judgment when he made no attempt to emulate the grandeur exhibited by his immediate predecessor. He did not indeed possess the means; for much of the property of the see was in the hands of the king, to whom according to custom it had been sequestered; and what Henry once grasped he did not easily relinquish.

Archbishop Cranmer dispensed with the attendance of some of the nobles who were accustomed to officiate on those occasions; but he signified his readiness to accept a present of venison, especially of red deer, for the banquet.* It would appear, from a letter still existing of the Prior of Canterbury, that a portion of the expense was defrayed by the convent.†

It is thus to the poverty, not to the will, of Cranmer that we are to attribute the absence of the splendour usually displayed at enthronization banquets. The younger son of a respectable but not opulent family had no resources of his own, and nothing was due to him on his taking possession of the see, as the last rents

---

* Letter lxxx. Harl. MS. 6,148, fol. 40. From some of his letters, it appears that Cranmer was particular about his venison, and the preservation of game.

† Ellis, Third Series, Letter ccxxi. Thomas Goldwell, Prior of Canterbury, in writing to Crumwell, apologises for not being able to send a present worthy of his acceptance, for "so it is that by reason of my Lord of Canterbury's enthronization, which was the last week, our swans and partridges and such other things be consumed and spent, so that I have nothing now to send unto you, but only fruits of the earth. We have one fruit growing here with us in Kent, the which is called a Pomeriall. He is called a very good apple, and good to drink wine withal, wherefore I do now send unto you, as to my special friend, twenty of them by my servant."

due to Warham were paid to his executors, and during the vacancy the revenues were appropriated by the king.* He had, at the same time, for very charity's sake, to keep up a large establishment at his palace and at his various manor houses. We may add, also, the fact of the unpopularity of his appointment, and of the impolicy of bringing together any large assembly of the people. It was known that he was made archbishop to facilitate the king's divorce, and the divorce was unpopular among all whose manly hearts or womanly affections felt indignant at the insult offered to the highest lady in the land under the most cruel persecution.†

Having thus traced the life of Cranmer from his earliest years to the day of his consecration to the see of Canterbury, it may be convenient to arrange his future history under three general sections. We will follow his political history to the close of Henry's life; we will then review the progress of his opinions; we shall afterwards resume his history during the reign of Edward VI.; and we shall dwell upon his trials and sufferings under Queen Mary.

I. We have assigned the reason for Cranmer's unexpected promotion. He was aware why he was selected fer the primacy, and he knew what he was expected to do. On his arrival in England he found everything prepared for action, through the untiring energy of Crumwell's government, and the determined will of

---

* Many of the letters of Cranmer at this period consist of applications for pecuniary assistance. On this subject we shall have more to say hereafter.

† Among the few unpublished documents relating to Cranmer, I have found a writ, preserved at Canterbury, from Henry VIII. in 1534, directed to the dukes, viscounts, barons, &c. to protect the Lord Archbishop of Canterbury during the visitation of his clergy. This shows the strong feeling there was against him.

the king. All preparatory measures had been already taken ; it only remained for him to give judgment, and to pronounce sentence.

The king was already married.

The king asserted—and who might dispute or gainsay the royal assertion ?—that the canonists and universities had pronounced the marriage of Katherine with the brother of her former husband contrary to the divine law. If so, it was beyond the reach of a papal dispensation. If so, the marriage was void *ab initio*, the king was a bachelor. If so, the bachelor king was at liberty to marry. And because it was so, he had married the Marchioness of Pembroke. As an act of delicacy, he kept his marriage with the Marchioness of Pembroke a secret, until the nullity of his marriage with the Infanta of Spain was publicly and officially declared. This was the state of the case as assumed by the king. Crumwell had obtained an act of parliament to prevent the possibility of the delay which the unhappy Katherine might have attempted to interpose by an appeal to Rome. He did not venture openly to avow the object of the bill which he introduced, for he was well aware of the unpopularity of the proceeding ; he simply asked of parliament to render more stringent certain acts which had been passed in former reigns. Not one reason assigned bore directly upon the present case. It was proposed that no appeals should be made out of this realm for these reasons, viz.—

"That whereas the kingdom of England was a just empire furnished with such able persons, both spiritual and temporal, as could decide all controversies arising in it. And whereas, Edward I, Edward III, Richard II, Henry IV, and other kings of this realm, have made sundry ordinances, laws, and statutes, for the conservation of the prerogative, liberties, and pre-eminences of the said imperial Crown, and of the jurisdictions, spiritual and temporal, of the same, to keep it from the annoyance of the see of Rome, as also from the authority of other foreign potentates attempting the domination or violation thereof, and because notwithstanding the said acts, divers appeals have been sued to the see of Rome in causes testamentary, cases of matrimony and divorces, right of tithes, oblations and obventions, to the great vexation and charge of the king's highness and his subjects, and the delay of justice; and forasmuch as the distance of the way to Rome is such, as the necessary proofs and true knowledge of the cause cannot be brought thither and represented so well as in this kingdom, and that therefore many persons be without remedy. It is therefore enacted that all causes testamentary, causes of matrimony and divorces, tithes, oblations, and obventions, either commenced or depending formerly, or which hereafter shall commence in any of the king's dominions, shall be heard, discussed, and definitively determined within the king's jurisdiction and authority in the courts spiritual and temporal of the same, any foreign inhibition or restraint to the contrary notwithstanding. So that, although any excommunication or interdiction on this occasion should follow from that see, the prelates and clergy of this realm should administer sacraments and say divine service, and do all other their duties, as formerly hath been used, upon penalty of one year's imprisonment and fine at the king's pleasure, and they who procured the said sentences should fall into a præmunire."

As for the order to be observed henceforth, it was enacted, that in suits commenced before the archdeacon or his officials, appeal might be made to the diocesan; and from thence within fifteen days to the Archbishop of Canterbury or Archbishop of York respectively in their provinces. Appeals were to be made to the archbishops in the king's other dominions; or if suit be commenced before the archdeacon of any archbishop or his commissioners, then appeal might be made within fifteen days to the Court of Arches, and so without any further appeal to the primate. In all these cases,

the prerogative of the Archbishop and Church of Canterbury was reserved. If any suit arose betwixt the
king and his subjects, appeal might be made within
fifteen days to the prelates of the Upper House in the
convocation then sitting or next called by the king's
writ, there to be finally determined. It was further
enacted that "they who should take out any appeal
contrary to the effect of this act or refuse to obey it,
should incur the penalty of the statute of 16 Rich. II.,
"and thus," says Herbert, "the spiritualty, finding
the power invested formerly in the pope to be derived
now in great part on them, did more easily suffer the
diminution of the papal authority."*

Not only was this greater stringency given to acts
of parliament, which had been so frequently evaded, and
evaded even by Henry VIII. himself, as to have become
now obsolete; but the indefatigable Crumwell had caused
the convocation to be assembled, and business had commenced in the synod of Canterbury, before the arrival
of the archbishop elect. During the vacancy of the
metropolitan see, the administration of the province
devolved upon the prior and chapter of Canterbury. In
obedience to a royal mandate, they summoned the convocation to meet at Westminster on the 26th of March.
On that day the proceedings were opened by the Bishop
of London, president *pro tempore*. By the command of
the king he laid before the two houses all the documents
relating to the marriage of Henry and Katherine; and
caused to be read publicly the determinations of the
foreign universities on the subject of the divorce. He
expressed the king's desire that convocation should pronounce its judgment on the case with as little delay as
possible. At the session of the 28th of March, he laid
before the two houses the determination of the faculty of

* Herbert, Life and Reign of Henry VIII. Kennet, 162.

theology at Paris, which was said to express the opinion prevalent in the Gallican Church. He demanded the udgment of the Upper House of Convocation, and again urged his brethren to come to a decision at once. Many of the prelates asked for time to deliberate upon so important a question. They were given till four o'clock the next day, when the president put to them the question whether the pope could grant a dispensation to marry with a deceased brother's wife. The majority gave answer in the negative; that is, in the king's favour. It is to be remembered that, in this decision, thirty-six abbots and priors voted in the majority, but only three bishops; namely, the bishops of London, St. Asaph, and Lincoln.*

When we consider the ruin which the monks saw to be impending over their establishments, we can easily imagine how strong the pressure must have been to obtain a majority on a question on which most of the bishops had the manliness to oppose the king.

Cranmer, everything being prepared for him, acted with the zeal of a partisan, and issued a commission to the bishops of London, Winchester, and Lincoln, to prorogue the convocation until the next day, when he assumed his place as president. The archbishop laid the whole subject before the two houses, and desired the Lower House to report their opinion on the following day. A speedy determination was required. To expedite the business, the Lower House appointed two committees; a committee of theologians, and a committee of canonists. The first was to decide whether marriage with a deceased brother's wife were prohibited by God's law, and consequently excluded from any papal dispensation; and the canonists were to decide

---

* Four abbots afterwards gave in their adhesion to the majority, if it were proved that the marriage had been consummated.

whether the depositions taken before the legates
amounted to canonical proof that the marriage between Arthur and Katherine had never been consummated. Long and vehement debates ensued : but, on
a division, fourteen gave judgment that the marriage
was prohibited by Scripture, and consequently beyond
the reach of any papal dispensation ; seven were of
opinion that the marriage was not in violation of any
divine law ; one doubted ; another declared his opinion
to be that it was against the divine law, but that the
divine law might be dispensed with by the Bishop of
Rome. On the 3d of April, the archbishop was for
some cause absent, and the Bishop of London presided,
when the prolocutor reported that the canonists unanimously agreed that the proofs adduced before the legates
were sufficient for them to decide that the marriage
between Arthur and Katherine was complete. Notwithstanding this apparent unanimity, there were
some protests recorded ; but on the 4th of April, the
Bishop of Winchester, Stephen Gardyner, and the
Bishop of Exeter, expressed their concurrence with the
opinion of the canonists,* while the Bishop of Bath

---

* The offensive question submitted to the canonists was necessary, because it was contended that, although the Pope could not
dispense with the divine law, which forbade marriage with a
deceased brother's wife, yet the marriage between Arthur and
Katherine was not a real marriage, but only a precontract, which
was dispensable. Whatever blame may be attached to the canonists
for refusing to believe the repeated assertions of the queen of her
virginity at the time of her marriage, two things have now
come clearly to light. We now know that the queen solemnly
asserted the fact under seal of confession to Campeggio, with permission to him to mention it to the pope, in confidence. This we
learn from the valuable collection of historical documents lately
published by Theiner from the Vatican, which fully confirms all
that we gather from the Simancas documents. We also know that
the difficulties of Henry arose from his not daring to deny the fact

and Wells dissented.[*] The vote of the whole convocation seems then to have been taken, when there was for the king a majority of 253, against a minority of 19.

On the 5th of April, the king's advocate, Dr. Tregonwell, appeared before the convocation to demand that public instruments might be forthwith prepared setting forth the decision of the convocation. The instruments were accordingly drawn, and, the Convocation of York concurring with that of Canterbury, the judgment of the Church of England was recorded that marriage with a deceased brother's wife is contrary to the law of God.

The archbishop, like the king, being anxious that everything should be done in consistency with legal forms, deferred his judgment on the marriage of the king and Queen Katherine until the decision of the clergy of York should be received. But he was not inactive. The king's object was to create a popular opinion that he was only induced to separate from the queen by a sense of public duty. One would suppose that even Cranmer, willing to imagine all good of the king, must have been scandalized by hypocrisy so transparent and base. But he was in the king's hands, and they consulted together, and for the sake of imposing on the public it was agreed that the archbishop should address a letter to the king, in which his majesty was to be humbly informed that his loyal subjects

to the legates. That excuses may be made for the subordinate agents in the disgraceful affair of the divorce is possible, but of the unfeeling brutality of Henry there can scarcely be two opinions.

[*] Wilkins, iii. 757. On the 13th of May, Dr. Rowland Lee appeared as the king's advocate before the Convocation of York, which concurred in the judgment of the Convocation of Canterbury. —Wilkins, iii. 767.

H H 2

were sore troubled at the dangers to which this realm would be exposed by a disputed succession; wherefore he whom his grace "had called, albeit a poor wretch and much unworthy, to the high and chargeable office of primate and archbishop," humbly prayed the king's licence to put an end to all doubts with respect to the validity of his marriage with Katherine, by permitting him to hear and determine the cause of the divorce in his archiepiscopal court.* To which humble request his majesty graciously condescended. He would submit to be judged by the primate, although he held himself to be in all causes and over all persons, ecclesiastical and civil, supreme.†

Notwithstanding all the precautions he had taken, we find, from a letter from Cranmer to Crumwell, that the former was fearful to the last, of some opposition to the intended proceedings on the part of Katherine, which it might be difficult to meet. It would seem that he desired the judgment to be delivered without notice to the queen. He thought it sufficient simply to notify the fact that the marriage was void. But Henry was far too wise to sanction any "hole and corner" transaction. He desired that she should have no oppor-

* State Papers, i. 390.

† Ibid. 392. That there was collusion between the king and the archbishop is proved by two letters written by Cranmer for licence to act. Both are at present in existence, both in Cranmer's handwriting, both bear marks of having been folded, sealed, and received by the king; that is to say, the king was consulted as to the letter which was to be addressed to himself. With the first, apparently, he was not well satisfied. Cranmer, in the extreme servility with which he wrote, overstrained his point in the first of the two letters. It is difficult to see any real difference between them, though I think Dr. Lingard is right when he says the king's object was to compel the archbishop to take the whole responsibility on himself.

tunity for pleading ignorance of the proceedings, or of complaining that they were conducted at a distance which might render it inconvenient for her to attend. The queen was at Ampthill, in Bedfordshire. Within a few miles of her residence was a priory of black canons ; and thither the archbishop repaired on the 8th of May. He was cordially welcomed by the prior, Gervase Markham, who was a strong partisan of the king.* The primate established his court in the Chapel of Our Lady attached to the church of the convent. He had for his assessor the diocesan, the Bishop of Lincoln, Dr. Longlands ; while the Bishop of Winchester, Stephen Gardyner, Dr. Bell, Dr. Clay-broke, Dr. Trygonnell, Dr. Hewis, Dr. Olyver, Dr. Brytten, and Mr. Bedyll, with other learned men of the law, appeared as counsel for the king. Everything was done which could add solemnity to the occasion, and the public were admitted to witness the proceedings.† The court thus arrayed with a large attendance of counsel for the king, impressed the minds of the people with the notion that a strong opposition might be expected on the part of the queen. But, though duly cited into the court, the queen did not attend, nor did any one appear on her behalf. There seems to have been some difficulty in deciding how to take the depositions of some ladies, who, instead of coming to Dunstable, remained in London ;‡ and the people were obliged, during the 11th of May, to be contented with the procession as it moved into court, and the splendid ceremonial of high mass, at which Cranmer officiated. But on the 12th of May, the citation having been duly proved, and the queen appearing neither in person nor by

* Dugdale, i. 238.
† Remains, Letter xiv. Harl. MSS. 6,148, fol. 23.
‡ State Papers, i. 394.

proxy, the archbishop pronounced her contumacious, a
fact of which he immediately apprised the king by letter,
adding, "so that she is, as the counsel informed me,
precluded from further monition to appear."* On the
17th the archbishop wrote to the king, who it would
seem had expressed some impatience, to advertise
him that "his grace's great matter was now brought
to a final sentence;" but because every day in the
ensuing week was ferial, except Friday and Saturday,
he could not give judgment before the day first
named.†

On Friday, the 23d, the archbishop delivered his
judgment. He recited briefly the circumstances of
the case, and the reasons which induced the court
to arrive at its conclusion; and then, in a document
drawn up in the usual form, with the advice of the
most learned in the law and of persons of most eminent
skill in divinity who had been consulted, he delivered
his judgment, that it was not lawful for the most illustrious and powerful prince, Henry VIII, and the most
serene Lady Katherine, to remain in the pretended
marriage, "and we do separate and divorce from each
other the said most illustrious and most powerful
king, Henry VIII, and the said most illustrious Lady
Katherine, inasmuch as they contracted and consummated the said pretended marriage *de facto* and not
de jure, and that they, so separated and divorced, are
absolutely free from all marriage bond, with regard to
the aforesaid pretended marriage; and we pronounce,
decree, and declare by this our definitive sentence and
final decree which we here give, and by the tenor of
these presents publish."‡

He caused the judgment to be read in the chapel on

---

* State Papers, i. 394.   † Ibid. i. 396.

‡ Herbert, 165.

the 23d of May, 1533, and then forwarded it to the king. There is a letter extant from the Clerk of the Council, Archdeacon Bedyll, to Crumwell, written on the 12th of May, pending the trial; from which it appears that there was by no means a feeling of security at head-quarters. It was suspected that the queen might still interpose difficulties; and under this impression daily reports of the proceedings were made through Bedyll to the king. The conclusion of his letter to Crumwell is remarkable: "I trust the process here will be somewhat shorter than it was devised afore the king's grace; assuring you truly that my Lord of Winchester and all other that be here as of the king's grace's counsel studieth as diligently as they possibly can to cause everything to be handled so as to be most consonant to the law, *as far as the matter will suffer.* And my Lord of Canterbury handleth himself very well, and very uprightly, *without any evident cause of suspicion to be noted in him,* by the counsel of the said Lady Katherine, if she had any present here."[*]

No words can be adduced more condemnatory of the conduct of Cranmer on this occasion. It is admitted, that he was simulating the character of a just judge, when he had deliberately come to deliver an iniquitous judgment. But he seems never to have been conscience-stricken for his conduct on this occasion. As there are some who say that everything is lawful at an election, so he seems to have thought that a partisan, when he has the power, might employ it, without compunction, for the furtherance of party purposes. He was a hypocrite as regarded the queen and her supporters; but he sought applause, by the avowed hypocritical action, from the men of his own side. They expected him to play a part; and an old unprincipled official,

[*] State Papers, i. 395.

in a patronising tone, asserts that the new man, unexpectedly elevated and unused to the ways of a court, had played his part better than could have been expected. The moral tone was low; the king's will supreme; party feeling ran high.

Immediately after the sentence of divorce, some form was adopted by the archbishop to give, or appear to give, an official sanction to the marriage which had already taken place between the king and his mistress.

The whole subject of this marriage is mystified, and the care taken in this reign to cook or to destroy public documents which might otherwise be produced to the king's disadvantage, renders it unlikely that the mystery will be cleared, unless we obtain a clue from some foreign source. It has been sometimes conjectured, that after the archbishop's sentence the marriage ceremony was repeated. But this is not likely to have been the case, for the object was to represent the Marchioness of Pembroke as having resisted the addresses of her royal lover, until he had quite made up his mind, that his marriage with Katherine was no marriage at all.

One would have liked to read a single sentence written by Cranmer, expressive of commiseration for the unhappy queen, now divorced from a base and cruel husband, who, though even in their happier days he had not been faithful to her bed, had won her affections. But the heart is hardened by partisanship and politics. Cranmer did not with his own eyes behold the weeping, praying, dying, injured woman, who, born a princess of the mightiest empire in the world, had, for a quarter of a century, lived an honest wife, a courteous queen, and a pious Christian, and was now to regard herself as a cast-off concubine, and

her daughter—her only surviving child—as a bastard.
Cranmer saw her not; he had scarcely ever seen her;
and his was not a vivid imagination, to depict the
sorrows of her heart; while, on the other hand, he
knew, and feared, and loved the king, to whom he
was bound by ties of gratitude, and before whose
superior intellect and will his whole soul lay prostrate.
While the indignation of the world is directed against
Henry, we must not forget the merits of the king in
our abhorrence of the man; and even of the man it is
to be said that the power of his intellect and the fas-
cination of his manners were such as to conceal much
of his moral deformity from his contemporaries. To
them his life, as it approached its end, became the more
valuable even as the political prospects of the future
became the more dark. The party for which no apology
can be made is that of the infidel and the Puritan, who,
regarding Katherine and Ann with the jaundiced eye
of faction, defame the saint and canonize the harlot.

The king was aware of the disgust which his marriage had excited in most of those earnest-minded
persons who were removed from the royal influence, or
who were not expectant of court favour. He met the
case, and sought to purchase the favour of the people
towards his new wife by the splendid pageantry of her
coronation. Nothing could have exceeded the magnificence or the hilarity of the new court. Through it
an impulse was given to trade, while the beauty of the
queen fascinated all who approached her; and they
who left her presence were able to speak of the par-
tiality she evinced toward the Protestants, by whom
partisanship was placed in the room of charity, and
was regarded as covering a multitude of sins.

Of the coronation of Queen Ann it is unnecessary to
speak in detail, because of all coronations this is best

known, from the circumstance of its having been introduced by Shakspeare into his play of " Henry VIII."
It were easy to describe what is minutely depicted
by Stowe in his Annals; it were more interesting to
observe how admirably Shakspeare selects the salient
points, and with one stroke of the master's pen
vivifies what, under the annalist, is as tedious as
a twice-told tale.   This, however, were beside our
purpose; yet the reader will be pleased to peruse
Cranmer's own account of the ceremony, as everything from a contemporary, descriptive of an action
with which he was himself concerned, must be read
with interest.   Having narrated in a letter to his
friend, Archdeacon Hawkyns, the splendour of the
new queen's progress from Greenwich to the Tower of
London on the Thursday preceding Whit-Sunday, and
her subsequent progress on the following Saturday
through the city, he writes thus :—

" Now then on Sunday was the coronation, which also was
of such a manner.

" In the morning there assembled with me at Westminster
Church, the Bishop of York, the Bishop of London, the Bishop
of Wynchester, the Bishop of Lincoln, the Bishop of Bath,
and the Bishop of St. Asse, the Abbot of Westminster, with
ten or twelve more abbots, which all revestred ourselves in
our pontificalibus, and so furnished with our crosses and
croziers, proceeded out of the abbey in a procession into
Westminstre Hall, where we received the queen apparelled
in a robe of purple velvet, and all the ladies and gentlemen
in robes and gowns of scarlet, according to the manner used
beforetime in such business; and so her grace, sustained of
each side with two bishops, the Bishop of London and the
Bishop of Wynchester, came forth in procession unto the
Church of Westminstre, she in her hair, my Lord of Suffolke
bearing before her the crown, and two other lords bearing
also before her a sceptre and a white rod, and so entered
up into the high altar, where, divers ceremonies used about

her, I did set the crown on her head, and then was sung
Te Deum, &c. And after that was sung a solemn mass, all
which while her grace sat crowned upon a scaffold, which
was made between the high altar and the choir in Westminstre Church; which mass and ceremonies done and
finished, all the assembly of noblemen brought her into
Westminster Hall again, where was kept a great solemn
feast all that day; the good order thereof were too long
to write at this time to you. But now, sir, you may not
imagine that this coronation was before her marriage, for
she was married much about St. Paul's day last, as the
condition thereof doth well appear, by reason she is now
somewhat big with child. Notwithstanding it hath been
reported throughout a great part of the realm that I married
her, which was plainly false, for I myself knew not thereof a
fortnight after it was done. And many other things be also
reported of me, which be mere lies and tales." *

There were many careless-minded men on whom
the sight of the queen in all her beauty, set forth to
advantage by a gracious manner, had the effect so
well expressed by one of the gentlemen introduced
upon the scene by Shakspeare :—

> " Heaven bless thee !
> Thou hast the sweetest face I ever looked on.—
> Sir, as I have a soul, she is an angel :
> The king has all the Indies in his arms,
> And more and richer, when he embraces her ;
> *I cannot blame his conscience.*"

The reader will mark the sarcasm of the last line,
and will not be surprised to hear that in the provinces
there was less readiness to give the king credit for a

---

* Letter xiv. Harl. MSS. 6,148, fol. 23. The archbishop was
not so polite to the fair sex as we might have supposed one so
lately married might have been. He tells us that after the queen
came four rich chariots, one of them empty, " and three other
furnished with divers ancient old ladies." He reserved his admiration for the other ladies and gentlemen who followed.

conscience really scrupulous.　In London, all the Londoners at that time, in some way or other, partook
of the royal festivities.　The court of England was not
confined to the royal family and the officers of state.
Henry VIII. rejoiced to see the people enjoying themselves.　He shared in their amusements, and they in
his.　High and low, rich and poor, mingled together in
the palace, or in the surrounding gardens.　They saw
the king all joyous, they shared in his joy ; and as the
lovely queen smiled upon them, they became her lovers.

> "In shows,
> And pageants, and sights of honour,"

they took delight, as most men do.　They did not
begrudge the expenses of the court, when in the
pleasures of the court they were, in some way or
other, permitted to have their share.

But the enthusiasm of the moment, which might
carry away the Londoner, had little effect upon persons
dwelling in the country, and removed from court interest.　There were some even in London who viewed
the king's conduct with feelings of disgust.　The lords
temporal and the statesmen listened with profound
attention to the king, when he discoursed on the
miseries which would ensue to the country if at his
death any doubts should be raised as to the succession
to the throne.　The courtiers applauded the patriotism
which could induce the king to sacrifice a wife of
whom he was weary, and to share his throne with an
English lady by whose grace and beauty it was adorned.
The lords spiritual, grateful for favours received or to
come, and living in fear lest their lands might be
seized and the value risked at a gaming-table, believed,
or affected to believe, that the tender conscience of the
king required that he should have recourse either to

bigamy, if the pope would allow it, or to that divorce which was conceded to him by Cranmer. But the matronage of England rose up in chaste indignation at Henry's treatment of his wife,—an indignation imparted to their children, and handed on from generation to generation, until it has covered with everlasting infamy the name of a once popular king.*

There was then, as there always has been in England, a class of whom the most daring statesmen stand in awe;—men and women piously discharging the duties of their station, asserting hereditary rights, and only opposed to changes when those changes subject them to inconvenience, or interfere with their established prejudices. The persons of this class took little interest in the divorce question, while it was in progress; it was a question of law, to be decided by the law courts, the appeal lying to Rome. But when it appeared to them, that the law had been set aside merely to gratify the royal appetite, their sense of justice was shocked, their love of liberty was aroused. They with their wives listened with eager attention to the tales of Queen Katherine's sorrows which the itinerant preacher had to repeat; and the itinerant preacher was in the interest of the old learning.

The reaction soon reached London. The king and queen heard themselves compared from the pulpit to Ahab and Jezebel; and by more than one plainspoken

* Hall, a violent partisan of the king, speaking of what had occurred long before the divorce had actually taken place, and with reference to the decrees of the universities, observes: " When these determinations (of the University of Tholouse) were published, all wise men of the realm abhorred that marriage; but women, and such as were more wilful than wise and learned, spake against the determination, and said that the universities were corrupt."—Hall, 780. How easily we predicate a monopoly of wisdom to those who agree with us in opinion.

preacher their conduct was, in terms still stronger, denounced. The court was indignant. They applauded the Earl of Essex when he threatened to throw two of the preachers, who had been apprehended, tied together, into the Thames. The resolution of the poor but honest preachers was announced to the intolerant peer, by the reply, that the way to heaven is as near by water as by land. The pulpit in that day served the same purpose as the modern press. If the Government desired any statement to be made, or any document to be published, orders were sent to the preachers. When it is supposed that the clergy at this period were men without influence, dumb dogs that could not bark, the supposition is at once refuted by the fact, that the Government of the day became so alarmed that the primate found it necessary to prohibit all preaching for a season. The preachers being many of them friars, mingled politics with religion, and perhaps it was necessary to silence them; nevertheless it was a despotic act, only justified by the plea of necessity.

It was unfortunate for Cranmer that the first act of his primacy should be what, whether justifiable or not, could only be regarded in general as an act of tyranny. He prohibited all preaching throughout his own diocese, where the feeling was especially strong against the judge who had pronounced the sentence of divorce and the prelate who assumed the mitre in order that he might become the judge. With respect to the other dioceses in his province, he took counsel with his " well-beloved brothers in God," the Bishop of London (Stokesley), the Bishop of Winchester (Stephen Gardyner), and the Bishop of Lincoln (Longlands). The result of the conference was, that every bishop should be required to withdraw all existing licences to preach, and that new licenses should only be granted under the injunction, "that they should have regard in their preaching to the Provincial Constitution in the title *De Hœreticis;* that is to say, that they should in no wise touch or intermeddle themselves to preach or teach any such thing that might slander or bring into doubt and opinion the *catholic and received doctrine of Christ's Church,** or speak such matters as touch the prince, his laws or succession."

In a letter addressed to his suffragans, the primate directed them immediately to issue a monition and inhibition to this effect.

This inhibition or restraint upon preaching continued, it is presumed, till the 9th of June, 1534, when a proclamation was issued requiring the clergy to denounce the Bishop of Rome, and to inculcate by preaching the king's title and jurisdiction as recognised by parliament and convocation. At the same time, they were required to justify the king's separation from the princess dowager, and his new contract with the Lady Ann. If any one were to halt or stumble in the performance of this the king's will and pleasure, he was duly warned, " Be ye assured that we, like a prince of justice, will so extremely punish you for the same, that all the world shall take by you example and beware, contrary to their allegiance, to disobey the lawful commandment of their sovereign lord and prince."

These strong measures speak volumes of the unpopularity of the divorce ; and we are not surprised to find, that when in October 1533, the new archbishop proposed to hold a visitation at Canterbury, his very life was in danger. He was obliged to seek protection from the Government, and a writ was directed to all

* It is to be remembered that Cranmer did not at this time even pretend to be a Protestant. All that he did was, with Gardyner, to uphold the royal supremacy.

dukes, viscounts, barons, &c. requiring them to protect the lord archbishop in the visitation of his
Church.*

There was no want of animal courage in Cranmer.
When backed by his superiors he was bold, as he
became cowardly when their support was withdrawn.
Moral courage he had none. Strong in the royal
protection, he preached boldly on the divorce and the
supremacy ; and set an example of obeying the royal
commands, though the opposition which he met was
by no means to be despised. His hands were, however, strengthened by the fact, that many of the leading persons in his diocese, including the members of
his own cathedral, had been more or less implicated
in the imposture of Elizabeth Barton, the Nun of Kent,
and so were liable to a prosecution by the Government.
Having had occasion to detail the circumstances of this
case in the Life of Warham, I shall do no more in this
place than remind the reader that it is only a repetition
of what has often occured. Deceived first, and then deceiving, the Nun of Kent began in fanaticism, and passing through the phase of half-conscious hypocrisy, she
became for a time a tool in the hands of designing men,
until, her conscience being awakened by her fears, she
became her own accuser; and in her confession she was
impelled, as is frequently the case, to exaggerate her
faults and to criminate others. I have shown the
reader how the case presented itself to the mind of
Warham. The following letter will show how it
appeared to Cranmer, a man of another generation.
The letter has that charm which always attaches to an

---

* This writ is still preserved among the archives of Canterbury
Cathedral. It is one of the only documents, three in number,
which have not, I believe, been published. Why Strype did not
publish it, may be easily surmised.

original communication; and I know not how the story can be more concisely told.

Writing to Archdeacon Hawkyns :—

"These be to ascertain you of such news as be here now in fame amonges us in England. And first ye shall understand, that at Canterbury, within my diocese, about eight years past, there was wrought a great miracle in a maid by the power of God and Our Lady, named Our Lady of Courte-upstret, by reason of the which miracle there is stablished a great pilgrimage, and ever since many devout people hath sought to that foresaid Lady of Courte of Strett. The miracle was this: The maid was taken with a grievous and a continual sickness, and induring her said sickness she had divers and many trances, speaking of many high and godly things, and telling also wondrously by the power of the Holy Ghost as it was thought, things done and said in other places, whereat neither she was herself, nor yet heard no report thereof. She had also in her trances many strange visions and revelations, as of heaven, hell, and purgatory, and of the state of certain souls departed, and amonges all other visions one was, that she should be conveyed to Our Lady of Courte of Strett, where she was promised to be healed of her sickness, and that Almighty God should work wonders in her; and when she was brought thither, and laid before the image of Our Lady, her face was wonderfully disfigured, her tongue hanging out, and her eyes being in a manner plucked out and laid upon her cheeks, and so greatly disordered. Then was there heard a voice speaking within her belly, as it had been in a tun, her lips not greatly moving: she all that while continuing by the space of three hours and more in a trance; the which voice, when it told anything of the joys of heaven, it spake so sweetly and heavenly that every man was ravished with the hearing thereof; and contrary, when it told anything of hell, it spake so horribly and terribly that it put the hearers in a great fear. It spake also many things for the confirmation of pilgrimages and trentals, hearing of masses and confession, and many such other things. And after she had lain there a long time, she came to herself again and was perfectly whole, and

so this miracle was finished and solemnly rung, and a book
written of all the whole story thereof and put into print,
which ever since that time hath been commonly sold and
gone abroad amonges all people. After this miracle done,
she had a commandment from God in a vision, as she said,
to profess herself a nun. And so she was professed, and
hath so continued, in a nunnery at Canterbury, called St.
Sepulcres, ever since. And then she chose a monk of Christ's
Church, a doctor in divinity, to be ghostly father, whose
counsel she hath used and evermore followed in all her
doing. And evermore since from time to time hath had
almost every week, or at the furthest every fortnight, new
visions and revelations, and she hath had oftentimes trances
and raptures, by reason whereof, and also of the great per-
fectness that was thought to be in her, divers and many as
well great men of the realm as mean men, and many learned
men, but specially divers and many religious men, had great
confidence in her, and often resorted unto her and communed
with her, to the intent they might by her know the will of
God; and chiefly concerning the king's marriage, the great
heresies and schisms within the realm, and the taking away
the liberties of the Church; for in these three points standeth
the great number of her visions, which were so many that
her ghostly father could scantly write them in three or four
quires of paper. And surely I think that she did marvel-
lously stop the going forward of the king's marriage by the
reason of her visions, which she said were of God, persuading
them that came unto her how highly God was displeased
therewith, and what vengeance Almighty God would take
upon all the favourers thereof; insomuch that she wrote
letters to the pope, calling upon him in God's behalf to stop
and let the said marriage, and to use his high and heavenly
power therein, as he would avoid the great stroke of God,
which then hanged ready over his head, if he did the contrary.
She had also communication with my Lord Cardinal and
with my Lord of Canterbury my predecessor in the matter,
and in mine opinion, with her feigned visions and godly
threatenings, she stayed them very much in the matter.
She had also secret knowledge of divers other things, and
then she feigned that she had knowledge thereof from God;

insomuch that she conceived letters and sent them forth, making divers people believe that those letters were written in heaven, and sent from thence to earthly creatures. Now about Midsummer last, I hearing of these matters, sent for this holy maid to examine her; and from me she was had to Master Cromewell, to be further examined there. And now she hath confessed all, and uttered the very truth, which is this : that she never had vision in all her life, but all that ever she said was feigned of her own imagination, only to satisfy the minds of them the which resorted unto her, and to obtain worldly praise : by reason of the which her confession, many and divers, both religious men and other, be now in trouble, forasmuch as they consented to her mischievous and feigned visions, which contained much perilous sedition and also treason, and would not utter it, but rather further the same to their power.

"She said that the king should not continue king a month after that he were married. And within six months after, God would strike the realm with such a plague as never was seen, and then the king should be destroyed. She took upon her also to show the condition and state of souls departed, as of my Lord Cardinal, my late Lord of Canterbury, with divers other. To show you the whole story of all the matter it were too long to write in two or three letters; you shall know further thereof at your coming home."

It would appear from this and other documents, that Cardinal Wolsey either believed, or, as is more probable, employed for his own purposes, this unfortunate female. There was no tendency to superstition in Cranmer's nature, and his political principles would lead him to suspect proceedings in which Warham, More, and Fisher, unconsciously influenced by their prejudices, too readily acquiesced. The nun, with Dr. Bocking and her other accomplices, was compelled to do penance before the open cross in London, and in the churchyard at Canterbury. In the April of 1534, she, together with Bocking and Dering two dignitaries of the

* Remains, i. 79.

Church being members of the chapter of Canterbury, was taken from prison, and dragged through the streets of London, after which they were all hanged for treason and heresy at Tyburn.

Cranmer first came into collision with Stephen Gardyner by insisting on his right to hold a provincial visitation, a proceeding on the unpopularity of which we have had frequent occasion to remark. Such visitations enriched the metropolitan and his court at the expense of the diocesan and his clergy. We know that Cranmer was pressed for money, and it may have been to replenish his treasury that he made a metropolitical visitation; and we know also that he was accused of avarice. When he determined, however, upon a provincial visitation, it is difficult to understand why he should have selected the diocese of Winchester, since, as we have seen, only five years before, this diocese had been visited, and on account of the visitation Warham was brought into controversy with Fox. It is not improbable, that this was only a continuation of a visitation which had already commenced under Warham. Fox resisted Warham's visitation; a controversy ensued, and now Cranmer took up the action where Warham had left it.* It does not appear that the opposition was raised from mortification on the part of Gardyner at having missed the archbishopric, though one may easily suspect that this circumstance added acrimony to the dispute. The Bishop of Winchester contended that when the Archbishop claimed a right to visit as Primate of All England, he violated that act of supremacy of which he

* There is no account of the controversy in Cranmer's *Register* at Lambeth. Of Gardyner's Register at Winchester, only a portion of it has been preserved, and that has never been bound. If there was an entry on the subject mentioned above, it must have been in the missing portion of the Register. We are, therefore, left to conjecture.

was an eager advocate, according to which each bishop was responsible—so Gardyner pretended—not to his metropolitan, but to his king.   It was strange ground for Gardyner to have taken up, if we look to the later transactions of his life; but he spoke with authority now, for he had been himself instrumental in bringing the subject of the supremacy before the Convocation. Some awkward questions might have been raised, and the matter, through the interposition of Crumwell, was permitted to drop.   Cranmer stated, in a letter to Crumwell, what we may fairly believe to be true, that if all the bishops were as indifferent as he was to the externals of his office, the king's highness would find little difficulty in the satisfactory adjustment of such matters.   Nevertheless, he laid himself open to the charge of having indulged himself in a vexatious exercise of power over a prelate till lately his superior, and who may have been regarded as a rival candidate for the archiepiscopal throne.   Cranmer put himself more decidedly in the wrong when he proposed to visit the diocese of London; and this we mention because it shows that he had as yet laid down for himself no definite course of action.   He summoned to his visitation not only the archdeacon and clergy of London, but also the abbots and priors.   Now, the right to visit them rested either with the diocesan or with the pope.   Of late years the archbishop had occasionally summoned them to a visitation; but it was only on the ground that, in addition to the powers he possessed as an archbishop, he also possessed a legatine authority.   But the jurisdiction of the pope had been abolished by a late Act of Parliament, and the right of visiting monasteries had been at the same time expressly transferred to the king.   The archbishop had, indeed, through inadvertence, incurred the penalty of a præmunire when he summoned the regulars to his visitation. This was the more remarkable since the object for which he summoned them was, that he might announce to them that the Bishop of Rome was not God's vicar upon earth; and that though the king retained such of the Bishop of Rome's laws as were good, they were to be obeyed only on the ground that they were commanded by the king. This was said to meet the charge brought against him by Gardyner. This difficulty, like the last, was also overcome by the mere fact of Crumwell's treating it as a matter of no importance. He could not afford to have the archbishop distracted by professional controversies bearing upon no public interests, when the service of the country had a demand upon his thoughts and time.

The conduct of Henry, in cutting the Gordian knot by taking into his own hands the question of the divorce, had perplexed the counsels of his friend and ally the King of France. But Francis I. did not even yet despair of effecting a reconciliation between England and Rome. If an untoward event—in the detention of an English ambassador, who was expected at Rome by the friends of peace at the papal court,— had not strengthened the hands of the Imperialists, the French king might have succeeded; for there was a party in the conclave favourable to the compromise; and Henry himself was willing to make concessions if the Archbishop of Canterbury's judgment in the divorce case had been confirmed.

It is obvious, however, that if Henry was willing to concede something for the sake of peace, he was, nevertheless, nearly persuaded that the breach between England and Rome was really irreparable. Legislation in Church matters was to proceed. Henry addressed his own powerful intellect to the subject, and to Cranmer the king confided the conduct of ecclesiastical affairs in Parliament. Cranmer, however, was, when thus acting, in the strictest sense of the word, the mere minister, servant, and agent of the king. Henry encouraged freedom of discussion, and was not impatient of contradiction; but when once his mind was made up and he had signified his will to his servants, he was to be obeyed. To the people at large the Parliament spoke; but within the walls every one felt *Henricus loquitur*, whose voice soever he was pleased to employ.

Everything proceeded in an orderly manner. In 1531, before the time of Cranmer, as we have seen in the Life of Warham, the convocations of Canterbury and York took the first step for establishing the independence of our Church by recognising the king " as the singular protector, the only supreme governor, and, *so far as Christ permits*, the supreme head of the English Church and clergy." The next step to our independence was in 1532, when the convocations consented to a revision of ecclesiastical law by thirty commissioners to be nominated by the king, without any reference to Rome. The altered circumstances of the Church seemed to require immediate legislation; and to this important object the attention of Parliament was directed when it met in 1534. It is to be remembered that the business was chiefly conducted in the House of Lords, where the lay lords were only between twenty and thirty in number, and where, the abbots being still in existence, the spiritual lords formed a majority. The legislation was, in fact, conducted by a majority consisting of ecclesiastics, who were thus almost unanimous in carrying out the first steps of the Reformation.

The legislative enactments of the Parliament of

1533-4 are of such great importance, and are so closely connected with the history of Cranmer, that we must revert to them as briefly as possible.

The first act of permanent importance relates to the appointment of bishops. The appointment to the bishoprics had for a long period rested virtually with the king, as we have had frequent occasion to remark. The king had claimed to nominate, the chapters to elect, the pope to confirm and afterwards to appoint by provision, although the grant of the papal bulls had, unless in some exceptional cases, been made as a matter of course, when the king, in violation of the statutes of the realm, was pleased to ask for them. This application and this issue of bulls were no longer to be tolerated. It was now ordained and established—

"(1) That at every avoidance of every archbishopric or bishopric within this realm, or in any other the king's dominions, the king our sovereign lord, his heirs and successors, may grant to the prior and convent or the dean and chapter of the cathedral churches or monasteries where the see of such archbishopric or bishopric shall happen to be void, a licence under the great seal, as of old time hath been accustomed, to proceed to election of an archbishop or bishop of the see so being void, with a letter missive containing the name of the person which they shall elect and choose. (2) By virtue of which licence the said dean and chapter, or prior and convent, to whom any such licence and letters missive shall be directed, shall with all speed and celerity in due form elect and choose the same person named in the said letters missive, to the dignity and office of the archbishopric or bishopric so being void, and none other. (3) And if they do defer or delay their election above twelve days next after such licence or letters missive to them delivered, that then for every such default the king's highness, his heirs and successors, at their liberty and pleasure, shall nominate and present, by their letters patent under their great seal, such a person to the said office and dignity so being void, as they shall think able and convenient for the same. (4) And that every such nomination and presentment to be made by the king's highness, his heirs and successors, if it be to the office and dignity of a bishop, shall be made to the archbishop and metropolitan of the province, where the see of the same bishopric is void, if the see of the said archbishopric be then full, and not void; and if it be void then to be made to such archbishop or metropolitan within this realm, or in any of the king's dominions, as shall please the king's highness, his heirs or successors. (5) And if any such nomination or presentment shall happen to be made for default of such election to the dignity or office of any archbishop, then the king's highness, his heirs or successors, by his letters patent under his great seal, shall nominate and present such person as they will dispose to have, the said office and dignity of archbishopric being void, to one such archbishop and two such bishops, or else to four such bishops within this realm, or in any of the king's dominions, as shall be assigned by our said sovereign lord, his heirs or successors." *

The archbishop or metropolitan of the province in which the see of the bishopric was void, is required to invest and consecrate to the vacant see the person so elected, and to give and use to him all benedictions, ceremonies, and other things requisite for the same, without any suing, procuring, or obtaining any bulls, letters, or other things from the see of Rome for the same in any behalf. The act concludes with enforcing the penalty for not electing or consecrating the person named in the letter missive, namely—

"That every dean and particular person of his chapter, and every archbishop and bishop, and all other persons, so offending and doing contrary to this act, or any part thereof, and their aiders, counsellors, and abettors, shall run into the dangers, pains, and penalties of the Statute of the Provision

* Statutes at Large, ii. 192.

and Præmunire, made in the five and twentieth year of the reign of King Edward the Third, and in the sixteenth year of King Richard the Second." *

The collection of Peterpence and other payments to Rome was prohibited; and the Archbishop of Canterbury was empowered to grant such licences and dispensations as had heretofore been obtained from the see of Rome, including those which had been made to the king   It was enacted—

" That the archbishop for the time being and his successors shall have power and authority, from time to time, by their discretions, to give, grant, and dispose, by an instrument under the seal of the said archbishop, unto your majesty, and to your heirs and successors, kings of this realm, as well all manner of such licences, dispensations, compositions, faculties, grants, rescripts, delegacies, instruments, and all other writings, for causes not being contrary or repugnant to the Holy Scriptures and laws of God, as heretofore hath been used and accustomed to be had and obtained by your highness, or any your most noble progenitors, or any of your or their subjects, at the see of Rome, or any person or persons by authority of the same: and all other licences, dispensations, faculties, compositions, grants, rescripts, delegacies, instruments, and other writings, in, for, and upon all such causes and matters as shall be convenient and necessary to be had, for the honour and surety of your highness, your heirs and successors, and the wealth and profit of this your realm, so that the said archbishop or any of his successors in no manner wise grant any dispensation, licence, rescript, or any other writing afore rehearsed, for any cause or matter repugnant to the law of Almighty God." †

* 25 Ed. III. stat. 5, c. 22 ; 16 Ric. II. c. 5 ; 26 Hen. VIII. c. 14 ; 31 Hen. VIII. c. 9 ; 8 Eliz. c. 1 ; Rep. 1 and 2 Ph. and M. c. 8 ; and revised by 1 Eliz. c. 1 ; and see further 23 Eliz. c. 1.

† Statutes at Large, ii. 194.—From the original documents, where they have been misrepresented or misunderstood, I abbreviate, and give the substance only of those which contain what is admitted by all writers.

Provision was made for the reservation of the rights of the Archbishop of York and the respective diocesans of the two provinces. But now a question arose as to the treatment of the exempt monasteries,—of those monasteries which, in bygone days, had poured countless sums of money into the papal treasury to become independent of the bishops, and to secure the pope for their visitor. Crumwell had already called the attention of his royal master to that mine of wealth which might be opened by the confiscation of monastic property ; and it was expressly enacted that the visitatorial powers, as regarded those monasteries, should not be restored to the bishop of the diocese, but that they should rest in the king.

Thus far had the Reformation advanced. Neither Henry nor Cranmer was a theorist. They had no particular schemes of their own to carry. They found the Church of England bowed down by the galling tyranny of Rome—through powers gradually usurped. When they had asserted the freedom of the national Church, and declared the king to be " in all causes and over all persons, civil and ecclesiastical, within his dominions supreme," they had to legislate, not with a view to further their preconceived opinions, but simply to meet the difficulties arising from the circumstances under which they were placed. In an age of inquiry they soon discovered that the Catholic faith, though always preserved in the three Creeds, had been obscured by superincumbent superstitions ; and they sought as they were discovered, one by one, to remove them.

They did not seek to eradicate the Catholic religion, but to the hour of their death they each of them professed to adhere to it and to advance the cause of Catholicism as the cause of truth. They would only separate it from Papistry.

The difference between the two friends was clearly seen by Henry. Henry was of a conservative temper, and would move slowly, while Cranmer, though slow to receive a truth, laboured eagerly when he had accepted it for its promulgation. Both were frequently inconsistent, the one urged on by his passions, and the other retarded by his weakness.

During the recess of parliament, the Archbishop was engaged in the discharge of his various ecclesiastical duties, and in invigorating his mind for the work which he saw before him.

The parliament and convocation resumed their sittings at the beginning of November. Before that time, the breach between the Church of England and the see of Rome had become irreparable. Through the intrigues of the Imperialists, favoured by a circumstance to which I have before alluded, the negotiations of Francis I. to create a good understanding between the courts of England and Rome had failed. The judgment of the Lord Primate of England had been reversed by the Bishop of Rome; and Henry was required under pain of excommunication to separate from his new queen.

The Reformation was now accomplished, so far as the independence of the Church of England was concerned.

The insult offered to the realm, through the excommunication of the king, filled every true English heart with indignation. The nation acted as if it had been one man. Cranmer and Gardyner, the secular and the regular, the men of the old learning and of the new, were all aroused. The Government was wide awake. The king emerged from his dissipations, and was a tower of strength. The whole country was in a state of ferment. The Privy Council directed the bishops to consult

as to the means to be adopted in this new position of
the Church. Convocation directed that the act of
parliament which subjected all who made appeal to
the court of Rome to the penalties of a præmunire,
should be put in force. It had already announced the
great dogma of the Council of Constance, that a
general council represented the Church, and was above
the pope and all other bishops; it now added that
"the Bishop of Rome has no greater jurisdiction given
him in this realm of England than any other foreign
bishop."*

Thus was the Church of England by a synodical act
separated for ever, except during a few years in Queen
Mary's reign, from the see of Rome, or certainly until
that see ceases to be guilty of Mariolatry, and abstains
from asserting the infallibility—that is, the continuous
miraculous inspiration—of the pope. The Convocation
of York, as soon as possible, concurred with the
southern province in the solemn renunciation of the
papal supremacy; and the example set by the two
convocations was followed by the two universities,
and by all the capitular, and even by the conventual
bodies throughout the realm.† The archbishop also
gave directions in convocation, that in all petitions,
citations or addresses made to him, the title of
Metropolitan was to be inserted, and that of Legate
omitted.

To the archbishop's energy, at this time, contemporary evidence is borne; and though his speeches in
parliament and convocation have not been reported,
they are said to have produced a powerful effect upon

* Wilkins, iii. 769.

† The renunciations were preserved for many years in the Court
of Exchequer. Numerous specimens may be read in the Fœdera.
Henry Wharton read many of them, and saw more.

the minds of his hearers. This was the most active, the most busy, and consequently the most brilliant epoch of his life. He was giving proof to those who had disparaged his abilities that he was rising to his position. The unanimity with which the pope was rejected was only what those who have perused these volumes would have expected. Cranmer's argument was this :—What was given . might be recalled by those who gave it. The papal jurisdiction was not of divine right, it was a gradual concession won from this Church and realm. The Church and realm resumed what they had for a time conceded. The " De verâ differentiâ Regiæ Potestatis et Ecclesiasticæ" of Edward Fox, bishop of Hereford, appeared in 1534, and the " De verâ Obedientiâ" of Stephen Gardyner, bishop of Winchester, was published in the following year. It was a national, not a party or a Protestant movement.*

Proclamation was made for the erasure of the Bishop of Rome's name from all office-books in the Church. An act of parliament at length conceded to the king what had long before been granted by convocation, the title of Supreme Head of the Church, together with the power, which the name implied, to correct grievances, and to call defaulters to account.

Availing himself of the state of public feeling, Crumwell suggested, and Cranmer was not the man to contravene the suggestion, that the exactions of the pope, such as the payment of first-fruits and tenths of all dignities spiritual, ought to be handed over to the king to renumerate him for the expense

---

* This fact is admitted by Butler, one of the most candid of partisans.—Historical Memoirs of English (Roman) Catholics, i. 162.

he would incur in discharging the office of supreme head.

. There was another bill introduced by the archbishop, which was rendered expedient, if not absolutely necessary, by the altered circumstances of the country. We have had often occasion to observe that, during the preceding two hundred years, bishops who were not diocesans had been frequently employed to perform the necessary episcopal acts when the diocesan was engaged in the service of the state, or incapacitated for duty. by the infirmities of old age. Bishops *in partibus*, foreign bishops who had been driven by faction from their own dioceses, bishops sent by the pope to officiate in those exempt monasteries which rejected the services of the diocesan, had been at various times and in various ways employed. Against these curate-bishops, as we may call them, a popular clamour had of late years been raised; a subject to which the reader's attention has been called more than once. People who lived on the lands of a diocesan, and who supported him by paying their dues, demanded that he should perform his duty in person. But if bishops were still to be employed in public affairs, as was the case with Cranmer and Gardyner, they would, while, as a general rule, they discharged their own duties, require, nevertheless, occasional assistance, which would also be requisite in cases of sickness or old age. It was proposed, therefore, to legalise the appointment, under definite regulations, of assistant-bishops, and at the same time to give them a certain status in the country.

As this subject has come frequently under discussion of late years, and some readers may like to see what was proposed to be done in this direction during the progress of the Reformation, I.shall present them with the main provisions of the act. The preamble refers to the consecrations and ordinations which had been regularly conducted from the commencement of the parliament then sitting, and proceeds to say that some provision was necessary for the appointment of suffragans, who had hitherto been employed in this realm :—

" For the more speedy administration of the sacraments and other good, wholesome, and devout things and laudable ceremonies, to the increase of God's honour, and for the commodity of good and devout people: Be it therefore enacted by authority of this present Parliament, that the towns of Thetford, Ipswich, Colchester, Dover, Guilford, Southampnot, Taunton, Shaftesbury, Molton, Marlborough, Bedford, Leicester, Gloucester, Shrewsbury, Bristow, Penrith, Bridgwater, Nottingham, Grantham, Hull, Huntington, Cambridge, and the towns of Pereth and Berwick, St. Germains in Cornwall, and the Isle of Wight, shall be taken and accepted for sees of bishops suffragans to be made in this realm, and in Wales, and the bishops of such sees shall be called suffragans of this realm ; and that every archbishop and bishop of this realm, and of Wales, and elsewhere within the king's dominions, being disposed to have any suffragans, shall and may at their liberties name and elect, that is to say, every of them for their peculiar diocese, two honest and discreet spiritual persons, being learned, and of good conversation, and those two persons so by them to be named, shall present to the king's highness, by their writing under their seals, making humble request to his majesty, to give to one such of the said two persons, as shall please his majesty, such title, name, style and dignity of bishop of such of the sees above specified, as the king's highness shall think most convenient for the same; and that the king's majesty, upon every such presentation, shall have full power and authority to give to one of those two persons so to his highness to be presented, the style, title, and name of a bishop of such of the sees aforesaid, as to his majesty shall be thought most convenient and expedient, so it be within the same province whereof the bishop that doth name him is. And that every such person to whom the king's highness shall give any such style and title of any of the sees aforesaid shall be called bishop suffragan of the same see whereunto he shall be named."*

By another provision of the act such suffragan is to be accounted to hold the same rank and dignity as any other archbishop or bishop. Of this act, although it is still in force, very little use has ever been made.

Cranmer saw nothing of the court at this period of his life. Although the king delighted in Cranmer's society, he felt that his court, when over it Queen Ann presided, and when the king was indulging his propensities for gambling, was not the fit place for a prelate, to whom, though he had no tendency to Puritanism, the sound of the dice-box could not be pleasant music. The queen, too, though aware that, to a considerable extent, she owed her crown to Cranmer, and although she found it expedient to be regarded as a patroness of the "New Learning" party, was not anxious for the restraint which the constant presence of Cranmer would have imposed upon a court very different, in its character, from that of Queen Katherine. At the same time, Crumwell was not desirous of having at court one who, now sufficiently subservient, might have become a rival. Cranmer's character was not at present well known, and he was evidently neglected. We gather this from his correspondence. He was treated with respect, but was regarded as a man who, having received his mitre for a special object, and having fulfilled the purposes of his appointment, was no longer required. After the Dunstable divorce, Cranmer was no longer called to the councils of the king. Some time elapsed before Henry discovered his merits, or fully appreciated the value of his friendship. A kind of

* Statutes at Large, ii. 216.

cloud overshadowed all who had been concerned in persecuting Queen Katherine. Even the king, when he had secured what he so long and iniquitously laboured to obtain, was evidently ashamed of his conduct. The notices we have of his sharp sayings to Queen Ann indicate this; and her heartless conduct towards Katherine caused, in some measure, the alienation of his affections from the latter.

And so Cranmer was permitted to retire from public life, and to relax himself in the bosom of his family. This, probably, was one of the happiest periods of his life. We find him at Adlington, a seat of the archbishop, near Ashford in Kent. Here we are told was a park and a chase of deer; and here he indulged in those field sports which, from his boyhood, had been to him a source of recreation and delight. But he chiefly took up his abode at Otford and Ford; here he enjoyed the society of his chosen companions and friends, and here we can have little doubt that he employed his learned leisure in realizing some of the important truths which were everywhere under discussion. He was a man of the "New Learning," and was at the head of the "New Learning" party. The new learning in England had not any definite principles; or rather its one principle consisted in a readiness to advance, a willingness to examine any subject brought upon the *tapis*. It was a time to inquire; the time to dogmatize had not arrived.

So completely was Cranmer put aside as a public man at this period, that he was kept in ignorance as to the ordinary news of the day, and knew not what was going on at court. He would probably have been long left to the unostentatious discharge of his pastoral duties, had not his services been again required.

He was thus usefully employed, and enjoying his

new honours, when, to his surprise and alarm, he suddenly and unexpectedly received a command to proceed, without loss of time, to the metropolis.

On the 2d of May he arrived at Lambeth. The first peer of the realm was alone in his glory. Nobody was waiting to receive him, or to explain the proceedings of the council; he was simply commanded to remain at home till sent for. There was probably an intention to overawe him; for if he had refused to obey the king's command, as was not improbable, there would have been an insuperable difficulty in carrying out the royal will with respect to the queen; and we must repeat the remark that Cranmer's character, in its weakness and its strength, was at this time untested and unknown.

The rumour reached the archbishop that Queen Ann was a prisoner in the Tower. It was strange, that no notice of this proceeding had been given to the chief member of the Privy Council; but the generous spirit of Cranmer thought not a moment of this. He would at once drop down the river to Greenwich, where his royal master was at that time residing, to plead for the queen and advise the king. He ordered his barge. It was notified to him, that peremptory orders had been given that, until summoned to court, the primate was to confine himself to his house. In his house, in fact, the archbishop was a prisoner. His heart, however, was too full for silence. He saw the difficulties of the case. He pitied the unfortunate queen, and addressed a letter to her husband —the letter of a generous, kind-hearted, timid man, anxious to plead the queen's cause. But as he wrote he became aware that he knew nothing of the case; and that he could only express his readiness to obey the king's commands—which,—his readiness to obey,

—was, in fact, all that the king required,—a doubt having been entertained whether coercion would, in his case, be necessary.

The letter had hardly been written when the lord chancellor's barge was seen at the landing-place. He was commissioned to lay before the archbishop certain revelations relating to the queen's conduct. The object was to see what impression these revelations would make on the archbishop's mind. The king was determined upon a divorce at least; would the archbishop act obsequiously in this case, as he had done in that of Queen Katherine? This was the question. Would the archbishop commit himself as a partisan on the side of the king? The chancellor saw at a glance, that Cranmer would not hesitate to do what the king might demand of him. That point gained, the rest was not worthy of a thought. The letter had better go. It was creditable for the archbishop to have written it; it would be creditable to the king to receive it. All that was really needful was done when the primate added to his letter that, under all circumstances, he was ready to act the part of a true and loyal subject. The archbishop might form his own opinion of the case; and the king, when he had made up his mind and felt secure of carrying his point, found amusement in having his opinions canvassed. The chancellor was quite satisfied, when he saw that the judge before whom the case would be tried would give the judgment required.

The primate was now invited to take his place in the Star Chamber.

The whole plan had been devised before the archbishop was secured. On the 25th of April, a court of inquiry had been opened, consisting of the lord chancellor, with the Earls of Oxford and Sussex;

and it was with the result of these investigations that
the primate was now made acquainted. It does not
come within my province to enter into the merits of
this *cause célèbre*. All the proceedings relating to
Ann Boleyn are involved in the greatest obscurity;
a remark which is applicable to all the state trials in
the reign of Henry VIII. Hereafter, perhaps, from
the publication of foreign documents, some light may
be thrown on the subject; but the domestic records of
her trial, and of the trial of those who were in the
same accusation, have been carefully destroyed. What
has come down to us has only been the gossip of the
day, from which the most opposite conclusions have
been deduced. The atrocity of the crimes laid to her
charge must, to every impartial mind, speak in her
favour. When men have recourse to their imagination and invent facts, they know not when or where
to stop. In order to support their lie they overstate
their case. That Ann Boleyn should have plunged at
once into such filth of wickedness as that by which
she is overwhelmed by her accusation, is inconsistent
with her antecedent history. Frivolous and vain she
was, but not a licentious woman; if she had not been
cold in her temperament, she would have yielded
sooner to the solicitations of Henry. Of her ambition,
of her heartless, unfeeling conduct towards her royal
mistress, whom she supplanted, of her vindictive passions, I have spoken freely; but we require far stronger
proofs than we possess to induce a belief that she was
guilty of the crimes laid to her charge. She was a
great deal too clever a woman to be guilty. It is much
easier to believe what is stated by a contemporary—
that she fell a victim to a conspiracy. Two parties
were combined against her, and probably conspired
for her ruin. Her hostility to Rome was premised,

CHAP.
III.

Thomas
Cranmer.
1533–56.

and the Reformers claimed her as their own. The party of the "Old Learning" were desirous, therefore, of withdrawing the infatuated king from an influence always employed against them. At the same time, her vindictive passions were as vehement, as her ambition to rule the country, through her husband, was unendurable. She never forgave. This Crumwell knew. The minister had offended the queen, and he had before his eyes full proof of her power and of her relentless malignity in the fate of Wolsey, of More, and of Fisher. If the king himself was, half-consciously, blind to the iniquities of his minister, yet that minister himself knew that when the growing discontent of the people had proceeded to a certain extent, he would then be thrown over by his master, like the prophet of old, to appease the storm. The queen had her eyes open ; she openly attacked Crumwell, and threatened to inform the king that, under the disguise of the Gospel and religion, he and those who acted under him were thinking of their own interests rather than of his ; that without accounting to him, Crumwell had amassed a large fortune ; that he had put everything up for sale ; and that he was accustomed to take bribes to confer ecclesiastical benefits on unworthy persons. She had thus the extreme imprudence to make Crumwell her enemy, vainly supposing that her influence over the king was greater than his. Crumwell felt that one of the two must be sacrificed. The means were soon provided. A league existed between him and Wriothesly. Though attached to the "old learning," Wriothesly was co-operating with Crumwell, and, through Crumwell's assistance, was enriching himself by the spoils of the monasteries. At the same time, between Wriothesly and Gardyner, bishop of Winchester and at this time ambassador at the court of

France, a close correspondence was kept up. The ambassador, in his correspondence, retailed the gossip to the French court, which was amused by the report, that the woman for whom King Henry had risked his crown, and imperilled his throne, had played him false; and the Bishop of Winchester added, that certain letters were produceable which would prove the adultery of the queen. All this has certainly a very suspicious appearance. These letters were sent over to England, and by the bishop's steward they were placed in the hands of Wriothesly. Wriothesly communicated them to Crumwell, who was probably already acquainted with the contents. Crumwell is described as being at this time "the king's ear and mind," to whom he had entrusted the entire government of the kingdom. What was made known to Crumwell was confidentially made known to the king. Henry's wrath, though deadly, was concealed until the case had been investigated by Crumwell in conjunction with Wriothesly. Their fear of the queen, we are expressly told, induced them to act the part of spies. They caused her private apartments to be watched day and night. Her servants were bribed. To the ladies of her bedchamber there was scarcely anything which they did not promise, if they would only criminate their mistress. The ladies were aware how bitterly the king had expressed his disappointment that Ann's child was not a boy, and they suspected that his affections had wandered elsewhere. By accusing the queen they were sure to gain the king's favour. At length the conspirators considered that they had proofs sufficient of the queen's guilt. The council was summoned to meet at Greenwich on the 30th of April, to devise measures for the queen's trial. The public were not yet apprised of the suspicions which had been entertained of their beautiful queen ; and she, though she knew that an attack was about to be made upon her, was not aware of the extent, or perhaps of the nature, of the charge. She was a consummate actress, and played her part well, though not successfully. While the council was assembling at the palace of Greenwich, each great man arriving with the display of pomp then customary, the king was seen at an open window looking down on the courtyard below, filled with spectators. He liked to show himself, and to participate in whatever afforded amusement to his subjects. Then the queen was seen approaching him with all her accustomed elegance and grace, bearing her babe in her arms, that babe being Elizabeth, the future Queen of England. She was seen to be entreating the king with great earnestness, to grant her some request. What was going on was of course unintelligible to the people in the courtyard ; they only perceived, from the face and gestures of the queen, that the king was angry, though such was his mastery over himself, that the extent of his anger—its deadliness—was concealed. We have all this from an eye-witness ; and we may infer that, up to this time, the queen was not aware of the terrible nature of the charges brought against her. The council sat long and late. The crowd remained to see the lords depart until it was dark. The council was left sitting when the people took boat and crossed to London. It was noised abroad that some deep and difficult question was under discussion, but still the object of the debate was unknown, until the Londoners were awakened by the booming of the cannon, which announced that some person of high rank had been committed to the Tower.*

---

* The authority for these statements is a letter of Alexander Aless to Queen Elizabeth, which has lately been discovered among

The archbishop was not summoned to the council.
He was appointed confessor to the queen.   He appears
to have been at this time, almost a prisoner at
Lambeth.

This is one of the many unaccountable circumstances
by which we are perplexed. It is clear that the
enemies of the queen designed to prevent Cranmer from
having an interview with the king lest he should urge
him to show mercy ; and the king, having made up his
mind to act, may have chosen to save himself from
useless solicitation on the subject. It was, however,
signified to Cranmer on the 16th of May, that on the
following morning he would have officially to act
towards Queen Ann as he had acted towards Queen
Katherine ;—that the king required of him that he
should pronounce his second marriage, like the first, to
have been from the beginning a nullity. The archbishop was an early riser. He rose rather earlier than
usual on the morning of the 17th of May. The anxiety
of his mind prevented him from taking rest, and before
four o'clock he was walking in his garden. To his
surprise he met there Alexander Aless, to whom we are
indebted for the statement just submitted to the
reader. Alexander had been himself disturbed in his
sleep. He had dreamt that the queen was beheaded ;
and crossing the Thames, he had sought to calm his
perturbed spirit by taking a walk in the Lambeth
garden. He apologized to the archbishop for his
intrusion, and narrated the circumstances of his dream.

the State Papers. He was himself among the crowd who witnessed
the last interview between Ann Boleyn and her husband. There
was no one more competent than Aless to relate these affairs, for
he was at this time intimate with Crumwell. He had no reason
to accuse Crumwell wrongfully, for Crumwell was his benefactor
and patron ; yet I cannot but suspect that he coloured his statements, that they might be the more acceptable to Elizabeth.

The archbishop listened in silence, until at length he said, "Don't you know what is to happen to-day?" Aless stated that since the day of the queen's imprisonment he had heard no public news. The archbishop solemnly raised his eyes to heaven and said, "She who has been Queen of England on earth, will this day become a queen in heaven," and he burst into tears.[*]

The question forces itself on the mind—Could Cranmer really have said this? Was this attestation of the queen's innocence invented by Aless, in flattery to Ann Boleyn's daughter? If the assertion be true, Cranmer's conduct was unspeakably bad.

Soon after nine o'clock, the barges of the Earls of Oxford and Sussex appeared at the steps of the castle at Lambeth. The Lord Chancellor, the Master of the Rolls, Thomas Crumwell, Vicar-general or Vicegerent, soon after followed, with many canonists and lawyers. Dr. Sampson, dean of the Chapel Royal, appeared as proctor for the king, Dr. Wotton and John Barbour for the queen. The archbishop appeared *in pontificalibus*, and a procession was formed which entered the chapel in the crypt. In that cold, dark, sepulchral apartment the primate took his seat, his assessors on either side. The proctors of the king and queen in solemn mockery stood before them, and demanded a sentence. Archbishop Cranmer addressed them: for certain just and lawful causes lately brought under his cognisance, after full investigation, and acting with judgment, which was to the effect, that the pretended advice of counsel learned in the law, he delivered marriage between our sovereign lord the king and the Lady Ann had always been without effect. The judgment was sealed on the 10th of June.[†] The solemn

---

[*] State Papers, Elizabeth, 528.
[†] Wilkins, iii. 803, 104.

farce did not end here.   Convocation was summoned.

Before the members of both houses the judgment was
laid, and by them it was, on the 28th of June, sub-
scribed.

The object of this mode of proceeding it is difficult
to surmise.   Antecedently to this, the queen had been
condemned by the lay judges; she was sentenced to
be either burned or beheaded at the king's pleasure,
that is, to be executed as he might decide.   It was left
to him to decide whether she should suffer as a heretic
or as a traitor.   But the king's rage against her appears
to have known no bounds.   His object now seems to
have been to bastardize her daughter, though in doing
so he stultified his previous conduct.   If Ann had
never been his wife, Elizabeth, though her daughter,
was illegitimate; and if the marriage was null *ab initio*,
then Ann, though she had been unfaithful to the king,
was not guilty of adultery.

Then, again, what was the impediment pleaded by
the king, not denied by the queen, and accepted by
Cranmer, which rendered this marriage a nullity? The
fact is indisputable, that the unhappy queen, acting
under a promise that her life would be spared, made
some admission, the nature of which has never tran-
spired.   On the strength of this promise she expected,
almost to the hour of her death, to receive a reprieve;
and talked of settling at Antwerp.   But when the
king had gained his object, a violation of his promise
on this occasion was added to the long catalogue of
his crimes.   It were waste of time to offer conjectures
as to the nature of the confession made by the queen
in regard to some fact which nullified her marriage,—
something distinct from the charge of adultery.   It
has been supposed that she consented to plead a pre-
contract with Lord Percy; but in the first place, there

is no reason why such a statement should be surrounded by mystery, and in the next place Lord
Percy twice made solemn oath on the sacrament,
that into such contract he had never entered. With
greater probability it has been conjectured that the
confession of Ann related to the horrible fact that
Henry had intrigued with her sister Mary long
before his engagement with Ann. The objection to
this view of the case is, that it would be for the king,
not for the queen, to make confession on this point;
and that Cranmer had argued powerfully to prove
that no such affinity was contracted by the illicit
intercourse of a man and woman as to vitiate
any subsequent marriage.* But the supposition of

---

* He argued this point most ably in the unpublished paper
in the Cottonian Library, to which allusion has been made
before. That Mary Boleyn had been the mistress of the king, is
now very generally believed. The fact was openly stated by Pole
in his *De Unitate Ecclesiæ;* and his words imply that the fact
was by no means a secret. Henry did not deny the truth of
the charge ; but, on the contrary, the greatest care seems to
have been taken in the correspondence with Rome, as well as
in Cranmer's paper, to make broad the distinction between con-
sanguinity and affinity. The only object appears to have been, to
guard against this being urged as an impediment to the king's
marriage with Ann. It appears to me not improbable that Ann
Boleyn's long resistance to the addresses of her royal lover may
have had reference to this fact. There are certainly some suspicious
passages in an act of parliament quoted by Lingard, which may
induce us to suppose that when Henry determined to rid himself
of Ann Boleyn, he placed affinity on the same footing as con-
sanguinity. I submitted the document containing Cranmer's
argument to a learned lawyer, and his opinion is that the consideration of the case of affinity forms so naturally a part of Cranmer's
able argument, that it is not of necessity to be inferred that he was
at that time aware of Mary Boleyn's case. But we know too little
of the facts of the case to form an opinion. I merely give the
statements.

his allusion to this story will account for the extreme anger of the king, who wished to conceal it. The whole is a sad and disgraceful story, from whatever point of view we regard it; and of Cranmer's conduct in the affair, the less that his admirers say, the greater will be their discretion.

END OF THE SIXTH VOLUME.

LONDON:
R. CLAY, SON, AND TAYLOR, PRINTERS,
BREAD STREET HILL.

MR. BENTLEY'S ANNOUNCEMENTS FOR THE NEW SEASON.

THE LATE EMPEROR MAXIMILIAN.
RECOLLECTIONS OF MY LIFE. By the late EMPEROR MAXI-MILIAN. 3 vols.

LORD LYTTON.
THE MISCELLANEOUS PROSE WORKS OF EDWARD BULWER, LORD LYTTON. Now first collected, including Charles Lamb—The Reign of Terror—Gray—Goldsmith—Pitt and Fox—Sir Thomas Browne—Schiller, &c. &c. &c. In 3 vols. 8vo.

SIR HENRY LYTTON BULWER.
HISTORICAL CHARACTERS: Talleyrand—Mackintosh—Cobbett—Canning. By the Rt. Hon. SIR HENRY LYTTON BULWER, G.C.B. 2 vols. demy 8vo. 30s.   [*Ready.*

LADY HERBERT OF LEA.
CRADLE LANDS; EGYPT, SYRIA, AND THE HOLY LAND. By the Right Hon. LADY HERBERT OF LEA. In royal 8vo. with numerous Illustrations.

VAN PRAET.
HISTORICAL ESSAYS ON LATTER TIMES: The Dukes of Burgundy—Charles the Fifth—Philip the Second and the Taciturn—Cardinal Richelieu—The First English Revolution—William the Third. By J. VAN PRAET. Edited by SIR EDMUND HEAD, Bart. In 1 vol. demy 8vo.

THE DEAN OF CHICHESTER.
THE LIVES OF THE ARCHBISHOPS OF CANTERBURY. By WALTER FARQUHAR HOOK, D.D. Dean of Chichester. Second Series, commencing with the Reformation. Vols. I. and II. Demy 8vo. (being Vols. VI. and VII. of the whole Work).

MRS. AUGUSTUS CRAVEN.
LOVE, MARRIAGE, AND DEATH (Recit d'une Sœur). A True Story. By MRS. AUGUSTUS CRAVEN. In 3 vols.

DR. FERGUSON AND DR. MORTON BROWN.
THE LIFE AND LABOURS OF JOHN CAMPBELL, D.D. By the Rev. ROBERT FERGUSON, LL.D. and the Rev. A. MORTON BROWN, LL.D. In 1 vol. Demy 8vo. with Portrait.

ZURCHAR AND MARGOLLÉ.
VOLCANOES AND EARTHQUAKES. From the French of ZURCHAR and MARGOLLÉ. By the Translator of "THE HEAVENS." In crown 8vo. with many Illustrations.

FLORENCE MARRYAT.

"GUP;" or, Sketches of Indian Life and Character. By FLORENCE MARRYAT (Mrs. Ross Church). In 1 vol. crown 8vo.

JOHN TIMBS, ESQ. F.S.A.

LONDON AND WESTMINSTER: City and Suburb. By JOHN TIMBS, Esq. F.S.A. Author of "Century of Anecdote," "Club Life of London," &c. &c. In 2 vols. post 8vo.

H. R. FOX BOURNE, ESQ.

ENGLISH SEAMEN UNDER THE TUDORS. By H. R. FOX BOURNE, Esq. Author of "Lives of English Merchants," &c. 2 vols. crown 8vo.

EDWARD J. WOOD, ESQ.

GIANTS AND DWARFS. By EDWARD J. WOOD, Esq. Author of "Curiosities of Clocks and Watches." In 1 vol. 8vo.

J. E. HILARY SKINNER, ESQ.

ROUGHING IT IN CRETE. By J. E. HILARY SKINNER, Esq. Author of "After the Storm," &c. &c. Post 8vo.

NEW EDITIONS.

DR. MOMMSEN.

THE HISTORY OF ROME TO THE FALL OF THE REPUBLIC. By Dr. THEODOR MOMMSEN. Translated by PROFESSOR DICKSON. A Library Edition. In 4 vols. demy 8vo.

FRANK BUCKLAND, ESQ.

CURIOSITIES OF NATURAL HISTORY. By FRANK BUCKLAND, Esq. Third Series. A New and Cheaper Edition. In 2 vols. fcap. 8vo. with Illustrations. 12s.

DR. M'CAUSLAND.

ADAM AND THE ADAMITE; or, the Harmony of Scripture and Ethnology. By DOMINICK M'CAUSLAND, Q.C. LL.D. Author of "Sermons in Stones," &c. A New and Cheaper Edition. In crown 8vo. with Illustrations. 6s.

M. GUIZOT.

THE LIFE OF OLIVER CROMWELL. By M. GUIZOT. A New Edition, with numerous Portraits. Crown 8vo. 6s.

LONDON: RICHARD BENTLEY, NEW BURLINGTON STREET,

PUBLISHER IN ORDINARY TO HER MAJESTY.